PREPARING FOR THE CALCULUS

AP® EXAM

WITH

CALCULUS: Graphical, Numerical, Algebraic

Fifth Edition

FINNEY, DEMANA, WAITS, KENNEDY, BRESSOUD

WRITTEN BY
BARTON
BRUNSTING
DIEHL
HILL
TYLER
WILSON

PEARSON

Boston   Columbus   Indianapolis   New York   San Francisco
Amsterdam   Cape Town   Dubai   London   Madrid   Milan   Munich   Paris   Montréal   Toronto
Delhi   Mexico City   São Paulo   Sydney   Hong Kong   Seoul   Singapore   Taipei   Tokyo

CREDITS: Pages 9–21, Concept Outline. *AP Calculus AB and AP Calculus BC Course and Exam Description, Effective Fall 2016.* © 2016. The College Board. www.collegeboard.org. Reproduced with permission.

ISBN-13: 978-0-328-90914-8
ISBN 10: 0-328-90914-9

6   18

www.pearsonschool.com/advanced

Preparing for the AP* Calculus Exam

TABLE OF CONTENTS

About the Authors

Ray Barton teaches AP* Calculus BC at Olympus High School in Salt Lake City, Utah. He has been an Advanced Placement Calculus exam reader and is an active instructor for Teachers Teaching with Technology. He is coauthor of *Advanced Placement Calculus with the TI-89* and *Differential Equations with the TI-86*. Ray received the Presidential Award for Excellence in Mathematics and Science Teaching in 1995. He is a strong proponent of using technology to teach mathematics.

John R. Brunsting taught AP* Calculus at Hinsdale Central High School in Hinsdale, Illinois. He has been an Advanced Placement Calculus exam reader and table leader, as well as an AP* Calculus Test Development Committee member. He is a consultant for the College Board and a past director of Illinois Advanced Placement Institutes and Mathematics & Technology Institutes, providing summer training for AP* teachers.

John J. Diehl has taught AP* Calculus and AP* Statistics at Hinsdale Central High School in Hinsdale, Illinois. He has been an Advanced Placement Statistics exam reader and table leader, as well as an AP* Statistics Test Development Committee member. John was a consultant for the Midwest Region of the College Board, a Teachers Teaching with Technology Institute instructor, and a member of the Casio Teacher Advisory Council. John is coauthor of *Advanced Placement Calculus with the TI-89*.

Greg Hill taught AP* Calculus at Hinsdale Central High School in Hinsdale, Illinois from 1986 until his retirement in 2014. He continues to be a College Board consultant, presenting one-day and week-long workshops throughout the Midwest. Greg has also been an AP* Calculus exam reader for more than 10 years. He has authored two other books on calculus and remains active in retirement in AP mathematics circles.

Karyl Tyler taught AP* Calculus AB and BC at Hinsdale Central High School in Hinsdale, Illinois. Her 34 years of teaching experience include 17 years of teaching calculus. Beyond her classroom, Karyl assisted with instruction at Teachers Teaching with Technology Institutes, sharing her passion for using technology in the mathematics classroom. Now that she is retired, she enjoys the leisurely pace at which she can visualize related rates problems while watching her coffee brew every morning.

Steven L. Wilson teaches AP* Calculus AB at Hinsdale Central High School in Hinsdale, Illinois. Many of his 24 years of teaching experience include teaching calculus. Outside of the classroom, Steve works with students who are training for mathematics oral competitions, and has also started up a robotics team at his school that competes in the FIRST® Robotics Competition.

About Your Pearson AP* Guide

Pearson Education is the leading publisher of textbooks worldwide. With operations on every continent, we make it our business to understand the changing needs of students at every level, from kindergarten to college.

This gives us a unique insight into what kind of study materials work for students. We talk to customers every day, soliciting feedback on our books. We think that this makes us especially qualified to offer this series of AP* test prep books, tied to some of our best-selling textbooks.

We know that as you study for your AP* course, you're preparing along the way for the AP* exam. By tying the material in the book directly to AP* course goals and exam topics, we help you focus your time most efficiently. And that's a good thing!

The AP* exam is an important milestone in your education. A high score will position you optimally for college acceptance—and possibly will give you college credits that put you a step ahead. Our goal at Pearson Education is to provide you with the tools you need to excel on the exam … the rest is up to you.

Good Luck!

Acknowledgments

We wish to thank the late Ross Finney, the late Bert Waits, and Frank Demana, Dan Kennedy, David M. Bressoud, Greg Foley, and David E. Bock for precalculus and calculus textbook contributions that made linking their books to AP* Calculus objectives a nearly effortless task. Thanks also to the College Board for its long-standing commitment to educational excellence as exemplified by the AP* Calculus curriculum and assessment standards.

We are indebted to the entire Pearson Education publishing team for their trust, guidance, and patience with us as a writing team.

We also acknowledge the support of Dan Kennedy and David Bressoud for their thoughtful input and wise counsel in shaping this project.

Part I

Introduction to the AP Calculus—AB or BC—Examination

Preparing for the Calculus AP* Exam has been written as a supplement to *Precalculus: Graphical, Numerical, Algebraic* by Demana, Waits, Foley, Kennedy, and Bock and *Calculus: Graphical, Numerical, Algebraic* by Finney, Demana, Waits, Kennedy, and Bressoud. The authors hope that users will find this work faithful to the themes, content, and spirit of those two texts. We also hope that users of other textbooks will recognize the broad-based approach and specific insights of this guide as useful preparation for their students.

This Book

So you are planning to take or have already enrolled in either AP* Calculus AB or AP* Calculus BC! Either AP* course will stretch and enrich your mathematics skills and knowledge and will culminate in an AP* examination.

Presently enrolled in a precalculus course?

Complement the foundational calculus topics encountered in your precalculus course by referencing the Precalculus Review of Calculus Prerequisites in the Appendix of this book. The Appendix describes each calculus prerequisite topic in terms of its Learning Objectives and places it into a calculus *Overview* context, provides succinct *Content* explanations, gives *Additional Practice* problems, and makes *Need More Help?* connections to the Pearson Education *Precalculus* and *Calculus* textbooks.

Presently enrolled in a calculus course?

This book will point out the corresponding AP* Calculus Exam Learning Objectives, identify the *Overview* context, provide succinct *Content* explanations, give *Additional Practice* problems and solutions, and wherever possible make *Need More Help?* connections to Pearson Education *Precalculus* and *Calculus* textbooks, as well as suggest supportive topics from the Appendix.

In either case, this workbook supplement to your textbook will help you clearly identify essential calculus concepts as well as improve both your understanding of such concepts and your ability to communicate your thinking so that you can be successful.

This book is not intended as a substitute for a full precalculus or calculus course or a comprehensive treatment of calculus topics. It is rather meant to act as a useful review for students who have previously studied the curriculum topics and now want to solidify their learning through recall and practice.

The Advanced Placement Calculus AB or BC Curriculum*

The AP* Calculus AB and AP* Calculus BC curricula are designed to provide courses in calculus that are equal in content to the best of collegiate courses. Each is developed by a team of educators from the high school and college communities and continues to adapt itself so that a broad base of college programs will offer credit for success in the respective examination. To find out whether your prospective institution will give credit for your AP* Calculus Examination performance, you should email or call the admissions office. You can log on to AP* Central at www.apcentral.collegeboard.com for up-to-date information about the Advanced Placement* Program.

A course in calculus is especially useful to those pursuing studies in mathematics, as well as an ever-widening variety of engineering, science, economic, and business fields.

Understanding the Advanced Placement Calculus AB or BC Examination*

AP* Calculus Examinations began in 1956 as one of the earliest examinations created by the College Board. Now offered as AP* Calculus AB and AP* Calculus BC, these examinations are given in May during the same two-week window as the other examinations. Your teacher or the AP* coordinator in your school district can give you the exact date for this year's examination. You can also check for this and other information on the AP* Central web site. Test schedules are determined long in advance and the dates and times are not flexible. In the event of an emergency you may qualify for an alternate examination, but the qualifying conditions are extremely rigid. Plan your calendar around the examination date, and register with your teacher or coordinator to reserve an examination. Standard fees as periodically adjusted by the College Board apply.

The AP* Examinations specify calculus content for AP* Calculus AB and AP* Calculus BC under the following three Big Idea headings:

- Limits
- Derivatives
- Integrals and the Fundamental Theorem of Calculus

Additionally, a fourth Big Idea heading for AP* Calculus BC only is

- Series

You may bring to the examination two calculators with graphical capabilities. A complete up-to-date list of acceptable graphing calculators can be found on the College Board web site. We highly recommend using one model throughout the calculus course and bringing that same model to the examination. The exam assumes that your calculator has built-in capabilities to

1. plot the graph of a function within an arbitrary viewing window.
2. find the zeros of functions (solve equations numerically).
3. numerically calculate the derivative of a function.
4. numerically calculate the value of a definite integral.

Many students bring a second calculator as a backup. Fresh batteries are a must! Since calculator memories need not be cleared before taking the examination, calculators may contain whatever additional programs students may desire.

The actual examination is currently formatted and has timing and grade weights as follows:

Section I. Multiple Choice Section	Total of 45 Questions/105 Minutes	50% of Test
Part A (Calculator Not Allowed)	30 questions/60 minutes	
Part B (Calculator Required)	15 questions/45 minutes	
Section II. Free Response	**Total of 6 Questions/90 Minutes**	**50% of Test**
Part A (Calculator Required)	2 questions/30 minutes	
Part B (Calculator Not Allowed)	4 questions/60 minutes	

The Multiple Choice and Free Response sections of the examination are equally weighted. They stand alone with a recommended break between. You should expect to work the full allotted time. You should, if at all possible, allow time in each part of each section to go back and check your work. The Multiple Choice section is done first; you should not expect to go back to it after break. Indeed, that part of the examination will be sealed and collected at the end of the 105-minute time period.

Both the Multiple Choice and Free Response sections come with separate directions for Calculator Not Allowed and Calculator Required portions. In the Multiple Choice section, a student may not return to the Part A section after beginning Part B. In the Free Response section, a student may continue working on the Part A section after beginning Part B, but **may no longer use a calculator.**

Calculus AB Subscore Grade for the Calculus BC Examination

Since the Calculus BC curriculum and examination encompass the Calculus AB curriculum, the Calculus BC is able to report a Calculus AB Subscore. A detailed explanation of the Calculus AB Subscore and its value can be found on the College Board web site.

Understanding the Grading Procedure for the Advanced Placement* Calculus AB or BC Examination

The scoring of an AP* Calculus Examination is done in part by machine (Section I—Multiple Choice) and in part by calculus educators (human beings!) who read the answers as you have communicated them (Section II—Free Response). The entire test is valued at 108 points with the Multiple Choice and Free Response sections each contributing 54 points.

In the Multiple Choice section you are awarded 1 point for each correct answer. There are no penalties for wrong answers, so students are encouraged to answer all questions. Your score is converted to a 54-point total (reflecting 50% of the grade), by multiplying the number of correct answers by 1.2. For example, if you answer 31 questions correctly, your multiple choice score is:

$$\text{MULTIPLE CHOICE SCORE} = 31 \times 1.2 = 37.2$$

In the Free Response section, the *reader* assigns a score from 0–9 as indicated by the rubric or grading rule developed by the Chief Reader and a select team of exam leaders. A rubric is developed for each question to attain scoring consistency.

Suppose your answers to the Free Response questions are scored in the following manner:

Question 1:	8 points
Question 2:	6 points
Question 3:	8 points
Question 4:	5 points
Question 5:	6 points
Question 6:	4 points

FREE RESPONSE SCORE = 37 points

Your Total Exam score would be the sum of the Multiple Choice and Free Response scores: $37.2 + 37 = 74.2$.

This composite score is then subject to the Chief Reader's interpretation of the cut points for that particular examination year's results. These cut points are set shortly after examinations are scored and are based on several factors, including statistical comparability with other years' examinations, the distributions of performance on the various parts of the current year's examination, and previous years of grade distributions.

Your test results will be available from the College Board, usually before mid-July. You must have an online College Board account to access your AP scores as score reports are not mailed. See www.apscore.org for more information. You may already have an account if you registered for the SAT or participated in other College Board programs. If you do not have ready access to the Internet at home, work with your school to create a College Board account and update your AP profile. If that is not possible, use the Internet at a public library. The College Board will send one score report for free to the college you designated on your first AP answer sheet. Scores can be sent to additional colleges using the online service for a fee.

Test-Taking Strategies for an Advanced Placement* Calculus Examination

You should approach the AP* Calculus Examination the same way you would any major test in your academic career. Just remember that *it is a one-shot deal*—you must be at your peak performance level on the day of the test. For that reason you should do everything that your "coach" tells you to do. In most cases your coach is your classroom teacher. It is very likely that your teacher has some experience, based on workshop information or previous students' performance, to share with you.

You should also analyze your own test-taking abilities. At this stage in your education, you probably know your strengths and weaknesses in test-taking situations. You may be very good at multiple choice but weaker in essays, or perhaps it is the other way around. Whatever your particular abilities are, evaluate them and respond accordingly. Spend more time on your weaker points. In other words, rather than spending time in your comfort zone where you need less work, try to improve your soft spots. In all cases, concentrate on *clear communication* of your strategies, techniques, and conclusions.

The following table presents some ideas in a quick and easy form. It is divided into two sections: general strategies for approaching the examination day and specific strategies for addressing particular types of questions on the examination.

General Strategies for AP* Examination Preparation

Time	DOs ☺	DON'Ts ☹
Through the Year	▪ Register with your teacher/coordinator ▪ Pay your fee (if applicable) on time ▪ Take good notes ▪ Work with others in study groups ▪ Review on a regular basis ▪ Evaluate your test-taking strengths and weaknesses—keep track of how successful you are when guessing	▪ Procrastinate ▪ Avoid homework and labs ▪ Wait until the last moment to pull it together for quizzes and tests ▪ Rely on others for your own progress ▪ Scatter your work products (notes, labs, reviews, tests) ▪ Ignore your weak areas—remediate as you go along
The Week Before	▪ Combine independent and group review ▪ Get tips from your teacher ▪ Do lots of mixed review problems ▪ Check your exam date, time, and location ▪ Review the appropriate AP* Calculus syllabus (AB or BC)	▪ Procrastinate ▪ Think you are the only one who is stressed ▪ Forget your priorities—this test is a one-shot deal
The Night Before	▪ Put new batteries in your calculator ▪ Lay out your clothes and supplies so that you are ready to go out the door ▪ Do a short review ▪ Go to bed at a reasonable hour	▪ Study all night ▪ Get caught without fresh batteries
Exam Day	▪ Get up a little earlier than usual ▪ Eat a good breakfast/lunch ▪ Put some hard candy in your pocket in case you need an energy boost during the test ▪ Get to your exam location 15 minutes early	▪ Sleep in ▪ Panic with last-minute cramming
Exam Night	▪ Relax—you earned it	▪ Worry—it's over

Specific Strategies to Use During the AP* Examination

Question Type	DOs ☺	DON'Ts ☹
Multiple Choice	▪ Underline key words and phrases; circle important information you will use ▪ Look at the answer format so that you do not do unnecessary steps ▪ Anticipate the likely errors for the type of question being asked—watch out for obvious choices ▪ When formulas and calculations are needed, write down what you are doing so you can check your procedure ▪ Eliminate as many answers as possible ▪ Guess when necessary from among the most likely answers ▪ Check the units of your answers	▪ Rush—reading the question correctly is the key to answering the question correctly ▪ Do unnecessary calculations (sometimes equations can be left in any form) ▪ Fall into the traps your teacher warned you about—a question that looks too easy may have one of these traps built in ▪ Scribble your work—if you need to review your procedure you wind up having to repeat it ▪ Guess haphazardly ▪ Spend more than 2–3 minutes on any one question—if you don't know, move on ▪ Close the book until time is up
Free Response (All Questions)	▪ Look over all the questions before you start and do the ones that seem easiest first ▪ Read the *entire* question *in all of its parts* ▪ Underline what is being asked ▪ Carry out your strategy by clearly indicating your steps ▪ Move on to the next part of the question if you cannot answer one part ▪ Make up a reasonable answer for one part if the next part requires the previous answer ("Suppose my answer to Part A had been 20 sq. units. Using that area value and the integral $\int_0^k f(x)\,dx = \frac{1}{2} \cdot (20)$, I will find the number k for which the line $x = k$ divides the region equally.") ▪ Write neatly, compactly, and clearly and use calculus vocabulary **correctly** ▪ When useful, include graphs/sketches that illustrate your answer; be sure to label axes ▪ Mark up sketches provided to illustrate your thinking ▪ COMMUNICATE CLEARLY—answer the question asked and place your answer in the CONTEXT of the question ▪ Review your response to make sure that it shows good **mathematical thinking**	▪ Feel all problems must be done in numerical order. ▪ Forget to answer the **question asked** in your haste to write an answer ▪ Begin without a plan ▪ Move on until you have read what you have written for each part to make sure you have not left out important words, punctuation, or numbers ▪ Get stuck on a question—if you have no idea how to proceed after thinking about it, move on ▪ Scribble—a human being must be able to decipher your response ▪ Waste time erasing unless space is an issue—anything crossed out will not be read as part of your answer ▪ Round during computation—wait until you reach a final answer to round ▪ Run on—you are likely to say something INCORRECTLY that will diminish your previously correct response ▪ Assume that the size of the space provided is proportional to the answer desired

AP* Calculus AB and BC— The Concept Outline

Big Idea 1: Limits

Many calculus concepts are developed by first considering a discrete model and then the consequences of a limiting case. Therefore, the idea of limits is essential for discovering and developing important ideas, definitions, formulas, and theorems in calculus. Students must have a solid, intuitive understanding of limits and be able to compute various limits, including one-sided limits, limits at infinity, the limit of a sequence, and infinite limits. They should be able to work with tables and graphs in order to estimate the limit of a function at a point. Students should know the algebraic properties of limits and techniques for finding limits of indeterminate forms, and they should be able to apply limits to understand the behavior of a function near a point. Students must also understand how limits are used to determine continuity, a fundamental property of functions.

Note: In the Concept Outline, subject matter that is included only in the BC course is indicated with gray shading.

Enduring Understandings (Students will understand that . . .)	Learning Objectives (Students will be able to . . .)	Essential Knowledge (Students will know that . . .)
EU 1.1: The concept of a limit can be used to understand the behavior of functions.	LO 1.1A(a): Express limits symbolically using correct notation.	EK 1.1A1: Given a function f, the limit of $f(x)$ as x approaches c is a real number R if $f(x)$ can be made arbitrarily close to R by taking x sufficiently close to c (but not equal to c). If the limit exists and is a real number, then the common notation is $\lim_{x \to c} f(x) = R$.
	LO 1.1A(b): Interpret limits expressed	**EXCLUSION STATEMENT (EK 1.1A1):** *The epsilon-delta definition of a limit is not assessed on the AP Calculus AB or BC Exam. However, teachers may include this topic in the course if time permits.*
		EK 1.1A2: The concept of a limit can be extended to include one-sided limits, limits at infinity, and infinite limits.
		EK 1.1A3: A limit might not exist for some functions at particular values of x. Some ways that the limit might not exist are if the function is unbounded, if the function is oscillating near this value, or if the limit from the left does not equal the limit from the right.

Source: AP Calculus AB and BC Course and Exam Description, Effective Fall 2016. © 2016. Used with permission.

Enduring Understandings (Students will understand that . . .)	Learning Objectives (Students will be able to . . .)	Essential Knowledge (Students will know that . . .)
EU 1.1: The concept of a limit can be used to understand the behavior of functions. *(continued)*		**EXAMPLES OF LIMITS THAT DO NOT EXIST:** $\lim\limits_{x \to 0} \dfrac{1}{x^2} = \infty$ $\qquad$ $\lim\limits_{x \to 0} \sin\left(\dfrac{1}{x}\right)$ *does not exist* $\lim\limits_{x \to 0} \dfrac{\lvert x \rvert}{x}$ *does not exist* $\qquad$ $\lim\limits_{x \to 0} \dfrac{1}{x}$ *does not exist*
	LO 1.1B: Estimate limits of functions.	**EK 1.1B1:** Numerical and graphical information can be used to estimate limits.
	LO 1.1C: Determine limits of functions.	**EK 1.1C1:** Limits of sums, differences, products, quotients, and composite functions can be found using the basic theorems of limits and algebraic rules.
		EK 1.1C2: The limit of a function may be found by using algebraic manipulation, alternate forms of trigonometric functions, or the squeeze theorem.
		EK 1.1C3: Limits of the indeterminate forms $\dfrac{0}{0}$ and $\dfrac{\infty}{\infty}$ may be evaluated using L'Hospital's Rule.
	LO 1.1D: Deduce and interpret behavior of functions using limits.	**EK 1.1D1:** Asymptotic and unbounded behavior of functions can be explained and described using limits.
		EK 1.1D2: Relative magnitudes of functions and their rates of change can be compared using limits.
EU 1.2: Continuity is a key property of functions that is defined using limits.	**LO 1.2A:** Analyze functions for intervals of continuity or points of discontinuity.	**EK 1.2A1:** A function f is continuous at $x = c$ provided that $f(c)$ exists, $\lim\limits_{x \to c} f(x)$ exists, and $\lim\limits_{x \to c} f(x) = f(c)$.
		EK 1.2A2: Polynomial, rational, power, exponential, logarithmic, and trigonometric functions are continuous at all points in their domains.
		EK 1.2A3: Types of discontinuities include removable discontinuities, jump discontinuities, and discontinuities due to vertical asymptotes.
	LO 1.2B: Determine the applicability of important calculus theorems using continuity.	**EK 1.2B1:** Continuity is an essential condition for theorems such as the Intermediate Value Theorem, the Extreme Value Theorem, and the Mean Value Theorem.

Big Idea 2: Derivatives

Using derivatives to describe the rate of change of one variable with respect to another variable allows students to understand change in a variety of contexts. In AP Calculus, students build the derivative using the concept of limits and use the derivative primarily to compute the instantaneous rate of change of a function. Applications of the derivative include finding the slope of a tangent line to a graph at a point, analyzing the graph of a function (for example, determining whether a function is increasing or decreasing and finding concavity and extreme values), and solving problems involving rectilinear motion. Students should be able to use different definitions of the derivative, estimate derivatives from tables and graphs, and apply various derivative rules and properties. In addition, students should be able to solve separable differential equations, understand and be able to apply the Mean Value Theorem, and be familiar with a variety of real-world applications, including related rates, optimization, and growth and decay models.

Enduring Understandings (Students will understand that . . .)	Learning Objectives (Students will be able to . . .)	Essential Knowledge (Students will know that . . .)
EU 2.1: The derivative of a function is defined as the limit of a difference quotient and can be determined using a variety of strategies.	**LO 2.1A:** Identify the derivative of a function as the limit of a difference quotient.	**EK 2.1A1:** The difference quotients $\dfrac{f(a + h) - f(a)}{h}$ and $\dfrac{f(x) - f(a)}{x - a}$ express the average rate of change of a function over an interval.
		EK 2.1A2: The instantaneous rate of change of a function at a point can be expressed by $\lim\limits_{h \to 0} \dfrac{f(a + h) - f(a)}{h}$ or $\lim\limits_{x \to a} \dfrac{f(x) - f(a)}{x - a}$, provided that the limit exists. These are common forms of the definition of the derivative and are denoted $f'(a)$.
		EK 2.1A3: The derivative of f is the function whose value at x is $\lim\limits_{h \to 0} \dfrac{f(x + h) - f(x)}{h}$ provided this limit exists.
		EK 2.1A4: For $y = f(x)$, notations for the derivative include $\dfrac{dy}{dx}$, $f'(x)$, and y'.
		EK 2.1A5: The derivative can be represented graphically, numerically, analytically, and verbally.
	LO 2.1B: Estimate derivatives.	**EK 2.1B1:** The derivative at a point can be estimated from information given in tables or graphs.

Enduring Understandings (Students will understand that . . .)	Learning Objectives (Students will be able to . . .)	Essential Knowledge (Students will know that . . .)
EU 2.1: The derivative of a function is defined as the limit of a difference quotient and can be determined using a variety of strategies. *(continued)*	LO 2.1C: Calculate derivatives.	EK 2.1C1: Direct application of the definition of the derivative can be used to find the derivative for selected functions, including polynomial, power, sine, cosine, exponential, and logarithmic functions.
		EK 2.1C2: Specific rules can be used to calculate derivatives for classes of functions, including polynomial, rational, power, exponential, logarithmic, trigonometric, and inverse trigonometric.
		EK 2.1C3: Sums, differences, products, and quotients of functions can be differentiated using derivative rules.
		EK 2.1C4: The chain rule provides a way to differentiate composite functions.
		EK 2.1C5: The chain rule is the basis for implicit differentiation.
		EK 2.1C6: The chain rule can be used to find the derivative of an inverse function, provided the derivative of that function exists.
		EK 2.1C7: (BC) Methods for calculating derivatives of real-valued functions can be extended to vector-valued functions, parametric functions, and functions in polar coordinates.
	LO 2.1D: Determine higher order derivatives.	EK 2.1D1: Differentiating f' produces the second derivative f'', provided the derivative of f' exists; repeating this process produces higher order derivatives of f.
		EK 2.1D2: Higher order derivatives are represented with a variety of notations. For $y = f(x)$, notations for the second derivative include $\dfrac{d^2y}{dx^2}$, $f''(x)$, and y''. Higher order derivatives can be denoted $\dfrac{d^ny}{dx^n}$ or $f^{(n)}(x)$.
EU 2.2: A function's derivative, which is itself a function, can be used to understand the behavior of the function.	LO 2.2A: Use derivatives to analyze properties of a function.	EK 2.2A1: First and second derivatives of a function can provide information about the function and its graph including intervals of increase or decrease, local (relative) and global (absolute) extrema, intervals of upward or downward concavity, and points of inflection.

Enduring Understandings (Students will understand that . . .)	Learning Objectives (Students will be able to . . .)	Essential Knowledge (Students will know that . . .)
EU 2.2: A function's derivative, which is itself a function, can be used to understand the behavior of the function. *(continued)*	LLO 2.2A: Use derivatives to analyze properties of a function. *(continued)*	EK 2.2A2: Key features of functions and their derivatives can be identified and related to their graphical, numerical, and analytical representations.
		EK 2.2A3: Key features of the graphs of f, f', and f'' are related to one another.
		EK 2.2A4: (BC) For a curve given by a polar equation $r = f(\theta)$, derivatives of r, x, and y with respect to θ and first and second derivatives of y with respect to x can provide information about the curve.
	LO 2.2B: Recognize the connection between differentiability and continuity.	EK 2.2B1: A continuous function may fail to be differentiable at a point in its domain.
		EK 2.2B2: If a function is differentiable at a point, then it is continuous at that point.
EU 2.3: The derivative has multiple interpretations and applications including those that involve instantaneous rates of change.	LO 2.3A: Interpret the meaning of a derivative within a problem.	EK 2.3A1: The unit for $f'(x)$ is the unit for f divided by the unit for x.
		EK 2.3A2: The derivative of a function can be interpreted as the instantaneous rate of change with respect to its independent variable.
	LO 2.3B: Solve problems involving the slope of a tangent line.	EK 2.3B1: The derivative at a point is the slope of the line tangent to a graph at that point on the graph.
		EK 2.3B2: The tangent line is the graph of a locally linear approximation of the function near the point of tangency.
	LO 2.3C: Solve problems involving related rates, optimization, rectilinear motion, (BC) and planar motion.	EK 2.3C1: The derivative can be used to solve rectilinear motion problems involving position, speed, velocity, and acceleration.
		EK 2.3C2: The derivative can be used to solve related rates problems, that is, finding a rate at which one quantity is changing by relating it to other quantities whose rates of change are known.
		EK 2.3C3: The derivative can be used to solve optimization problems, that is, finding a maximum or minimum value of a function over a given interval.
		EK 2.3C4: (BC) Derivatives can be used to determine velocity, speed, and acceleration for a particle moving along curves given by parametric or vector-valued functions.

Enduring Understandings (Students will understand that . . .)	Learning Objectives (Students will be able to . . .)	Essential Knowledge (Students will know that . . .)
EU 2.3: The derivative has multiple interpretations and applications including those that involve instantaneous rates of change. *(continued)*	LO 2.3D: Solve problems involving rates of change in applied contexts.	EK 2.3D1: The derivative can be used to express information about rates of change in applied contexts.
	LO 2.3E: Verify solutions to differential equations.	EK 2.3E1: Solutions to differential equations are functions or families of functions.
		EK 2.3E2: Derivatives can be used to verify that a function is a solution to a given differential equation.
	LO 2.3F: Estimate solutions to differential equations.	EK 2.3F1: Slope fields provide visual clues to the behavior of solutions to first order differential equations.
		EK 2.3F2: (BC) For differential equations, Euler's method provides a procedure for approximating a solution or a point on a solution curve.
EU 2.4: The Mean Value Theorem connects the behavior of a differentiable function over an interval to the behavior of the derivative of that function at a particular point in the interval.	LO 2.4A: Apply the Mean Value Theorem to describe the behavior of a function over an interval.	EK 2.4A1: If a function f is continuous over the interval $[a, b]$ and differentiable over the interval (a, b), the Mean Value Theorem guarantees a point within that open interval where the instantaneous rate of change equals the average rate of change over the interval.

Big Idea 3: Integrals and the Fundamental Theorem of Calculus

Integrals are used in a wide variety of practical and theoretical applications. AP Calculus students should understand the definition of a definite integral involving a Riemann sum, be able to approximate a definite integral using different methods, and be able to compute definite integrals using geometry. They should be familiar with basic techniques of integration and properties of integrals. The interpretation of a definite integral is an important skill, and students should be familiar with area, volume, and motion applications, as well as with the use of the definite integral as an accumulation function. It is critical that students grasp the relationship between integration and differentiation as expressed in the Fundamental Theorem of Calculus — a central idea in AP Calculus. Students should be able to work with and analyze functions defined by an integral.

Enduring Understandings (Students will understand that . . .)	Learning Objectives (Students will be able to . . .)	Essential Knowledge (Students will know that . . .)
EU 3.1: Antidifferentiation is the inverse process of differentiation.	LO 3.1A: Recognize antiderivatives of basic functions.	EK 3.1A1: An antiderivative of a function f is a function g whose derivative is f.
		EK 3.1A2: Differentiation rules provide the foundation for finding antiderivatives.
EU 3.2: The definite integral of a function over an interval is the limit of a Riemann sum over that interval and can be calculated using a variety of strategies.	LO 3.2A(a): Interpret the definite integral as the limit of a Riemann sum.	EK 3.2A1: A Riemann sum, which requires a partition of an interval I, is the sum of products, each of which is the value of the function at a point in a subinterval multiplied by the length of that subinterval of the partition.
	LO 3.2A(b): Express the limit of a Riemann sum in integral notation.	EK 3.2A2: The definite integral of a continuous function f over the interval $[a, b]$, denoted by $\int_a^b f(x)dx$, is the limit of Riemann sums as the widths of the subintervals approach 0. That is, $\int_a^b f(x)dx = \lim_{\max \Delta x_i \to 0} \sum_{i=1}^n f(x_i^*)\Delta x_i$ where x_i^* is a value in the ith subinterval, Δx_i is the width of the ith subinterval, n is the number of subintervals, and $\max \Delta x_i$ is the width of the largest subinterval. Another form of the definition is $\int_a^b f(x)dx = \lim_{n \to \infty} \sum_{i=1}^n f(x_i^*)\Delta x_i$, where $\Delta x_i = \dfrac{b-a}{n}$ and x_i^* is a value in the ith subinterval.
		EK 3.2A3: The information in a definite integral can be translated into the limit of a related Riemann sum, and the limit of a Riemann sum can be written as a definite integral.

Enduring Understandings (Students will understand that . . .)	Learning Objectives (Students will be able to . . .)	Essential Knowledge (Students will know that . . .)
EU 3.2: The definite integral of a function over an interval is the limit of a Riemann sum over that interval and can be calculated using a variety of strategies. *(continued)*	**LO 3.2B:** Approximate a definite integral.	**EK 3.2B1:** Definite integrals can be approximated for functions that are represented graphically, numerically, algebraically, and verbally.
		EK 3.2B2: Definite integrals can be approximated using a left Riemann sum, a right Riemann sum, a midpoint Riemann sum, or a trapezoidal sum; approximations can be computed using either uniform or nonuniform partitions.
	LO 3.2C: Calculate a definite integral using areas and properties of definite integrals.	**EK 3.2C1:** In some cases, a definite integral can be evaluated by using geometry and the connection between the definite integral and area.
		EK 3.2C2: Properties of definite integrals include the integral of a constant times a function, the integral of the sum of two functions, reversal of limits of integration, and the integral of a function over adjacent intervals.
		EK 3.2C3: The definition of the definite integral may be extended to functions with removable or jump discontinuities.
	LO 3.2D: (BC) Evaluate an improper integral or show that an improper integral diverges.	**EK 3.2D1: (BC)** An improper integral is an integral that has one or both limits infinite or has an integrand that is unbounded in the interval of integration.
		EK 3.2D2: (BC) Improper integrals can be determined using limits of definite integrals.
EU 3.3: The Fundamental Theorem of Calculus, which has two distinct formulations, connects differentiation and integration.	**LO 3.3A:** Analyze functions defined by an integral.	**EK 3.3A1:** The definite integral can be used to define new functions; for example, $f(x) = \int_0^x e^{-t^2} dt$
		EK 3.3A2: If f is a continuous function on the interval $[a, b]$, then $\frac{d}{dx}\left(\int_a^x f(t)dt\right) = f(x)$, where x is between a and b.
		EK 3.3A3: Graphical, numerical, analytical, and verbal representations of a function f provide information about the function g defined as $g(x) = \int_a^x f(t)dt$.
	LO 3.3B(a): Calculate antiderivatives.	**EK 3.3B1:** The function defined by $F(x) = \int_a^x f(t)dt$ is an antiderivative of f.
	LO 3.3B(b): Evaluate definite integrals.	**EK 3.3B2:** If f is continuous on the interval $[a, b]$ and F is an antiderivative of f, then $\int_a^b f(x)dx = F(b) - F(a)$.

Enduring Understandings (Students will understand that . . .)	Learning Objectives (Students will be able to . . .)	Essential Knowledge (Students will know that . . .)
EU 3.3: The Fundamental Theorem of Calculus, which has two distinct formulations, connects differentiation and integration. *(continued)*	**LO 3.3B(a):** Calculate antiderivatives. **LO 3.3B(b):** Evaluate definite integrals. *(continued)*	**EK 3.3B3:** The notation $\int f(x)dx = F(x) + C$ means that $F'(x) = f(x)$, and $\int f(x)dx$ is called an indefinite integral of the function f. **EK 3.3B4:** Many functions do not have closed form antiderivatives. **EK 3.3B5:** Techniques for finding antiderivatives include algebraic manipulation such as long division and completing the square, substitution of variables, **(BC)** integration by parts, and nonrepeating linear partial fractions.
EU 3.4: The definite integral of a function over an interval is a mathematical tool with many interpretations and applications involving accumulation.	**LO 3.4A:** Interpret the meaning of a definite integral within a problem.	**EK 3.4A1:** A function defined as an integral represents an accumulation of a rate of change. **EK 3.4A2:** The definite integral of the rate of change of a quantity over an interval gives the net change of that quantity over that interval. **EK 3.4A3:** The limit of an approximating Riemann sum can be interpreted as a definite integral.
	LO 3.4B: Apply definite integrals to problems involving the average value of a function.	**EK 3.4B1:** The average value of a function f over an interval $[a, b]$ is $\dfrac{1}{b-a}\displaystyle\int_a^b f(x)dx$.
	LO 3.4C: Apply definite integrals to problems involving motion.	**EK 3.4C1:** For a particle in rectilinear motion over an interval of time, the definite integral of velocity represents the particle's displacement over the interval of time, and the definite integral of speed represents the particle's total distance traveled over the interval of time. **EK 3.4C2: (BC)** The definite integral can be used to determine displacement, distance, and position of a particle moving along a curve given by parametric or vector-valued functions.

Enduring Understandings (Students will understand that . . .)	Learning Objectives (Students will be able to . . .)	Essential Knowledge (Students will know that . . .)
EU 3.4: The definite integral of a function over an interval is a mathematical tool with many interpretations and applications involving accumulation. *(continued)*	**LO 3.4D:** Apply definite integrals to problems involving area, volume, **(BC)** and length of a curve.	**EK 3.4D1:** Areas of certain regions in the plane can be calculated with definite integrals. **(BC)** Areas bounded by polar curves can be calculated with definite integrals.
		EK 3.4D2: Volumes of solids with known cross sections, including discs and washers, can be calculated with definite integrals.
		EK 3.4D3: (BC) The length of a planar curve defined by a function or by a parametrically defined curve can be calculated using a definite integral.
	LO 3.4E: Use the definite integral to solve problems in various contexts.	**EK 3.4E1:** The definite integral can be used to express information about accumulation and net change in many applied contexts.
EU 3.5: Antidifferentiation is an underlying concept involved in solving separable differential equations. Solving separable differential equations involves determining a function or relation given its rate of change.	**LO 3.5A:** Analyze differential equations to obtain general and specific solutions.	**EK 3.5A1:** Antidifferentiation can be used to find specific solutions to differential equations with given initial conditions, including applications to motion along a line, exponential growth and decay, **(BC)** and logistic growth.
		EK 3.5A2: Some differential equations can be solved by separation of variables.
		EK 3.5A3: Solutions to differential equations may be subject to domain restrictions.
		EK 3.5A4: The function F defined by $F(x) = c + \int_a^x f(t)dt$ is a general solution to the differential equation $\frac{dy}{dx} = f(x)$, and $F(x) = y_0 + \int_a^x f(t)dt$ is a particular solution to the differential equation $\frac{dy}{dx} = f(x)$ satisfying $F(a) = y_0$.
	LO 3.5B: Interpret, create and solve differential equations from problems in context.	**EK 3.5B1:** The model for exponential growth and decay that arises from the statement "The rate of change of a quantity is proportional to the size of the quantity" is $\frac{dy}{dt} = ky$.
		EK 3.5B2: (BC) The model for logistic growth that arises from the statement "The rate of change of a quantity is jointly proportional to the size of the quantity and the difference between the quantity and the carrying capacity" is $\frac{dy}{dt} = ky(a - y)$.

Big Idea 4: Series (BC)

The AP Calculus BC curriculum includes the study of series of numbers, power series, and various methods to determine convergence or divergence of a series. Students should be familiar with Maclaurin series for common functions and general Taylor series representations. Other topics include the radius and interval of convergence and operations on power series. The technique of using power series to approximate an arbitrary function near a specific value allows for an important connection to the tangent-line problem and is a natural extension that helps achieve a better approximation. The concept of approximation is a common theme throughout AP Calculus, and power series provide a unifying, comprehensive conclusion.

Enduring Understandings (Students will understand that . . .)	Learning Objectives (Students will be able to . . .)	Essential Knowledge (Students will know that . . .)
EU 4.1: The sum of an infinite number of real numbers may converge.	LO 4.1A: Determine whether a series converges or diverges.	EK 4.1A1: The nth partial sum is defined as the sum of the first n terms of a sequence.
		EK 4.1A2: An infinite series of numbers converges to a real number S (or has sum S), if and only if the limit of its sequence of partial sums exists and equals S.
		EK 4.1A3: Common series of numbers include geometric series, the harmonic series, and p-series.
		EK 4.1A4: A series may be absolutely convergent, conditionally convergent, or divergent.
		EK 4.1A5: If a series converges absolutely, then it converges.
		EK 4.1A6: In addition to examining the limit of the sequence of partial sums of the series, methods for determining whether a series of numbers converges or diverges are the nth term test, the comparison test, the limit comparison test, the integral test, the ratio test, and the alternating series test.
		EXCLUSION STATEMENT (EK 4.1A6): *Other methods for determining convergence or divergence of a series of numbers are not assessed on the AP Calculus AB or BC Exam. However, teachers may include these topics in the course if time permits.*

Enduring Understandings (Students will understand that . . .)	Learning Objectives (Students will be able to . . .)	Essential Knowledge (Students will know that . . .)
EU 4.1: The sum of an infinite number of real numbers may converge. *(continued)*	LO 4.1B: Determine or estimate the sum of a series.	EK 4.1B1: If a is a real number and r is a real number such that $|r| < 1$, then the geometric series $\sum_{n=0}^{\infty} ar^n = \dfrac{a}{1-r}$.
		EK 4.1B2: If an alternating series converges by the alternating series test, then the alternating series error bound can be used to estimate how close a partial sum is to the value of the infinite series.
		EK 4.1B3: If a series converges absolutely, then any series obtained from it by regrouping or rearranging the terms has the same value.
EU 4.2: A function can be represented by an associated power series over the interval of convergence for the power series.	LO 4.2A: Construct and use Taylor polynomials.	EK 4.2A1: The coefficient of the nth-degree term in a Taylor polynomial centered at $x = a$ for the function f is $\dfrac{f^{(n)}(a)}{n!}$.
		EK 4.2A2: Taylor polynomials for a function f centered at $x = a$ can be used to approximate function values of f near $x = a$.
		EK 4.2A3: In many cases, as the degree of a Taylor polynomial increases, the nth-degree polynomial will converge to the original function over some interval.
		EK 4.2A4: The Lagrange error bound can be used to bound the error of a Taylor polynomial approximation to a function.
		EK 4.2A5: In some situations where the signs of a Taylor polynomial are alternating, the alternating series error bound can be used to bound the error of a Taylor polynomial approximation to the function.
	LO 4.2B: Write a power series representing a given function.	EK 4.2B1: A power series is a series of the form $\sum_{n=0}^{\infty} a_n(x - r)^n$ where n is a non-negative integer, $\{a_n\}$ is a sequence of real numbers, and r is a real number.
		EK 4.2B2: The Maclaurin series for $\sin(x)$, $\cos(x)$, and e^x provide the foundation for constructing the Maclaurin series for other functions.
		EK 4.2B3: The Maclaurin series for $\dfrac{1}{1-x}$ is a geometric series.
		EK 4.2B4: A Taylor polynomial for $f(x)$ is a partial sum of the Taylor series for $f(x)$.

Enduring Understandings (Students will understand that . . .)	Learning Objectives (Students will be able to . . .)	Essential Knowledge (Students will know that . . .)
EU 4.2: A function can be represented by an associated power series over the interval of convergence for the power series. *(continued)*	LO 4.2B: Write a power series representing a given function. *(continued)*	EK 4.2B5: A power series for a given function can be derived by various methods (e.g., algebraic processes, substitutions, using properties of geometric series, and operations on known series such as term-by-term integration or term-by-term differentiation).
	LO 4.2C: Determine the radius and interval of convergence of a power series.	EK 4.2C1: If a power series converges, it either converges at a single point or has an interval of convergence.
		EK 4.2C2: The ratio test can be used to determine the radius of convergence of a power series.
		EK 4.2C3: If a power series has a positive radius of convergence, then the power series is the Taylor series of the function to which it converges over the open interval.
		EK 4.2C4: The radius of convergence of a power series obtained by term-by-term differentiation or term-by-term integration is the same as the radius of convergence of the original power series.

Part II

Review of AP Calculus AB and BC Topics*

To help you prepare for the AP* Calculus AB or AP* Calculus BC Examination this section is organized under the topical heading themes associated with each of those courses. Working through the respective set of AP* Learning Objectives will help you confidently answer the essential question:

What am I expected to know and be able to do on the AP* Calculus Examination?

Limits of Functions

AP* Learning Objectives: • Express limits symbolically using correct notation. (LO 1.1A(a))
• Interpret limits expressed symbolically. (LO 1.1A(b))
• Estimate limits of functions. (LO 1.1B)
• Determine limits of functions. (LO 1.1C)
• Deduce and interpret behavior of functions using limits. (LO 1.1D)

Overview

To determine the behavior of a function, we evaluate its *limits* at significant points of its domain. We can use limits to determine where a function is continuous and where it has asymptotes, as well as to predict its values and end behavior. The concept of limits allows us to find instantaneous rates of change, a study that leads to differential calculus. We also use limits to estimate areas under curves, which leads to integral calculus. You should be able to determine limits using methods of substitution, algebra, graphing, or numerical approximation.

Content and Practice

When we are finding the limit of a function, we are determining the value that the function, $f(x)$, approaches as x gets very close to some particular value. This does not mean that $f(x)$ takes on that value at x, but rather that it *approaches* that value. Additionally, we sometimes find a limit of a function as x approaches either infinity or negative infinity (see example 5).

For a limit to exist as x approaches some value c, the limit of the function must be the same regardless if x approaches c from the right or from the left. If c is either a right- or left-hand endpoint, we may be able to find a one-sided limit at that point.

A function $f(x)$ has a limit, L, as x approaches c if and only if

$$\lim_{x \to c^-} f(x) = \lim_{x \to c^+} f(x) = L.$$

Simply write $\lim_{x \to c} f(x) = L.$

You will notice that the definition specifies that three different conditions be met.

$$\lim_{x \to c^-} f(x) = \lim_{x \to c^+} f(x) = L$$

This is easily done by evaluating the three parts separately, as the following example illustrates.

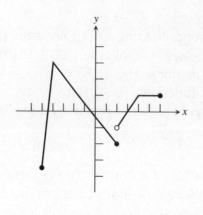

$$y = f(x)$$
$$[-6, 6] \text{ by } [-4, 4]$$

$$\lim_{x \to 2^-} f(x) = -2$$

$$\lim_{x \to 2^+} f(x) = -1$$

Since $\lim_{x \to 2^-} f(x) \neq \lim_{x \to 2^+} f(x)$,

$\lim_{x \to 2} f(x)$ does not exist.

We shall review finding two-sided and one-sided limits as well as limits that involve infinity.

Two-Sided Limits

One method that can sometimes be used to find a limit of a function is to substitute that value into the function. Find the following limits using substitution.

1. $\displaystyle \lim_{x \to 2} (x^3 - 5) =$

2. $\displaystyle \lim_{x \to -4} \left(\frac{x^2}{x - 2} \right) =$

3. (a) $\displaystyle \lim_{x \to 3} \left(\frac{x^2 - 9}{x^2 - 5x + 6} \right) =$

    (b) The substitution method was not helpful in part (a). Why?

(c) Use algebra to solve this problem.

$$\lim_{x \to 3} \frac{x^2 - 9}{x^2 - 5x + 6} =$$

$$\lim_{x \to 3} \frac{(\qquad)(\qquad)}{(\qquad)(\qquad)} =$$

$$\lim_{x \to 3} \frac{\qquad}{\qquad} =$$

(d) Use a table of function values to approximate $\lim_{x \to 3} f(x)$.

x	$f(x)$
2.7	8.1429
2.8	7.25
2.9	6.5556
3	
3.1	5.5455
3.2	5.1667

One-Sided Limits

4.

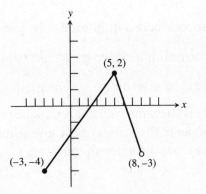

At the endpoints, we can find only the right-hand limit as x approaches -3 and the left-hand limit as x approaches 8.

(a) $\displaystyle\lim_{x \to -3^+} f(x) =$

(b) $\displaystyle\lim_{x \to 8^-} f(x) =$

Limits Involving Infinity

5.

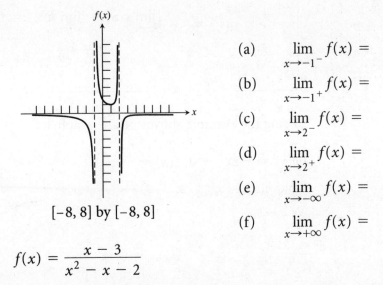

$[-8, 8]$ by $[-8, 8]$

$$f(x) = \frac{x - 3}{x^2 - x - 2}$$

(a) $\displaystyle\lim_{x \to -1^-} f(x) =$

(b) $\displaystyle\lim_{x \to -1^+} f(x) =$

(c) $\displaystyle\lim_{x \to 2^-} f(x) =$

(d) $\displaystyle\lim_{x \to 2^+} f(x) =$

(e) $\displaystyle\lim_{x \to -\infty} f(x) =$

(f) $\displaystyle\lim_{x \to +\infty} f(x) =$

Problem 5 illustrates the following properties.

> If either $\lim\limits_{x \to a^-} f(x) = \pm\infty$ or $\lim\limits_{x \to a^+} f(x) = \pm\infty$, then the line $x = a$ is a *vertical asymptote* of the graph of the function $y = f(x)$.

> If either $\lim\limits_{x \to +\infty} f(x) = b$ or $\lim\limits_{x \to -\infty} f(x) = b$, then the line $y = b$ is a *horizontal asymptote* of the graph of the function $y = f(x)$.

Squeeze Theorem

There are instances where a limit cannot be found directly, so indirect methods are required. For example, if we try to use substitution to find $\lim\limits_{x \to 0} \frac{\sin 2x}{x}$, we obtain the inconclusive result of $\frac{0}{0}$. One method that can be used to determine limits indirectly is the Squeeze Theorem. The objective is to find two functions whose values squeeze the values of the given function and whose limits are the same as x approaches the value in question.

> **The Squeeze Theorem**
>
> If $g(x) \leq f(x) \leq h(x)$ for all $x \neq c$ in some interval about c, and
>
> $$\lim_{x \to c} g(x) = \lim_{x \to c} h(x) = L, \text{ then}$$
>
> $$\lim_{x \to c} f(x) = L.$$

Using the example above and the graph, let

$g(x) = -2x^2 + 2, f(x) = \frac{\sin 2x}{x}$

and $h(x) = x^2 + 2$.

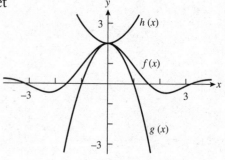

Notice that $g(x) \le f(x) \le h(x)$ for all x. Therefore

$$\lim_{x \to 0} (-2x^2 + 2) \le \lim_{x \to 0} \frac{\sin 2x}{x} \le \lim_{x \to 0} (x^2 + 2).$$

Substitution yields

$$2 \le \lim_{x \to 0} \frac{\sin 2x}{x} \le 2.$$

As a result, we may conclude that

$$\lim_{x \to 0} \frac{\sin 2x}{x} = 2.$$

The Squeeze Theorem proves $\lim_{x \to 0} \dfrac{\sin(ax)}{ax} = 1$. This fact is often used to determine the limits of composite functions that involve trigonometry.

Find $\lim_{x \to 0} \dfrac{\tan(3x)}{2x}$.

$$
\begin{aligned}
\lim_{x \to 0} \frac{\tan(3x)}{2x} &= \lim_{x \to 0} \frac{\sin(3x)}{2x \cos(3x)} \\[2mm]
&= \lim_{x \to 0} \left(\frac{\sin(3x)}{x} \cdot \frac{1}{2\cos(3x)} \right) \\[2mm]
&= \lim_{x \to 0} \left(\frac{\sin(3x)}{x} \cdot \frac{1}{2\cos(3x)} \cdot \frac{3}{3} \right) \\[2mm]
&= \lim_{x \to 0} \left(\frac{\sin(3x)}{3x} \cdot \frac{3}{2\cos(3x)} \right) \\[2mm]
&= \lim_{x \to 0} \left(\frac{\sin(3x)}{3x} \right) \cdot \lim_{x \to 0} \left(\frac{3}{2\cos(3x)} \right) \\[2mm]
&= 1 \cdot \left(\frac{3}{2} \right) \\[2mm]
&= \frac{3}{2}
\end{aligned}
$$

6. Use the Squeeze Theorem to find $\lim\limits_{x \to 0} \left(3 - x^4 \sin\left(\dfrac{1}{x}\right) \right)$.

$$\underline{\hspace{2cm}} \le \sin\left(\dfrac{1}{x}\right) \le \underline{\hspace{2cm}}$$

$$\underline{\hspace{2cm}} \le x^4 \sin\left(\dfrac{1}{x}\right) \le \underline{\hspace{2cm}}$$

$$\underline{\hspace{2cm}} \le -x^4 \sin\left(\dfrac{1}{x}\right) \le \underline{\hspace{2cm}}$$

$$\underline{\hspace{2cm}} \ge -x^4 \sin\left(\dfrac{1}{x}\right) \ge \underline{\hspace{2cm}}$$

$$\underline{\hspace{2cm}} \le 3 - x^4 \sin\left(\dfrac{1}{x}\right) \le \underline{\hspace{2cm}}$$

$$\lim_{x \to 0} \underline{\hspace{1.5cm}} \le \lim_{x \to 0} \left(3 - x^4 \sin\left(\dfrac{1}{x}\right) \right) \le \lim_{x \to 0} \underline{\hspace{1.5cm}}$$

$$\underline{\hspace{2cm}} \le \lim_{x \to 0} \left(3 - x^4 \sin\left(\dfrac{1}{x}\right) \right) \le \underline{\hspace{2cm}}$$

$$\lim_{x \to 0} \left(3 - x^4 \sin\left(\dfrac{1}{x}\right) \right) = \underline{\hspace{2cm}}$$

Additional Practice

1. $f(x) = \begin{cases} 2x - 3, & x \le 2 \\ x^2 - 1, & x > 2 \end{cases}$

   (a) $\lim\limits_{x \to 2^-} f(x) =$

   (b) $\lim\limits_{x \to 2^+} f(x) =$

   (c) What does this imply about the $\lim\limits_{x \to 2} f(x)$? Explain. $\underline{\hspace{3cm}}$

   $\underline{\hspace{10cm}}$

2. Let $f(x) = \begin{cases} 2x - 3, & x \le 2 \\ x^2 + a, & x > 2. \end{cases}$

   Use one-sided limits to find the value of a so that $\lim\limits_{x \to 2} f(x) = 1$.

3.

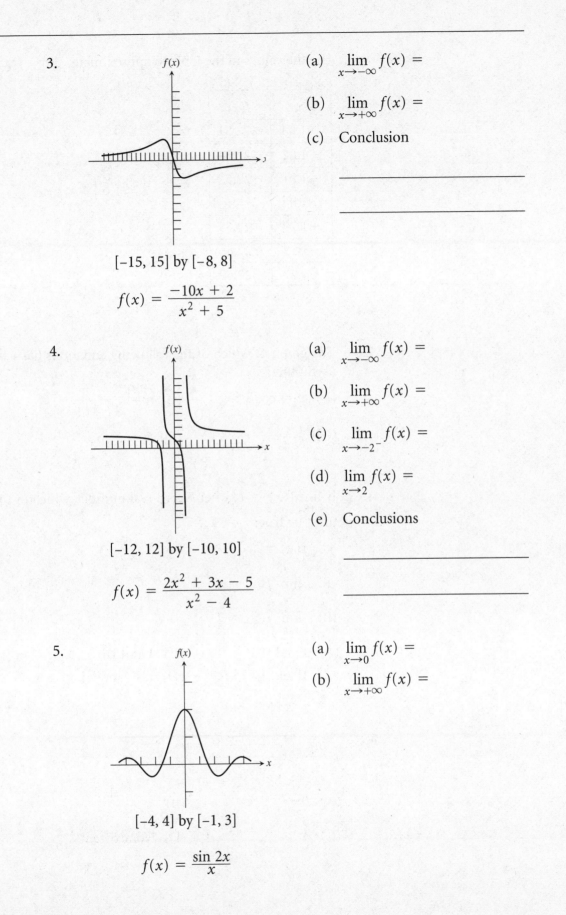

(a) $\lim\limits_{x \to -\infty} f(x) =$

(b) $\lim\limits_{x \to +\infty} f(x) =$

(c) Conclusion

_____

_____

$[-15, 15]$ by $[-8, 8]$

$$f(x) = \frac{-10x + 2}{x^2 + 5}$$

4.

(a) $\lim\limits_{x \to -\infty} f(x) =$

(b) $\lim\limits_{x \to +\infty} f(x) =$

(c) $\lim\limits_{x \to -2^-} f(x) =$

(d) $\lim\limits_{x \to 2} f(x) =$

(e) Conclusions

_____

_____

$[-12, 12]$ by $[-10, 10]$

$$f(x) = \frac{2x^2 + 3x - 5}{x^2 - 4}$$

5.

(a) $\lim\limits_{x \to 0} f(x) =$

(b) $\lim\limits_{x \to +\infty} f(x) =$

$[-4, 4]$ by $[-1, 3]$

$$f(x) = \frac{\sin 2x}{x}$$

6. Use the values in the table to approximate $\lim\limits_{x \to -1.8} f(x)$.

x	$f(x)$
-1.83	-22.51
-1.82	-22.54
-1.81	-22.57
-1.8	
-1.79	-22.63
-1.78	-22.66
-1.77	-22.69

7. The graph of which of the following equations has $y = 1$ as an asymptote?

(A) $y = \cos x$

(B) $y = \dfrac{x^3}{x^2 + 1}$

(C) $y = \dfrac{x^2}{x^2 - 5}$

(D) $y = -\ln x$

8. If $\lim\limits_{x \to a} f(x) = L$, where L is a real number, which of the following must be true?

I. $f(a) = L$

II. $\lim\limits_{x \to a^-} f(x) = L$

III. $\lim\limits_{x \to a^+} f(x) = L$

(A) I and II

(B) I and III

(C) II and III

(D) I, II, and III

9. $\lim\limits_{x \to -\infty} \dfrac{4x^2 + x - 7}{x^2 - 5x - 3} =$

(A) 0

(B) $\dfrac{7}{3}$

(C) 4

(D) Nonexistent

10. If the graph of $y = \dfrac{ax + b}{x + c}$ has a horizontal asymptote $y = -2$, a vertical asymptote $x = 4$, and an x-intercept of 1.5, then $a - b + c =$

   (A) -9 (B) -3 (C) 1 (D) 5

11. Let $\lim\limits_{x \to -2} f(x) = 6$ and $\lim\limits_{x \to -2} g(x) = -3$. Find $\lim\limits_{x \to -2} \dfrac{f(x)}{5 - [g(x)]^2}$.

   (A) $-\dfrac{3}{2}$ (B) $\dfrac{3}{7}$ (C) $\dfrac{3}{4}$ (D) $\dfrac{3}{2}$

12. Find $\lim\limits_{x \to 0} \dfrac{5}{3x \csc(2x)}$ and verify your answer algebraically.

Need More Help With . . .

   Limits?

See . . .

   Precalculus, Section 11.3

   Calculus, Sections 2.1, 2.2

Asymptotic and Unbounded Behavior

AP* Learning Objectives:
- Express limits symbolically using correct notation. (LO 1.1A(a))
- Interpret limits expressed symbolically. (LO 1.1A(b))
- Deduce and interpret behavior of functions using limits. (LO 1.1D)

Overview

Graphical models help us visualize the relationships between the variable quantities of the numerical or algebraic models. By understanding the behaviors of the graphs, we can make predictions in their real-world applications. Graphs of past and present business data can help predict future growth. Calculus studies include many different types of optimization and related rate problems, which analyze practical situations. A good knowledge of basic graphs and their behavior is invaluable in solving these problems.

Content and Practice

When we are looking for restrictions on a function's domain, we need to determine if there are any *vertical asymptotes*. Similarly, finding *horizontal asymptotes* will help us determine a function's range. The concept of boundedness of a graph also gives us insight as to the range. If we know a function's domain and range, we know on what intervals we can expect to evaluate and analyze a function.

Vertical Asymptotes

Consider the following function.

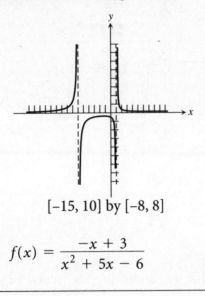

[–15, 10] by [–8, 8]

$$\lim_{x \to -6^-} f(x) = \infty \quad \text{and}$$
$$\lim_{x \to -6^+} f(x) = -\infty$$

We may conclude that the line $x = -6$ is a vertical asymptote of the graph of $f(x)$.

$$\lim_{x \to 1^-} f(x) = -\infty \quad \text{and} \quad \lim_{x \to 1^+} f(x) = \infty$$

We may conclude that the line $x = 1$ is a vertical asymptote of the graph of $f(x)$.

$$f(x) = \frac{-x + 3}{x^2 + 5x - 6}$$

> If either $\lim_{x \to a^-} f(x) = \pm\infty$ or $\lim_{x \to a^+} f(x) = \pm\infty$, then the line $x = a$ is a *vertical asymptote* of the graph of the function $y = f(x)$.

Horizontal Asymptotes

Looking at the graph of $f(x)$ above, we see that $\lim_{x \to -\infty} f(x) = 0$ and $\lim_{x \to \infty} f(x) = 0$. We may conclude that the line $y = 0$ is a horizontal asymptote of the graph of $f(x)$.

> If either $\lim_{x \to +\infty} f(x) = b$ or $\lim_{x \to -\infty} f(x) = b$, then the line $y = b$ is a *horizontal asymptote* of the graph of the function $y = f(x)$.

Consider the following functions.

I.   II.   III.

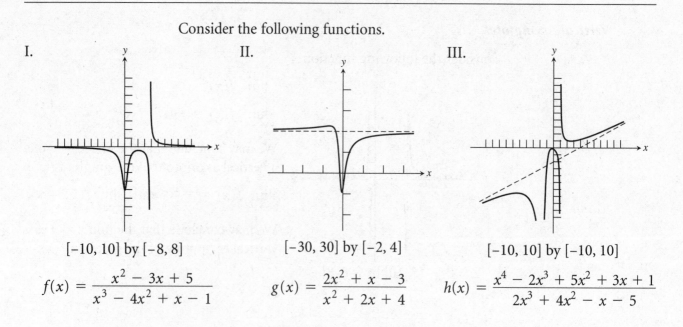

$$[-10, 10] \text{ by } [-8, 8] \qquad\qquad [-30, 30] \text{ by } [-2, 4] \qquad\qquad [-10, 10] \text{ by } [-10, 10]$$

$$f(x) = \frac{x^2 - 3x + 5}{x^3 - 4x^2 + x - 1} \qquad g(x) = \frac{2x^2 + x - 3}{x^2 + 2x + 4} \qquad h(x) = \frac{x^4 - 2x^3 + 5x^2 + 3x + 1}{2x^3 + 4x^2 - x - 5}$$

You may remember the following shortcuts for determining the horizontal asymptotes of rational functions.

1.   If the degree of the numerator is less than the degree of the denominator, the horizontal asymptote is $y = 0$.

2.   If the degree of the numerator is equal to the degree of the denominator, the horizontal asymptote is $y = \dfrac{\text{leading coefficient of numerator}}{\text{leading coefficient of denominator}}$.

3.   If the degree of the numerator is greater than the degree of the denominator, there is no horizontal asymptote.

Note that the graph of $h(x)$ above has a *slant asymptote*. A slant asymptote will be found when the degree of the numerator is 1 greater than the degree of the denominator. Using long division, $h(x)$ may be rewritten as

$$h(x) = \frac{1}{2}x - 2 + \frac{\frac{5}{2}x^2 + \frac{15}{2}x - 9}{2x^3 - 4x^2 - x - 5}.$$

For large values of x, $h(x)$ approaches the line $y = \dfrac{1}{2}x - 2$, which is the equation of its slant asymptote.

End Behavior Model

Suppose we want to determine the behavior of a function f where $|x|$ is very large. We use limits to define and determine the existence of an end behavior model.

> **A function _g_ is a**
>
> left end behavior model for _f_ if and only if $\lim\limits_{x \to -\infty} \dfrac{f(x)}{g(x)} = 1$.
>
> right end behavior model for _f_ if and only if $\lim\limits_{x \to +\infty} \dfrac{f(x)}{g(x)} = 1$.

Comparing function graphs or table values of ordered pairs can be useful in suggesting or confirming the end behavior model of a given function.

Consider the following functions.

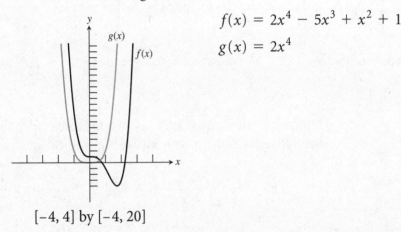

$$f(x) = 2x^4 - 5x^3 + x^2 + 1$$
$$g(x) = 2x^4$$

[−4, 4] by [−4, 20]

For large values of _x_ the graph of _f_ will begin to look much like the graph of _g_. Considering the limits in our end behavior definition above, we use

division to express $\dfrac{f(x)}{g(x)}$ as a sum, $\dfrac{f(x)}{g(x)} = \dfrac{2x^4 - 5x^3 + x^2 + 1}{2x^4} =$

$\left(1 + \dfrac{-5x^3 + x^2 + 1}{2x^4}\right)$. It follows easily that $\lim\limits_{x \to -\infty} \dfrac{f(x)}{g(x)} = 1$ and

$\lim\limits_{x \to \infty} \dfrac{f(x)}{g(x)} = 1$. We therefore conclude that $g(x) = 2x^4$ is both a left end

and right end behavior model for $f(x) = 2x^4 - 5x^3 + x^2 + 1$.

Boundedness

A function _f_ is bounded below if there is some number _b_ that is less than or equal to every number in the range of _f_. Any such number _b_ is called a lower bound of _f_.

A function f is bounded above if there is some number B that is greater than or equal to every number in the range of f. Any such number B is called an upper bound of f.

A function f is bounded if it is bounded both above and below.

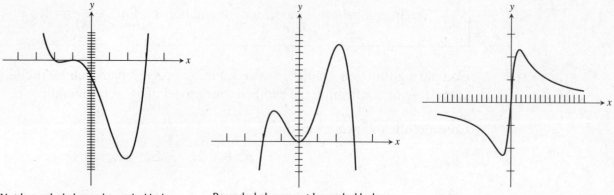

Not bounded above; bounded below   Bounded above; not bounded below   Bounded above; bounded below

Determine the equations of asymptotes for the following functions algebraically. Confirm your answers graphically.

1. $f(x) = \dfrac{x^2 + 7x + 12}{x^2 - 16}$ 2. $g(x) = \dfrac{2x^2 + 3x - 5}{x - 3}$

3. $h(x) = \dfrac{4x^3}{x^4 + 1}$

4. Which of the functions in Problems 1–3 is bounded above and below?

5. Which of the following is a left end behavior model for $f(x) = x^2 - 3e^{-x}$?

(A) $y = x^2$ (B) $y = -3e^{-x}$

(C) $y = 3e^{-x}$ (D) $y = e^{-x}$

Additional Practice

✎ 1. The function $f(x) = \dfrac{4x^2 - 3}{2x^2 + 1}$ is

    I. unbounded.

    II. bounded below by $y = -3$.

    III. bounded above by $y = 2$.

    (A) I   (B) II only

    (C) III only   (D) II and III

✎ 2. If $f(x) = e^x + 2$, which of the following lines is an asymptote to the graph of f?

    (A) $x = 0$ (B) $y = 2$

    (C) $x = 2$ (D) $y = 0$

Need More Help With . . .	*See . . .*
Asymptotes and end behavior models?	*Precalculus,* Sections 1.2, 2.3, 2.6 *Calculus,* Section 2.2 Appendix, "Analysis of Graphs"
Boundedness?	*Precalculus,* Section 1.2 Appendix, "Analysis of Graphs"

Function Magnitudes and Their Rates of Change

AP* Learning Objective: • Deduce and interpret behavior of functions using limits. (LO 1.1D)

Overview

There are many functions that have values that increase as their *x*-values increase. To get a better understanding of the behavior of these functions, we often compare them to the exponential function, which grows very rapidly, or to the logarithmic function, which grows very slowly.

Content and Practice

To compare exponential, polynomial, and logarithmic functions, we shall use the following definitions.

Let $f(x)$ and $g(x)$ be positive for sufficiently large values of x.

1. f grows faster than g (and g grows slower than f) as $x \to \infty$ if

$$\lim_{x \to \infty} \frac{f(x)}{g(x)} = \infty \quad \text{or} \quad \lim_{x \to \infty} \frac{g(x)}{f(x)} = 0.$$

2. f and g grow at the same rate as $x \to \infty$ if

$$\lim_{x \to \infty} \frac{f(x)}{g(x)} = L \neq 0. \quad (L \text{ is finite.})$$

Example 1: Let $f(x) = g(x) + h(x)$, where $g(x) = 5x^3$ and $h(x) = -x^2 + 3x - 6$. Using the definition above,

$$\lim_{x \to \infty} \frac{5x^3 - x^2 + 3x - 6}{5x^3} = \lim_{x \to \infty} \left(\frac{5x^3}{5x^3} + \frac{-x^2 + 3x - 6}{5x^3} \right)$$

$$= \lim_{x \to \infty} \left(1 + \frac{-x^2 + 3x - 6}{5x^3} \right)$$

$$= 1 + 0$$

$$= 1.$$

From this we see that $f(x)$ and $g(x)$ grow at the same rate. This is why, for large values of x, we can ignore the terms of $h(x)$ in $f(x)$. This is also why we can say that $g(x)$ is a right end behavior model of $f(x)$.

Example 2: Compare the growth rates of x^5 and e^x as $x \to \infty$.

$$\lim_{x \to \infty} \frac{x^5}{e^x} = \lim_{x \to \infty} \frac{5x^4}{e^x} \qquad \text{Use L'Hospital's Rule.}$$

$$= \lim_{x \to \infty} \frac{20x^3}{e^x}$$

$$= \lim_{x \to \infty} \frac{60x^2}{e^x}$$

$$= \lim_{x \to \infty} \frac{120x}{e^x}$$

$$= \lim_{x \to \infty} \frac{120}{e^x}$$

$$= 0$$

Therefore, x^5 grows slower than e^x as $x \to \infty$.

Example 3: Compare the growth rates of $\log \sqrt[3]{x}$ and $\ln x$ as $x \to \infty$.

$$\lim_{x \to \infty} \frac{\log \sqrt[3]{x}}{\ln x} = \lim_{x \to \infty} \frac{\dfrac{\ln x}{3 \ln 10}}{\ln x}$$

$$= \frac{1}{3 \ln 10}$$

Therefore $\log \sqrt[3]{x}$ and $\ln x$ grow at the same rate as $x \to \infty$.

1. List the functions e^x, 3^x, and x^3 in order from slowest-growing to fastest-growing as $x \rightarrow \infty$.

   (A) $3^x, x^3, e^x$ (B) $x^3, e^x, 3^x$

   (C) $x^3, 3^x, e^x$ (D) $e^x, x^3, 3^x$

2. Which of the following functions grow at the same rate as $x \rightarrow \infty$?

   I. $f(x) = x^3$

   II. $g(x) = \sqrt{x^6 + x^2}$

   III. $h(x) = \sqrt[3]{x^6 + 9x^3}$

   IV. $j(x) = \dfrac{x^5 - 4x^2 + 3}{x^2 + 2x - 9}$

   (A) I and II only   (B) I and IV only

   (C) I, II, and IV only   (D) I, II, and III only

Need More Help With . . .

Relative rates of growth?

See . . .

Calculus, Section 9.3

Continuity

AP* Learning Objective: • Analyze functions for intervals of continuity or points of discontinuity.
(LO 1.2A)

Overview

In precalculus, your first experience with *continuity* was studying functions and their properties. This study included finding various limits of a function over its domain. Continuity is presented early in the *Calculus* text since most theorems in the course rely on this property. Remember, a function can be examined for continuity at a point, on an interval, or over its entire domain.

Content and Practice

Intuitively we think of a function as continuous over an interval if its graph can be sketched in one continuous motion without lifting the pencil. In studying functions that are discontinuous, we can learn more about the behaviors of continuous functions.

By considering the graph, identify all points of discontinuity in each of the following.

1. $f(x) = \tan x$

2. $g(x) = \dfrac{x^2 - 2x - 3}{x + 1}$

3. $h(x) = \begin{cases} 2x - 3, & x \leq -1 \\ x^2 - 5, & x > -1 \end{cases}$

In your own words, write a sentence to explain how you identified the discontinuities of each function in Problems 1–3.

4. $f(x)$ _____

5. $g(x)$ _____

6. $h(x)$ _____

The *Calculus* book presents the following definition of continuity at an interior point of a domain.

> A function $y = f(x)$ is continuous at an interior point c of its domain if
> $$\lim_{x \to c} f(x) = f(c)$$
> If c is an endpoint of its domain, only the appropriate one-sided limit is checked.

Many students find it helpful to recognize that this definition asks three distinct questions:

I. Does $f(c)$ exist? (What do I get at $x = c$?)

II. Does $\lim\limits_{x \to c} f(x)$ exist? (What do I expect to get as x approaches c?)

III. Does $\lim\limits_{x \to c} f(x) = f(c)$? (Is what I get at $x = c$ equal to what I expected to get as x approaches c?)

Look again at the functions in Problems 1–3. Determine which part of the definition of continuity is not satisfied in each.

7. $f(x)$ _____

8. $g(x)$ _____

9. $h(x)$ _____

Additional Practice

In Problems 1–3, use the definition of continuity to decide whether each of the following functions is continuous at the specified value of x. If it is not continuous, explain why the function does not meet the definition.

1. $f(x) = \lfloor x \rfloor$ at $x = 3$

2. $g(x) = \begin{cases} x + 5, & x \neq 0 \\ 4, & x = 0 \end{cases}$ at $x = 0$

3. $h(x) = \begin{cases} -x^2 + 8, & x < 2 \\ \frac{1}{2}x + 3, & x \geq 2 \end{cases}$ at $x = 2$

4. Let f be the function defined as follows:

$$f(x) = \begin{cases} |x - 3| + 1, & x < 3 \\ ax^2 + bx, & x \geq 3 \end{cases}$$

(a) If $a = 3$ and $b = 2$, is f continuous for all x? Justify your answer.

(b) Describe all values of a and b for which f is a continuous function.

5. Which of the following functions are continuous for all real numbers x?

I. $f(x) = |x|$

II. $f(x) = \tan x$

III. $f(x) = 3x^2 + x - 7$

(A) I only   (B) III only

(C) I and II   (D) I and III

6. Let $f(x) = \dfrac{x^3 - 2x^2 - 29x - 42}{x^2 - 9}$. Which of the following statements is true?

(A) $f(x)$ has a removable discontinuity at $x = -3$.

(B) $f(x)$ has a jump discontinuity at $x = 3$.

(C) $f(x)$ has nonremovable discontinuities at $x = -3$ and $x = 3$.

(D) $\lim\limits_{x \to -3} f(x) = \infty$

Need More Help With . . .

Continuity?

See . . .

Precalculus, Section 1.2

Calculus, Section 2.3

Intermediate and Extreme Value Theorems

AP* Learning Objective: • Determine the applicability of important calculus theorems using continuity. (LO 1.2B)

Overview

Considerable time is spent in algebra II and precalculus courses learning how to find the zeros of a function and then using this information to sketch its graph. As you extended your mathematical knowledge in calculus, you learned that the zeros of the graph of a function's derivative will enable us to determine a function's maximum minimum values. These are values we need when solving optimization problems.

In precalculus, you used synthetic division to determine if a number was a zero of a polynomial function. The Intermediate Value Theorem helps us determine where such zeros exist. The Extreme Value Theorem gives us insight as to whether a function has maxima or minima. It is important to remember that the extreme values are the maximum or minimum y-values of the function.

Content and Practice

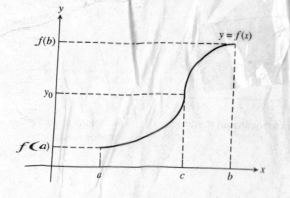

The Intermediate Value Theorem

A function $y = f(x)$ that is continuous on a closed interval $[a, b]$ takes on every value between $f(a)$ and $f(b)$ on (a, b).

If y_0 is between $f(a)$ and $f(b)$, then $y_0 = f(c)$ for some c in (a, b).

It is essential that f be a continuous function in order to apply the Intermediate Value Theorem, as illustrated below.

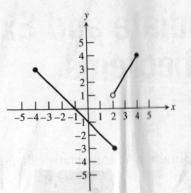

$$f(x) = \begin{cases} -x - 1, & -4 \leq x \leq 2 \\ \dfrac{3}{2}x - 2, & 2 < x \leq 4 \end{cases}$$

We see that $f(1) = -2$ and $f(4) = 4$. However, $f(x)$ does not take on all values between -2 and 4 on the interval $[1, 4]$. This is because $f(x)$ is not a continuous function on the interval $[1, 4]$.

However, looking at the interval $[-4, 2]$ where f is continuous, we see that $f(x)$ does take on every value between $f(-4)$ and $f(2)$.

The Extreme Value Theorem

If f is continuous on a closed interval $[a, b]$, then f has both a maximum value and a minimum value on the interval.

Maxima and minima can occur at interior points or at the endpoints, as illustrated in the figures.

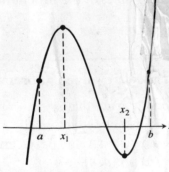

Maximum and minimum at interior points

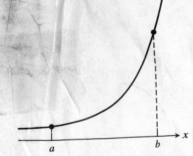

Maximum and minimum at endpoints

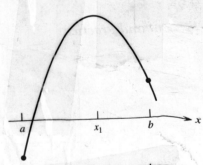

Minimum at endpoint; maximum at interior point

We can see that f must be continuous on a closed interval in order to apply the Extreme Value Theorem by analyzing the following graph.

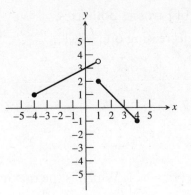

$$f(x) = \begin{cases} \frac{1}{2}x + 3, & -4 \leq x < 1 \\ -x + 3, & 1 \leq x \leq 4 \end{cases}$$

On the interval $[-4, 4]$, there is no maximum value for $f(x)$. There is also no maximum on $[-4, 1)$ since this is not a closed interval. There is a maximum on $[-4, 0.9]$.

Additional Practice

Use the graph of f to the right for Problems 1 and 2.

1. Explain how the Intermediate Value Theorem is used to verify that f has a zero between $x = 2$ and $x = 3$.

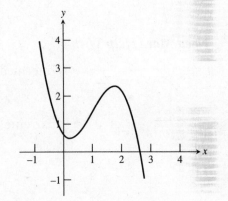

2. Approximate the maximum and minimum values of f on the interval $[0, 2]$.

3. The function f is continuous on the closed interval $[-2, 1]$. Some values of f are shown in the table.

x	-2	-1	0	1
$f(x)$	-3	7	k	3

The equation $f(x) = \frac{3}{2}$ must have at least two solutions in the interval $[-1, 1]$ if $k =$

(A) 1 (B) $\frac{3}{2}$ (C) 2 (D) $\frac{5}{2}$

4. A function f is continuous on $[-4, 1]$ and has its maximum at $(-3, 5)$ and its minimum at $\left(\frac{1}{2}, -6\right)$. Which of the following statements must be false?

(A) The graph of f crosses both axes.

(B) f is always decreasing on $[-4, 1]$.

(C) $f(-2) = 0$

(D) $f(0) = 2$

5. Let $f(x) = \left|\cos(x) - \dfrac{1}{2}\right|$. Which is the maximum value attained by f?

(A) $\dfrac{1}{2}$ (B) $\dfrac{3}{2}$ (C) π (D) 2π

Need More Help With . . .	*See* . . .
Intermediate Value Theorem?	*Precalculus,* Section 2.3
	Calculus, Section 2.3
Extreme Value Theorem?	*Calculus,* Section 5.1

Concept of the Derivative

AP* Learning Objective: • Identify the derivative of a function as the limit of a difference quotient. (LO 2.1A)

Overview

The concept of the *derivative* is a critical part of almost everything we do in calculus; it is important to familiarize ourselves with the derivative as seen from different perspectives: graphically, numerically, and analytically. This familiarity will in turn allow us to understand and apply the derivative in a variety of situations. In addition to helping us understand the rate at which something is changing, a derivative also informs us about the sensitivity of changes in one variable to changes in a related variable.

Content and Practice

From a graphical perspective, a function's derivative at any specific point can be thought of as the slope of the graph of that function at that point. Shown below is the graph of a quadratic function (in bold) and of its derivative. Notice that high positive or negative derivative values indicate rapid growth or decline in the function and a steeply sloping graph, whereas derivative values close to zero indicate little or no change in the values of the original function and an approximately horizontal graph.

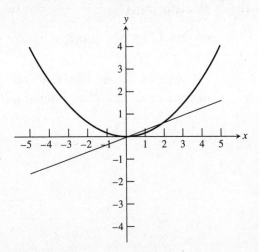

1. Consider the graph of $f(x)$ shown at right.

    (a) Find $f'(-3)$, the value of the derivative of this function at $x = -3$.

    (b) Find $f'(1)$, the value of the derivative of this function at $x = 1$.

Similarly, the derivative of a function can be thought of as the rate at which the function's value is changing at a specific instant. For example, if $f(t)$ measures the position of a moving particle at time t, then $f'(5)$ represents the velocity of that particle at the moment when $t = 5$.

2. If $y = f(x)$ is a profit function measuring the amount of profit (in dollars) as a result of manufacturing and selling x basketballs, what is the significance of $f'(550)$? Make sure you use specific units.

Since we generally require two points to calculate slope, the task of finding slope at a single point will require a new strategy. We will use the standard slope formula $\dfrac{f(b) - f(a)}{b - a}$ for two points on the curve, and then take the limit of this difference quotient as one point approaches the other.

Eventually, we will be able to develop analytical techniques for finding the derivative as a *function* related to the original function.

1. Let $y = g(x)$ be a function that measures the water depth in a pool x minutes after the pool begins to fill. Then $g'(25)$ represents:

   I. The rate at which the depth is increasing 25 minutes after the pool starts to fill.

   II. The average rate at which the depth changes over the first 25 minutes.

   III. The slope of the graph of g at the point where $x = 25$.

   (A) I only   (B) III only

   (C) I and II   (D) I and III

2. The function $y = f(x)$ measures the fish population in Blue Lake at time x, where x is measured in years since January 1, 1950. If $f'(25) = 500$, it means that

   (A) there were 500 fish in the lake in 1975.

   (B) there were 500 more fish in 1975 than there were in 1950.

   (C) on the average, the fish population increased by 500 per year over the first 25 years following 1950.

   (D) on January 1, 1975, the fish population was growing at a rate of 500 fish per year.

Need More Help With . . .

Concept of derivative?

See . . .

Precalculus, Section 11.1

Calculus, Sections 2.1, 2.4, 3.1–3.5

Differentiability and Continuity

AP* Learning Objective: • Recognize the connection between differentiability and continuity. (LO 2.2B)

Overview

Most, but not all, of the functions we encounter in calculus will be differentiable over their entire domains. Before we can confidently apply the rules regarding derivatives, we need to be able to recognize the exceptions to the rule.

Content and Practice

A function that is differentiable at a point or over an interval will always be continuous there, but the converse is not true: There are situations where a continuous function may not have a derivative. To rephrase this, a function that is *dis*continuous at a point will definitely *not* have a derivative at that point. A continuous function, on the other hand, will still fail to have a derivative at any point where it has a corner, a cusp, or a vertical tangent.

1. Consider the function shown at right. At what domain values does the function appear to be

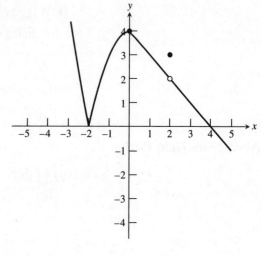

   (a) differentiable?

   (b) continuous but not differentiable?

   (c) neither continuous nor differentiable?

1. Consider the function $y = f(x)$ shown at right.

    (a) At what x-values is f discontinuous?

    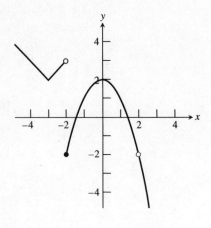

    (b) At what x-values would this function *not* be differentiable?

2. Let f be a function with $f'(5) = 8$. Which of the following statements is true?

    (A) f must be continuous at $x = 5$.

    (B) f is definitely not continuous at $x = 5$.

    (C) There is not enough information to determine whether or not $f(x)$ is continuous at $x = 5$.

3. Suppose f is a function such that $f'(9)$ is undefined. Which of the following statements is true?

    (A) f must be continuous at $x = 9$.

    (B) f is definitely not continuous at $x = 9$.

    (C) There is not enough information to determine whether or not f is continuous at $x = 9$.

4. Suppose that f is a function that is continuous at $x = -11$. Which of the following statements is true?

    (A) f must be differentiable at $x = -11$.

    (B) f is definitely not differentiable at $x = -11$.

    (C) There is not enough information to determine whether or not $f(x)$ is differentiable at $x = -11$.

5. Which of the following statements are always true?

   I. A function that is continuous at $x = c$ must be differentiable at $x = c$.

   II. A function that is differentiable at $x = c$ must be continuous at $x = c$.

   III. A function that is *not* continuous at $x = c$ must *not* be differentiable at $x = c$.

   IV. A function that is *not* differentiable at $x = c$ must *not* be continuous at $x = c$.

   (A) I and III   (B) II and IV

   (C) I and IV   (D) II and III

Need More Help With . . .   *See . . .*

Differentiability?   *Precalculus,* Section 11.1

Continuity and differentiability?   *Calculus,* Sections 2.3, 3.1, 3.2

Slope of a Curve at a Point

AP* Learning Objective: • Solve problems involving the slope of a tangent line. (LO 2.3B)

Overview

We often use graphs to help us visualize the relationship between variables (distance versus time, for instance). We know from previous courses that when we do this for a linear function, the constant slope of that function represents the **rate of change** of one variable with respect to the other. By defining slope for nonlinear functions, we can extend this same concept to a much broader range of situations.

Content and Practice

The value of a function's derivative at a specific point can be thought of as the slope of the tangent line to the function's graph at that point. This interpretation can be quite helpful, both as a means of approximating the value of a derivative and as a means for identifying points at which the derivative will be undefined.

1. Estimate the slope of each curve at point *P*.

(a)   (b)   (c)

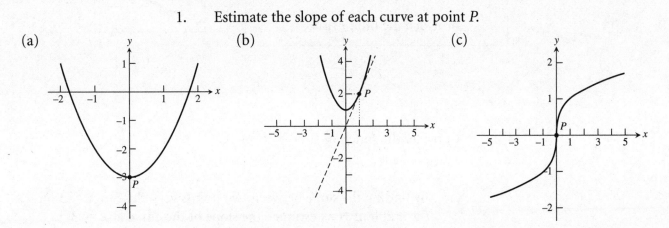

Although the conventional formula for slope requires two distinct points, the slope of the tangent line to a function at a specific point can be determined by finding the slope between that point and a nearby point on the curve, and then finding the limit as the nearby point approaches the original point.

The **slope** of the curve $y = f(x)$ at the point $(a, f(a))$ is

$$\lim_{h \to 0} \frac{f(a + h) - f(a)}{h},$$

if and only if it exists.

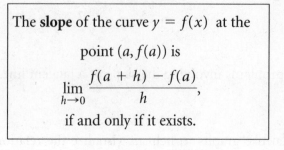

The tangent slope is

$$\lim_{h \to 0} \frac{f(a + h) - f(a)}{h}.$$

An alternate form for the slope of the function f at the point $x = a$ is

$$f'(a) = \lim_{x \to a} \frac{f(x) - f(a)}{x - a},$$

provided the limit exists.

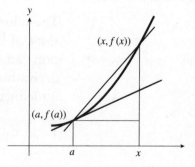

2. Consider the function $f(x) = x^2 + 3$.

(a) By finding the slope between two points very close to $x = 3$ on the graph of $f(x)$, estimate the slope of the curve at $x = 3$.

(b) Justify your answer analytically, using the definition of the slope of a curve.

3. The slope of this function of f
   at the point P is
   (A) 1.
   (B) -1.
   (C) 0.
   (D) undefined.

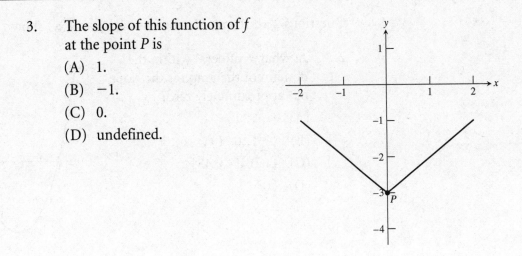

4. Explain how your answer to Problem 3 is consistent with the definition of the slope of a curve.

From the above examples, we can see that there are at least two situations in which a function's slope may not be defined at a certain point: the tangent line to the function at that point may be vertical (and therefore have no slope), or there may simply be no tangent line at that point.

Additional Practice

 1. Find all values of x at which the slope of the function $f(x) = \frac{1}{x}$ is equal to $-\frac{1}{4}$.

Questions 2 and 3 refer to the function $y = f(x)$ shown in the figure.

2. At what x-value(s) within the domain of the graph is the slope of f approximately zero?

   (A) $\{-1, 1\}$

   (B) $\{-1, 0, 1\}$

   (C) $\{-0.45, 0.45\}$

   (D) $\{0\}$

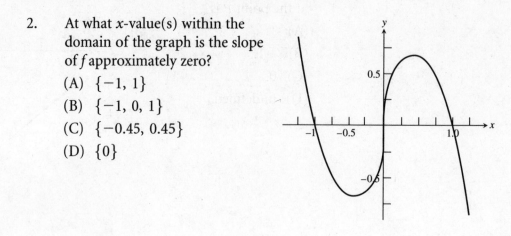

3. At what x-values within the domain of the graph would the slope of f be undefined?

   (A) Never

   (B) $\{-1, 0, 1\}$

   (C) $\{-0.45, 0.45\}$

   (D) $\{0\}$

Need More Help With . . .

Derivative at a point?

See . . .

Precalculus, Section 11.1

Calculus, Sections 2.4, 3.1

Local Linearity

AP* Learning Objective: • Solve problems involving the slope of a tangent line. (LO 2.3B)

Overview

You first encountered the derivative $y = f'(x)$ as the limiting slope of a secant to the curve as one point of intersection approached the other. As those points converged, the secant line became a tangent to the curve. For differentiable functions, that tangent line can be used as a simple approximation, or model, for the curve near the tangent point. This is a significant practical application; it is also helpful in developing an intuitive understanding of what makes a curve differentiable.

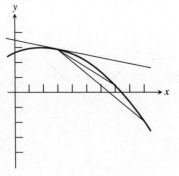

Content and Practice

The derivative of a function at a specific point, $f'(a)$, gives us the slope of a tangent line to the function f at the point where $x = a$. We can construct the equation of that tangent line from the values of $f(a)$ and $f'(a)$.

1. Write the equation of the tangent line to f at $x = 5$, given that $f(5) = 3$ and $f'(5) = 0.5$.

This tangent line can be used as a model to find approximate values for the original function close to the point of tangency.

2. Use your tangent line from Problem 1 to approximate $f(5.023)$.

Why is this approximation close to the value of the original function? Because the derivative is defined as the (two-sided) limit of the slope at that point, the derivative can only exist at a point if the limiting slopes on both sides of that point are identical—if there is any kind of corner or cusp at that point, it will *not* be differentiable!

Consider the function $f(x) = |x| + 1$, which is not differentiable at $x = 0$, and $g(x) = \sqrt{x^2 + 0.0001} + 0.99$, which *is* differentiable at $x = 0$. In many viewing windows, this pair of functions will appear almost identical around $x = 0$. If we zoom in, as shown below, and consider only a very small interval surrounding $x = 0$, we can see that the differentiable function g flattens out and begins to appear linear over that interval. The nondifferentiable function f maintains its sharp corner even at this resolution.

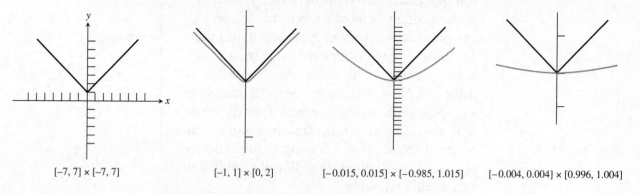

[–7, 7] × [–7, 7]   [–1, 1] × [0, 2]   [–0.015, 0.015] × [–0.985, 1.015]   [–0.004, 0.004] × [0.996, 1.004]

As this example illustrates, a differentiable function—even one that appears to be changing direction suddenly—will begin to look and act like its tangent line if we zoom in close enough and look at a very small interval around the point of tangency. This characteristic of differentiable functions is known as *local linearity.*

Additional Practice

1. Let $f(x) = e^x$. Use the built in functionality of your graphing calculator to find the value of the derivative of $f(x)$ at $x = 2$, then write the equation of the line tangent to f at $x = 2$.

2. For each of the following functions,

    I. State whether or not the function is differentiable at $x = 1$. (How do you know by looking at the graph?)

    II. If the function is differentiable, give an equation for the line tangent to the function at $x = 1$.

    (a) $f(x) = x^2 + 1$

    (b) $f(x) = 2x$

    (c) $f(x) = \begin{cases} x^2 + 1 & x \le 1 \\ 2x & x > 1 \end{cases}$

3. Consider the function $f(x) = \sin(kx) + 3$. Given that $f'(0) = k$, what is the approximate value of $f(0.03)$?

    (A) 3.03   (B) $3.03k$

    (C) $k + 3.03$ (D) $0.03k + 3$

4. Consider the function $f(x) = a \ln(x + 2)$. Given that $f'(1) = \frac{a}{3}$, what is the *approximate* value of $f(0.98)$?

    (A) $\left(\dfrac{a}{3}\right) \cdot (-0.02) + a \cdot \ln(3)$

    (B) $\dfrac{-0.02a}{3}$

    (C) $(0.98) \cdot \ln\left(\dfrac{a}{3}\right)$

    (D) $\left(\dfrac{a}{3}\right) \cdot 0.98 + a \cdot \ln(3)$

Need More Help With . . .	*See* . . .
Derivatives?	*Precalculus*, Section 11.1
Derivatives and local linearity?	*Calculus*, Section 3.2

Instantaneous Rate of Change

AP* Learning Objective: · Interpret the meaning of a derivative within a problem. (LO 2.3A)

Overview

Many of our applications are concerned with *rates of change*. While the difference quotient gives us a way to measure the average rate of change over an interval, often we are more interested in the rate of change at one given instant. The use of limits will allow us to find such a rate.

Content and Practice

Suppose we have a particle that is moving in such a way that its position at time t is given by the function $f(t) = 3t^2$, with t measured in seconds. Also let us assume that we are interested in calculating the rate at which the particle is moving at the instant $t = 1$. We can calculate the **average** rate of change of $f(t)$ over any interval using the difference quotient $\dfrac{f(t + h) - f(t)}{h}$, where h is the length of the interval. For instance, the average rate of change for the 10-second period beginning at $t = 1$ would be

$$\text{average rate} = \frac{f(1 + 10) - f(1)}{10}$$

$$= \frac{f(11) - f(1)}{10}$$

$$= \frac{363 - 3}{10}$$

$$= 36 \text{ units/sec}$$

1. Repeat the above calculation for the (a) 5-second, (b) 3-second, and (c) 1-second intervals beginning at $t = 1$. What do you think the rate of change is at precisely $t = 1$?

The **instantaneous rate of change** of $f(x)$ at the moment when $x = a$ can be calculated by finding the average rate of change of $f(x)$ over the small interval between $x = a$ and a nearby value $x = a + h$ and then taking the limit as this interval is made increasingly smaller.

$$\text{Instantaneous Rate of Change} = \lim_{h \to 0} \frac{f(a + h) - f(a)}{h}.$$

2. Calculate the instantaneous rate of change for $a = 1$ analytically, using the above definition. (*Hint:* Simplify the numerator until you can factor out h.) How does this result compare to your result in Problem 1?

When we are working from a graph or table, it is not always possible to evaluate the function at any point we choose. It is still possible, however, to approximate the value of an instantaneous rate of change at a point by calculating the average rate of change over a small interval including that point.

3. Find an approximate value for the rate of change of $f(x)$ at $x = 3$ based on the information in the table. Choose the most appropriate value. In this type of problem, do not attempt to find and use a regression formula, but use only the data in the table.

x	$f(x)$
0	5.75
2	6.15
4	8.32
6	12.66

(A) 7.235
(B) 2.170
(C) 1.085
(D) 0.645

Additional Practice

1. Let $f(x) = 6 - x^2$. Use analytical methods to find the instantaneous rate of change when $x = -2$.

⊞ 2. Consider the following table of values for the advertising budget of ACME Cola.

Year	Budget
1994	28.9
1996	33.3
1998	35.5
2000	39.0
2002	44.8
2004	54.5

(a) Find the average rate of change for the period 1994–2004.

(b) Find the average rate of change for the period 1996–2002.

(c) Find the average rate of change for the period 1998–2000.

(d) Give an estimate for the instantaneous rate of change in 1999.

3. Consider the function $y = f(x)$ shown at right. Approximate the instantaneous rate of change at $x = 2$.

(A) -4

(B) -2

(C) 2

(D) 4

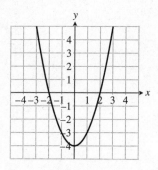

Need More Help With . . .

Instantaneous velocity?

Instantaneous rate of change?

See . . .

Precalculus, Section 11.1

Calculus, Sections 2.4, 3.4

Relationships between the Graphs of *f* and *f'*

AP* Learning Objective: • Use derivatives to analyze properties of a function. (LO 2.2A)

Overview

A large part of what we study in calculus hinges on the relationship between a function and its derivative. One important aspect of this relationship is the connection between the graphs of the two functions—the graph of *f* can give us important information about the graph of *f'*, and vice versa. A basic knowledge of what each graph can reveal about the other is critical in order to understand many of the theorems you will encounter in calculus. It is also an important tool for applications such as optimization and modeling.

Content and Practice

At any given point, the value of a function's derivative can be thought of as the slope of that function. Therefore, if we know what the graph of a specific function *f* looks like, we can get a good idea of what its derivative function *f'* looks like simply by estimating the slope of *f* at various points along the graph and plotting each slope at its corresponding *x*-value. After plotting a number of these points, a smooth curve can be drawn through the points to approximate the graph of the derivative function *f'*.

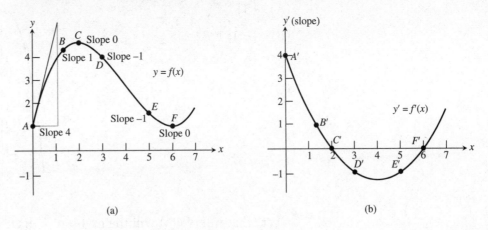

(a)   (b)

1. What do you notice about the values of the derivative function on those intervals where the original function f shown above is

   (a) increasing?

   (b) decreasing?

2. Explain why these observations make sense in terms of the slope of f.

3. When the graph of f' crosses the x-axis, what does this tell you about the graph of f? Explain, in terms of slope, why this happens.

Additional Practice

Questions 1 and 2 relate to the function f shown in the figure.

1. Give the approximate value(s) of the x-intercepts of f'.

   (A) $\{3\}$

   (B) $\{-1, 1, 3\}$

   (C) $\{0, 2\}$

   (D) $\{-3, 3\}$

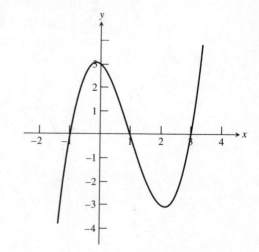

2. Over what interval(s) will the graph of f' have only negative values?

   (A) $(-\infty, \infty)$
   (B) $(-\infty, 0) \cup (2, \infty)$

   (C) $(0, 2)$
   (D) $(-\infty, -1) \cup (1, 3)$

⊞ 3. Based on the appearance of their graphs, which of these functions looks like it could be equal to its own derivative?

(A) $f(x) = \sin x$ (B) $f(x) = \cos x$

(C) $f(x) = e^x - 5$ (D) $f(x) = e^{x-5}$

Need More Help With . . .

Concept of derivative?	*Precalculus*, Section 11.1 *Calculus*, Sections 2.1, 2.4, 3.1–3.5
Relationship between graphs of f and f'?	*Calculus*, Sections 3.1, 3.2

See . . .

Basic Derivatives

AP* Learning Objective: • Calculate derivatives. (LO 2.1C)

Overview

Basic derivative formulas are the building blocks of the mechanics of calculus. Without the ability to differentiate functions correctly, you will be at a roadblock in the course. The basic formulas for derivatives must be committed to memory. These formulas will be tested in the Multiple Choice portion of the AP* exam and will also be necessary to complete certain portions of the Free Response portion of the exam. Additionally, success in integral calculus is strongly dependent on knowing these formulas.

Content and Practice

As a means to review some of your basic derivative formulas, complete the following table by filling in each empty cell. If you have not yet studied all these formulas, it is still productive to look them up and begin committing them to memory. As you move through Chapter 3 of the *Calculus* text, the number of formulas will increase and will address the use of the Chain Rule when differentiating.

	Function	Derivative
1.	$y = x^n$ (*n* is any real number.)	$\dfrac{dy}{dx} = nx^{n-1}$
2.	$y = k$ (*k* is a constant.)	
3.	$y = \sin x$	
4.	$y = \cos x$	
5.	$y = \tan x$	
6.		$\dfrac{dy}{dx} = -\csc^2 x$

continued on next page

	Function	Derivative
7.	$y = \sec x$	
8.		$\dfrac{dy}{dx} = -\csc x \cot x$
9.	$y = \ln x$	
10.		$\dfrac{dy}{dx} = e^x$

Not only should the formulas be known and easily applied, the concept of a derivative as slope of a curve and as an instantaneous rate of change must also be understood. Any time an independent and dependent variable exist, an instantaneous rate of change of one variable with respect to the other can be examined. The most common independent variable is x, but it can be any variable we choose. We just differentiate with respect to that variable. For example, the area of a circle is dependent on the radius. With $A = \pi r^2$, we can express the instantaneous rate of change of the area with respect to the radius. Differentiating the area equation produces $dA/dr = 2\pi r$.

Practice taking a few derivatives other than differentiating y with respect to x.

11. $P = \tan w$ $\qquad \dfrac{dP}{dw} =$

12. $V = \dfrac{1}{3}\pi r^2 h$ (Consider h constant.) $\quad \dfrac{dV}{dr} =$

13. $E = mc^2$ (c is constant.) $\qquad \dfrac{dE}{dm} =$

14. $S = 6t^2$ $\qquad \dfrac{dS}{dt} =$

Additional Practice

1. What is the slope of the graph of $y = \sin x$ at $x = \pi/3$?

   (A) $-\dfrac{\sqrt{3}}{2}$ (B) $-\dfrac{1}{2}$

   (C) $\dfrac{1}{2}$ (D) $\dfrac{\sqrt{3}}{2}$

2. What is the instantaneous rate of change of y with respect to x on the graph of $y = e^x$ at $x = a$?

(A) e
(B) a
(C) e^a
(D) e^x

3. The area of a circle is $A = \pi r^2$. How does the instantaneous rate of change of the area with respect to the radius when $r = 2$ compare to the average rate of change of the area as the radius changes from $r = 1$ to $r = 3$?

(A) The instantaneous rate of change is twice the average rate of change.

(B) The instantaneous rate of change is equal to the average rate of change.

(C) The instantaneous rate of change is half the average rate of change.

(D) The instantaneous rate of change is three times the average rate of change.

4. Find the equation of the line tangent to the graph of $y = \sqrt{x}$ at the point on the curve where the y-coordinate is exactly one-third the value of the x-coordinate given $x > 0$. Show the work that leads to your answer.

Need More Help With . . .   *See . . .*

Derivative formulas?   *Calculus,* Sections 3.3, 3.5

Memorizing?   Make a set of flash cards to study.

Average rate of change vs. instantaneous rate of change?   *Calculus,* Section 2.4

Concept of derivative?   *Calculus,* Sections 2.1, 2.4, 3.1–3.5

Derivative Rules

AP* Learning Objective: • Calculate derivatives. (LO 2.1C)

Overview

Frequently, the functions we need to differentiate are irreducible sums, differences, products, or quotients of functions. Mastery of the formulas for these cases is another key skill in the early part of any calculus course. These formulas will be tested in the Multiple Choice portion of the AP* Calculus exam and will also be necessary to complete certain portions of the Free Response portion of the exam. Additionally, success in integral calculus is strongly dependent on knowing these formulas.

Content and Practice

As a means to review derivative formulas, complete the following table below by filling in each empty cell. If you have not yet studied all these formulas, it is still productive to look them up and begin committing them to memory. As you move through Chapters 3 and 4 of the *Calculus* text, the number of formulas will increase and will address the use of the Chain Rule when differentiating.

Formula Name	Derivative Formula	Word Description
Difference Formula	$y = f(x) - g(x)$ $\dfrac{dy}{dx} = f'(x) - g'(x)$	The derivative of a difference of functions is the difference of their individual derivatives.
Sum Formula	$y = f(x) + g(x)$ $\dfrac{dy}{dx} = f'(x) + g'(x)$	
Product Rule	$y = f(x) \cdot g(x)$ $\dfrac{dy}{dx} = f'(x) \cdot g(x) + f(x) \cdot g'(x)$	
Quotient Rule	$y = \dfrac{f(x)}{g(x)}$ $\dfrac{dy}{dx} = \dfrac{g(x) \cdot f'(x) - f(x) \cdot g'(x)}{[g(x)]^2}$	

Complete the following derivatives using the appropriate formula. The most common independent variable is x, but it can be any variable we choose. We just differentiate with respect to that variable.

1. $y = 5x^3 + \ln(x)$ $\dfrac{dy}{dx} =$

2. $y = x^3 \cdot \ln(x)$ $\dfrac{dy}{dx} =$

3. $s = \dfrac{5}{t^4}$ $\dfrac{ds}{dt} =$

4. $k = \dfrac{\sin p}{\sqrt{p}}$ $\dfrac{dk}{dp} =$

5. $w = z^4 - (z + 2)^7 \cdot \cos z$ $\dfrac{dw}{dz} =$

6. $y = x^2(x^3 - 2)$ Find $\dfrac{dy}{dx}$ two different ways. Distribute x^2 before differentiating. Use product rule on the two factors. Show the two answers are equivalent.

Additional Practice

1. Given $f(x) = e^x \cdot \cos x$, choose a solution to $f'(x) = 0$:

    (A) 0

    (B) $\dfrac{\pi}{4}$

    (C) $\dfrac{\pi}{2}$

    (D) π

2. Find the equation of the line tangent to $y = \dfrac{x + 3}{x^2 + 1}$ at $x = 1$.

(A) $y = -\dfrac{5}{2}x + \dfrac{9}{2}$ (B) $y = \dfrac{5}{2}x - \dfrac{1}{2}$

(C) $y = \dfrac{1}{2}x + \dfrac{3}{2}$ (D) $y = -\dfrac{3}{2}x + \dfrac{7}{2}$

Use the table below for solving Problems 3 and 4.

x	$f(x)$	$g(x)$	$f'(x)$	$g'(x)$
1	4	2	5	$\dfrac{1}{2}$
3	7	-4	$\dfrac{3}{2}$	-1

3. The value of $\dfrac{d}{dx}(f \cdot g)$ at $x = 3$ is:

(A) $\dfrac{5}{2}$ (B) $-\dfrac{3}{2}$

(C) -13 (D) 12

4. The value of $\dfrac{d}{dx}\left(\dfrac{f}{g}\right)$ at $x = 1$ is:

(A) 2 (B) 3

(C) 5 (D) 6

Need More Help With . . .

Formulas used here?
Practice problems?

See . . .

Calculus, Section 3.3
Make up some of your own product and quotient rule problems and check your answers with a computer algebra system (CAS).

Chain Rule

AP* Learning Objective: • Calculate derivatives. (LO 2.1C)

Overview

In precalculus, you practiced decomposing functions. This skill is useful in understanding and applying the Chain Rule. Using the Chain Rule correctly is one of the most important skills in the calculus course. It is applied to derivatives and integrals throughout much of the rest of the year.

Content and Practice

Suppose we wanted to find dy/dx if $y = \sin(x^2 + 3x)$. Think of y as $f(x)$ and recognize $f(x)$ as a composite of two functions: $f(x) = h(g(x))$, where $g(x) = x^2 + 3x$ and $h(x) = \sin x$. In this case we can write $y = \sin u$, where $u = x^2 + 3x$. Using the Chain Rule, we have

$$\frac{dy}{dx} = \frac{dy}{du} \cdot \frac{du}{dx}$$

$$= \frac{d(\sin u)}{du} \cdot \frac{d(x^2 + 3x)}{dx}$$

$$= \cos u \cdot (2x + 3)$$

$$= \cos(x^2 + 3x) \cdot (2x + 3).$$

The *Calculus* text also presents this as the derivative of the "outside" function, sine, times the derivative of the "inside" function, the polynomial. In some cases, it is also possible to have more than just two factors involved in the Chain Rule, for example, $dy/dx = dy/du \cdot du/dt \cdot dt/dx$.

1. Find dy/dx if $y = (4x + 2)^3$, using y as a composite of $y = u^3$ and $u = 4x + 2$.

2.   Following the first example, write $h = \sqrt{1 - \sin v}$ as a composition of two functions, g (the inner function of v) and h (the outer function of g), so that $h(v) = h(g(v))$. Use your answers to find dh/dv using $dh/dv = dh/dg \cdot dg/dv$.

3.   Use composition to show $dy/dt = 6t \sin^2 (t^2 + 5) \cos (t^2 + 5)$ if $y = [\sin (t^2 + 5)]^3$. This is an example where you may have three factors involved in the process.

4.   What is $f'(x)$ if $f(x) = \sin^2 (3x)$?
     (A) $2 \sin 3x$
     (B) $6 \sin 3x$
     (C) $2 \sin (3x) \cdot \cos (3x)$
     (D) $6 \sin (3x) \cdot \cos (3x)$

5.   The derivative formulas you learned recently were simple functions of x and did not require the Chain Rule. Those functions and numerous additional functions now take on the form seen in the table on the next page. A few lines are completed for you. Fill in the remaining blanks, then check the formulas in your book. If there are formulas you have not yet learned, look them up and begin committing them to memory.

	Function	Derivative
	$y = u^n$ (n is any real number.)	$\dfrac{dy}{dx} = nu^{n-1}\dfrac{du}{dx}$
(a)	$y = k$ (k is a constant.)	
	$y = \sin u$	$\dfrac{dy}{dx} = \cos u \cdot \dfrac{du}{dx}$
(b)	$y = \cos u$	
(c)	$y = \tan u$	
(d)		$\dfrac{dy}{dx} = -\csc^2 u \cdot \dfrac{du}{dx}$
(e)	$y = \sec u$	
(f)		$\dfrac{dy}{dx} = -\csc u \cot u \cdot \dfrac{du}{dx}$
(g)	$y = e^u$	
(h)		$\dfrac{dy}{dx} = \dfrac{1}{u} \cdot \dfrac{du}{dx}$
(i)	$y = a^u$ ($a > 0, a \neq 1$)	
(j)	$y = \sin^{-1} u$ (This is inverse sine.)	
(k)		$\dfrac{dy}{dx} = \dfrac{-1}{1 + u^2} \cdot \dfrac{du}{dx}$
(l)	$y = \sec^{-1} u$	
(m)		$\dfrac{dy}{dx} = \dfrac{-1}{|u|\sqrt{u^2 - 1}} \cdot \dfrac{du}{dx}$
(n)	$y = \tan^{-1} u$	
(o)	$y = \cos^{-1} u$	
(p)	$y = \log_a u$	

Additional Practice

The functions f and g and their derivatives have the following values at $x = 1$ and $x = 2$.

x	$f(x)$	$g(x)$	$f'(x)$	$g'(x)$
1	3	2	0	$\frac{3}{4}$
2	7	-4	$\frac{1}{3}$	-1

Use the information above to find the value of the first derivative of the following at the given value of x.

1. $[f(x)]^2$ at $x = 2$

(A) 0   (B) $\frac{2}{3}$

(C) $\frac{14}{3}$ (D) 6

2. $f(g(x))$ at $x = 1$

(A) $-\frac{1}{3}$ (B) 0

(C) $\frac{1}{4}$ (D) $\frac{9}{4}$

Need More Help With . . .   ***See . . .***

Decomposing functions?   *Precalculus,* Section 1.4

Basic derivatives?   *Calculus,* Sections 3.3, 3.5, 4.3, 4.4

Chain Rule?   *Calculus,* Section 4.1

Derivatives of Parametric, Polar, and Vector Functions

AP* Learning Objectives:
- Calculate derivatives. (LO 2.1C)
- Solve problems involving related rates, optimization, rectilinear motion, (BC) and planar motion. (LO 2.3C)

Overview

This BC only topic applies the rules for derivatives to parametric, polar, and vector functions. In addition, you should also know the Chain Rule for parametric equations.

Chain Rule for Parametric Equations

If x and y are given as parametric functions of t, then

$$\frac{dy}{dx} = \frac{dy/dt}{dx/dt} \text{ and } \frac{d^2y}{dx^2} = \frac{d/dt\,(dy/dx)}{dx/dt}.$$

To differentiate a vector function, simply differentiate the components.

$$\text{If} \quad \mathbf{r} = x(t)\mathbf{i} + y(t)\mathbf{j}, \quad \text{then} \quad \frac{d\mathbf{r}}{dt} = \frac{dx}{dt}\mathbf{i} + \frac{dy}{dt}\mathbf{j}.$$

Content and Practice

1. If $x(t) = t^2 - t$ and $y(t) = t^3 + 1$, find dy/dx and d^2y/dx^2 in terms of t.

$$\frac{dy}{dx} = \frac{3t^2}{2t - 1}$$

$$\frac{d^2y}{dx^2} = \frac{\dfrac{d}{dt}\left(\dfrac{3t^2}{2t-1}\right)}{2t-1} = \frac{\dfrac{6t(t-1)}{(2t-1)^2}}{(2t-1)} = \frac{6t(t-1)}{(2t-1)^3}$$

2. If $x(t) = 4 \cos t$ and $y(t) = \sin 2t$, find d^2y/dx^2 when $t = \pi/2$.

3. If f is a vector-valued function defined by $f(t) = <e^{2t}, \cos t>$, then $f''(t) = $ _____.

Additional Practice

1. An object moving along a curve in the xy-plane has position $(x(t), y(t))$ at time $t \geq 0$ with $dx/dt = 3 + \sin t^2$. The derivative dy/dt is not explicitly given. At time $t = 2$, the object has position $(1, 3)$ and $dy/dt = -5$. Find an equation for the line tangent to the curve at the point $(x(2), y(2))$.

2. If $x(t) = t^2 - t$ and $y(t) = \sqrt{3t + 1}$, then dy/dx at $t = 1$ is

   (A) $-\dfrac{1}{2}$ (B) $\dfrac{1}{2}$

   (C) $\dfrac{3}{4}$ (D) 1

3. If $\mathbf{f}$ is a vector-valued function defined by $\mathbf{f}(t) = \ln(t)\mathbf{i} + \sqrt{t}\,\mathbf{j}$, then $\mathbf{f}''(1) = $

   (A) $-\mathbf{i} - \dfrac{1}{4}\mathbf{j}$ (B) $\mathbf{i} - \dfrac{1}{4}\mathbf{j}$

   (C) $-\mathbf{i} - \dfrac{1}{2}\mathbf{j}$ (D) $\mathbf{i} - \dfrac{1}{2}\mathbf{j}$

Need More Help With . . .	See . . .
Derivatives of parametric or vector functions?	*Calculus,* Sections 11.1, 11.2

Equations Involving Derivatives

AP* Learning Objectives: • Identify the derivative of a function as the limit of a difference quotient. (LO 2.1A)

• Apply the Mean Value Theorem to describe the behavior of a function over an interval. (LO 2.4A)

Overview

Being able to write and comprehend basic equations involving derivatives is a necessary prerequisite for later applications, including related rate problems and solving differential equations. As was mentioned earlier, the derivative measures the sensitivity of change of the dependent variable to small changes in the independent variable. Fluency with such equations also makes it easier to recognize and deal with exponential growth and decay situations, since one of the characteristics of such a situation is the fact that the derivative (growth rate) is proportional to the function value itself.

Content and Practice

We know that the derivative $f'(x)$ measures the rate at which the quantity represented by $f(x)$ changes with respect to change in x. Likewise, dy/dx measures the rate at which y changes with respect to the change in x. This information can help us write and interpret statements involving derivatives. For instance, suppose that we have a function $T(x)$ that measures surface temperature of an object (x is time, measured in hours). If we are told that the object's surface is cooling off at a steady 5°C per hour, then we can write $T'(x) = -5$.

1. The water level $W(t)$ (where t is measured in hours) is falling 3 inches every hour. Write an equation involving a derivative to describe the situation.

2.   The rabbit population $R(t)$ (where t is measured in years) is increasing at a rate of 10 percent every year. Which of the following equations is consistent with that description?

(A) $R'(t) = 10$

(B) $R'(t) = -10$

(C) $R'(t) = 0.10R$

(D) $R'(t) = 10R$

It is equally important to be able to translate such statements in the reverse direction; when you are presented with an equation involving derivatives, you should be able to interpret what information this gives you about the problem situation.

3.   A plane is descending for a landing. Its altitude $A(t)$ is measured in feet with t measuring time in minutes. Given that $A'(t) = -200$, describe the plane's behavior.

In many situations, a change in one quantity affects a change in another quantity. For example, as the radius of an artery decreases, the amount of blood flow decreases. Sensitivity is what we call the connection between the changes. Sensitivity identifies how one variable reacts to small changes in another variable.

The volume of blood flow depends on the radius of an artery. If V denotes the volume of blood flow and r denotes the radius of an artery, then the sensitivity is given by

$$\text{sensitivity} = \lim_{\Delta r \to 0} \frac{\Delta V}{\Delta r}.$$

If the sensitivity is known and there is a very small change in the radius of the artery, then the approximate change in the volume of blood flow is given by

$$\Delta V \approx \text{sensitivity} \times \Delta r.$$

Suppose we are given that $V = 2.8r^4$ and we are asked to find and interpret the sensitivity of the volume of blood flow to the radius of the artery when $r = 1.5$ mm.

Since $\frac{\Delta V}{\Delta r} = 11.2r^3$, the sensitivity at $r = 1.5$ mm is 37.8. This means that when the radius is 1.5 mm, a small additional change in the radius, Δr mm, will result in an increase in the volume of blood flow of approximately $37.8\Delta r$ cubic millimeters.

4. The surface area of a cube, S, as a function of the measure of a side, x, is given by $S = 6x^2$. Find and interpret the sensitivity of the surface area to the measure of a side when $x = 3$ cm.

Additional Practice

1. At time $t = 5$ sec, the sensitivity of the change of the volume of a sphere to a small additional change in the radius is 8. Write an equation to match this statement.

2. The cost of operating the widget factory $C(w)$ increases \$23 for every widget produced. Write an equation involving a derivative to describe the situation.

3. Let $A(t)$ represent the deer population in a local forest preserve at time t years, when $t \geq 0$. The population is increasing at a rate directly proportional to $1200 - A(t)$, where the constant of proportionality is k. Which of the following statements accurately reflects the situation?

    (A) $A(t) = k[1200 - A'(t)]$

    (B) $A'(t) = k[1200 - A(t)]$

    (C) $A'(t) = [1200 - kA(t)]$

    (D) $A'(t) = \dfrac{[1200 - A(t)]}{k}$

Need More Help With . . .   ***See . . .***

Derivative equations?   *Calculus,* Sections 5.5, 5.6, 7.4

Extreme Values of Functions

AP* Learning Objective: • Use derivatives to analyze properties of a function. (LO 2.2A)

Overview

Determining *maximum and minimum values* on open and closed intervals is a foundational skill that applies to many other topics such as optimization and motion. The places we search for maximum and minimum values are at critical points and endpoints of closed intervals. Critical points are where the first derivative of a function is zero or where the first derivative does not exist. Three frequently overlooked aspects of optimization are checking places where the derivative is undefined, checking endpoints, and justifying that a point is indeed a maximum or minimum by looking for a sign change in the derivative or using the second derivative test. Another important distinction is the difference between local and absolute extrema. Mastering this concept on simple functions and graphs will contribute greatly to your success on later topics.

Content and Practice

A key skill is the ability to distinguish between *local* (or relative) maximum or minimum values and *absolute* extrema. Whenever you work with a continuous function on a closed interval, endpoints must be examined as possible local and absolute extrema. Questions on this topic can be graphical, analytic, numerical, or conceptual, as the following sample questions show.

1. Identify each point on the curve as a location of a local maximum or minimum, absolute maximum or minimum, both a local and an absolute, or neither.

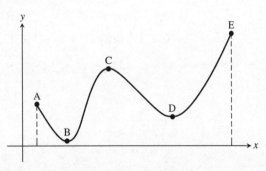

2. Is it possible for $f'(x)$ to equal 0 at $x = c$ but f not have a local maximum or minimum at $x = c$? Explain.

3. Is it possible for $f'(x)$ to fail to exist at $x = a$ but f still have a maximum or minimum at $x = a$? Explain.

4. Without a calculator, find the absolute maximum value of $g(x) = \frac{1}{3}x^3 - 4x$ on the interval $[-1, 4]$. Justify your answer.

5. Let f be a differentiable and monotonic function on the domain $[3, 8]$. The table shows four function values of f.

x	3	4	6	7
$f(x)$	-4	1	5	8

Which of the following statements must be true?
I. $f(8) > 9$
II. $f'(5) > 0$
III. $f'(c) = 3$ for exactly one c in $[3, 7]$

(A) II only   (B) II and III only
(C) III only   (D) I and III only

1. Let g be a function defined and continuous on the closed interval $[a, b]$. If g has a local minimum at c where $a < c < b$, which of the following statements must be true?

    I. If $g'(c)$ exists, then $g'(c) = 0$.

    II. $g(c) < g(b)$

    III. g is monotonic on $[a, b]$.

    (A) I only   (B) II only

    (C) I and II only   (D) I and III only

2. On the interval $[-5, 5]$, f is continuous and differentiable. If $f'(x) = (x - 1)(2x + 1)(x + 3)^2$, briefly explain the following conclusions.

    (a) There is a local maximum on f at $x = -\frac{1}{2}$.

    (b) There is a horizontal tangent but no extrema at $x = -3$.

    (c) If $f(2) = 7$, then $f(3) > 7$.

Need More Help With . . .	See . . .
Polynomial function behavior?	*Precalculus*, Section 2.3
Taking derivatives?	*Calculus*, Sections 3.3, 3.5, 4.3, 4.4
Extreme values of functions?	*Calculus*, Sections 5.1, 5.3, 5.4

Concavity of Functions

AP* Learning Objective: • Use derivatives to analyze properties of a function. (LO 2.2A)

Overview

A major component of function analysis is concavity, which is related to the second derivative of a function. Concavity also represents the rate of change of the slope of a given function. Visually we see this displayed in the curvature of the function. The second derivative is also important for locating inflection points and, in combination with the first derivative, may be used to justify local extrema. Common student errors in finding inflection points are to overlook places where the second derivative is undefined—and to fail to check for changes in the sign of the second derivative.

Content and Practice

Questions on this topic can be graphical, analytic, numerical, or conceptual, as the following sample questions show.

1. Using the capital letters below the *x*-axis, identify the intervals where the plotted function, *f*, is concave down. Convention dictates that intervals of concavity are reported as *open* intervals.

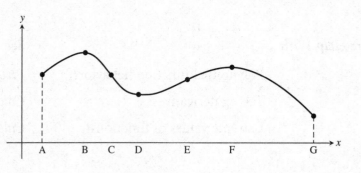

2. If the graph in Problem 1 is a plot of h' on the domain [A, G], identify all places where h has points of inflection on the given domain. Explain your choice(s).

3. Is it possible for $f''(x)$ to equal 0 at $x = c$ but not have an inflection point at $x = c$? Explain.

4. Is it possible for $f''(x)$ to fail to exist at $x = a$ but still have an inflection point at $x = a$? Explain.

5. Without a calculator, find the intervals where $g(x) = \ln(4 + x^2)$ is concave down. Show work that leads to your answer.

6. Let f'' be a continuous and monotonic decreasing function on the domain [1, 7]. The table below shows four function values of f''.

x	1	3	5	7
$f''(x)$	5	2	1	-2

Which of the following statements must be true?

I.   If $f'(2) = 11$, then $f'(3) > 11$.
II. f has an inflection point between $x = 5$ and $x = 7$.
III. f is concave up at $x = 6$.

(A) II only   (B) II and III only

(C) I and II only   (D) I and III only

In the graph on the right, it appears that the function has a local maximum when $x = a$ and a local minimum when $x = b$. Notice that the curve is concave down where this maximum occurs and concave up where this minimum occurs. Remember that a graph of a function $f(x)$ is concave down on any interval where $f''(x)$ is negative and concave up on any interval where $f''(x)$ is positive. This illustrates how the second derivative can be used to determine the extrema of a function.

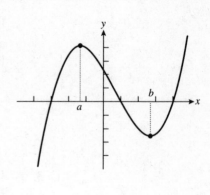

Second Derivative Test for Local Extrema

If $f'(c) = 0$ and $f''(c) < 0$, then f has a local maximum at $x = c$.

If $f'(c) = 0$ and $f''(c) > 0$, then f has a local minimum at $x = c$.

It is important to satisfy *both* conditions for each type of extrema. If you only know $f'(c) = 0$, you do not know if a maximum or a minimum occurs at $x = c$. If you only know that $f''(c) < 0$ or $f''(c) > 0$, then you cannot be certain that $x = c$ is where a critical point occurs. It could simply be a point on a concave down or a concave up interval of the curve.

7.   Let $f(x) = x^3 + \dfrac{11}{2}x^2 - 4x + \dfrac{9}{2}$. Use the second derivative test to determine where the extrema occur.

1. The graph of *g*, a twice-differentiable function, is shown below. Choose the correct order for the values of $g(1)$, $g'(1)$, and $g''(1)$.

   (A) $g(1) < g'(1) < g''(1)$

   (B) $g'(1) < g''(1) < g(1)$

   (C) $g''(1) < g(1) < g'(1)$

   (D) $g'(1) < g(1) < g''(1)$

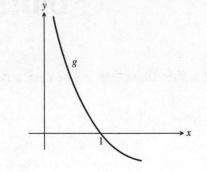

2. Use the second derivative test for local extrema to justify that $h(x) = x^2 e^x$ has a local maximum at $x = -2$.

Need More Help With . . .   *See . . .*

Polynomial function behavior?   *Precalculus,* Section 2.3

Derivatives?   *Calculus,* Sections 3.1–3.5

Concavity?   *Calculus,* Section 5.3

Points of Inflection

AP* Learning Objective: • Use derivatives to analyze properties of a function. (LO 2.2A)

Overview

We are interested in *points of inflection* because they help us describe the behavior of a graph (along with the extrema of the function). They also represent points of greatest sensitivity to change in the independent variable as a result of small changes in the dependent variable. For this reason, it can be quite useful to locate the points of inflection in some applications (it can represent, for instance, a shift in demand or price movement).

Content and Practice

A point where the graph of a function has a tangent line and where the concavity changes is a **point of inflection.** Points of inflection can be found by looking for changes in sign in the second derivative. Since the Intermediate Value Theorem applies here, the second derivative will either have a value of zero or be undefined at the points of inflection.

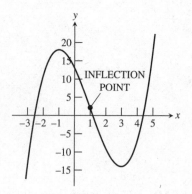

$$f(x) = x^3 - 3x^2 - 9x + 13$$

To identify points of inflection:
   I.   Locate the *x*-values at which the second derivative function is zero or undefined.
   II.   Test values in between those points to determine the sign of the second derivative for that interval.
   III.   At those points where the sign changes, if the original function has a tangent line, then that is a point of inflection.

1. Consider the function $f(x) = -x^4 + 4x^3 + 3x + 5$.

   (a) Find the second derivative, f''.

   (b) At what x-values is f'' zero or undefined?

   (c) Over what intervals is f'' positive? Negative?

   (d) Identify any points of inflection.

Additional Practice

1. A function $f(x)$ exists such that $f''(x) = (x - 2)^2(x + 1)$. How many points of inflection does $f(x)$ have?
   (A) None (B) One
   (C) Two (D) Three

2. Find the x-coordinates of all points of inflection of the function $f(x) = 2x^3 - 3x^2 + 6x - 10$.

3.   Suppose f is continuous on $[0, 6]$ and satisfies the following:

x	0	3	5	6
f	-1	4	-1	-3
f'	5	0	-8	0
f''	-1	-3	Does not exist	3

x	$0 < x < 3$	$3 < x < 5$	$5 < x < 6$
f'	$+$	$-$	$-$
f''	$-$	$-$	$+$

(a)   Identify all points of inflection.

   (A) $(5, -1)$ only

   (B) $(3, 4)$ and $(6, -3)$

   (C) $(3, 4)$ only

   (D) $(3, 4)$, $(6, -3)$, and $(5, -1)$

(b)   Explain the reason for your choice in part (a).

Need More Help With . . .   ***See . . .***

   Points of inflection?   *Calculus*, Section 5.3

Correspondences among the Graphs of *f*, *f′*, and *f″*

AP* Learning Objective: • Use derivatives to analyze properties of a function. (LO 2.2A)

Overview

We will often use the derivative and second derivative functions to give us information about the graph of *f*, and vice versa. We can use the signs of *f′* and *f″* to understand characteristics about the increasing and decreasing behavior of *f* and about its concavity. The relationships among these functions allow us to perform optimization (where we seek to find the maximum or minimum value of a function).

Content and Practice

A function's derivative measures the slope of that function. This simple fact can lead to a number of connections between the graph of *f* and *f′* (for now, let's assume that *f* is a differentiable function).

1.   Complete each of the following statements for a differentiable function *f*:

   (a)   When *f′* is positive, it means that *f* is

   _____ .

   (b)   When *f′* is negative, it means that *f* is

   _____ .

   (c)   When *f′* is changing from negative to positive, *f* is at a
   _____ value.

   (d)   When *f′* is changing from positive to negative, *f* is at a
   _____ value.

In the figure at right, the bold function is f and the other function is f'. Note that f' is negative on the interval $(-2, 2)$ (where the graph of f is decreasing) and positive on both $(-\infty, -2)$ and $(2, \infty)$ (where the graph of f is increasing). Points where the first derivative is changing sign correspond to maximum or minimum values of the original function.

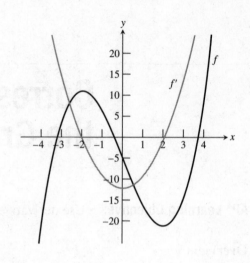

Since f'' measures the slope of f', we can apply the same basic reasoning again. When f'' is positive, for instance, it means that f' is increasing. This, in turn, means that the graph of f must be concave up.

Shown at right is the same function f (again in bold) along with its second derivative, f''. Note that $f''(x)$ is negative on $(-\infty, 0)$, where the original function is concave down; similarly, it is positive on $(0, \infty)$, where the original function is concave up. Points where the second derivative has a change of sign represent points of inflection in the graph of f if a tangent to f exists at that point.

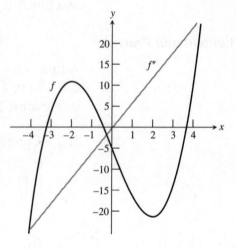

1. Consider the graph of $f(x) = x \sin x$ shown at right. Draw schematic diagrams to approximate where the first and second derivatives are positive, negative, and zero. Include scales on your diagrams along with $+$ or $-$ signs in the appropriate intervals.

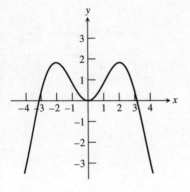

   (a) f' ⟷

   (b) f'' ⟷

   (c) State the reasoning behind your diagrams in parts (a) and (b). How did you determine where each function would be positive, negative, or zero? Be specific.

2. Let the graph shown in Problem 1 be g'.

   (a) Estimate the intervals on which $g(x)$ is increasing.

   (b) Estimate the intervals on which $g(x)$ is decreasing.

   (c) Estimate where $g(x)$ has local extreme values.

3. *f* is continuous on [0, 8] and satisfies the following:

x	$0 \leq x < 3$	3	$3 < x < 5$	5	$5 < x < 6$	6	$6 < x \leq 8$
f''	−	0	+	Does not exist	−	0	−

(a) Based on this information, is there a point of inflection at $x = 3$?
  (i) Definitely
  (ii) Possibly
  (iii) Definitely not

(b) Based on this information, is there a point of inflection at $x = 5$?
  (i) Definitely
  (ii) Possibly
  (iii) Definitely not

(c) Based on this information, is there a point of inflection at $x = 6$?
  (i) Definitely
  (ii) Possibly
  (iii) Definitely not

4. Shown at right is a graph of f' (in bold) and f''. Sketch a possible graph of f on the same axes.

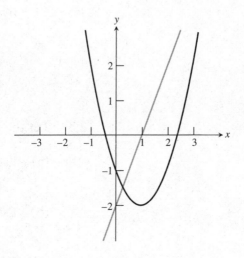

Need More Help With . . .

Functions and their properties?

Graphical relationships among $f, f',$ and f''?

See . . .

Precalculus, Section 1.2

Calculus, Section 5.3

The Mean Value Theorem

AP* Learning Objective: • Apply the Mean Value Theorem to describe the behavior of a function over an interval. (LO 2.4A)

Overview

One consequence of the Mean Value Theorem is that it provides a method of determining the intervals where the graph of a function rises or falls. This skill is useful in many situations where we have a model that we wish to analyze (for instance, we can examine a position function and determine at what times the object was moving to the left or the right).

Content and Practice

The statement of the Mean Value Theorem is as follows:

Mean Value Theorem for Derivatives

If $y = f(x)$ is continuous at every point of the closed interval $[a, b]$ and differentiable at every point of its interior (a, b), then there is at least one point c in (a, b) at which

$$f'(c) = \frac{f(b) - f(a)}{b - a}.$$

This theorem says that, under these conditions, there must be at least one point in the interval where the instantaneous rate of change, $f'(c)$, equals the average rate of change, $\frac{f(b) - f(a)}{b - a}$, for the interval.

Graphically, if A and B are two points on a differentiable curve, then somewhere between points A and B there is at least one tangent line to the curve that is parallel to chord AB.

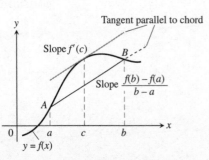

Figure for the Mean Value Theorem

99

1. Consider the function $f(x) = x^2$ on the interval $[1, 5]$.

   (a) Are the conditions of the Mean Value Theorem met?

   (b) Find $f'(x)$ as a function in terms of x.

   (c) Find the average rate of change $\dfrac{f(b) - f(a)}{b - a}$ over the interval $(a = 1$ and $b = 5)$.

   (d) Use your answers to parts (b) and (c) to find each value of c in the interval that satisfies the equation of the Mean Value Theorem, $f'(c) = \dfrac{f(b) - f(a)}{b - a}$.

One important consequence of the Mean Value Theorem is that it simplifies the process of determining where a graph rises or falls.

Corollary

Let f be continuous on $[a, b]$ and differentiable on (a, b).

1. If $f' > 0$ at each point of (a, b), then f increases on $[a, b]$.
2. If $f' < 0$ at each point of (a, b), then f decreases on $[a, b]$.

Two other important conclusions can be drawn from the Mean Value Theorem:

 I. If $f' = 0$ over an interval, then f is constant over that interval.

 II. If $f' = g'$ over an interval, then $f = g + C$ over the interval for some constant C.

1. Consider the function $f(x) = \sqrt{x - 2}$. On what interval are the hypotheses of the Mean Value Theorem satisfied?

    (A) $[0, 2]$ (B) $[1, 5]$ (C) $[2, 7]$ (D) None of these

2. Verify that the function $f(x) = \sin x$ satisfies the hypotheses of the Mean Value Theorem on the interval $[2, 11]$. Then approximate to three decimal places all values of c in $(2, 11)$ that satisfy the Mean Value Theorem equation.

3. Consider the following graph of $f(x) = x \sin x$ on the domain $[-4, 4]$. How many values of c in $(-4, 4)$ appear to satisfy the Mean Value Theorem equation?

    (A) None
    (B) One
    (C) Two
    (D) Three

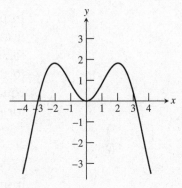

Need More Help With . . .

Average rate of change?

Mean Value Theorem?

See . . .

Precalculus, Sections 2.1, 11.1

Calculus, Section 5.2

Optimization

AP* Learning Objective: • Solve problems involving related rates, optimization, rectilinear motion, (BC) and planar motion. (LO 2.3C)

Overview

Optimization is one of the many applications of derivatives of functions. They are most commonly presented as word problems and encompass a wide variety of interesting applications. It is important to develop mastery of the *process* of solving this type of problem and not to try to memorize a small set of problem types.

Content and Practice

In precalculus you solved optimization problems by setting up equations and using a calculator to determine a maximum or minimum value of the function to be optimized. Since the AP* Calculus exam does not expect or allow students to use that feature of a calculator, you must be able to set the first derivative equal to zero and justify extreme values using calculus methods. The strategy for solving max-min problems is presented in Section 5.4 of the *Calculus* text.

Let's look at an example and connect it to steps from the strategy.

Example: A rectangle is inscribed under the graph of $h(x) = 9 - x^2$. Find the maximum possible area for that rectangle.

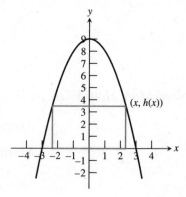

Understand the problem:

Recognize that the area of the rectangle changes based on the placement of the corners. Find the area of the largest possible rectangle.

Develop a mathematical model:

The total width of the rectangle is $2x$ since it is symmetric to the y-axis. The height of the rectangle is determined by the function value on the parabola. Therefore the area as a function of x is $A(x) = 2x(9 - x^2)$.

Identify the critical points and endpoints:

Expanding $A(x) = 18x - 2x^3$, so $A'(x) = 18 - 6x^2$. The zeros of $A'(x)$ are $x = \pm\sqrt{3}$. The only candidates for x to produce a maximum area are the endpoints $x = 0$ and $x = 3$, and the positive solution to $A'(x) = 0$, which is $x = \sqrt{3}$.

Solve the mathematical model:

The values $x = 0$ and $x = 3$ make the area of the rectangle equal to 0. Using a signed number line for $A'(x)$ shows $x = \sqrt{3}$ is a location of a maximum on A. A number line is a good organizer, but not accepted as justification. A brief sentence explanation as shown beneath the number line below is required.

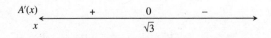

Since the first derivative changes from positive to the left of $x = \sqrt{3}$, to zero at $x = \sqrt{3}$, and to negative to the right of $x = \sqrt{3}$, a local maximum of the area function occurs at $x = \sqrt{3}$.

Interpret the solution:

Stopping at $x = \sqrt{3}$ is a very common mistake. The problem asks for the *maximum area*. The area of the rectangle is $A(x) = 2x(9 - x^2)$, so the maximum area is $A(\sqrt{3}) = 12\sqrt{3}$.

Sometimes a problem requires writing two equations. One is usually based on a fixed quantity and is used for substitution purposes. The other equation is frequently the quantity we wish to optimize. Try the next one yourself using the hint for guidance.

1. An open-topped box with square base must be constructed with a volume of 12 cubic inches. What dimensions use the least amount of material?

    (*Hint:* Define your variables for dimensions of the box. Now write two equations, one for volume and one for surface area. Which one will be optimized?)

1. A rectangle is inscribed under the arch of $y = \sin(x)$ on the domain $[0, \pi]$ with its base on the x-axis and its upper vertices on the curve. Find the maximum area of the rectangle.

 2. From an 8 inch by 10 inch rectangular sheet of paper, squares of equal size will be cut from each corner. The flaps will then be folded up to form an open-topped box. Find the maximum possible volume of the box.

3. A particle moves from $(0, 1)$ to the right, following the path of $f(x) = e^{x/2}$. What are the coordinates of the particle when its distance to the point $(2, 0)$ is at a minimum?

   (A) $(0.841, 1.523)$ (B) $(0.841, 1.914)$

   (C) $(1.415, 1.411)$ (D) $(1.415, 2.030)$

4. The steps of the optimization process are reworded slightly and listed in random order below. Number them from 1 to 8 as they should be completed.

____ Justify that your solution provides a maximum or minimum.

____ Find the derivative of the varying quantity.

____ If necessary, substitute from the fixed quantity into the varying quantity.

____ Make sure you have answered the original question, with appropriate units of measure.

____ Define variables to be used.

____ Read and understand the problem, noting especially what is to be optimized.

____ Find the zeros of the derivative equation.

____ Write equations for all fixed and varying quantities.

Need More Help With . . .	**See . . .**
Writing mathematical models?	*Precalculus,* Section 1.7
Taking derivatives?	*Calculus,* Sections 3.3, 3.5, 4.3, 4.4
Optimization?	*Calculus,* Sections 5.1, 5.3, 5.4

Implicit Differentiation

AP* Learning Objective: • Calculate derivatives. (LO 2.1C)

Overview

There are situations where it is not possible to analytically isolate y as a function of x. One example of this is $y^3 + \sin y = \cos x + x^2$. In this case we must find dy/dx using *implicit differentiation*. No matter what variables you are working with, any time the dependent variable in an equation cannot be isolated, implicit differentiation may be necessary. One of its most important uses is to help establish the formulas for the derivatives of inverse trigonometric functions. Although you are expected to know the formulas themselves the actual derivation of those formulas has rarely, if ever, appeared on the AP* exam. Review Section 4.2 of the *Calculus* text for examples of the derivations.

Content and Practice

There are three key skills for successfully differentiating implicitly with respect to x:

1. Any time you differentiate a variable with respect to a different variable you will get a Chain Rule factor. For example,
$$\frac{d}{da}(\sin(p)) = \cos(p)\frac{dp}{da}.$$

2. Be alert to use the product rule or the quotient rule when independent and dependent variables are connected by multiplication or division respectively. For example,
$$\frac{d}{dx}\left(e^{(x/y)}\right) = e^{(x/y)} \cdot \frac{y - x \cdot \dfrac{dy}{dx}}{y^2}.$$

3. Remember to use the Chain Rule factor, when needed, after applying the power rule. For example,
$$\frac{d}{dx}\cos(x \cdot y^2) = -\sin(x \cdot y^2)\left(y^2 + x \cdot 2y\frac{dy}{dx}\right).$$

When first learning differentiation, students often use a very fundamental skill for successful implicit differentiation without realizing it. To find the derivative of a simple explicit function such as $y = x^3$, we naturally write $dy/dx = 3x^2$. Our attention is often on the right-hand side of that equation, but let's focus on the left-hand side for a minute. You have actually differentiated the y term with respect to x. It would be no different if the equation had started out as $y - x^3 = 0$. There are 3 "terms" to differentiate: x^3, 0, and y. When you differentiate *y with respect to x*, you get the dy/dx term, producing $dy/dx - 3x^2 = 0$. We do not see anything after $3x^2$ because we are differentiating with respect to x, so in effect we get $3x^2\, dx/dx = 3x^2 \cdot 1$.

The steps for finding dy/dx implicitly can be summarized as follows:

   (i)   Differentiate each term.
   (ii) Collect all terms with dy/dx on one side of the equation.
  (iii) Factor out dy/dx as a common factor.
  (iv) Move all remaining factors to the other side of the equation using division.

1.   Show that if $x^2 + y^2 = 2y^3$, then $\dfrac{dy}{dx} = \dfrac{2x}{6y^2 - 2y}$.

2.   Given: $xy^2 + 2y^4 = x^2y$.

   (a) Verify that the point $(2, 1)$ is on the curve.

   (b) Find the slope of the line tangent to the curve at $(2, 1)$.

1. Which is the slope of the line tangent to $y^2 + xy - x^2 = 11$ at $(2, 3)$?

   (A) $-\dfrac{5}{2}$ (B) $\dfrac{1}{8}$

   (C) $\dfrac{4}{7}$ (D) $\dfrac{9}{7}$

2. If $ac^2 - c^3 = a^2 - 5$, then $\dfrac{dc}{da} =$

   (A) $\dfrac{2a - c^2}{2ac - 3c^2}$ (B) $\dfrac{c^2 - 2a + 5}{3c^2 - 2ac}$

   (C) $\dfrac{2a - 5}{2c - 3c^2}$ (D) $\dfrac{2a}{2c - 3c^2}$

3. Consider the curve given by $x^2 - x^2 y = y^2 - 1$.

   (a) Show that $\dfrac{dy}{dx} = \dfrac{2x - 2xy}{x^2 + 2y}$.

   (b) Find all points on the curve where $x = 2$. Show there is a horizontal tangent to the curve at one of those points.

4. Given $\ln(1 + y) = \dfrac{1}{2} x^2 + 5$, find $\dfrac{d^2 y}{dx^2}$.

Need More Help With . . .   *See . . .*

Implicit differentiation?   *Calculus,* Section 4.2

Related Rates

AP* Learning Objective: • Solve problems involving related rates, optimization, rectilinear motion, (BC) and planar motion. (LO 2.3C)

Overview

Related rates explore a relationship among several derivatives. Related rates is one of the more challenging topics during the first half of a calculus course. A methodical approach will provide the best opportunity for success. It is likely you will need practice to master this concept. Related rates may show up on either the Multiple Choice or the Free Response section of the AP* Calculus exam. Carefully defining variables and summarizing a lot of preliminary information will keep you organized.

Content and Practice

The goal of the technique used to solve related rates problems is to identify a mathematical relationship between the quantities that vary. It is crucial to understand which quantities are changing and which are constant throughout the problem. In the solution process, express rates as derivatives and quantities as simple variables. In many problems, there is a secondary equation from which a substitution of variables is made prior to the differentiation process. The strategy for solving related rates problems is presented in Section 5.6 of the *Calculus* text.

Let's look at an example and connect it to steps from the strategy.

   Example 1: Air is being blown into a sphere at a rate of 6 cubic inches per minute. How fast is the radius changing when the radius of the sphere is 2 inches?

Understand the problem:
Let r be the radius and V be the volume of the sphere. The units, "cubic inches per minute," denote a rate of change of volume, so $\dfrac{dV}{dt} = 6$. "How fast is the radius changing . . ." means we need to solve for $\dfrac{dr}{dt}$.

109

Develop a mathematical model of the problem:

The radius and the volume of the sphere are both changing. Therefore we must work with the variables r and V. We cannot substitute 2 inches for the radius until *after* differentiation because the radius length is not constant.

Write an equation relating the variable whose rate of change you seek with the variable(s) whose rate of change you know:

We need a formula that relates the volume, V, and the radius, r, of a sphere.

$$V_{\text{sphere}} = \frac{4}{3}\pi r^3$$

Differentiate both sides of the equation implicitly with respect to time t:

$$\frac{dV}{dt} = 4\pi r^2 \frac{dr}{dt}$$

Substitute values for any quantities that depend on time and solve:

$$6 \text{ in.}^3/\text{min} = 4\pi (2 \text{ in.})^2 \frac{dr}{dt}$$

$$\frac{dr}{dt} = \frac{3}{8\pi} \text{ in./min}$$

Interpret the solution:

When the radius of the sphere is 2 inches, the radius of the sphere is changing at a rate of $\frac{3}{8\pi}$ in./min.

Example 2: A toddler is holding the string to a helium filled balloon that is 6 feet directly above him. A sudden noise startles him and he lets go of the string while running away. The balloon rises 2 ft/sec and the child runs 1 ft/sec. How fast is the distance between the toddler and the balloon changing when 5 seconds have elapsed?

Understand the problem:

Let x be the distance the toddler runs, let y be the distance the balloon rises, and let z be the distance between the balloon and the toddler. We need to solve for $\frac{dz}{dt}$ while we know $\frac{dy}{dt} = 2$ ft/sec and $\frac{dx}{dt} = 1$ ft/sec.

Develop a mathematical model of the problem:

The diagram of the situation shows how all the variables are related. The three distances are all changing but the balloon starts moving upward from a fixed height of 6 feet. Therefore we cannot make any substitutions for x, y, or z until *after* differentiation.

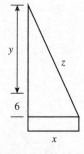

Write an equation relating the variable whose rate of change you seek with the variable(s) whose rate of change you know:

The Pythagorean Theorem relates the three variables.

$$x^2 + (y + 6)^2 = z^2$$

Differentiate both sides of the equation implicitly with respect to time t:

$$2x\frac{dx}{dt} + 2(y + 6)\frac{dy}{dt} = 2z\frac{dz}{dt}$$

Substitute values for any quantities that depend on time and solve:

After 5 seconds, $x = 5$ feet and $y = 10$ feet. Solving for z we have:

$$5^2 + 16^2 = z^2 \text{ so } z = \sqrt{281}.$$

Substituting into the derivative equation, we have:

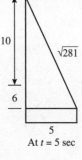

10

$\sqrt{281}$

6

5

At $t = 5$ sec

$$2 \cdot 5 \cdot 1 + 2 \cdot 16 \cdot 2 = 2\sqrt{281}\frac{dz}{dt}$$

$$\frac{dz}{dt} = \frac{37}{\sqrt{281}} \approx 2.207$$

Interpret the solution:

After 5 seconds have elapsed, the distance between the toddler and the balloon is changing at a rate of 2.207 feet/second.

Follow this procedure for the following problems.

1. The edge of a cube is increasing at a rate of 2 inches per minute. At the instant the edge is 3 inches, how fast is the volume increasing?

2. A point moves along the curve $y = (x - 3)^2$ such that its x-coordinate is increasing at 4 units per second.

   (a) At the moment $x = 1$, how fast is its y-coordinate changing? Interpret your answer based on the shape of the graph and the location of the point.

   (b) At the moment $x = 1$, how fast is the point's distance from the origin changing?

In part (b) of the previous problem you may have encountered three rates, the change in x and y, and the distance from the origin. The next problem requires working with three rates. Be aware of your need for the Product Rule when differentiating.

3. Two ships leave a port at the same time, traveling on paths that differ by 50°. The first ship holds a steady course at 35 miles per hour. The second ship holds its course going 28 miles per hour. After two hours, how fast is the distance between the ships increasing? (*Hint:* Use the Law of Cosines: $a^2 = w^2 + h^2 - 2wh \cos \theta$.)

There are times when the equation which is to be differentiated has more than one independent variable. In such instances, a relationship between the independent variables should be determined so that a substitution can be made prior to differentiating. Sometimes that relationship comes from similarities, as in the next example, or it may come from information in the word problem. Although there are exceptions, it is usually easier to differentiate an equation with only one independent variable.

4. Water is flowing into an inverted right circular cone at a rate of 4 cubic inches per minute. The cone is 16 inches tall and its base has a radius of 4 inches. At the moment the water has a depth of 5 inches, how fast is the radius at the surface of the water increasing?

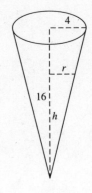

(*Hint:* The volume of a cone is $V = \frac{1}{3}\pi r^2 h$, but based on proportions in the cone, substitute an expression for h so your equation is in terms of only V and r prior to differentiating.)

Additional Practice

1. The diagonal of a square is increasing at a rate of 3 inches per minute. When the area of the square is 18 square inches, how fast (in inches per minute) is the perimeter increasing?

   (A) $3\sqrt{2}$　　　　　(B) $\dfrac{3\sqrt{2}}{2}$

   (C) 6　　　　　　　(D) $6\sqrt{2}$

2. A spherical snowball with diameter 4 inches is removed from the freezer in June and begins melting uniformly such that it is shrinking 2 cubic inches per minute. How fast (in square inches per minute) is its surface area decreasing when the radius is 1 inch?

   (A) $\dfrac{1}{2\pi}$　　　　　(B) $\dfrac{1}{\pi}$

   (C) 1　　　　　　　(D) 4

3. The steps of the related rates process are reworded slightly and listed in random order below. Number them from 1 to 6 as they should be completed.

_____ Draw a diagram that illustrates the problem, identifying quantities that are variables and those that are constant.

_____ Substitute values for variables.

_____ Solve for the desired quantity, using appropriate units in your answer.

_____ Differentiate both sides of the equation implicitly with respect to time t.

_____ Read and understand the problem, identifying the variable(s) whose rate of change is known and the variable whose rate of change is to be found.

_____ Write an equation that relates the variables of the problem.

Need More Help With . . .   *See . . .*

Related rates?   *Calculus,* Section 5.6

Derivative as a Rate of Change

AP* Learning Objectives:
- Identify the derivative of a function as the limit of a difference quotient. (LO 2.1A)
- Interpret the meaning of a derivative within a problem. (LO 2.3A)

Overview

Although there are countless applications using the derivative to measure change, one of the most important is its use in relating position, velocity, and acceleration. You need to have a clear understanding of velocity as the derivative of position and acceleration as the derivative of velocity. The AP* test may evaluate this understanding in all three common forms—analytically, graphically, and numerically. You can also count on being tested on the subtle difference between average and instantaneous rates of change. Remember, an average rate of change occurs over an interval, while a derivative (instantaneous) occurs at a single point.

Content and Practice

Recall that the *average rate of change* of the position function is the slope of a secant line on the graph of the position function. It is average velocity and requires no calculus to compute. As the time interval becomes shorter and shorter, the limit of the slope of the secant becomes the slope of the tangent line. This is the instantaneous rate of change of position, *velocity*. Velocity therefore is the derivative of the position function. Velocity can be positive or negative, so we say it has both magnitude and direction. For instance, often a falling object is said to have negative velocity. Similarly, the derivative of velocity is acceleration. Remember also that speed is defined as the absolute value of velocity.

1. The position of a particle as a function of time is given by the equation $s(t) = t^2 - 3t$ for $t \geq 0$, where t is in seconds and s is in inches.

    (a) Find the velocity of the particle at the instant $t = 5$ seconds. Include units.

(b) Find the average velocity over the first 4 seconds of motion. (No calculus needed!)

(c) What is the speed of the particle at $t = 1$ second?

2. Consider the following graph of a velocity function. Velocity is in feet per second and time in seconds.

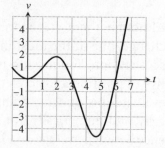

(a) On the domain $0 \leq t \leq 6$ seconds, approximate the time interval(s) when acceleration is positive. Explain your answer. (*Think:* What characteristic of a velocity graph reveals acceleration?)

(b) On the domain $0 \leq t \leq 6$ seconds, approximate the time interval(s) when the speed is decreasing. Explain your answer. (*Hint:* You may want to sketch the absolute value of velocity on the same axes.)

(c) Find an approximation of the average acceleration on the interval [1, 5] seconds. Include units. (*Hint:* No calculus necessary.)

1. The distance of a particle from its initial position is given by
$s(t) = t - 5 + \dfrac{9}{(t+1)}$, where s is feet and t is minutes. Find the velocity at $t = 1$ minute in feet per minute.

(A) $-\dfrac{5}{4}$ (B) $\dfrac{13}{4}$

(C) $\dfrac{1}{2}$ (D) $-\dfrac{9}{4}$

2. The distance of a particle from its initial position is measured every 5 seconds and provided in the table below. Use the data to answer the questions that follow.

Time (sec)	0	5	10	15	20
Distance (ft)	0	7	17	25	30

(a) Estimate the velocity of the particle at $t = 13$ seconds. Include units.

(b) What is the average velocity on the time interval [5, 20] seconds?

3. The graph of the velocity of a particle is given below. On the same axes, draw the acceleration graph.

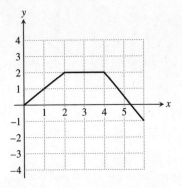

4. The number of liters of water remaining in a tank t minutes after the tank has started to drain is $R(t) = 2t^3 - 20t^2 - 72t + 820$. At what moment is the water draining the fastest?

(A) 0 min   (B) 2 min

(C) $3\frac{1}{3}$ min   (D) $5\frac{1}{3}$ min

Need More Help With . . .

Derivative as a rate of change?

See . . .

Calculus, Section 3.4

Slope Fields

AP* Learning Objective: • Estimate solutions to differential equations. (LO 2.3F)

Overview

As you have learned, the solution to a differential equation of the form $dy/dx = f(x)$ is found by antidifferentiation. When the integral is indefinite, your teacher has most likely emphasized the "+C" at the end of your answer. This is because there are an infinite number of solution curves, all differing by a simple constant. If you just slide a graph up or down, it does not change the graph's slope at any given x-value. Therefore, it is true for all those solutions that at any given value of x, their derivatives (and thus their slopes) are the same. A slope field is a series of very small segments representing the slopes of those solution curves at various points throughout the coordinate plane. This allows us to see the family of solution curves even when we cannot calculate an antiderivative. You should be able to plot a slope field given a differential equation, match a slope field to a differential equation, draw a particular solution onto a slope field given an initial condition, and match a slope field to one possible solution function.

Content and Practice

Consider the differential equation $dy/dx = \frac{1}{2}x$. To create a slope field, we calculate the slope at various points in the coordinate plane and plot a small segment with that slope at the given location.

x	y	$\dfrac{dy}{dx} = \dfrac{1}{2}x$
-1	0	-0.5
-1	1	-0.5
-1	2	-0.5
0	0	0
0	1	0
0	2	0
1	0	0.5
1	1	0.5
1	2	0.5
2	0	1
2	1	1
2	2	1

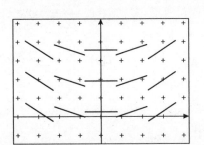

Grid marks are every 0.5 units.

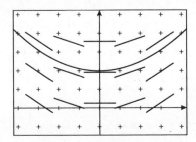

One particular solution plotted on the field,

$y = \dfrac{1}{4}x^2 + 1.$

Notice that the slopes at various points are dependent only on the value of x. As we look at a column of marks (y-changing), the slopes do not change. This is not always the case, but in this first example, only x

119

appears in the differential equation. What you should notice in the plot is that the pattern of slope marks begin to look like a series of parabolas. This is true because the solution to the given differential equation is $y = \frac{1}{4}x^2 + C$. You are looking at the changing slopes of the family of translated parabolas. In the second figure, an equation with $C = 1$ has been plotted on the slope field.

1.   Given $dy/dx = 1/x$, create a slope field at the 20 given points on the grid.

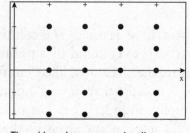

The grid marks are every 1 unit.

2.   Indicate which differential equation is represented in the slope field graph. *Briefly* explain your choice.

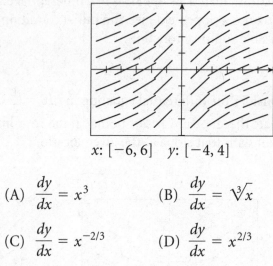

x: $[-6, 6]$ y: $[-4, 4]$

(A) $\dfrac{dy}{dx} = x^3$ (B) $\dfrac{dy}{dx} = \sqrt[3]{x}$

(C) $\dfrac{dy}{dx} = x^{-2/3}$ (D) $\dfrac{dy}{dx} = x^{2/3}$

Explanation:

3. A differential equation may also be a function of just y or a combination of x and y. As an example, the slope field below was created from the differential equation $dy/dx = x/y$. Describe any patterns you notice for regions of positive, negative, or zero slope as they may be determined by values of x and y.

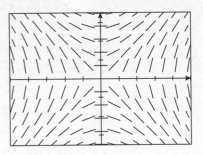

4. Create a slope field on the 12 points in the graph for the differential equation $dy/dx = y^2(x - 1)$.

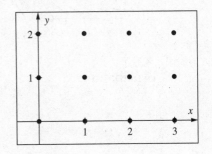

Additional Practice

1. On each slope field, draw the solution curve that satisfies the initial condition $f(-1) = 2$. (Marks on the axes are every 1 unit.)

(a)   (b)

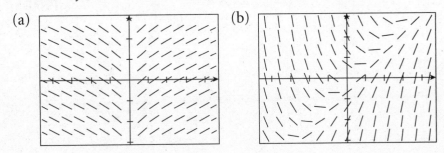

2. Which of the following slope fields could be a solution to the differential equation $dy/dx = x^{1/3}$? Briefly explain your choice. (All windows are $[-4.7, 4.7]$ and $[-3.1, 3.1]$.)

(A)   (B)

(C)   (D)

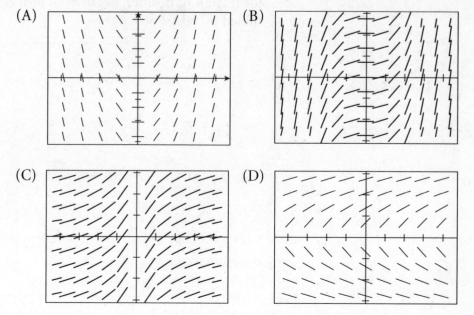

Explanation:

Need More Help With . . .

Slope fields?

See . . .

Calculus, Section 7.1

2004 AP* Calculus AB Exam, Problem 6

Euler's Method

AP* Learning Objective: • Estimate solutions to differential equations. (LO 2.3F)

Overview

Euler's method is another strictly AP* Calculus BC topic. Like a tangent line, Euler's method is used to numerically approximate a function near a known point but is generally more accurate over a wider domain.

Content and Practice

Early in the course you learned that a tangent line will approximate a function over varying intervals depending on the shape of the function, but often that tangent line became a poor approximation of the function as the slope of the function changed while the slope of the tangent did not. Euler's method basically adjusts the slope of the tangent to more closely follow the curve of the function. Imagine a line tangent to a function. To approximate the function, you follow the line over a designated short domain, called Δx. At that point, you "change course" and follow a path parallel to the slope of the function based on your new location. It is useful to organize your information in a table, as shown.

(x, y)	$f'(x, y)$	Δx or h	$\Delta y = f'(x, y)\Delta x$	$(x + \Delta x, y + \Delta y)$

Graphically, connecting consecutive Euler points produces a segmented curve, which will follow the shape of the curve with varying degrees of accuracy over a limited domain.

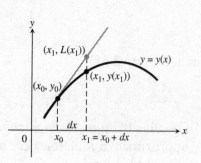

The first Euler step approximates $y(x_1)$ with $L(x_1)$.

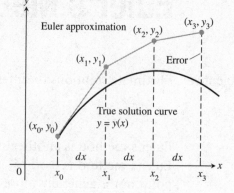

Three steps in the Euler approximation to the solution of the initial value problem $y' = f(x, y)$, $y(x_0) = y_0$. As we take more steps, the errors involved usually accumulate, but not in the exaggerated way shown here.

1. Given that $f(1) = 1$, and $dy/dx = 2x + 1$, generate the next two points of the Euler line using $\Delta x = 0.5$. Show your work in the table provided. If your teacher has given you a program to generate Euler points on your calculator, use it to verify your results. This happens to be a differential equation you can solve analytically, so find the specific function and sketch the function and the Euler line together on the given coordinate plane.

(x, y)	$f'(x, y)$	Δx or h	$\Delta y = f'(x, y)\Delta x$	$(x + \Delta x, y + \Delta y)$
$(1, 1)$		0.5		
		0.5		

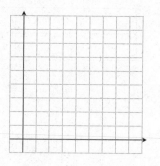

2. In the previous problem, what could be changed in the process of generating points to increase the accuracy of the Euler line?

Often, the differential equation will be a function of both x and y, and you may not be able to solve it by simple separation of variables. Euler's method is particularly useful in these cases to help visualize the function around the known point.

3. Given $f(0) = 1$ and $dy/dx = 2x + y$, use $\Delta x = 0.5$ to generate the next three Euler points. Sketch the curve on the given coordinate plane. Then plot the solution curve $y = 3e^x - 2(x + 1)$ on the same graph.

(x, y)	$f'(x, y)$	Δx or h	$\Delta y = f'(x, y)\Delta x$	$(x + \Delta x, y + \Delta y)$
		0.5		

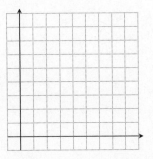

Additional Practice

1. Given $f'(x, y) = \frac{x}{y}$, $f(2) = 1$, and using two steps of equal size, which of the following is the Euler approximation of $f(3)$?

(A) 2.000   (B) 2.449

(C) 2.625   (D) 2.970

2. The error in generating Euler approximations is the absolute value of the difference between the Euler value and the actual function value at a given x. If $dy/dx = 2x + 3$ and $(1, 3)$ lies on the curve, use $\Delta x = 0.2$ and find the error when approximating $f(1.4)$.

(A) 0.04

(B) 0.08

(C) 1.08

(D) 1.40

Need More Help With . . .

Euler's method?

See . . .

Calculus, Section 7.1

L'Hospital's Rule

AP* Learning Objective: • Determine limits of functions. (LO 1.1C)

Overview

There are times when we encounter limits that seem to have no obvious solution—for example, a fraction whose numerator and denominator are both approaching zero. A form such as this may not lend itself to easy evaluation. *L'Hospital's Rule* can often help evaluate these difficult limits.

Content and Practice

When finding limits, there is a group of forms that sometimes require the use of L'Hospital's Rule. These are called *indeterminate* forms. We look for limits of the form 0/0, ∞/∞ or expressions that can easily be written in one of these forms. As you know, zero divided by zero is undefined, but it is vital to keep in mind that for a limit of this form, the numerator and denominator are *approaching* zero, not actually equal to zero, and L'Hospital's Rule allows us to determine a limiting value.

An example of a limit that approaches ∞/∞ is the $\lim\limits_{x\to\infty}\left(\dfrac{5x}{x^2}\right)$. Both the numerator and denominator are growing infinitely large, but a simple reduction of the fraction produces $\lim\limits_{x\to\infty}\left(\dfrac{5}{x}\right) = 0$. If the original denominator were simply x, the limit would have been 5. If the original numerator had been $5x^3$, the limit would have grown infinitely large. Here we have three cases where both the numerator and denominator are growing infinitely large but, with small changes to exponents, we arrived at three different limits.

The stronger form of L'Hospital's Rule is stated as follows.

L'Hospital's Rule

Suppose that $f(a) = g(a) = 0$, that f and g are differentiable on an open interval I containing a, and that $g'(x) \neq 0$ on I if $x \neq a$. Then

$$\lim_{x\to a}\frac{f(x)}{g(x)} = \lim_{x\to a}\frac{f'(x)}{g'(x)}.$$

If a limit has either the form 0/0 or ∞/∞, L'Hospital's Rule can be applied. You may encounter a few other simple forms that can be rewritten to fit these two cases. Remember also, that after applying L'Hospital's Rule once, you should always check the resulting limit. If it is still an indeterminate form, you may use L'Hospital's Rule again until the limit can be evaluated.

Find the following limits.

1. $\displaystyle \lim_{x \to \infty} \frac{\ln(x+1)}{\ln(3+x^2)} =$

2. $\displaystyle \lim_{x \to 0} \frac{\sin x - 2x}{e^{3x} - 1} =$

(*Hint:* In #3 and #4 below, rewrite each expression as a fraction.)

3. $\displaystyle \lim_{x \to 0^+} (\csc x - \cot x) =$

4. $\displaystyle \lim_{x \to \infty} \left(\frac{1}{x}\right)[\ln(x+1) + 5x] =$

Additional Practice

1. $\displaystyle \lim_{x \to 0} \frac{\sqrt[3]{1+x} - \frac{x}{3} - 1}{x^2} =$

    (A) -1 (B) $-\dfrac{1}{9}$

    (C) 0 (D) $\dfrac{1}{3}$

2. $\displaystyle \lim_{x \to \infty} \frac{\ln \sqrt{x}}{\ln(2+3x)} =$

    (A) 0 (B) $\dfrac{1}{3}$

    (C) $\dfrac{1}{2}$ (D) $\dfrac{2}{3}$

3.   Use the following table to determine $\lim\limits_{x \to 1} \dfrac{f(g(x))}{h(x)}$.

x	$f(x)$	$g(x)$	$h(x)$	$f'(x)$	$g'(x)$	$h'(x)$
1	-3	2	0	-1	4	7
2	0	5	8	3	9	6

Need More Help With . . .   ***See . . .***

L'Hospital's Rule?   *Calculus,* Section 9.2

Analysis of Parametric, Polar, and Vector Curves

AP* Learning Objective: • Use derivatives to analyze properties of a function. (LO 2.2A)

Overview

This BC only topic extends single variable calculus to three types of two-variable contexts.

If the position of a particle in the plane is given by the vector/parametric function

$$\mathbf{r}(t) = <x(t), y(t)>$$

with alternate notation

$$\mathbf{r}(t) = x(t)\mathbf{i} + y(t)\mathbf{j},$$

then the velocity and acceleration vectors are

$$\mathbf{v}(t) = <x'(t), y'(t)> \text{ and } \mathbf{a}(t) = <x''(t), y''(t)>$$

with alternate notation

$$\mathbf{v}(t) = x'(t)\mathbf{i} + y'(t)\mathbf{j} \text{ and } \mathbf{a}(t) = x''(t)\mathbf{i} + y''(t)\mathbf{j}.$$

The slope of the path of the particle is $\dfrac{dy}{dx} = \dfrac{dy/dt}{dx/dt}$.

A polar curve of the form $r = f(\theta)$ can be defined parametrically by

$$x = r\cos(\theta) = f(\theta)\cos(\theta)$$
$$y = r\sin(\theta) = f(\theta)\sin(\theta).$$

Using the slope of the path of a particle for a parametic curve it is easier to derive, rather than memorize, the equation for the slope of a tangent to a polar curve. Instead of dy/dt and dx/dt we find $dy/d\theta$ and $dx/d\theta$, remembering to use the Product Rule. The result is

$$\frac{dy}{dx} = \frac{f'(\theta)\sin(\theta) + f(\theta)\cos(\theta)}{f'(\theta)\cos(\theta) - f(\theta)\sin(\theta)}.$$

Content and Practice

1. A particle moves along a curve defined by the vector function $\mathbf{r}(t) = <t^2 - 1, \sin(2t)>$.

   (a) Find the velocity vector.

   (b) Find the acceleration vector.

   (c) Find the slope of the path of the particle at $t = \pi/6$.

2. A particle moves along a planar curve according to the parametric equations

   $$x(t) = t^3 - t, \ y(t) = (2t - 1)^3, \text{ where } t \geq 0.$$

   (a) What is the velocity vector at $t = 1$?

   (b) Find the acceleration vector of the particle when the particle's vertical position is 0.

3. At which values of θ in the interval $[0, 2\pi]$ does the polar curve $r = 1 + \cos\theta$ have horizontal tangents?

Additional Practice

1. The position of a particle is given by $\mathbf{r}(t) = <2t, \ln t>$.
   (a) Find the acceleration vector of the particle.

   (b) Find the speed of the particle at $t = \dfrac{1}{2}$.

2. For what values of t does the curve given by the parametric equations

$$x(t) = \frac{t^3}{3} + \frac{t^2}{2} - 6t + 1$$
$$y(t) = t^2 + t + 1$$

have a vertical tangent?

(A) 2 only

(B) -3 and 2 only

(C) -3, 0, and 2

(D) $\frac{1}{2}$

3. A particle moves along the parametric curve

$$x(t) = t^3 - t, y(t) = t^2, \text{ where } 0 \leq t \leq 3.$$

For what values of t is the particle moving to the left?

(A) $\left(0, \sqrt{3}\right)$

(B) $\left(\sqrt{3}, 3\right)$

(C) $\left[0, \frac{1}{\sqrt{3}}\right)$

(D) $\left[\frac{1}{\sqrt{3}}, 3\right]$

Need More Help With . . .	See . . .
Position, velocity, and acceleration vectors?	*Calculus*, Section 11.2
Slopes of polar curves?	*Calculus*, Section 11.3

Riemann Sums

AP* Learning Objectives: • Interpret the definite integral as the limit of a Riemann sum. (LO 3.2A(a))
 • Express the limit of a Riemann sum in integral notation. (LO 3.2A(b))
 • Interpret the meaning of a definite integral within a problem. (LO 3.4A)

Overview

Many important tasks in calculus involve finding the area under a curve. Areas represent answers to many real-world problems such as the distance traveled by an object with variable velocity or the work done by a variable force. The area under a curve can be divided into narrow strips. Each of these strips can be approximated by a narrow rectangle. The sum of the areas of the rectangles approximates the area under the curve. This sum is called a *Riemann sum*. The exact area can be found by taking a limit of the Riemann sum as the widths of the rectangles approach zero. This limit is called a *definite integral*.

Content and Practice

The area under the curve $y = 4 - x^2$ on the interval $-2 \le x \le 2$ can be approximated by three different rectangular methods. Using ten subdivisions, the graphs below visually suggest these rectangular approximation methods.

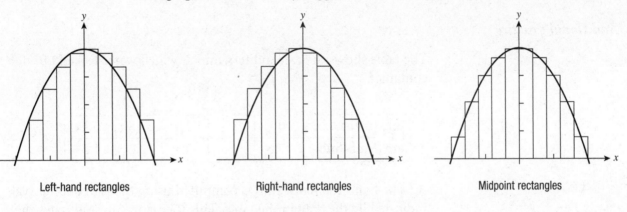

Left-hand rectangles   Right-hand rectangles   Midpoint rectangles

1.   Approximate the area bounded by $f(x) = 4 - x^2$ and the x-axis using

   (a)   left-hand rectangles and four equal subdivisions.

(b) right-hand rectangles and four equal subdivisions.

(c) midpoint rectangles and four equal subdivisions.

2. The table shows the velocity of a remote-controlled toy car as it traveled down a hallway for 10 seconds.

Time (sec)	0	1	2	3	4	5	6	7	8	9	10
Velocity (in./sec)	0	6	10	16	14	12	18	22	12	4	2

Estimate the distanced traveled by the car using 10 subintervals of length 1 and the methods shown.

(a) Left-hand rectangles

(b) Right-hand rectangles

Additional Practice

1. The table shows the rate in liters/min at which water leaked out of a container.

Time (min)	0	1.2	2.3	3.8	5.4
Rate (liters/min)	5.6	4.3	3.1	2.2	1.5

A right-hand Riemann sum is computed using the four subintervals indicated by the data in the table. This Riemann sum estimates the total amount of water that has leaked out of the container. What is the estimate?

(A) 12.70 liters   (B) 14.27 liters

(C) 16.70 liters   (D) 19.62 liters

2.   The temperature, in degrees Celsius (°C), of a turkey in an oven is a continuous function of time t. Some values of this function are given in the table.

Time (min)	0	5	10	15	20	25
Temperature (°C)	24	76	106	124	135	141

Approximate the average temperature (in degrees Celsius) of the turkey over the time interval $0 \le t \le 25$ using a left-hand Riemann sum with subintervals of length 5 minutes.

Need More Help With . . .   *See . . .*

Riemann sums?   *Calculus,* Sections 6.1, 6.2

There is also a calculator program to compute Riemann sums in the *Technology Resource Manual* that accompanies *Calculus.* This program is called RAM.

Average value of a function?   *Calculus,* Section 6.3

Definite Integral of a Rate of Change

AP* Learning Objective: • Interpret the meaning of a definite integral within a problem. (LO 3.4A)

$$\int_a^b f'(x)\, dx = f(b) - f(a)$$

Overview

If you are given a function that describes the rate of change of a quantity, the definite integral of this function gives the net change in the quantity. The definite integral of a rate of change can be used to find the net change in quantities such as position, velocity, growth, decay, production, and consumption.

Content and Practice

Suppose the velocity in cm/sec of a particle moving along the horizontal x-axis is given by the equation $dx/dt = f'(t) = 4 - t^2$ for $0 \le t \le 3$. The figure below shows the graph of this velocity.

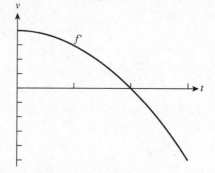

Velocity is the rate of change of position. Integrating this rate of change will give the net change in position. The net change in position for this particle after 3 seconds is

$$\int_0^3 (4 - t^2)\, dt = 3 \text{ cm.}$$

1. If the starting point for the particle is $x = 1$, find the position of the particle after

   (a) 3 seconds

   (b) 2 seconds

2. From 1990 to 2004 the production of apples in a certain orchard was $P(t) = 1.3 + 1.025^t$ thousand bushels per year, where t is the number of years from the beginning of 1990. Find the total number of bushels produced from the beginning of 1990 to the beginning of 2004.

Additional Practice

1. Water is pumped from a storage tank to meet the needs of a town. The flow of water from the tank is given by $C(t) = 25e^{-0.05(t-15)^2}$ thousand gallons per hour, where t is the number of hours since midnight. Which of the following best approximates the total water consumption for one day (in thousands of gallons)?

   (A) 164.202   (B) 197.727

   (C) 198.166   (D) 202.144

2. The rate at which a bison herd is increasing is given by
$B(t) = 26.7 \times 1.036^t$ bison per year where t is the time in years since the beginning of year 2000.

(a) If the herd contains 756 bison at the beginning of 2000, predict the size of the herd at the beginning of 2015.

(b) Predict the average annual increase in the bison herd from 2000 to 2015.

Need More Help With . . .   *See . . .*

Integrating a rate of change?   *Calculus,* Section 8.1

Displacement and total distance?   *Calculus,* Section 8.1

Average value of a function?   *Calculus,* Section 6.3

Basic Properties of Definite Integrals

AP* Learning Objective: • Calculate a definite integral using areas and properties of definite integrals. (LO 3.2C)

Overview

The basic properties of definite integrals allow you to evaluate variations on a definite integral such as switching limits of integration, multiplying by a constant, adding two definite integrals, or breaking a definite integral over an interval into separate parts.

Content and Practice

Rules for Definite Integrals

1. $\int_b^a f(x)\, dx = -\int_a^b f(x)\, dx$

2. $\int_a^a f(x)\, dx = 0$

3. $\int_a^b kf(x)\, dx = k\int_a^b f(x)\, dx$

4. $\int_a^b (f(x) \pm g(x))\, dx = \int_a^b f(x)\, dx \pm \int_a^b g(x)\, dx$

5. $\int_a^b f(x)\, dx + \int_b^c f(x)\, dx = \int_a^c f(x)\, dx$

6. If max f and min f are the maximum and minimum values of f on $[a, b]$, then $\min f \cdot (b - a) \le \int_a^b f(x)\, dx \le \max f \cdot (b - a)$

7. $f(x) \ge g(x)$ on $[a, b] \Rightarrow \int_a^b f(x)\, dx \ge \int_a^b g(x)\, dx$

8. $f(x) \ge 0$ on $[a, b] \Rightarrow \int_a^b f(x)\, dx \ge 0$

---

1. Let $\int_1^2 f(x)\,dx = -3$, $\int_1^5 f(x)\,dx = 5$, and $\int_1^5 g(x)\,dx = 9$. Find

(a) $\int_2^2 g(x)\,dx$

(b) $\int_1^2 (3f(x) + 1)\,dx$

(c) $\int_2^5 f(x)\,dx$

2. If $f(x)$ is continuous on $[1, 3]$ and $2 \leq f(x) \leq 4$, what is the greatest possible value of $\int_1^3 f(x)\,dx$?

3. The graph of f is the semicircle shown below. Let g be the function given by $\int_0^x f(t)\,dt$. What is the value of $g(-2)$?

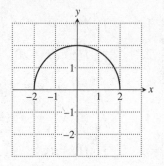

Additional Practice

1. If f is increasing on the interval $[a, b]$, which of the following must be true?

I. $\int_a^b f(x)\,dx \leq f(b)(b - a)$

II. $\int_a^b f(x)\,dx \geq f(a)(b - a)$

III. $\int_a^b f(x)\,dx \geq 0$

(A) I only   (B) II only

(C) I, II, and III   (D) I and II only

2.   Suppose that h is continuous and that $\int_{-1}^{1} h(r)\, dr = -2$ and $\int_{-1}^{3} h(r)\, dr = 7$. Find

   (a) $\int_{1}^{3} h(r)\, dr$

   (b) $\int_{3}^{1} h(r)\, dr$

Need More Help With . . .   ***See . . .***

   Properties of definite integrals?   *Calculus*, Sections 6.2, 6.3

   Analyzing antiderivatives graphically?   *Calculus*, Sections 6.2, 6.4

Fundamental Theorem of Calculus, Antiderivative Part

AP* Learning Objective: • Analyze functions defined by an integral. (LO 3.3A)

Overview

The Fundamental Theorem of Calculus describes a remarkable connection between integration and differentiation. It is one of the most important ideas in mathematics. It relates areas or accumulations to antidifferentiation and the resulting function. The Fundamental Theorem has two parts. Because of its importance, it will be reviewed in consecutive sections. One part says that the definite integral of a continuous function is a differentiable function of its upper limit of integration. It also tells us how to differentiate this definite integral. The other part tells us how to evaluate a definite integral. This section addresses the first part of this crucial theorem.

Content and Practice

The Antiderivative Part of the Fundamental Theorem says if a function f is continuous on an interval $[a, b]$, then the definite integral produces a differentiable function F on $[a, b]$ where $F(x) = \int_a^x f(t)dt$ and $\dfrac{dF}{dx} = \dfrac{d}{dx} \int_a^x f(t)dt = f(x)$.

It is important to remember that an antiderivative does not need to be found to differentiate a definite integral of this form.

The Evaluation Part of the Fundamental Theorem says for a continuous function f on $[a, b]$, $\int_a^b f(x)dx = F(b) - F(a)$ where F is any antiderivative of f. This part is reviewed immediately following this section.

1. Find $\dfrac{dy}{dx}$ given $y = \int_3^x t \cdot \ln(t - 1)dt$ for $x > 1$.

2. Find $G'(2)$ if $G(x) = \int_4^x \sqrt{3 + \sin(t)}\, dt$.

If the variable appears in the lower limit, simply use the property of definite integrals that allows you to switch the limits of integration and change the sign of the integral, $\int_x^a f(t)dt = -\int_a^x f(t)dt$.

3.   Find $\dfrac{dy}{dx}$ given $y = \int_x^5 t^2 \cdot e^t\, dt$.

If the variable in the limit has a derivative other than 1, the Chain Rule must be used. For example, $y = \int_2^{x^3} e^t\, dt$ then $\dfrac{dy}{dx} = e^{(x^3)} \cdot 3x^2$. This is justified by decomposing the integral expression into $y = \int_2^u e^t\, dt$ and $u = x^3$. Now, $\dfrac{dy}{du} = e^u, \dfrac{du}{dx} = 3x^2$ and $\dfrac{dy}{dx} = \dfrac{dy}{du} \cdot \dfrac{du}{dx}$. This particular integral example also allows us to antidifferentiate easily and then take the derivative of the result. If $y = \int_2^{x^3} e^t\, dt$, then by the Evaluation Part of the Fundamental Theorem recall $y = e^{(x^3)} - e^2$ and $\dfrac{dy}{dx} = 3x^2 \cdot e^{(x^3)}$.

4.   Find $f'(x)$ given $f(x) = \int_3^{\sin(x)} \sqrt[3]{t^2 + 2}\, dt$.

   (A) $\sqrt[3]{\sin^2(x) + 2}$ (B) $\cos(x) \cdot \sqrt[3]{\sin^2(x) + 2}$

   (C) $\sin(x) \cdot \sqrt[3]{\sin^2(x) + 2}$ (D) $\cos(x) \cdot \sqrt[3]{\sin^2(x) + 2} - \sqrt[3]{11}$

Fundamental Theorem questions can also be graphical as the following guided problem shows. A function is frequently defined as the definite integral of a given graph.

5. Let $g(x) = \int_0^x f(t)dt$, where f is the continuous function on $[0, 3]$ whose graph is shown. The area of the first quadrant region, A, is 4 and the area of the fourth quadrant region, B, is 5. $f(x)$ has a local minimum at $x = 2$.

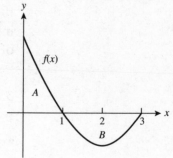

(a) At what x-value does $g(x)$ achieve its maximum value? Justify your answer. (*Hint:* $g'(x) = f(x)$ so the given graph is the derivative of g.)

(b) If $h(x) = 2 + g(x)$, find $h(1)$.

(c) Where does $g(x)$ achieve its minimum value? Explain your reasoning. (*Hint:* Think about accumulated signed area.)

(d) On what interval is $g(x)$ concave down? (*Hint:* Find an expression for $g''(x)$.)

Additional Practice

1. Given $f(x) = \int_1^{x^2} g(t)dt$. If $f(2) = -3$ and $g(4) = 5$, write the equation of the line tangent to $f(x)$ at $x = 2$.

2. Given $h(x) = \int_3^x (\ln(t + 2) - t^2 + 4)dt$ for $x \geq 0$, find $h'(x)$ by hand, then use your calculator to find the x-coordinate of the local maximum of h.

(A) 0 (B) 0.225 (C) 2.338 (D) 3

3. Find an expression in terms of g and g' for $f''(x)$ if $f(x) = \int_{7}^{2\sqrt{x}} g(t^2)\, dt$.

4. The graph of $p(t)$ is shown to the right and consists of four segments on $[-5, 5]$.

    Let $H(x) = \int_{-1}^{x} p(t)\, dt$

    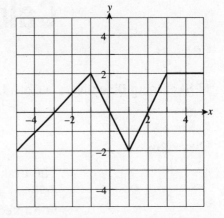

    (a) Write an expression for $H'(x)$.

    (b) Find $H(4)$.

    (c) Find $H(-3)$.

    (d) Find $H'(1)$.

    (e) Find $H''(-2.3)$

    (f) On what intervals is $H(x)$ increasing? Briefly explain your choice.

    (g) On what intervals is $H(x)$ concave up? Briefly explain your choice.

Need More Help With . . .   *See* . . .

Fundamental Theorem of Calculus?   *Calculus,* Section 6.4

Fundamental Theorem of Calculus, Evaluation Part

AP* Learning Objectives:
- Calculate antiderivatives. (LO 3.3B(a))
- Evaluate a definite integral. (LO 3.3B(b))

Overview

The Evaluation Part of the Fundamental Theorem of Calculus is used almost daily in the second half of the calculus course. Its applications are nearly unlimited. It can be used to evaluate areas, volumes, distances traveled, and a vast number of other accumulations. Anything to which a continuous symbolic function can be assigned can be used as the integrand in a definite integral. These integrals will be evaluated either by finding an antiderivative by hand or using the built in functionality of your graphing calculator.

Content and Practice

The Evaluation Part of the Fundamental Theorem says for a continuous function f on $[a, b]$, $\int_a^b f(x)dx = F(b) - F(a)$ where F is any antiderivative of f. Complete mastery of the derivative rules makes finding antiderivatives by hand much easier. There are a few more required integration techniques for Calculus BC. Those problems will be noted in the *Additional Practice* set.

(*Note:* If you are using this as a review and have already learned integration techniques, try the problems by hand to improve your antidifferentiation skills. If you have not yet learned integration techniques, use a calculator as necessary.)

1. Evaluate $\int_1^3 (2x + e^x)dx$.

2. Evaluate $\int_0^1 \frac{dx}{1 + x^2}$.

   (A) $\frac{1}{2}\ln(2)$ (B) $\ln(2)$

   (C) $\frac{\pi}{4}$ (D) $\frac{\pi}{2}$

3. Use your calculator to find the area between $y = 2 + \cos^3(x)$ and the x-axis on the interval $[2, 5]$.

There are times when you will be asked to tackle an initial value problem using a definite integral. Other problems may require you to generalize the process and construct a function using a definite integral. A minor rearrangement of the Evaluation Part sheds light on this task.

Since we know that $F(b) - F(a) = \int_a^b f(x)dx$ where F is any antiderivative of f, adding $F(a)$ to the both sides of the equation produces $F(b) = F(a) + \int_a^b f(x)dx$. In simple terms, a resulting value of F at b comes from the initial value of F at a plus the accumulated change over any given interval. The generalization from a to any value x may look like $g(x) = g(a) + \int_a^x g'(t)dt$. For example, find $g(8)$ given that $g(0) = 5$ and $\frac{dg}{dx} = \frac{x^2}{e^x}$. Symbolically $g(b) = g(a) + \int_a^b g'(x)dx$, so $g(8) = g(0) + \int_0^8 \frac{x^2}{e^x}dx$. Using your calculator to evaluate the definite integral gives 6.972.

4. Construct a function of the form $y = \int_a^x f(t)dt + C$ given $\frac{dy}{dx} = x^3 e^{\sin(x)}$ and $y = 2$ when $x = -4$.

Additional Practice

1. Given $f(2) = 7$ and $f(10) = -15$
   (a) Find the average value of $y = f'(x)$ on $[2, 10]$.

   (b) Interpret the result in terms of f.

2. Use your calculator to evaluate $\int_0^3 [x^2 \cdot \ln(x + 3)]dx$.

3. The rate of change of position of a particle moving along the x-axis is $\frac{dx}{dt} = t \cdot \sin(t)$. The initial position of the particle is $x(0) = 6$.

   (a) Use your calculator to find its position at time $t = 5$.

   (b) Write an integral expression to represent the position of the particle at any time $t = c$.

The following are Calculus BC questions only.

4. Evaluate $\int_0^{\pi/2} x \sin(2x)dx$ using antidifferentiation by parts.

5. Evaluate $\int_1^3 \frac{12}{x^2 + 6x} dx$ using partial fractions.

Need More Help With . . .   *See . . .*

Fundamental Theorem of Calculus   *Calculus*, Section 6.4

Antiderivative Basics

AP* Learning Objectives:
- Calculate antiderivatives. (LO3.3B(a))
- Evaluate definite integrals. (LO3.3B(b))

Overview

The second major portion of the calculus course depends largely on the skill of finding antiderivatives. The process can range from simply looking at an expression and knowing the function whose derivative has been taken, to many advanced techniques. You also learn that the limiting process of Riemann sums results in integrals, and the Fundamental Theorem of Calculus connects integrals to antiderivatives.

Content and Practice

The key to successful antidifferentiation is to master the derivatives of basic functions. Below is a list similar to what appeared in the section on basic derivatives, but you will notice three changes: the column headings, the order of the columns, and the presence of a "$+C$." One challenging aspect of working with antiderivatives is to not confuse which "direction" you are going. Students frequently take a derivative when they think they are taking an antiderivative.

Fill in the empty spaces in the table. It will help you review the basic relationships and force you to practice going different directions with the process.

	Derivative	Antiderivative
	$n \cdot x^{n-1}$	$x^n + C$ (n is any real number.)
(a)		$\sin x + C$
(b)		$-\cos x + C$
(c)		$\tan x + C$
(d)	$-\csc^2 x$	
(e)		$\sec x + C$
(f)	$-\csc x \cot x$	
(g)		
(h)		
(i)	$a^x \ln a$ (a is a constant.)	

By observation, attempt to determine the antiderivative of each of the following functions. Check your answer by taking its derivative. Remember the Chain Rule when checking your answers. You may need to adjust your answer by multiplying or dividing by a constant.

	Function	Antiderivative
1.	$\sin 2x$	
2.	$8x^3 + \sqrt{x}$	
3.	$3 + e^{5t}$	
4.	$x \cos x^2$	
5.	$8x - \csc x \cot x$	
6.	$\sec^2 5x$	
7.	$6(2x + 7)^5$	
8.	$3^{4x} \ln 3$	

9. In your own words, write a sentence or two expressing what you understand an antiderivative to be.

10. Why is the "$+ C$" placed on antiderivatives when they are not associated with definite integrals?

Additional Practice

1. $\int (2x + 7) \, dx =$

   (A) $x^2 + 7x + C$ (B) $x^2 + C$

   (C) $2 + C$ (D) $\dfrac{x^2}{2} + 7x + C$

2. $\int_0^{\pi/6} \sin 2x \, dx =$

   (A) $-\dfrac{1}{2}$ (B) $-\dfrac{1}{4}$

   (C) $\dfrac{1}{4}$ (D) $\dfrac{1}{2}$

3.   If $f'(x) = \dfrac{2x}{x^2 + 1}$, then $f(x)$ could be

(A) $3 + \ln(x^2 + 1)$

(B) $\dfrac{x^2}{\frac{1}{3}x^3 + x} + 8$

(C) $\dfrac{2 - 2x^2}{(x^2 + 1)^2} + C$

(D) $x + \ln(x^2 + 1) + C$

Need More Help With . . .   *See . . .*

Definition of an antiderivative?   *Calculus,* Section 5.2

Working with antiderivatives?   *Calculus,* Sections 6.3, 6.4

Antiderivative formulas?   *Calculus,* Sections 7.2, 7.3

Antidifferentiation by Substitution

AP* Learning Objectives: • Calculate antiderivatives. (LO3.3B(a))
• Evaluate definite integrals. (LO3.3B(b))

Overview

As integrals become more complicated, it is often not possible to determine an antiderivative by observation. Some work must be done to see the form of the integral. One basic method is substitution of variables. A proper substitution will reveal the form of an integral and make antidifferentiation much easier.

Content and Practice

If an integral is to be handled by substitution, the process requires identifying within the integrand a function and a constant multiple of its derivative. We then substitute a single variable for the main function and the appropriate differential for the remaining factors in the integrand. As stated earlier in this text, the better you know the derivative formulas, the easier the substitution method will be. Study the example below before attempting the subsequent problems.

Suppose we wanted to integrate the indefinite integral

$$\int 4x(x^2 + 5)^8 \, dx.$$

One way would be to expand the power of the binomial, distribute the $4x$, and integrate each of the nine terms individually. In a mere 30 minutes or so the problem would be solved! Substitution provides a more efficient solution.

Solving the Integral by Substitution	
Recognize that $4x$ is a multiple of the derivative of $x^2 + 5$. An exponent on a function is often *not* chosen as part of the main function. We will therefore choose $x^2 + 5$ to be our main function and $4x\,dx$ to be a multiple of its derivative.	$\int 4x(x^2 + 5)^8\,dx$
Notice the integrand contains $4x\,dx$, not $2x\,dx$. There are numerous ways to account for this. We will choose to simply multiply both sides of the differential equation by 2.	Let $u = x^2 + 5$, then $du = 2x\,dx$ so $2\,du = 4x\,dx$.
Substituting for the base of the power function and the other factors in the integrand allows us to see the form of the integrand much more clearly.	$\int u^8 2\,du = 2\int u^8\,du$
Find the antiderivative using the Power Rule for integration.	$2\left(\dfrac{u^9}{9}\right) + C$
Re-substitute for u from our original choice, $u = x^2 + 5$. Clearly this is much more efficient than expanding an eighth power of a binomial!	$\dfrac{2}{9}(x^2 + 5)^9 + C$

Identifying u and du in the integrand is one of the most important skills in the substitution method of integration. It will be helpful to practice. For each of the following integrals, choose which part of the integrand will be u, then determine du, and perform the substitution. You do not need to find the antiderivative.

1. $\int 3x^2 \sin x^3\,dx$

2. $\int \dfrac{5\,dx}{4x + 3}$

3. $\int 7\tan^5 x \sec^2 x\,dx$

4. $\int \dfrac{4x\,dx}{\sqrt{x^2 - 4}}$

5. $\int \csc x^2 \cdot \cot x^2 \cdot 8x\,dx$

6. $\int \dfrac{3^{\ln(x)}}{x}\,dx$

7. Integrate by the substitution method.

$$\int \frac{6x^2 + 10}{x^3 + 5x}\, dx$$

The substitution method can also be used on definite integrals. When doing so, you should also substitute for the limits of integration. The relationship between u and your choice of main function in the integrand determines the new limits. Initial steps of an example are presented below.

$$\int_0^2 (x^3 + 1)^{\frac{3}{2}} \cdot x^2\, dx$$

Let $u = x^3 + 1$, so $du = 3x^2\, dx$, and $\frac{1}{3}\, du = x^2\, dx$.

Also, if $x = 0$, then $u = 1$; and if $x = 2$, then $u = 9$.

By substitution into the integrand and limits, the integral becomes

$$\frac{1}{3}\int_{u=1}^{u=9} u^{\frac{3}{2}}\, du.$$

We can now finish the problem without ever substituting back in terms of x.

$$\frac{1}{3} \cdot \frac{2}{5} u^{\frac{5}{2}}\Big|_1^9 = \frac{2}{15}\left(9^{\frac{5}{2}} - 1\right) = \frac{484}{15}$$

Additional Practice

1. $\int e^{\cos x} \sin x\, dx =$

    (A) $-e^{\cos (x)+1} + C$ (B) $e^{\cos x} + C$

    (C) $-e^{\cos x} + C$ (D) $e^{\sin x} + C$

2. Given: $\int_0^{\frac{\pi}{6}} \sin 2x \cos 2x \, dx$. Letting $u = \sin 2x$, the integral becomes

(A) $\int_0^{\frac{1}{2}} u \, du$ (B) $\frac{1}{2} \int_0^{\frac{1}{2}} u \, du$

(C) $2 \int_0^{\frac{\sqrt{3}}{2}} u \, du$ (D) $\frac{1}{2} \int_0^{\frac{\sqrt{3}}{2}} u \, du$

3. Evaluate the integral $\int_1^2 \frac{2x^3 + 1}{x^4 + 2x} \, dx$.

(A) $\ln 20 - \ln 3$ (B) $\ln \sqrt{\frac{20}{3}}$

(C) $\frac{1}{2} \ln 2$ (D) $\ln 2$

4. Suppose $\int_2^4 f(2x) \, dx = 10$. Then $\int_4^8 f(u) \, du =$
(A) 5   (B) 10
(C) 20   (D) Cannot be determined

Need More Help With . . .	*See . . .*
Integration using the substitution method?	*Calculus*, Section 7.2

Antidifferentiation by Parts

AP* Learning Objectives: • Calculate antiderivatives. (LO3.3B(a))
   • Evaluate definite integrals. (LO3.3B(b))

Overview

Antidifferention by parts is strictly an AP* Calculus BC topic. This process must be considered when direct substitution does not work. It is frequently tested in the Multiple Choice portion of the AP* exam.

Content and Practice

There are times when integration by substitution does not work because when we choose a function to substitute for, a multiple of its derivative does not exist in the integrand. In other words, the factors in the integrand consist of a function and the derivative of a different function. It is symbolized by an integral of the form $\int u \, dv$, where u is the primary function and dv is the derivative of another function.

There are two keys to using antidifferentiation by parts successfully. First, recognize when no other integration method will apply. Second, choose the correct parts of the integrand as u and dv. An acronym for the priority order for choosing u is LIPET.

   L: Logarithms
   I: Inverse trigonometric functions
   P: Polynomials
   E: Exponential functions
   T: Trigonometric functions

Once u and dv have been chosen, du and v must be identified. At this point it is important to keep straight whether you are finding a derivative or an antiderivative. Once you have determined all four parts, substitute them into the formula $\int u \, dv = uv - \int v \, du$.

In the following integrals, identify what you would choose as u and dv. Do not attempt to integrate. One of the five integrals can be done by direct substitution. For that one, choose u and du.

156

1. $\int x^2 \ln x \, dx$

2. $\int x \tan^{-1} x \, dx$

3. $\int x \cos x \, dx$

4. $\int \dfrac{e^{\sqrt{x}} \, dx}{\sqrt{x}}$

5. $\int 5^x x \, dx$

6. Integrate by parts: $\int x \ln x^2 \, dx$.

As shown in the next examples, when antidifferentiation by parts is necessary on a definite integral, it is usually best to find the entire antiderivative before evaluating with the limits.

$$\int_1^2 xe^x \, dx \qquad\qquad \text{Let } u = x \text{ and } dv = e^x \, dx, \text{ so}$$
$$\qquad\qquad\qquad\qquad du = dx \text{ and } v = e^x.$$

$$\int_1^2 xe^x \, dx = xe^x \Big|_1^2 - \int_1^2 e^x \, dx$$
$$= (xe^x - e^x)\Big|_1^2$$
$$= 2e^2 - e^2 - (1e^1 - e^1)$$
$$= e^2$$

Tabular Integration

There are times when it is necessary to repeat the integration by parts process in order to complete the problem. If an integral is in the form of $\int f(x)g(x)dx$, $f(x)$ is a function whose successive derivatives become zero, and $g(x)$ is a function whose successive integrals are easy to determine, then tabular integration can simplify the process.

Let's look at how this process simplifies the problem above. Find successive derivatives of $f(x)$ until they become zero, and then find the same number of successive integrals of $g(x)$. Alternately add and subtract the products of the functions that the arrows connect as indicated by the operation sign above the arrow.

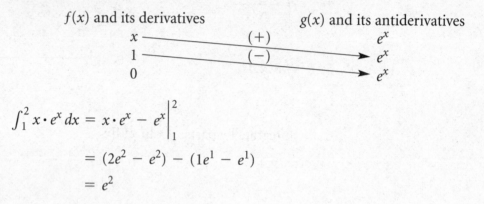

$$\int_1^2 x \cdot e^x \, dx = x \cdot e^x - e^x \Big|_1^2$$

$$= (2e^2 - e^2) - (1e^1 - e^1)$$

$$= e^2$$

Additional Practice

1. $\displaystyle\int \frac{\ln x}{x^2} \, dx =$

    (A) $\dfrac{\ln x}{x^2} - \dfrac{1}{x} + C$ 　　　　(B) $-\dfrac{\ln x}{x} - \dfrac{1}{x} + C$

    (C) $\dfrac{\ln x}{x} - \dfrac{1}{x} + C$ 　　　　(D) $-\dfrac{\ln x}{x} + \dfrac{1}{x^2} + C$

2. $\int \sin^{-1} x \, dx =$

(A) $x \sin^{-1} x + \sqrt{x^2 - 1} + C$

(B) $x \sin^{-1} x - \sqrt{x^2 - 1} + C$

(C) $x \sin^{-1} x + \sqrt{1 - x^2} + C$

(D) None of the above

3. Find the area enclosed by the graphs of $y = x \sin x$, $y = x - \pi$, and to the right of the y-axis.

(A) $\dfrac{\pi^2}{2} + \pi$ (B) $\dfrac{\pi^2}{2} - \pi$

(C) $\pi - \dfrac{3}{2} \pi^2$ (D) $\pi + \dfrac{3}{2} \pi^2$

Need More Help With . . .   ***See*** . . .

     Antidifferentiation by parts?   *Calculus,* Section 7.3

Antidifferentiation by Simple Partial Fractions

AP* Learning Objectives: • Calculate antiderivatives. (LO3.3B(a))

                                      • Evaluate definite integrals. (LO3.3B(b))

Overview

Antidifferiation by partial fractions is strictly an AP* Calculus BC topic. It is another advanced technique of integration. Although it does not often appear in the Free Response portion of the AP* exam, it is a regularly tested item in the Multiple Choice section.

Content and Practice

As you learn the various techniques of integration, you should become skilled at deciding which technique must be applied in each situation. This process takes much practice. One clue for when the partial fraction method may be required is when an integrand's denominator can be factored into two or more different linear factors.

Since the AP* Calculus course limits the cases to nonrepeated linear factors, the general process is to break a single fraction into the sum of numerous fractions, each with a constant numerator and a linear denominator. Each individual fraction is then integrated, resulting in a sum or difference of natural logarithm antiderivatives. You need to know the rules for simplifying logarithms, since you may have to reconcile your answer to multiple choice options that may look slightly different from your result.

Study the example below, then try the following problems.

$$\int \frac{dw}{w^2 - 2w - 8}$$

$$\frac{1}{w^2 - 2w - 8} = \frac{1}{(w - 4)(w + 2)}$$

$$\frac{1}{(w - 4)(w + 2)} = \frac{A}{w - 4} + \frac{B}{w + 2}$$

Now multiply both sides of the equation by $(w - 4)(w + 2)$ to obtain $1 = A(w + 2) + B(w - 4)$. Some books present solving for A and B by setting up a system of equations, but a simple substitution method is somewhat more efficient.

Let $w = 4$, and the equation becomes

$$1 = A(4 + 2) + B(4 - 4)$$

so $A = \frac{1}{6}$ since B drops out.

Similarly, let $w = -2$, and the equation becomes

$$1 = A(-2 + 2) + B(-2 - 4)$$

so $B = -\frac{1}{6}$.

Thus

$$\frac{1}{(w - 4)(w + 2)} = \frac{\frac{1}{6}}{w - 4} + \frac{\frac{-1}{6}}{w + 2}$$

and the original integral can be rewritten as

$$\int \frac{dw}{w^2 - 2w - 8} = \frac{1}{6}\int \frac{dw}{w - 4} + \frac{-1}{6}\int \frac{dw}{w + 2}$$

$$= \frac{1}{6}\ln|w - 4| - \frac{1}{6}\ln|w + 2| + C.$$

Why are there absolute value bars on the final answer? Are they always necessary? Unless the expressions (i.e., $(w - 4)$ or $(w + 2)$) are known to have only positive values, absolute value bars are required so that any value of the expressions will fit the domain of the natural logarithm.

Decompose the following fractions by the partial fraction method. You can check your answer by adding the resulting fractions or by using a computer algebra system and applying an *Expand* command to the original problem.

1. $\dfrac{8}{2x^2 - 3x - 2}$

2. $\dfrac{7x - 1}{x^2 + 4x - 21}$

1. $\int \dfrac{4}{x^2 + 8x + 15}\, dx =$

    (A) $2(\ln|x + 3| + \ln|x + 5|) + C$

    (B) $2(\ln|x + 3| - \ln|x + 5|) + C$

    (C) $2(\ln|x + 5| - \ln|x + 3|) + C$

    (D) $4\ln(x^2 + 8x + 15) + C$

2. Which is the solution to the initial value problem $\dfrac{dy}{dx} = \dfrac{3x + 1}{x^2 + x}$ and $y(1) = \ln 8$?

    (A) $y = \ln|x| - 2 \cdot \ln|x + 1| + \ln 32$

    (B) $y = \ln\left|\dfrac{(x + 1)^3}{x}\right|$

    (C) $y = \dfrac{3}{2}\ln\left|x^2 + x\right| + \dfrac{1}{2}\ln 8$

    (D) $y = \ln\left|2x(x + 1)^2\right|$

Need More Help With . . .

Properties of logarithms?

Decomposition of fractions?

See . . .

Precalculus, Sections 3.3, 3.4

Precalculus, Section 7.3

Calculus, Sections 7.5, 9.4

Applications of Integrals

AP* Learning Objectives: • Apply definite integrals to problems involving the average value of a function. (LO 3.4B)
• Apply definite integrals to problems involving motion. (LO 3.4C)
• Apply definite integrals to problems involving area, volume, (BC) and length of a curve. (LO 3.4D)
• Use the definite integral to solve problems in various contexts. (LO 3.4E)

Overview

Applications of integrals occur in a wide variety of settings. Regardless of the setting, the emphasis should be on using the integral of a rate of change to give accumulated change or setting up an approximating Riemann sum and representing its limit as a definite integral.

Content and Practice

Some common applications of integrals on the AP* Calculus Exam include area, volume, average value of a function, distance traveled by a particle, and curve length. (Curve length is only found on the BC exam.) In many cases it may be helpful to slice the problem into small sections and set up the appropriate Riemann sum. This sum can then be used to find the corresponding definite integral.

Area

Example 1: Find the area bounded by the curve $y = 4 - x^2$ and the x-axis.

Solution: The area can be approximated using rectangular slices. Each rectangle has a height of $4 - x^2$ and a width of Δx. The Riemann sum for the area of these slices is $\sum_{k=1}^{n}(4 - x_k^2)\Delta x$. The limit of this sum gives the definite integral $\int_{-2}^{2}(4 - x^2)dx = 10\frac{2}{3}$. Notice that there is symmetry with respect to the y-axis so that the area could also be found by evaluating the integral $2\int_{0}^{2}(4 - x^2)dx$.

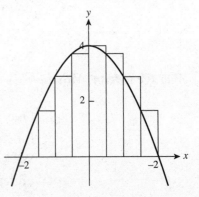

163

Area Between Curves

If f and g are continuous with $f(x) \geq g(x)$ throughout $[a, b]$,

then the area between the curves $y = f(x)$ and $y = g(x)$

from a to b is the integral of $[f - g]$ from a to b,

$$A = \int_a^b [f(x) - g(x)]dx.$$

Example 2: Find the area between the line $f(x) = -x - 3$ and the curve $g(x) = x^3 + 2x^2 - 3x - 4$.

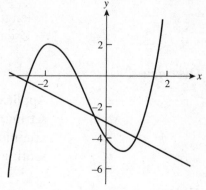

Solution: The two functions intersect at $x = -2.618, x = -0.382$, and $x = 1$. In the region on the left $g(x) \geq f(x)$, while on the right $f(x) \geq g(x)$. Therefore the area of the two regions is

$$\int_{-2.618}^{-0.382} (g(x) - f(x))dx + \int_{-0.382}^{1} (f(x) - g(x))dx = 5.946.$$

Example 3: Find the area between the curves $x = f(y) = y^2 - 4y$ and $x = g(y) = 2y - \dfrac{y^2}{2}$.

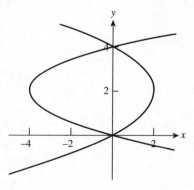

Solution: This area is easier to compute using horizontal slices. The lengths of the rectangular slices are $g(y) - f(y)$ and the widths are each Δy. Being mindful that the integral is taken with respect to y, the lower and upper bounds are 0 and 4.

$$A = \int_0^4 (g(y) - f(y))dy = 16.$$

Average (Mean) Value

One way to visualize the average value of a function is to analyze the problem graphically.
We know that if a positive function can be integrated on $[a, b]$ then its area under the curve is $\int_a^b f(x)dx$. When we are solving for the average value of a

function, we are looking for the value of y, $av(f)$, that creates a rectangle over the interval $[a, b]$ equal in area to the area under the curve.

Therefore, $av(f) \cdot (b - a) = \int_a^b f(x)dx$ so

$$av(f) = \frac{1}{b - a} \int_a^b f(x)dx$$

Example: The average daily temperature in Springfield, Illinois, is modeled by the function $T(x) = 50 - 42\cos(0.017x - 0.534)$, where x is the number of days after the start of the new year and T is the temperature in degrees Fahrenheit.

    (a)   Find the average temperature for January.

    (b)   On what day is the temperature the same as January's average temperature?

Solution:

    (a) $av(T) = \dfrac{1}{31 - 0} \int_0^{31} [50 - 42\cos(0.017x - 0.534)]dx = 9.994°\text{F}$.

    (b)   The graphs intersect at $x = 13.213$, so it will occur on January 14.

Distance Traveled

The displacement of an object over a given time interval is the distance between the object's starting point and ending point. Since an object can change directions in that time interval, the total distance traveled may be greater than the displacement. An object's displacement is calculated by evaluating the integral of the velocity over the given time interval. The total distance traveled by an object can be found in two different ways. Using technology, one could evaluate the integral of the absolute value of the velocity over time. Without a calculator, one needs to separate the problem into the positive and negative integrals. The total distance traveled is found by adding the positive values and subtracting the negative values on the interval requested.

Example: A particle moves along a line so that its velocity at any time $t \geq 0$ is given by the function $v(t) = 2t^2 - 13t + 15$, where v is measured in meters per second and t is measured in seconds. Find the total distance traveled during the first 6 seconds.

Solution: The velocity is positive on $[0, 1.5]$ and $[5, 6]$, and negative on $[1.5, 5]$. The total distance traveled is

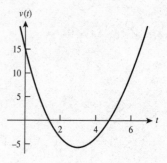

$$\int_0^{1.5} v(t)dt - \int_{1.5}^5 v(t)dt + \int_5^6 v(t)dt = \frac{343}{12} \text{ meters.}$$

Volume

Cross Sections

When using cross sections to find the volume of a solid, find the formula for the area of the cross section, determine the limits of integration, and integrate the area over that interval.

Example: Let R be the region bounded by the graphs of $y = x^2$, $y = 1 - x$, and the y-axis. The region R is the base of a solid where each cross section perpendicular to the x-axis is a rectangle whose widths, w, run from the line to the curve and whose heights, h, are three times the widths. Find the volume of this solid.

Solution: Since $w = 1 - x - x^2$ and $h = 3(1 - x - x^2)$, $A = 3(1 - x - x^2)^2$. The curves intersect at $x = 0.618$, so the volume is

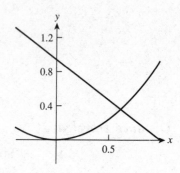

$$V = \int_0^{0.618} 3(1 - x - x^2)^2 dx = 0.745.$$

Solids of Revolution

You will be expected to know how to find the volume of a solid of revolution using circular cross sections, or disks, and washer cross sections. These methods are applied when the cross sections are perpendicular to the axis of revolution. It is critical that you correctly identify each radius, especially if the axis of revolution is something other than the x-axis or y-axis. Including a sketch of the radii on the graph will be helpful.

Example 1: The region in the first quadrant enclosed by the axes and the graph of $y = \cos x$ is revolved about the x-axis to form a solid. Find the volume of the solid.

Solution: The graph illustrates that the solid will be a circular cross section whose radius is $r = \cos x$. Therefore the volume will be

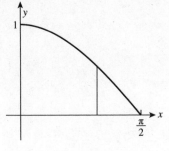

$$V = \pi \int_0^{\pi/2} (\cos x)^2 \, dx = 2.467.$$

Example 2: The region in the first quadrant enclosed by the x-axis, the graph of $y = 2x - 1$, and the line $x = 2$ is revolved about the line $x = 2$ to form a solid. Find the volume of the solid.

Solution: The radius of each cross section is $2 - x$. However we see that the radius is horizontal, not vertical, so we need to integrate with respect to y. Solving the linear equation for x and making a substitution gives a radius of $\dfrac{3 - y}{2}$. The region is bounded below by $y = 0$ and bounded above by $y = 3$. Therefore

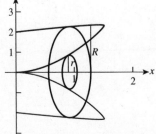

$$V = \pi \int_0^3 \left(\frac{3 - y}{2} \right)^2 dy = 7.069.$$

Example 3: The region in the first quadrant enclosed by the y-axis and the graphs of $y = \sqrt{x + 4}$ and $y = x^2$ is revolved about the x-axis to form a solid. Find the volume of the solid.

Solution: The two graphs intersect when $x = 1.5337$. Each cross section in this problem is a washer whose larger radius, R, is $\sqrt{x + 4}$ and whose smaller radius, r, is x^2. The area of a washer is $\pi(R^2 - r^2)$ so the volume is

$$V = \pi \int_\theta^{1.5337} \left(\left(\sqrt{x + 4} \right)^2 - (x^2)^2 \right) dx = 17.636.$$

1. Find the area bounded by the curves $y = \cos x$, $y = x$, and the y-axis.

2. Find the volume generated when the region bounded by the curves $y = \sqrt{x}$ and $y = \frac{1}{2}x$ is rotated about the x-axis.

The following integral applications are required topics for BC Calculus students.

Lengths of Curves

If a smooth curve begins at (a, c) and ends at (b, d), $a < b$, $c < d$, then the length (arc length) of the curve is

$$L = \int_a^b \sqrt{1 + \left(\frac{dy}{dx}\right)^2}\, dx \text{ if } y \text{ is a smooth function of } x \text{ on } [a, b];$$

$$L = \int_a^b \sqrt{1 + \left(\frac{dx}{dy}\right)^2}\, dx \text{ if } x \text{ is a smooth function of } y \text{ on } [c, d].$$

If $\frac{dx}{dt}$ and $\frac{dy}{dt}$ are continuous functions of t, then the length of a parametric curve that is traversed exactly once as t increases from t_1 to t_2 is

$$L = \int_{t_1}^{t_2} \sqrt{\left(\frac{dx}{dt}\right)^2 + \left(\frac{dy}{dt}\right)^2}\, dt.$$

Polar Area

The area of the region between the origin and the curve $r = f(\theta)$ for $\alpha \leq \theta \leq \beta$ is

$$A = \int_\alpha^\beta \frac{1}{2} r^2 d\theta = \int_\alpha^\beta \frac{1}{2}(f(\theta))^2\, d\theta.$$

Example: Find the area of one petal of the three-petaled rose $r = 2\sin(3\theta)$.

Solution: One petal is generated as θ increases from 0 to $\dfrac{\pi}{3}$, so

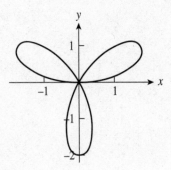

$$A = \int_0^{\pi/3} \frac{1}{2}(2\sin(3\theta))^2\,d\theta = 1.047.$$

3. Set up but do not evaluate the integral that gives the length of the path described by the parametric equations $x = t^2$ and $y = t^3$, where $0 \le t \le 1$.

Additional Practice

1. The base of a solid is a region in the first quadrant bounded by the x-axis, the y-axis, and the line $y = 1 - x$. If cross sections of the solid perpendicular to the x-axis are semicircles, what is the volume of the solid?

2. What is the average value of the function $y = 3x^2\sqrt{x^3 + 1}$ on the interval $[0, 2]$?

    (A) $\dfrac{26}{3}$

    (B) $\dfrac{52}{3}$

    (C) 18

    (D) 24

3. Find the *total distance* traveled by the particle moving along a straight line with velocity $v = \sin \pi t$ for $0 \leq t \leq 2$.

4. (BC only) *Polar area:* Find the area inside the polar curve $r = 4 \cos \theta$ and outside the polar curve $r = 2$.

5. (BC only) *Curve length:* Find the length of the curve described by $y = \frac{2}{3} x^{3/2}$ from $x = 0$ to $x = 3$.

    (A) $\frac{7}{3}$ (B) $\frac{14}{3}$ (C) $\frac{16}{3}$ (D) 7

***Need More Help With* . . .**   *See* . . .

Average value of a function?	*Calculus,* Section 6.3
Total distance?	*Calculus,* Section 8.1
Area under a curve?	*Calculus,* Section 8.2
Finding volumes?	*Calculus,* Section 8.3
Length of a curve?	*Calculus,* Section 8.4
Length of parametric curves?	*Calculus,* Section 11.1
Polar areas?	*Calculus,* Section 11.3

Improper Integrals

AP* Learning Objective: • (BC) Evaluate an improper integral or show that an improper integral diverges. (LO 3.2D)

Overview

Drawing together many of your calculus skills, *improper integrals* require recognition of discontinuities, skillful use of integration techniques, and limits sometimes involving L'Hospital's Rule. They also lay a foundation for some of your work with converging and diverging series. It is an AP* Calculus BC only topic that often shows up on the Multiple Choice portion of the exam.

Content and Practice

A definite integral is improper if it has either an infinite limit of integration or any value from the lower limit of integration to the upper limit that causes an infinite discontinuity in the integrand. Proper form and use of limits is crucial to success with improper integrals. Any limit of integration value that causes an integral to be improper must be replaced with a variable and a limit approaching that value. You may also need to use L'Hospital's Rule to evaluate some of the limits.

Study the following examples, then try the following problems.

- $\int_1^5 \dfrac{1}{\sqrt{x-1}} \, dx$ is improper because the lower limit 1 causes division by 0 in the integrand. So we rewrite the integral as

$$\lim_{a \to 1^+} \int_a^5 \frac{1}{\sqrt{x-1}} \, dx.$$

- Notice that a approaches 1 from above since the interval of integration is $[1, 5]$.

- $\int_0^7 \dfrac{1}{x-2} \, dx$ is improper since at $x = 2$, the integrand has an asymptote. This problem must be split into two integrals with limits:

$$\lim_{a \to 2^-} \int_0^a \frac{1}{x-2} \, dx + \lim_{a \to 2^+} \int_a^7 \frac{1}{x-2} \, dx.$$

171

Rewrite each integral in proper form using limits. *Do not integrate.*

1. $\int_0^\infty \tan^{-1} x \, dx$

2. $\int_0^5 \frac{1}{e^x - 1} \, dx$

3. $\int_0^6 \frac{dx}{\sqrt[3]{4 - x^2}}$

Improper integrals are also used to develop a small "library" of known convergent and divergent integrals. Using direct or limit comparison tests, these integrals can then be used to determine the convergence or divergence of more difficult integrals. Although too long to redevelop in this context, you should know that

- $\int_0^1 \frac{1}{x^p} \, dx$ converges for $0 < p < 1$ and diverges for $p \geq 1$.

- $\int_1^\infty \frac{1}{x^p} \, dx$ diverges for $0 < p \leq 1$ and converges for $p > 1$.

You also need to know the direct comparison test.

Direct Comparison Test

Let f and g be continuous on $[a, \infty)$ with $0 \leq f(x) \leq g(x)$
for all $x \geq a$. Then

1. $\int_a^\infty f(x) \, dx$ converges if $\int_a^\infty g(x) \, dx$ converges.

2. $\int_a^\infty g(x) \, dx$ diverges if $\int_a^\infty f(x) \, dx$ diverges.

Use the direct comparison test to determine if the following integrals converge or diverge.

4. $\int_1^\infty \frac{dx}{1 + x^3}$

5. $\int_0^1 \frac{dx}{1 + \sqrt{x}}$

6. $\int_2^\infty \frac{dx}{\ln x}$

1. Find the first quadrant area under $y = \dfrac{3}{2e^{\frac{x}{2}}}$.

    (A) ∞ (B) $\dfrac{3}{2}e$

    (C) 3 (D) $\dfrac{3}{2}$

2. $\displaystyle\int_2^\infty \dfrac{dx}{x^2 + 5x + 6}$

    (A) 1 (B) $\ln 20$

    (C) $\ln\dfrac{5}{4}$ (D) ∞

3. $\displaystyle\int_0^1 x \ln x \, dx =$

    (A) -1 (B) $-\dfrac{1}{2}$

    (C) $-\dfrac{1}{4}$ (D) $-\infty$

Need More Help With . . . *See . . .*

L'Hospital's Rule? *Calculus,* Section 9.2

Improper integrals? *Calculus,* Section 9.4

Initial Value Problems

AP* Learning Objective: • Analyze differential equations to obtain general and specific solutions. (LO 3.5A)

Overview

An equation containing a derivative dy/dx is called a *differential equation*. The general solution to the differential equation is the family of functions $y = f(x)$ that satisfy the differential equation. If in addition to the derivative dy/dx we are also given a point (x_0, y_0) that satisfies the function $y = f(x)$, we have an *initial value problem*. The value $y_0 = f(x_0)$ is called an initial value. The solution to the initial value problem is a function $y = f(x)$ that satisfies the differential equation on an appropriate interval and also contains the initial value. This solution is called a *particular solution*.

Content and Practice

The general solution to a differential equation is often found by integrating the derivative. This integral will include a constant of integration. The constant of integration can be found by substituting the initial value into the general solution. If the general solution is differentiable, this pins down the solution on the entire domain and once the constant of integration is found, we have the particular solution.

Example 1: Find the solution to the initial value problem
$dy/dx = \cos 2x, \, y(0) = 1$.

Solution: The general solution is found by antidifferentiation.

$$y = \int \cos 2x \, dx = \frac{1}{2} \sin 2x + C$$

The constant of integration is found by substituting the initial value:

$$1 = \frac{1}{2} \sin (2 \cdot 0) + C, \text{ so } C = 1$$

The particular solution is

$$y = \frac{1}{2} \sin 2x + 1.$$

Example 2: Find the solution to the initial value problem $\dfrac{dy}{dx} = \dfrac{1}{x}, y(-1) = 2$.

Solution: The general solution is $y(x) = \ln|x| + C$. Using initial conditions, $2 = \ln|-1| + C$ so $C = 2$, which gives us $y(x) = \ln|x| + 2$. Although this function satisfies the differential equation and the initial values, it is NOT the solution to the initial value problem because the general solution is not continuous at $x = 0$. The general solution has branches for $x < 0$ and for $x > 0$. The initial condition pins down only the branch for $x < 0$ so we must specify this domain restriction. The solution is $y(x) = \ln|x| + 2, x < 0$.

Example 3: If is the antiderivative of $g(x) = \dfrac{x^3}{1 + x^5}$ such that $f(1) = -2$, then $f(5) = $ _____.

Solution: At first this may appear to be a simple initial value problem in which you solve for $y = f(x)$ and then find $f(5)$. However, solving for $y = f(x)$ is difficult. In fact, it was not intended that students solve for $y = f(x)$. Instead, define a function $f(x) = \int_1^x \dfrac{t^3}{1 + t^5} dt$. By the Antiderivative Part of the Fundamental Theorem, $f'(x) = \dfrac{x^3}{1 + x^5}$, so f is an antiderivative of $\dfrac{x^3}{1 + x^5}$. By the Evaluation Part of the Fundamental Theorem, $f(5) = \int_1^5 \dfrac{t^3}{1 + t^5} dt + f(1)$, which can be evaluated with a calculator. Therefore $f(5) = -1.312$.

1. An arrow is fired straight up into the air with an initial velocity of $v(0) = 155$ feet/second.

   (a) If the acceleration is $dv/dt = -32$ feet/second^2, find the velocity as a function of time.

   (b) If the arrow is fired from an initial height of 5 feet, find the height as a function of time.

2. Find the solution to the initial value problem $\dfrac{dy}{dx} = \dfrac{1}{x^2}, y(-2) = 1$.

3. If f is the antiderivative of $g(x) = \sin(x^2)$ such that $f(0) = 1$, find $f(3)$.

Additional Practice

⊞ 1. At time $t \geq 0$, the acceleration of a particle moving on the x-axis is $a(t) = t + \cos t$. At $t = 0$, the velocity of the particle is -3. For what value of t will the velocity of the particle be zero?

 (A) 2.057 (B) 2.713

 (C) 2.954 (D) 3.720

2. The acceleration of a particle moving along the x-axis is $a = \cos(t)$. If $v(0) = 0$ and $x(0) = 1$, find the position $x(t)$ of the particle.

3. Find the particular solution to the differential equation $\dfrac{dy}{dx} = 1 + \sec^2 x$ whose graph passes through the point $(0, 1)$.

Need More Help With . . .	See . . .
Initial value problems?	*Calculus*, Section 7.1
Particle motion problems?	*Calculus*, Sections 3.4, 8.1

Separable Differential Equations

AP* Learning Objective: • Analyze differential equations to obtain general and specific solutions.
(LO 3.5A)

Overview

A differential equation of the form $\dfrac{dy}{dx} = g(x)h(y)$ is said to be *separable*. We solve the differential equation by dividing both sides of the equation by $h(y)$ and then integrating both sides of the resulting equation.

$$\int \frac{1}{h(y)}\, dy = \int g(x)\, dx$$

Content and Practice

The differential equation $\dfrac{dy}{dt} = ky$ is a separable differential equation that describes exponential growth (k positive) or decay (k negative). The general solution follows.

$$\int \frac{1}{y}\, dy = \int k\, dt \qquad \text{Separate variables.}$$

$$\ln|y| = kt + C \qquad \text{Integrate both sides.}$$

$$|y| = e^{kt+C} \qquad \text{Solve for } y.$$

$$|y| = e^{C}e^{kt} \qquad \text{Properties of exponents}$$

$$y = y_0 e^{kt} \qquad e^{c} = y_0$$

The value of y_0 can be found from initial conditions. We may need to find the value of k from another given point on the curve $y = f(t)$.

Consider the differential equation $\dfrac{dy}{dx} = \dfrac{y^2}{x}$, where $x \neq 0$. Find the particular solution $y = f(x)$ to the differential equation with the initial condition $f(-1) = 1$ and state its domain.

$$\int \frac{1}{y^2}\, dy = \int \frac{1}{x}\, dx \qquad \text{Separate variables.}$$

$$-\frac{1}{y} = \ln|x| + C \qquad \text{Integrate both sides.}$$

$$y = \frac{-1}{\ln|x| + C} \qquad \text{Solve for } y.$$

$$1 = \frac{-1}{\ln|-1| + C} \qquad \text{Use initial condition.}$$

$$C = -1 \qquad \text{Solve for } C.$$

We have $y = \dfrac{-1}{\ln|x| - 1}$, but this particular solution is not complete until we include the domain. The function $y = \dfrac{-1}{\ln|x| - 1}$ is not continuous at

$x = -e, x = 0$, and $x = e$. It has branches between these discontinuities and is defined for $x < -e$, $-e < x < 0$, $0 < x < e$, and $x > e$. The initial condition only pins down the branch for $-e < x < 0$, so the domain of the particular solution is $-e < x < 0$.

1. A bacteria colony with population y grows according to the differential equation $\dfrac{dy}{dt} = 2.3y$. There are 2000 bacteria initially.

   (a) Find the equation for population y as a function of time.

   (b) Find the number of bacteria at time = 7.

2. Consider the differential equation $\dfrac{dy}{dx} = \dfrac{2}{\sqrt{y}}$. Find the particular solution $y = f(x)$ to the differential equation with the initial condition $y(0) = 9$ and state its domain.

The differential equation $dP/dt = kP(M - P)$ is called a *logistic differential equation*. The equation describes the growth rate of a population P with carrying capacity M. Calculus AB students are not expected to solve this differential equation as it requires partial fractions, a skill unique to the BC curriculum. Recognizing that the equation represents logistic growth, and finding carrying capacity and k by algebraic methods is expected of all students. The solution is

$$P = \frac{M}{1 + Ae^{-kMt}}$$

Notice $\lim_{t \to \infty} P(t) = M$ since the Ae^{-kMt} term goes to 0 as t goes to infinity. Thus, if by observation, a student can identify M and k in the differential equation, most of the critical information has been determined. For example: $\frac{dP}{dt} = 3P - 0.003P^2$ can be factored into $\frac{dP}{dt} = 0.003P(1000 - P)$. By comparison to the standard differential equation we can determine $M = 1000$ and $k = 0.003$.

3. (BC) Consider the logistic differential equation $\dfrac{dP}{dt} = \dfrac{P}{3}\left(1 - \dfrac{P}{12}\right)$.

    (a) Write the differential equation in the standard form shown above.

    (b) If $P(0) = 5$, what is $\lim_{t \to \infty} P(t)$?

Additional Practice

1. Find $y(t)$ if $\dfrac{dy}{dt} = \dfrac{y}{3}\left(1 - \dfrac{t}{4}\right)$ and $y(0) = 2$.

2. Population y grows according to the equation $\frac{dy}{dt} = ky$, where k is a constant and t is measured in years. If the population doubles every 8 years, which of the following could be the value of k?

   (A) 0.087   (B) 0.349
   (C) 0.799   (D) 1.071

3. Solve the differential equation $\frac{dy}{dx} = -2xy$ and $y(1) = 4$.

4. (BC) Without integrating, find the carrying capacity for a population growth rate modeled by $\frac{dp}{dt} = 6P - 0.012\,P^2$.

   (A) 500   (B) 50
   (C) 0.012   (D) None of these

Need More Help With . . .	*See . . .*
Separable differential equations?	*Calculus,* Section 7.4
Exponential growth and decay?	*Calculus,* Sections 1.3, 7.4
Logistic growth?	*Calculus,* Section 7.5
Partial fractions?	*Calculus,* Section 7.5

Numerical Approximations to Definite Integrals

AP* Learning Objective: • Approximate a definite integral. (LO 3.2B)

Overview

In theory, *definite integrals* can be used in a wide variety of real-world applications including area, volume, work, distance, and velocity. In practice, these definite integrals may be difficult or impossible to evaluate directly. This is why it is helpful to know methods that closely approximate definite integrals. Some of these methods include left-hand, right-hand, and midpoint Riemann sums as well as the Trapezoidal Rule.

Content and Practice

The section in this workbook titled "Riemann Sums" described left-hand, right-hand, and midpoint rectangular methods to approximate definite integrals. You may want to review that section before continuing. Each of these three methods uses rectangles to approximate a definite integral. Another geometric shape that may give a more accurate approximation is the trapezoid.

Trapezoidal Rule

If the interval $[a, b]$ is partitioned into n equal subintervals of width $h = \dfrac{b - a}{n}$, the Trapezoidal Rule to approximate the definite integral of $y = f(x)$ on the interval $[a, b]$ is

$$\int_a^b f(x)\, dx \approx \frac{h}{2}\left[y_0 + 2y_1 + 2y_2 + \cdots + 2y_{n-1} + y_n\right].$$

Note that the trapezoidal approximation is equal to the average of the left- and right-hand rectangular approximation methods.

If the subintervals are not of equal length, you must find the area of each trapezoid separately and sum the areas to approximate the definite integral. The area of a single trapezoid is

$$\frac{h}{2}[y_i + y_{i+1}].$$

1. Consider the area bounded by $f(x) = 4 - x^2$ and the x-axis.

   (a) Approximate this area using the Trapezoidal Rule with $n = 4$.

   (b) Find the left- and right-hand Riemann sums using $n = 4$ and verify that the average of these two approximations gives the same result as the Trapezoidal Rule.

2. The table below shows the velocity of a remote-controlled toy car as it traveled down a hallway for 10 seconds.

Time (sec)	0	1	2	3	4	5	6	7	8	9	10
Velocity (in./sec)	0	6	10	16	14	12	18	22	12	4	2

Using the Trapezoidal Rule, estimate the distance traveled by the car. Use 10 subintervals of length 1.

Additional Practice

1. The graph of $y = f(x)$ is shown. Use the Trapezoidal Rule with $n = 4$ to estimate the area bounded by the graph of $y = f(x)$ and the x-axis on the interval $[-2, 2]$.

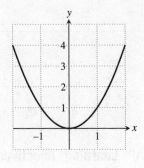

2. The function f is continuous on the closed interval $[1, 7]$ and has the values given in the table.

x	1	4	6	7
$f(x)$	10	20	40	30

Using the subintervals $[1, 4]$, $[4, 6]$, and $[6, 7]$, what is the trapezoidal approximation of $\int_1^7 f(x)\, dx$?

(A) 120   (B) 130   (C) 140   (D) 150

Need More Help With . . .   **See . . .**

Rectangular approximation methods?   *Calculus,* Section 6.1

Trapezoidal Rule?   *Calculus,* Section 6.5

Concept of Series

AP* Learning Objective: • Determine whether a series converges or diverges. (LO 4.1A)

Overview

A *series* is defined as a sequence of partial sums, and *convergence* is defined in terms of the limit of the sequence of partial sums. Technology can be used to explore convergence or divergence.

Content and Practice

An infinite series is an expression of the form

$$a_1 + a_2 + a_3 + \cdots + a_n + \cdots = \sum_{k=1}^{\infty} a_k.$$

The partial sums of the series form a sequence

$$s_1 = a_1$$
$$s_2 = a_1 + a_2$$
$$s_3 = a_1 + a_2 + a_3$$
$$\vdots$$
$$s_n = \sum_{k=1}^{n} a_k$$

of real numbers. If the sequence of partial sums converges to a value S, then the infinite series converges to the sum S, which can be written $\sum_{k=1}^{\infty} a_k = S$.

The infinite geometric series $\sum_{k=1}^{\infty} \left(\dfrac{1}{2}\right)^k$ converges to 1. A table and graph of the sequence of partial sums provide evidence for convergence.

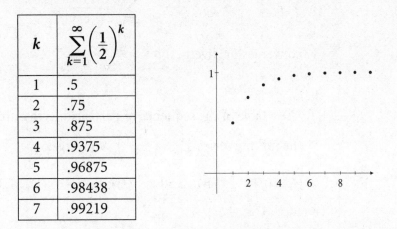

k	$\sum_{k=1}^{\infty} \left(\dfrac{1}{2}\right)^k$
1	.5
2	.75
3	.875
4	.9375
5	.96875
6	.98438
7	.99219

Make a table and graph of the sequence of partial sums for each of the following series. Use the sequence of partial sums to predict whether the infinite series converges or diverges. If the infinite series converges, estimate the value to which it converges.

1. $\displaystyle\sum_{k=1}^{\infty} \frac{1}{k^2}$

2. $\displaystyle\sum_{k=1}^{\infty} \frac{k}{k+2}$

If the infinite series $\displaystyle\sum_{k=1}^{\infty} a_k = a_1 + a_2 + \cdots + a_k + \cdots$ converges, then $\displaystyle\lim_{k \to \infty} a_k = 0$. This means that if $\displaystyle\lim_{k \to \infty} a_k \neq 0$ the series must diverge.

The nth-Term Test for Divergence

$\displaystyle\sum_{n=1}^{\infty} a_n$ diverges if $\displaystyle\lim_{n \to \infty} a_n$ fails to exist or is different from zero.

In problem 2 above, the sequence of partial sums for $\displaystyle\sum_{k=1}^{\infty} \frac{k}{k+2}$ diverges, so the series diverges. It is also possible to show this series diverges by the nth-Term Test since $\displaystyle\lim_{k \to \infty} \frac{k}{k+2} = 1$.

1. Use a graph of the sequence of partial sums to predict whether the infinite series

    $$\sum_{k=1}^{\infty} \frac{(-1)^{k+1}}{k}$$

    converges or diverges.

2. Use a table of the sequence of partial sums to estimate the value to which the infinite series $\sum_{k=0}^{\infty} \left(\frac{-1}{3}\right)^{k}$ converges.

    (A) 0.33   (B) 0.50   (C) 0.75   (D) 1.33

3. Does the series $\sum_{k=1}^{\infty} \left(1 + \frac{1}{k}\right)^{k}$ converge or diverge?

Need More Help With . . .   **See . . .**

   Infinite series?   *Calculus,* Section 10.1

Geometric, Harmonic, and Alternating Series

AP* Learning Objectives: • Determine whether a series converges or diverges. (LO 4.1A)

• Determine or estimate the sum of a series. (LO 4.1B)

Overview

Geometric, harmonic, and alternating series have very specific forms and properties. If you can identify which type of series you are dealing with, it is easy to decide questions about convergence.

Content and Practice

A geometric series takes the form

$$a + ar + ar^2 + ar^3 + \cdots + ar^{n-1} + \cdots = \sum_{n=1}^{\infty} ar^{n-1}.$$

If $|r| < 1$, the series converges to $\dfrac{a}{1-r}$; otherwise, the series diverges.

The harmonic series takes the form

$$1 + \frac{1}{2} + \frac{1}{3} + \frac{1}{4} + \cdots + \frac{1}{n} + \cdots = \sum_{n=1}^{\infty} \frac{1}{n}.$$

The harmonic series diverges.

An alternating series takes the form

$$u_1 - u_2 + u_3 - u_4 + \cdots = \sum_{n=1}^{\infty} (-1)^{n+1} u_n,$$

where each u_n is positive. If $u_n \geq u_{n+1}$ for all $n \geq N$ for some integer N and if $\lim_{n \to \infty} u_n = 0$, the series converges.

1. Which of the following series converge?

I. $\displaystyle\sum_{n=1}^{\infty}\left(\frac{4}{3}\right)^n$ II. $\displaystyle\sum_{n=1}^{\infty}\frac{\cos n\pi}{n}$ III. $\displaystyle\sum_{n=1}^{\infty}\frac{1}{n}$

(A) None

(B) II only

(C) III only

(D) I and II only

2. $\displaystyle\sum_{n=1}^{\infty}5\left(\frac{2}{3}\right)^{n-1} = \underline{\hspace{2cm}}.$

Additional Practice

1. What is the sum of the infinite geometric series

$$\frac{3}{2}+\frac{9}{16}+\frac{27}{128}+\frac{81}{1024}+\cdots?$$

(A) $\dfrac{7}{4}$

(B) $\dfrac{12}{5}$

(C) $\dfrac{5}{2}$

(D) There is no finite sum.

 2. Consider the infinite series $\displaystyle\sum_{n=1}^{\infty}4\left(\frac{-1}{3}\right)^{n-1}$.

What is the sum of this series?

Need More Help With . . .	See . . .
Geometric series?	*Calculus*, Section 10.1
Harmonic and alternating series?	*Calculus*, Section 10.5

Power Series

• Write a power series representing a given function. (LO 4.2B)
• Determine the radius and interval of convergence of a power series. (LO 4.2C)

Overview

Power series are the foundation upon which we build Maclaurin and Taylor series. They are also a good starting point for understanding the concept of series representing functions graphically and the idea of convergence. Power series flow directly from our work with geometric series.

Content and Practice

A power series is an expression of the form

$$\sum_{j=0}^{\infty} c_j x^j = c_0 + c_1 x + c_2 x^2 + \cdots + c_j x^j + \cdots.$$

All c_j's are real constants and may at times be 0. We say the series is centered at $x = 0$.

If we center the series somewhere other than zero, say $x = a$, we replace all x's with $(x - a)$:

$$\sum_{j=0}^{\infty} c_j (x - a)^j = c_0 + c_1 (x - a) + c_2 (x - a)^2 + \cdots + c_j (x - a)^j + \cdots.$$

Consider the power series

$$P(x) = 2 + 4x^2 + 8x^4 + 16x^6 + \cdots.$$

If we recognize it as an infinite geometric series, its sum will be $S_\infty = \dfrac{a}{1 - r}$. The first term is $a = 2$ and the common ratio is $r = 2x^2$, so the sum of the function is

$$f(x) = \frac{2}{1 - 2x^2}.$$

If a power series is geometric, we can determine an interval of convergence by setting $|r| < 1$. Unfortunately, not all power series are geometric, and in those cases it can be extremely difficult to determine an infinite sum and an interval of convergence.

Power series may also be differentiated or integrated term by term to produce new series to model different functions. Consider our previous example. On a certain domain,

$$\frac{2}{1 - 2x^2} = 2 + 4x^2 + 8x^4 + 16x^6 + \cdots.$$

Differentiating both sides of the equation produces

$$\frac{8x}{(1 - 2x^2)^2} = 8x + 32x^3 + 96x^5 + \cdots.$$

Notice the new series is not geometric. Had we just been given the series alone, it would have been very difficult to determine its infinite sum. Similarly, if we knew the function and wanted to generate the series, because the function is not in the form of a sum of an infinite geometric series we would have an extremely difficult task before us.

1. Given the infinite geometric series $x - 3x^2 + 9x^3 - 27x^4 + \cdots$, identify a and r and determine the function represented by the sum of the series.

2. By writing it in the form $\dfrac{a}{1 - r}$, generate a power series for the function $f(x) = \dfrac{4}{2 - 3x}$ that is centered at each of the following values.

    (a) $x = 0$

    (b) $x = \dfrac{1}{3}$

1. The seventh-order power series representation of $g(x) = \sin^{-1}x$ at $x = 0$ is $x + \dfrac{x^3}{6} + \dfrac{3x^5}{40} + \dfrac{5x^7}{112}$. Which is a power series representation of $f(x) = \dfrac{x}{\sqrt{1 - x^2}}$ at $x = 0$?

   (A) $1 + \dfrac{x^2}{2} + \dfrac{3x^4}{8} + \dfrac{5x^6}{16}$ (B) $\dfrac{x^2}{2} + \dfrac{x^4}{24} + \dfrac{x^6}{80} + \dfrac{5x^8}{896}$

   (C) $x + \dfrac{x^3}{2} + \dfrac{3x^5}{8} + \dfrac{5x^7}{16}$ (D) Cannot be determined

2. Determine the coefficient of the 12th-degree term of the power series representation of $h(x) = \dfrac{3}{1 + 2x^3}$ centered at $x = 0$.

   (A) $-3 \cdot 2^{12}$ (B) -48

   (C) 48 (D) $3 \cdot 2^{12}$

3. What is the interval of convergence of the power series $\displaystyle\sum_{n=0}^{\infty} \dfrac{(x - 3)^n}{2^{n+1}}$?

   (A) $1 < x < 5$ (B) $2 < x < 4$
   (C) $-1 < x < 1$ (D) $-2 < x < 2$

Need More Help With . . .

Power series?

See . . .

Calculus, Section 10.1

Taylor Polynomials

AP* Learning Objective: • Construct and use Taylor polynomials. (LO 4.2A)

Overview

Early in the course we approximated a function near a given point by using a tangent line. The problem was that it quickly became very inaccurate for most functions. We find that as we increase the number of terms and degree of the approximating polynomial, the polynomial can approximate a nonpolynomial function with greater accuracy. In the study of Taylor series we examine these concepts, look at construction of these polynomials, explore domains over which they approximate other functions, and consider the error involved in using polynomials for approximation. This is a topic required only in the AP* Calculus BC curriculum.

Content and Practice

Graphed below are the functions $y = \cos x$ and an increasing number of the terms of the polynomial $P(x) = 1 - \dfrac{x^2}{2!} + \dfrac{x^4}{4!} - \dfrac{x^6}{6!} + \cdots$. Notice how the polynomial begins to approximate the cosine function on a wider and wider domain.

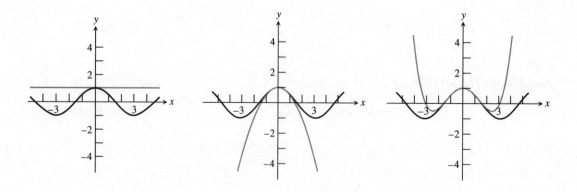

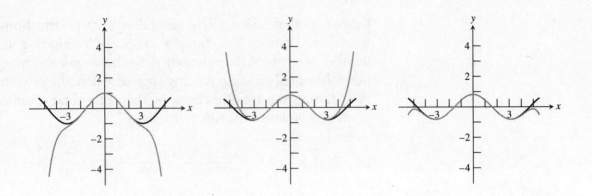

We can show that the infinite polynomial series converges to the cosine function for all real numbers. If we truncate the series, the only place it will exactly equal the cosine is at the original point of tangency, the center of the series. But a higher-order polynomial will certainly provide greater accuracy over a wider domain than a linear approximation.

1. Examine the relationship between $y = \ln(x - 1)$ and an increasing number of terms of the polynomial

$$P(x) = (x - 2) - \frac{(x - 2)^2}{2} + \frac{(x - 2)^3}{3} - \frac{(x - 2)^4}{4} + \cdots.$$

Graph $y = \ln(x - 1)$ and $P(x)$ together on the same screen. First use only the linear factor of $(x - 2)$. Then add the quadratic term and examine the graph again. Next add the cubic term, and so on.

(a) Where is the polynomial exactly equal to the natural logarithm function?

(b) Does adding more terms appear to create a polynomial that "fits" the curve better?

(c) Over how large a domain can you get the polynomial to approximate the natural logarithm function?

2. Below is a list of Taylor polynomials along with the functions that match the series. Examine their graphs gradually by plotting an increasing number of terms of the polynomial. See how soon you recognize which nonpolynomial function is being approximated. Check your conjecture by graphing the two functions at the same time. Comment on the domain over which the functions match.

(a) $P(x) = x + \dfrac{(x-1)^2}{2!} + \dfrac{(x-1)^3}{3!} + \dfrac{(x-1)^4}{4!} + \cdots$

(b) $P(x) = x - \dfrac{x^3}{3} + \dfrac{x^5}{5} - \dfrac{x^7}{7} + \cdots$

(c) $P(x) = x - \dfrac{x^3}{3!} + \dfrac{x^5}{5!} - \dfrac{x^7}{7!} + \cdots$

(d) $\sum_{n=1}^{\infty} \dfrac{x^{n-1}}{(-2)^{n-1}}$

(e) $P(x) = x + \dfrac{x^3}{3} + \dfrac{2x^5}{15} + \dfrac{17x^7}{315} + \cdots$

(i) $y = \dfrac{2}{2+x}$ (ii) $y = \sin x$ (iii) $y = \tan x$

(iv) $y = \tan^{-1} x$ (v) $y = e^{x-1}$

Additional Practice

1. The Taylor polynomial

$$P(x) = \frac{x}{3} + \frac{x^2}{9} + \frac{x^3}{27} + \frac{x^4}{81} + \cdots$$

is used to approximate the function $f(x) = \dfrac{x}{3-x}$. How many terms of the polynomial are needed so that the error between the polynomial approximation and the function at $x = 0.4$ is less than $\dfrac{1}{1000}$?

(A) 1   (B) 2   (C) 3   (D) 4

2. The Taylor polynomial

$$P(x) = 1 - 2x^2 + \frac{2x^4}{3} - \frac{4x^6}{45} + \frac{2x^8}{315} - \frac{4x^{10}}{14175}$$

approximates the function $f(x) =$

(A) $\cos 2x$ (B) $\sin 2x$

(C) $\cos x^2$ (D) $\cos x$

Need More Help With . . .

Taylor polynomials?

See . . .

Calculus, Section 10.2

Maclaurin and Taylor Series

AP* Learning Objectives: • Construct and use Taylor polynomials. (LO 4.2A)

• Write a power series representing a function. (LO 4.2B)

Overview

Maclaurin and Taylor series are the entire focus of Chapter 10 in the *Calculus* text. Familiarity with the Maclaurin series for the functions e^x, $\sin x$, $\cos x$, and $1/(1 - x)$ is necessary, as they represent the most common series used throughout the course. You can almost always count on a Taylor series question on the Free Response portion of the AP* exam, and a series question or two among the Multiple Choice problems. Series are also important building blocks for further study beyond the scope of this course.

Content and Practice

Once a visual understanding of a series approximating a function is established, we move into actually learning to produce those series. We are extending the idea of a linear approximation at a point of tangency to a higher-degree polynomial. The original point of tangency is the center of the series. Students often miss the simple idea that a Maclaurin series is just a special case of a Taylor series. A Maclaurin series is centered at 0, while a Taylor series can be centered at any value $x = a$ in the domain of the original function.

The general form of a Taylor series for a function f centered at $x = a$ is:

$$\sum_{k=0}^{\infty} \frac{f^{(k)}(a)}{k!} (x - a)^k = f(a) + f'(a)(x - a) + \frac{f''(a)}{2!} (x - a)^2 + \cdots + \frac{f^{(k)}(a)}{k!} (x - a)^k + \cdots$$

The infinite series requires the function to have derivatives of all orders. If we acknowledge that our approximation will have less accuracy than an infinite series, a Taylor polynomial of finite order n can be used. It is simply a partial sum from the series above. The order of a series is the highest order of the derivative of f used in forming the series.

$$\sum_{k=0}^{n} \frac{f^{(k)}(a)}{k!} (x - a)^k = f(a) + f'(a)(x - a) + \frac{f''(a)}{2!} (x - a)^2 + \cdots + \frac{f^{(n)}(a)}{n!} (x - a)^n$$

Notice that the first two terms of the series form the linearization we worked with through much of the course.

The development of why the formula works is presented more thoroughly in the *Calculus* text. The Maclaurin series for $f(x) = e^x$ is one of the easiest to develop from scratch. We simply need to evaluate its derivatives at $a = 0$. Let's review the process.

(i)   Evaluate the function and its successive derivatives at the center $a = 0$.

$$f(0) = e^0 = 1 \text{ and since the derivative of } e^x$$
$$\text{is still } e^x, \text{ the value of all derivatives at 0 is 1.}$$

(ii)   Substitute the value of the function, its derivatives, and a into the Taylor formula.

$$e^x = \sum_{k=0}^{\infty} \frac{f^{(k)}(0)}{k!}(x-0)^k = f(0) + f'(0)(x-0) + \frac{f''(0)}{2!}(x-0)^2 + \cdots$$

$$+ \frac{f^{(k)}(0)}{k!}(x-0)^k + \cdots$$

(iii)   Simplify with all the derivatives of f at 0 equal to 1.

$$e^x = \sum_{k=0}^{\infty} \frac{(x)^k}{k!} = 1 + x + \frac{x^2}{2!} + \frac{x^3}{3!} + \cdots + \frac{x^{(k)}}{k!} + \cdots$$

This is the infinite Maclaurin series for e^x. It converges to e^x for all real numbers x.

To develop the Maclaurin series for $\frac{1}{1-x}$, we could use the same procedure, but as you will recall from earlier in this workbook, this function has the form of a geometric series. It is significantly less work to recognize it has the form $S_\infty = \frac{a}{1-r}$ where $a = 1$ and $r = x$. Then the series generates nicely to $\frac{1}{1-x} = 1 + x + x^2 + x^3 + \cdots + x^n + \cdots$. Remember also that it converges only when $|r| < 1$, so the series only converges to the function on the interval $-1 < x < 1$.

Additional Practice

1. Let g be a function that has derivatives of all orders. Assuming $g(0) = 4, g'(0) = 7, g''(0) = -2, g'''(0) = 5$, and $g^{(4)}(0) = -8$, write a fourth order Maclaurin polynomial for g.

2. Determine the infinite Taylor series for $f(x) = 1/x$ centered at $a = 1$.

3. For a given function $h(x)$, a 12th-order Taylor polynomial is written in ascending powers of x, so that the last term of the polynomial is $\dfrac{x^{12}}{3960}$. Which is the value of the 12th derivative of h at $x = 0$, $h^{12}(0)$?

   (A) $9!$ (B) $3 \cdot 8!$

   (C) $12!$ (D) 3960^2

Need More Help With . . .	*See . . .*
Taylor or Maclaurin series?	*Calculus*, Section 10.2

Manipulating Taylor Series

AP* Learning Objectives: • Construct and use Taylor polynomials. (LO 4.2A)
• Write a power series representing a given function. (LO 4.2B)

Overview

Just as there are rules of acceptable processes in algebra (such as always keeping a balanced equation), there are rules to govern what can and cannot be done with Taylor series. Your goal is to understand those rules to work most efficiently and confidently with series.

Content and Practice

If we wanted to create a Taylor series for e^{2x} centered at $a = 0$, we would evaluate its derivatives at 0 and substitute into the Taylor series formula below. Showing just the first few steps reveals an interesting pattern.

$$\sum_{k=0}^{\infty} \frac{f^{(k)}(a)}{k!}(x-a)^k = f(a) + f'(a)(x-a) + \frac{f''(a)}{2!}(x-a)^2 + \cdots + \frac{f^{(k)}(a)}{k!}(x-a)^k + \cdots$$

$$
\begin{aligned}
f(x) &= e^{2x} & &\text{so} & f(0) &= e^0 = 1 \\
f'(x) &= 2e^{2x} & &\text{so} & f'(0) &= 2e^0 = 2 \\
f''(x) &= 4e^{2x} & &\text{so} & f''(0) &= 4e^0 = 4 \\
f'''(x) &= 8e^{2x} & &\text{so} & f'''(0) &= 8e^0 = 8
\end{aligned}
$$

So a third-order Taylor polynomial for e^{2x} centered at $a = 0$ is

$$e^{2x} \approx 1 + 2x + \frac{4}{2!}x^2 + \frac{8}{3!}x^3,$$

or, rewriting,

$$e^{2x} \approx 1 + 2x + \frac{(2x)^2}{2!} + \frac{(2x)^3}{3!}.$$

Compare this to the series for e^x,

$$e^x = \sum_{k=0}^{\infty} \frac{(x)^k}{k!} = 1 + x + \frac{x^2}{2!} + \frac{x^3}{3!} + \cdots + \frac{x^k}{k!} + \cdots.$$

Notice that x in the series for e^x has just been replaced by $2x$ to obtain a series for e^{2x}.

The question that must now be answered is, "When is a replacement of variables into a known series allowed, and when is it not?" The simplest solution is to keep your attention focused on the center of each series. If the centers of the series are the same, a new series can be generated from a known series by substitution. Let's look at a couple of examples where substituting does and does not work.

Example 1: The series for $f(x) = \sin x$ centered at $a = 0$ is

$$\sin x = \sum_{n=0}^{\infty} (-1)^n \frac{x^{2n+1}}{(2n+1)!} = x - \frac{x^3}{3!} + \frac{x^5}{5!} - \cdots.$$

Example 2: The series for $g(x) = \sin 3x$ centered at $a = 0$ is

$$\sin 3x = \sum_{n=0}^{\infty} (-1)^n \frac{(3x)^{2n+1}}{(2n+1)!} = 3x - \frac{(3x)^3}{3!} + \frac{(3x)^5}{5!} - \cdots.$$

Example 3: The series for $h(x) = \sin(3x + 1)$ centered at $a = 0$ *is not*

$$\sin(3x + 1) = \sum_{n=0}^{\infty} (-1)^n \frac{(3x + 1)^{2n+1}}{(2n+1)!} = (3x + 1) - \frac{(3x + 1)^3}{3!} + \frac{(3x + 1)^5}{5!} - \cdots.$$

This is a series for $\sin(3x + 1)$, but it is centered at $a = -1/3$. To understand why it is not centered at 0, think of $h'(0)$. $h'(x) = 3\cos(3x + 1)$ and $h'(0) = 3\cos 1$, but this value and successive derivatives of $\sin(3x + 1)$ at $x = 0$ could not possibly show up in the series by substituting only for x.

We can also generate new series by differentiating or integrating. For example, differentiating the Taylor series for $\sin(x)$ will produce the series for $\cos(x)$.

$$\sin x = \sum_{n=0}^{\infty} (-1)^n \frac{x^{2n+1}}{(2n+1)!} = x - \frac{x^3}{3!} + \frac{x^5}{5!} - \cdots$$

$$\frac{d}{dx} \sin x = \frac{d}{dx} \sum_{n=0}^{\infty} (-1)^n \frac{x^{2n+1}}{(2n+1)!} = \frac{d}{dx}\left(x - \frac{x^3}{3!} + \frac{x^5}{5!} - \cdots \right)$$

$$\cos x = \sum_{n=0}^{\infty} (-1)^n \frac{x^{2n}}{(2n)!} = 1 - \frac{x^2}{2!} + \frac{x^4}{4!} - \cdots$$

A common mistake made by students when integrating a series is failing to account for the arbitrary constant. Consider the series for $f(x) = \dfrac{1}{2-x}$ centered at $a = 1$. If we write $f(x) = \dfrac{1}{1-(x-1)}$, we can write a geometric series with first term 1 and common ratio $(x-1)$:

$$\frac{1}{2-x} = 1 + (x-1) + (x-1)^2 + (x-1)^3 + \cdots.$$

Integrating both sides of the equation we get

$$-\ln(2-x) = x + \frac{(x-1)^2}{2} + \frac{(x-1)^3}{3} + \frac{(x-1)^4}{4} + \cdots + C$$

We now substitute the only point where the series exactly equals the function, at the center $x = 1$, to get $0 = 1 + 0 + 0 + 0 + \cdots + C$. So $C = -1$ and the series becomes

$$-\ln(2-x) = (x-1) + \frac{(x-1)^2}{2} + \frac{(x-1)^3}{3} + \frac{(x-1)^4}{4} + \cdots.$$

We have used one series and integration to develop a series for a new function centered in the same place. Had we not considered the constant, our new series would have been missing a term.

1. The geometric series

$$\frac{1}{1+x^2} = \sum_{n=0}^{\infty} (-1)^n x^{2n} = 1 - x^2 + x^4 - x^6 + \cdots$$

   can be integrated to produce a series for a new function. Find the function, the new series, a general term, and identify the center of the series.

2. From the Maclaurin series for e^x, can substitution be used to generate a Maclaurin series for e^{2x-1}? Explain your answer in a few sentences.

1. Given the Maclaurin series

    $$e^{x^2} = 1 + x^2 + \frac{x^4}{2!} + \cdots + \frac{(x)^{2n}}{n!} + \cdots,$$

    find a series representation for xe^{x^2}. Write the first three terms and the general term.

2. Which is the center of the series $\displaystyle\sum_{n=0}^{\infty} (-1)^n \frac{(4x-1)^{2n}}{n!}$?

    (A) -4 (B) $-\dfrac{1}{4}$ (C) $\dfrac{1}{4}$ (D) 4

3. Let $P(x) = 7 - 3(x-4) + 5(x-4)^2 - 2(x-4)^3 + 6(x-4)^4$ be the fourth-degree Taylor polynomial for the function f about 4. Assume f has derivatives of all orders for all real numbers. What is the third-degree Taylor polynomial for $g(x) = \int_4^x f(t)\, dt$ about 4?

    (A) $7 - 3(x-4) + 5(x-4)^2 - 2(x-4)^3$

    (B) $7x - \dfrac{3(x-4)^2}{2} + \dfrac{5(x-4)^3}{3} - 28$

    (C) $-3 + 10(x-4) - 6(x-4)^2 + 24(x-4)^3$

    (D) $7x - \dfrac{3(x-4)^2}{2} + \dfrac{5(x-4)^3}{3}$

Need More Help With . . .   **See . . .**

    Manipulation of series?   *Calculus,* Sections 10.1, 10.2

Integral Test, Ratio Test, and Comparison Test

AP* Learning Objective: • Determine whether a series converges or diverges. (LO 4.1A)

Overview

Integral Test: Suppose that $a_n = f(n)$, where f is a continuous, positive, decreasing function of x for all $x \geq N$ (N a positive integer). Then the series $\sum_{n=N}^{\infty} a_n$ and the integral $\int_N^{\infty} f(x)\, dx$ either both converge or both diverge.

Ratio Test: Let $\sum a_n$ be a series with all positive terms and with

$$\lim_{n \to \infty} \frac{a_{n+1}}{a_n} = L.$$

• If $L < 1$, the series converges.

• If $L > 1$, the series diverges.

• If $L = 1$, the test is inconclusive.

Comparison Test: Let $\sum a_n$ be a series with no negative terms.

• $\sum a_n$ converges if there is a convergent series $\sum c_n$ with $a_n \leq c_n$ for all $n > N$ for some integer N.

• $\sum a_n$ diverges if there is a divergent series $\sum d_n$ of nonnegative terms with $a_n \geq d_n$ for all $n > N$ for some integer N.

Example 1: Does $\sum_{n=1}^{\infty} \dfrac{1}{n^2}$ converge or diverge?

Solution: Consider the corresponding improper integral:

$$\int_1^{\infty} \frac{1}{x^2}\, dx = \lim_{b \to \infty} \int_1^b \frac{1}{x^2}\, dx$$

$$= \lim_{b \to \infty} \left(1 - \frac{1}{b} \right) = 1$$

Since the improper integral converges, it follows that $\sum_{n=1}^{\infty} \dfrac{1}{n^2}$ converges.

It can be shown by the Integral Test that any series of the form $\sum_{n=1}^{\infty} \dfrac{1}{n^p}$ converges if $p > 1$ and diverges if $p \le 1$. A series of the form $\sum_{n=1}^{\infty} \dfrac{1}{n^p}$ is called a *p-series*.

Example 2: Does $\displaystyle\sum_{n=1}^{\infty} \frac{2^n}{n!}$ converge or diverge?

Solution: Using the Ratio Test,

$$\lim_{n \to \infty} \frac{\dfrac{2^{n+1}}{(n+1)!}}{\dfrac{2^n}{n!}} = \lim_{n \to \infty} \frac{2^{n+1}}{(n+1)!} \cdot \frac{n!}{2^n} = \lim_{n \to \infty} \frac{2}{n+1} = 0, \text{ so } L = 0.$$

Since $L < 1$, the series converges by the Ratio Test.

Example 3: Does $\displaystyle\sum_{n=1}^{\infty} \frac{1}{n^3 + 1}$ converge or diverge?

Solution: $\displaystyle\sum_{n=1}^{\infty} \frac{1}{n^3 + 1} < \sum_{n=1}^{\infty} \frac{1}{n^3}$. The series $\displaystyle\sum_{n=1}^{\infty} \frac{1}{n^3}$ is a *p*-series with $p = 3$, so it converges.

Therefore $\displaystyle\sum_{n=1}^{\infty} \frac{1}{n^3 + 1}$ converges by comparison.

1. Does the series $\sum_{n=1}^{\infty} \dfrac{3^n}{n!}$ converge or diverge?

2. Does the series $\sum_{n=1}^{\infty} \dfrac{1}{n^2 + n + 1}$ converge or diverge?

Additional Practice

1. Which of the following series converge?

   I. $\displaystyle\sum_{n=1}^{\infty} \dfrac{1}{\sqrt{n}}$ II. $\displaystyle\sum_{n=1}^{\infty} \dfrac{n!}{n^n}$ III. $\displaystyle\sum_{n=1}^{\infty} \dfrac{1}{n^3 + 1}$

   (A) I and II only   (B) I and III only

   (C) II and III only   (D) III only

Need More Help With . . .	See . . .
Ratio Test or Comparison Test?	*Calculus,* Section 10.4
Integral Test?	*Calculus,* Section 10.5

Limit Comparison Test

AP* Learning Objective: • Determine whether a series converges or diverges. (LO 4.1A)

Overview

There are times when some of the more efficient tests for convergence such as the p-Series Test, Ratio Test, Direct Comparison Test, or Integral Test cannot be applied. In those cases the Limit Comparison Test may be tried. This test is usually used after considering some of the other tests simply because it is slightly more involved. The test has three possible outcomes and an appropriate comparison series must be chosen.

Limit Comparison Test

Suppose that $a_n > 0$ and $b_n > 0$ for all $n \geq N$ (N a positive integer).

1.   If $\lim\limits_{n \to \infty} \dfrac{a_n}{b_n} = c, 0 < c < \infty$, then $\sum a_n$ and $\sum b_n$ both converge or both diverge.

2.   If $\lim\limits_{n \to \infty} \dfrac{a_n}{b_n} = 0$ and $\sum b_n$ converges, then $\sum a_n$ converges.

3.   If $\lim\limits_{n \to \infty} \dfrac{a_n}{b_n} = \infty$ and $\sum b_n$ diverges, then $\sum a_n$ diverges.

It is most helpful to choose a series, $\sum b_n$, for which you can easily determine convergence or divergence.

Content and Practice

When trying to determine if a series converges, quickly examine the simpler tests first. For example the nth-Term Test for divergence will quickly verify

$$\sum_{n=1}^{\infty} \frac{2e^n + 1}{4e^n} \text{ diverges.}$$

Now consider the series $\sum\limits_{n=2}^{\infty} \dfrac{n+1}{n^3-2}$. The Ratio Test will produce a value of 1, which means the test is inconclusive. The integral of the expression is very difficult to antidifferentiate. The Comparison Test might work with a cleverly chosen function, but the end behavior model, which is often the easiest for comparison, is not helpful since the series $\sum\limits_{n=2}^{\infty} \dfrac{1}{n^2}$ converges but $\dfrac{n+1}{n^3-2} > \dfrac{1}{n^2}$. So after a quick examination of other methods, one can try the Limit Comparison Test using the end behavior model.

$$\lim_{n\to\infty} \dfrac{\dfrac{n+1}{n^3-2}}{\dfrac{1}{n^2}} = \lim_{n\to\infty} \dfrac{n+1}{n^3-2} \cdot \dfrac{n^2}{1}$$

$$= \lim_{n\to\infty} \dfrac{n^3+n^2}{n^3-2} = 1$$

The limit of the ratio is positive and finite, so both series either converge or diverge. The series $\sum\limits_{n=2}^{\infty} \dfrac{1}{n^2}$ converges by the p-Series Test, so $\sum\limits_{n=2}^{\infty} \dfrac{n+1}{n^3-2}$ converges as well.

Being consistent in setting up the ratio for this test will make it easier to remember the three possible results of the limit of each ratio and the conclusion to be drawn from that result. Put the series you are exploring in the numerator and the series about which you have knowledge in the denominator. Notice in the statement of the Limit Comparison Test above, the last two parts of the test draw their conclusions based on what the denominator, $\sum b_n$, does.

1.   Briefly explain why each test would be difficult to use to determine the behavior of the series $\sum\limits_{n=1}^{\infty} \dfrac{n}{\sin^2(n) + n^2}$.

   (a)   Ratio Test

   (b)   Direct Comparison Test with $\sum\limits_{n=1}^{\infty} \dfrac{n}{n^2}$

   (c)   Integral Test

2. Use the Limit Comparison Test on the series $\sum_{n=1}^{\infty} \dfrac{n}{\sin^2(n) + n^2}$ to determine if it converges or diverges.

Additional Practice

Which convergence test(s) would work on the following series?

(The behavior of each series is not given in the solution, just the test names.)

1. $\sum_{n=1}^{\infty} \dfrac{3^n}{n!}$

2. $\sum_{n=2}^{\infty} \dfrac{2n^2 + 1}{3n + 5n^2}$

3. $\sum_{n=2}^{\infty} \dfrac{3^n}{5^n - n}$

4. $\sum_{n=1}^{\infty} \dfrac{e^n}{e^{3n} - 4}$

5. $\sum_{n=2}^{\infty} \dfrac{1 + \ln(n)}{n}$

6. Use the Limit Comparison Test to determine whether $\sum_{n=2}^{\infty} \dfrac{1}{\sqrt{n^3 - n}}$ converges or diverges.

7. Use the Limit Comparison test to determine whether $\sum_{n=1}^{\infty} \dfrac{1}{\sqrt{n} + \sqrt{n + 1}}$ converges or diverges.

Need More Help With . . .	*See . . .*
Limit Comparison Test?	*Calculus*, Section 10.5
Other convergence tests?	*Calculus*, Sections 10.4, 10.5

Absolute and Conditional Convergence

AP* Learning Objective: • Determine whether a series converges or diverges. (LO 4.1A)

Overview

The majority of tests you learn are tests for convergence of series of all positive terms. When varying signs appear in a series, a new condition must be considered. Fortunately, there exists a theorem that says if a series has absolute convergence, changing the sign of any number of its terms will not cause the altered series to diverge. However, if a series of all positive terms diverges, the alternating form of that series may converge. If this happens, the alternating series is said to converge conditionally.

Content and Practice

Recall that the Alternating Series Test requires three conditions be met.

An alternating series, $\displaystyle\sum_{n=1}^{\infty} (-1)^{n+1} u_n$ will converge if:

1.   each u_n is positive;

2. $u_n \geq u_{n+1}$ for all $n \geq N$, for some integer N;

3. $\displaystyle\lim_{n\to\infty} u_n = 0.$

Conditional convergence of an alternating series can be examined either by finding that the absolute form of the series diverges, and then applying the alternating series test, or by reversing that order.

This review will use the absolute test first, as it is the natural order when testing endpoints of an interval of convergence of a power series. The Ratio Test is applied to find the open interval of absolute convergence, then the endpoints are tested.

1. Determine if $\displaystyle\sum_{n=1}^{\infty} \frac{(-1)^{n+1}}{\sqrt{n}}$ converges absolutely, converges conditionally, or diverges.

2. Determine if $\displaystyle\sum_{n=1}^{\infty} (-1)^{n+1} \frac{2^n}{n^2}$ converges absolutely, converges conditionally, or diverges.

If a power series has a finite interval of absolute convergence, each endpoint must be tested for absolute convergence, conditional convergence, or divergence.

3. The interval of absolute convergence for $\displaystyle\sum_{n=1}^{\infty} \frac{(x-3)^n}{n+1}$ is $2 < x < 4$. Determine the convergence or divergence of each endpoint.

Additional Practice

1. Determine if $\displaystyle\sum_{n=1}^{\infty} \frac{\cos(n\pi)}{\sqrt{n^2+1}}$ converges absolutely, converges conditionally, or diverges.

2. Which of the following series converge conditionally, but not absolutely?

I. $\sum_{n=1}^{\infty} \frac{(-1)^{n+1}}{n^2}$ II. $\sum_{n=1}^{\infty} \frac{(-1)^{n+1}}{n}$ III. $\sum_{n=2}^{\infty} \frac{(-1)^{n+1}}{\ln(n)}$

(A) II only

(B) III only

(C) I and II only

(D) II and III only

3. Find the interval of convergence of $\sum_{n=1}^{\infty} \frac{(2x-1)^n}{n \cdot 2^{3n}}$.

(A) $-\frac{7}{2} < x < \frac{9}{2}$

(B) $-\frac{7}{2} \le x < \frac{9}{2}$

(C) $-\frac{7}{2} < x \le \frac{9}{2}$

(D) $-\frac{7}{2} \le x \le \frac{9}{2}$

Need More Help With . . .

Absolute and conditional convergence?

See . . .

Calculus, Section 10.5

Radius and Interval of Convergence

AP* Learning Objective: • Determine the radius and interval of convergence of a power series. (LO 4.2C)

Overview

Although a power series is useful for approximating functions, we must pay close attention to the domain over which the series converges to the function. Some power series converge for all real numbers, while some converge over a limited domain.

Content and Practice

While developing a graphical understanding of convergence, you should have visually determined that series converge to the functions they are modeling on intervals that can vary greatly. Some converge on $-1 < x < 1$, others converge on somewhat wider domains, and others converge for all real numbers. As we noted in the section on Geometric, Harmonic, and Alternating Series, it is not terribly difficult to analytically find the interval of convergence for an infinite power series that is geometric. We identify the common ratio, r, and then solve the inequality $|r| < 1$. The conjunction obtained will be of the form $b < x < c$ and this is the interval over which the power series converges to the function it represents.

Outside this interval, we cannot rely on the series to provide an accurate approximation of the function. Just as the radius of a circle is the distance from its center to the circle, the radius of convergence is the distance from the center of the interval of convergence to one end of the interval. Another way to see the radius of convergence is to write the above conjunction in the form $|x - a| < R$, where a is the center of the series and R is the radius of convergence. If we differentiate or integrate a power series, the radius and center of convergence remain the same for the new series obtained.

212

1. Consider the infinite geometric series $\sum_{n=0}^{\infty}(x-3)^n$.

    (a) Find the function represented by the series.

    (b) Find the interval of convergence.

    (c) Find the center of the series.

    (d) Find the radius of convergence.

2. If the interval of convergence of an infinite series is $-3 < x < 11$, which is its radius of convergence?

    (A) 4   (B) 7   (C) 11   (D) 14

3. If the interval of convergence of the series representing $f(x)$ is $\frac{3}{2} < x < \frac{11}{2}$, then the interval of convergence of the series representing $f'(x)$ is _____.

If a power series is not geometric, then we can often use the Ratio Test to determine the interval of convergence.

Let's examine the series defined by $\sum_{n=0}^{\infty}n(3x-5)^n$. If we expand it, the factor of n prevents the series from being geometric. The first few terms are $(3x-5) + 2(3x-5)^2 + 3(3x-5)^3 + \cdots$. We apply the Ratio Test to the general term.

$$\lim_{n\to\infty}\left|\frac{(n+1)(3x-5)^{n+1}}{n(3x-5)^n}\right| < 1$$

$$\lim_{n\to\infty}\left|\frac{n+1}{n}(3x-5)\right| < 1$$

$$\left|1(3x-5)\right| < 1$$

$$-1 < 3x-5 < 1$$

$$\frac{4}{3} < x < 2$$

Testing the endpoints in the series, we find that it fails to converge at both endpoints by the nth-Term Test.

4.	Apply the Ratio Test to find the interval of convergence of the series $\sum_{k=0}^{\infty} \dfrac{n(x-1)^n}{5^n}$.

Additional Practice

1.	Which is the sum of the infinite power series $\sum_{n=1}^{\infty} \dfrac{(x-1)^n}{2^n}$?

(A) $\dfrac{x-1}{3-x}$ (B) $\dfrac{2}{3-x}$

(C) $\dfrac{x-1}{2-x}$ (D) $\dfrac{x-1}{1+x}$

2.	If $f(x)$ is an infinite power series with an interval of convergence $-4 < x < 2$, which is the interval of convergence of the series for $f(2x)$?

(A) $-4 < x < 2$ (B) $-8 < x < 4$

(C) $-2 < x < 1$ (D) $-2 < x < 4$

3. Find the interval of convergence for the series $\displaystyle\sum_{n=0}^{\infty} \frac{(x + 2)^n}{n + 1}$.

(A) $-3 < x < -1$

(B) $-3 \leq x \leq -1$

(C) $-3 < x \leq -1$

(D) $-3 \leq x < -1$

Need More Help With . . .   *See . . .*

Power series?   *Calculus*, Section 10.1

Ratio Test?   *Calculus*, Section 10.4

Error Bounds

• Determine or estimate the sum of a series. (LO 4.1B)
• Construct and use Taylor polynomials. (LO 4.2A)

Overview

When approximating the sum of an infinite series, error estimation is an important skill. Two error estimation methods that are found often on the AP* Calculus Exam are the Alternating Series Error Bound and the Lagrange Error Bound. The first error bound method is used with convergent alternating series and the second method is used with convergent Taylor series.

Content and Practice

Alternating Series Error Bound

If the terms of a series have the following three properties:

1. the terms alternate in sign;

2. the terms decrease in absolute value;

3. the terms approach 0 as a limit;

then the series converges, and the truncation error after n terms is less than the absolute value of the first unused term and has the same sign as the first unused term.

Lagrange Error Bound

If a Taylor polynomial $P_n(x) = f(a) + f'(a)(x - a) +$

$\dfrac{f''(a)}{2!}(x - a)^2 + \cdots + \dfrac{f''(a)}{n!}(x - a)^n$ is used to approximate a function $f(x)$, then the truncation error involved in using this approximation is $\dfrac{f^{(n+1)}(c)}{(n + 1)!}(x - a)^{n+1}$ for some c between a and x.

When using this truncation error formula you will know n, a, and x but you won't know c. However, you can still find an upper bound for the error if you can find an upper bound for $f^{(n+1)}(c)$ for all c between a and x. The upper bound for the error is called a *Lagrange Error Bound*.

1. Show that $1 - \dfrac{1}{3!}$ approximates $\displaystyle\sum_{n=0}^{\infty} \dfrac{(-1)^n}{(2n+1)!}$ with an error less than $\dfrac{1}{100}$. Is the approximation an overestimate or an underestimate?

2. A second-order approximation for e^x on the domain $|x| \le 0.5$ is $e^x \approx 1 + x + \dfrac{x^2}{2!}$. Find a Lagrange Error Bound for the approximation. (*Hint:* $n = 2$, $a = 0$, and all the derivatives for e^x are e^x.)

3. A third-order Taylor polynomial is used to approximate $f(x)$ about $x = 2$ on the interval $[1, 3]$. If $f^{(4)}(x) < 1.65$ for all x in the interval $[1, 3]$, show that $|f(x) - P_4(x)| < 0.07$.

Additional Practice

1. Consider the infinite series $\displaystyle\sum_{n=1}^{\infty} 4\left(\dfrac{-1}{3}\right)^{n-1}$. How many terms are required in the partial sum to approximate the sum of the infinite series with an alternating series error bound less than 0.001?

2. The hyperbolic sine is defined as $\sinh x = \dfrac{e^x - e^{-x}}{2}$. A third-order Taylor polynomial approximation is $\sinh x \approx x + \dfrac{x^3}{3!}$. If this is used to approximate $\sinh x$ for $|x| < 2$, which is the Lagrange Error Bound?

(A) 4.836

(B) 3.627

(C) 2.718

(D) 2.418

3. What is the smallest order of Taylor polynomial centered at $x = 1$ that will approximate e^{x-1} on the domain $-1 \leq x \leq 3$ with Lagrange Error Bound less than 1?

(A) 3

(B) 5

(C) 7

(D) 9

***Need More Help With* . . .**

Error bounds?

***See* . . .**

Calculus, Section 10.3

Part III

Practice Examinations

Calculus AB—Exam 1

Section I, Part A

Time: 60 minutes
Number of questions: 30

NO CALCULATOR MAY BE USED IN THIS PART OF THE EXAMINATION.

<u>Directions:</u> Solve each of the following problems. After examining the form of the choices, decide which is the best of the choices given.

<u>In this test:</u> Unless otherwise specified, the domain of a function f is assumed to be the set of all real numbers x for which $f(x)$ is a real number.

1. Let f be the function defined below, where a and b are constants. If f is differentiable at $x = 3$, what is the value of $a - b$?

$$f(x) = \begin{cases} ax - b & \text{for } x < 3 \\ x^2 + bx & \text{for } x \geq 3 \end{cases}$$

   (A) 6   (B) 9   (C) 15   (D) 24

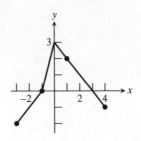

2. The graph of a piecewise-linear function f, for $-3 \leq x \leq 4$, is shown above. If $g(x) = \int_{-1}^{x} f(t)\, dt$, which of the following values is the least?

   (A) $g(-3)$ (B) $g(0)$ (C) $g(1)$ (D) $g(4)$

3. $\int_{2}^{3} \dfrac{1}{x^3}\, dx =$

   (A) $-\dfrac{5}{72}$ (B) $-\dfrac{5}{36}$ (C) $\dfrac{5}{144}$ (D) $\dfrac{5}{72}$

221

4. f is continuous for $a \leq x \leq b$ but not differentiable for some c such that $a < c < b$. Which of the following could be true?

(A) $x = c$ is a vertical asymptote of the graph of f.

(B) $\lim\limits_{x \to c} f(x) \neq f(c)$

(C) The graph of f has a cusp at $x = c$.

(D) $f(c)$ is undefined.

5. $\int_{\pi/2}^{x} \cos t \, dt =$

(A) $-\sin x$ (B) $-\sin x - 1$

(C) $\sin x - 1$ (D) $1 - \sin x$

6. If $x^3 + 2x^2 y - 4y = 7$, then when $x = 1, \dfrac{dy}{dx} =$

(A) -8 (B) $-\dfrac{9}{2}$

(C) -3 (D) $\dfrac{7}{2}$

7. $\int_{1}^{e^2} \dfrac{x^3 + 1}{x} \, dx =$

(A) $\dfrac{1}{3} e^6 + \dfrac{5}{3}$ (B) $\dfrac{1}{3} e^6 - \dfrac{1}{2e^2} + \dfrac{1}{6}$

(C) $\dfrac{1}{3} e^6 - \dfrac{1}{2e^4} + \dfrac{1}{6}$ (D) $\dfrac{1}{3} e^6 + \dfrac{7}{3}$

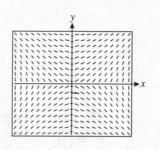

8. Shown above is a slope field for which of the following differential equations?

(A) $\dfrac{dy}{dx} = x - y$ (B) $\dfrac{dy}{dx} = \dfrac{x}{y}$

(C) $\dfrac{dy}{dx} = x + 1$ (D) $\dfrac{dy}{dx} = xy$

9. $\displaystyle\lim_{x\to\pi/2}\frac{1+\sin 3x}{1-\cos 4x}=$

(A) $-\dfrac{9}{16}$ (B) $-\dfrac{3}{4}$ (C) 0 (D) $\dfrac{9}{16}$

10. What is the instantaneous rate of change at $x=3$ of the function f given by $f(x)=\dfrac{x^2-2}{x+1}$?

(A) $-\dfrac{17}{16}$ (B) $-\dfrac{1}{8}$ (C) $\dfrac{13}{16}$ (D) $\dfrac{17}{16}$

11. If f is a linear function where $0<a<b$ and m is a nonzero constant, then $\int_b^a f''(x)\,dx=$

(A) 0 (B) $\dfrac{ab}{2}$ (C) $m(a-b)$ (D) $\dfrac{a^2-b^2}{2}$

12. If $f(x)=\begin{cases}\ln(3x) & \text{for } 0<x\le 3\\ x\ln 3 & \text{for } 3<x\le 4\end{cases}$, then $\displaystyle\lim_{x\to 3}f(x)$ is

(A) $\ln 9$ (B) $\ln 27$

(C) $3\ln 3$ (D) nonexistent

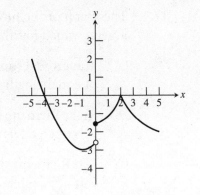

13. The graph of the function f shown in the figure has a horizontal tangent at the point $(-1,-3)$ and a cusp at $(2,0)$. For what values of x, $-5<x<5$, is f not differentiable?

(A) 0 only   (B) 0 and 2 only

(C) -1 and 0 only   (D) $-1, 0,$ and 2

14. A particle moves along the x-axis with velocity given by $v(t) = 3t^2 + 5t - 2$ for $t \geq 0$. If the particle is at position $x = 3$ at time $t = 0$, what is the position of the particle at time $t = 1$?

(A) 1.5   (B) 4.5   (C) 6   (D) 11

15. If $F(x) = \int_1^{x^2} \sqrt{t^2 + 3}\, dt$, then $F'(2) =$

(A) $\sqrt{7}$ (B) $4\sqrt{7}$ (C) $2\sqrt{19}$ (D) $4\sqrt{19}$

16. If $f(x) = \cos(e^{2x})$, then $f'(x) =$

(A) $-2\sin(e^{2x})$ (B) $-2e^{2x}\sin(e^{2x})$

(C) $2\sin(e^{2x})$ (D) $\sin(e^{2x})$

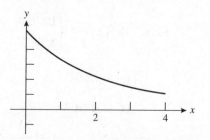

17. The graph of the function f for $0 \leq x \leq 4$ is shown above. Of the following, which has the greatest value?

(A) Trapezoidal sum approximation of $\int_0^4 f(x)\,dx$ with 4 subintervals of equal length

(B) Right Riemann sum approximation of $\int_0^4 f(x)\,dx$ with 4 subintervals of equal length

(C) Left Riemann sum approximation of $\int_0^4 f(x)\,dx$ with 4 subintervals of equal length

(D) $\int_0^4 f(x)\,dx$

18. An equation of the line tangent to the graph of $y = 3x - \cos x$ at $x = 0$ is

(A) $y = 2x$ (B) $y = 2x - 1$

(C) $y = 3x + 1$ (D) $y = 3x - 1$

19. If $f''(x) = (x - 1)(x + 2)^3(x - 4)^2$, then the graph of f has inflection points when $x =$

    (A) 1 only   (B) 1 and 4 only

    (C) −2 and 1 only   (D) −2, 1, and 4

20. If $\int_2^{-3} f(x)dx = -13$ and $\int_5^{-3} f(x)dx = -10$, what is the value of $\int_2^5 f(x)dx$?

    (A) −23   (B) −3

    (C) 3   (D) 23

21. If $\dfrac{dy}{dt} = my$ and m is a nonzero constant, then y could be

    (A) $4e^{mty}$ (B) $4e^{mt}$

    (C) $e^{mt} + 4$ (D) $\dfrac{m}{2}y^2 + 4$

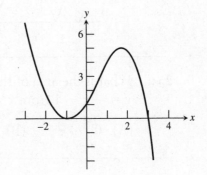

22. The graph of the function f shown above has horizontal tangents at $x = -1$ and $x = \frac{5}{3}$. Let g be the function defined by $g(x) = \int_0^x f(t)dt$. For what values of x does the graph of g have a point of inflection?

    (A) 0 only   (B) $\dfrac{5}{3}$ only

    (C) 3 only   (D) -1 and $\dfrac{5}{3}$

23. The minimum acceleration attained on the interval $0 \le t \le 4$ by the particle whose velocity is given by $v(t) = t^3 - 4t^2 - 3t + 2$ is

    (A) −16   (B) −10   (C) $-\dfrac{25}{3}$ (D) −3

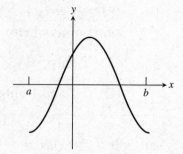

24. The graph of f is shown in the figure above. Which of the following could be the graph of the derivative of f?

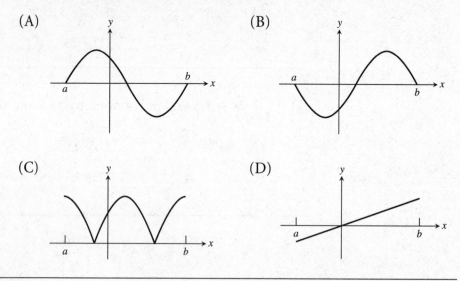

(A)

(B)

(C)

(D)

25. What is the area of the region between the graphs of $y = x^3$ and $y = -x - 1$ from $x = 0$ to $x = 2$?

(A) 0   (B) 4   (C) 5   (D) 8

x	-1	0	1	2	3
$f'(x)$	-3	2	0	4	2

26. The polynomial function f has selected values of its first derivative f' given in the table above. Which of the following statements must be true?

(A) f changes concavity at least twice on the interval $(-1, 3)$.

(B) f has a local minimum at $x = 1$.

(C) f is increasing on the interval $(1, 3)$.

(D) f has a local maximum at $x = 2$.

27. What is the average value of $y = x^3\sqrt{x^4 + 9}$ on the interval $[0, 2]$?

    (A) $\dfrac{98}{3}$ (B) $\dfrac{49}{3}$ (C) $\dfrac{125}{12}$ (D) $\dfrac{49}{6}$

28. If $f(x) = \tan(3x)$, then $f'\left(\dfrac{\pi}{9}\right) =$

    (A) $\dfrac{4}{3}$ (B) 4   (C) 12   (D) $6\sqrt{3}$

29. The side of a cube is increasing at a constant rate of 0.2 centimeter per second. In terms of the surface area S, what is the rate of change of the volume of the cube, in square centimeters per second?

    (A) $0.1S$ (B) $0.2S$ (C) $0.6S$ (D) $0.04S$

30. A particle moves along a straight line. The graph of the particle's position $x(t)$ at time t for $0 < t < 8$ is shown above. The graph has horizontal tangents at $t = 1$ and $t = \dfrac{17}{3}$ and a point of inflection at $t = \dfrac{10}{3}$. For what values of t is the velocity of the particle decreasing?

    (A) $0 < t < \dfrac{10}{3}$ (B) $1 < t < \dfrac{17}{3}$

    (C) $4 < t < 7$ (D) $\dfrac{10}{3} < t < 8$

⬧ **End of Part A of Section I** ⬧

Calculus AB—Exam 1
Section I, Part B

Time: 45 minutes
Number of questions: 15

A GRAPHING CALCULATOR IS REQUIRED FOR SOME QUESTIONS IN THIS PART OF THE EXAMINATION.

<u>Directions:</u> Solve each of the following problems. After examining the form of the choices, decide which is the best of the choices given.

<u>In this test:</u>

1. The exact numerical value of the correct answer does not always appear among the choices given. When this happens, select from among the choices the number that best approximates the exact numerical value.

2. Unless otherwise specified, the domain of a function f is assumed to be the set of all real numbers x for which $f(x)$ is a real number.

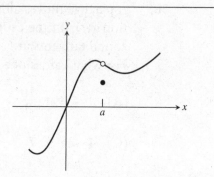

31. The graph of a function f is shown above. Which of the following statements about f is false?

    (A) $\lim\limits_{x \to a} f(x)$ exists.

    (B) f has a relative minimum at $x = a$.

    (C) $f(a)$ exists.

    (D) f is continuous at $x = a$.

32. Let $f(x) = 2e^{3x}$ and $g(x) = 5x^3$. At what value of x do the graphs of f and g have parallel tangents?

    (A) -0.366 (B) -0.344 (C) -0.251 (D) -0.165

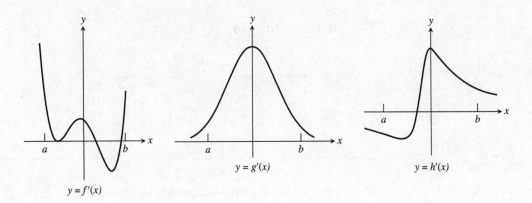

$y = f'(x)$

$y = g'(x)$

$y = h'(x)$

33. The graphs of the derivatives of the functions f, g, and h are shown above. Which of the functions f, g, or h have a relative minimum on the open interval $a < x < b$?

(A) g only

(B) h only

(C) f and h only

(D) f, g, and h

34. The first derivative of the function f is given by $f'(x) = \dfrac{\sin^2 x}{x} - \dfrac{2}{9}$. How many critical values does f have on the open interval $(0, 10)$?

(A) Two

(B) Three

(C) Four

(D) Six

35. Let f be the function given by $f(x) = x^{2/3}$. Which of the following statements about f are true?

   I. f is continuous at $x = 0$.
   II. f is differentiable at $x = 0$.
   III. f has an absolute minimum at $x = 0$.

(A) I only

(B) II only

(C) I and II only

(D) I and III only

36. If f is a continuous function and if $F'(x) = f(x)$ for all real numbers x, then $\int_{-1}^{2} f(3x)\,dx =$

(A) $3F(2) - 3F(-1)$

(B) $\dfrac{1}{3}F(2) - \dfrac{1}{3}F(-1)$

(C) $3F(6) - 3F(-3)$

(D) $\dfrac{1}{3}F(6) - \dfrac{1}{3}F(-3)$

37. If $a \neq 0$, then $\displaystyle\lim_{x \to a} \frac{x^3 - a^3}{a^6 - x^6}$ is

(A) nonexistent

(B) $-\dfrac{1}{2a^3}$

(C) 0

(D) $\dfrac{1}{2a^3}$

---

38. Population P grows according to the equation $\dfrac{dP}{dt} = kP$, where k is a constant and t is measured in years. If the population doubles every 12 years, then the value of k is

(A) 0.058   (B) 0.279   (C) 0.693   (D) 1.792

---

x	1	3	6	9
$f(x)$	15	25	40	30

39. The function f is continuous on the closed interval $[1, 9]$ and has values that are given in the table above. Using the subintervals $[1, 3]$, $[3, 6]$, and $[6, 9]$, what is the trapezoidal approximation of $\int_1^9 f(x)dx$?

(A) 110

(B) 175

(C) 242.5

(D) 262.5

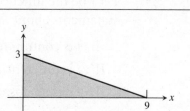

40. The base of a solid is a region in the first quadrant bounded by the x-axis, the y-axis, and the line $x + 3y = 9$, as shown in the figure above. If cross sections of the solid perpendicular to the y-axis are isosceles right triangles with the hypotenuses in the xy-plane, what is the volume of the solid?

(A) 6.75   (B) 13.5   (C) 20.25   (D) 40.5

41. Which of the following is an equation of the line tangent to the graph of $f(x) = x^6 - x^4$ at the point where $f'(x) = -1$?

(A) $y = -x - 1.031$

(B) $y = -x - 0.836$

(C) $y = -x + 0.934$

(D) $y = -x + 1.031$

42. Let $G(x)$ be an antiderivative of $f(x)$. If $G(2) = 3$, then $G(8) =$

(A) $f'(8)$

(B) $3 + f'(8)$

(C) $\int_2^8 (3 + f(t))dt$

(D) $3 + \int_2^8 f(t)dt$

43. A particle moves along a straight line with velocity given by $v(t) = 5 + 1.492^{-t^3}$ at time $t \geq 0$. What is the acceleration of the particle at time $t = 2$?

(A) -0.196 (B) 0.7433 (C) 5.041 (D) 11.205

44. Let f be a function that is differentiable on the open interval $(-3, 7)$. If $f(-1) = 4$, $f(2) = -5$, and $f(6) = 8$, which of the following must be true?

 I. For some c, $-1 < c < 2$, $f'(c) = -3$.

 II. f has a relative minimum at $x = 2$.

 III. For some c, $2 < c < 6$, $f(c) = 4$.

(A) I only

(B) I and II only

(C) I and III only

(D) I, II, and III

45. If $0 \leq k \leq \dfrac{\pi}{2}$ and the area under the curve $y = \sin x$ from $x = k$ to $x = \dfrac{\pi}{2}$ is 0.75, then $k =$

(A) 0.253 (B) 0.723 (C) 0.848 (D) 1.318

Calculus AB—Exam 1
Section II, Part A

Time: 30 minutes
Number of problems: 2

A GRAPHING CALCULATOR IS REQUIRED FOR SOME PROBLEMS IN THIS PART OF THE EXAMINATION.

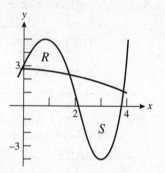

1. Let f and g be the functions defined by
    $f(x) = 0.5x^4 - 2.2x^3 + 4x + 2.75$ and $g(x) = 2.75 \cos\left(\frac{x}{\pi}\right)$. Let R and S be the two regions enclosed by the graphs of f and g shown in the figure above.

    (a) Find the sum of the areas of the regions R and S.

    (b) Find the volume of the solid generated when R is rotated about the x-axis.

    (c) The region S is the base of a solid whose cross sections perpendicular to the x-axis are squares. Find the volume of the solid.

2. For $0 \leq t \leq 4$, a particle is moving along the x-axis. The velocity of the particle is given by $v(t) = 3\cos(e^{t/2}) + 1.5$. The acceleration of the particle is given by $a(t) = -\frac{3}{2}e^{t/2}\sin(e^{t/2})$ and $x(0) = 2.7$.

(a) Is the speed of the particle increasing or decreasing at time $t = 2.4$? Give a reason for your answer.

(b) Find the average velocity of the particle for the time period $0 \leq t \leq 4$.

(c) Find the total distance traveled by the particle from time $t = 0$ to $t = 4$.

(d) For $0 \leq t \leq 4$, the particle changes direction twice. Find the position of the particle at the time when it changes from moving left to moving right.

✧ **End of Part A of Section II** ✧

Calculus AB—Exam 1
Section II, Part B

Time: 60 minutes
Number of problems: 4

NO CALCULATOR MAY BE USED IN THIS PART OF THE EXAMINATION.

T (days)	0	1	3	4	6
$h(t)$ (cm)	5.1	6.8	11	13.5	20.1

3. Jill bought an amaryllis plant hoping it would soon bloom. She decided to chart its growth before it flowered. The length of a leaf is modeled by a differentiable function h that is increasing and concave up for $0 \le t \le 6$. The table above gives selected values of $h(t)$, where t is measured in days and $h(t)$ is measured in centimeters.

    (a) Use the data in the table to estimate $h'(3.5)$. Show the computations that lead to your answer.

    (b) Using correct units, explain the meaning of $\frac{1}{6}\int_0^6 h(t)dt$ in the context of this problem. Use a right Riemann sum with the four subintervals indicated by the table to estimate $\frac{1}{6}\int_0^6 h(t)dt$.

    (c) Is your approximation in part (b) greater than or less than $\frac{1}{6}\int_0^6 h(t)dt$? Give a reason for your answer.

    (d) Evaluate $\int_0^6 h'(t)dt$. Explain the meaning of this expression.

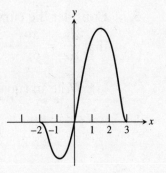

4.   The figure above shows the graph of f', the derivative of a twice-differentiable function f, on the interval $[-2, 3]$. The graph of f' has horizontal tangents at $x = -2$, $x = -0.8$, $x = 1.4$, and $x = 3$. The areas of the regions bounded by the x-axis and the graph of f' on the intervals $[-2, 0]$ and $[0, 3]$ are 2 and 7 respectively.

(a) Find all x-coordinates at which f has a relative minimum. Give a reason for your answer.

(b) On what open intervals contained in $-2 < x < 3$ is the graph of f both concave up and increasing? Give a reason for your answer.

(c) Find the x-coordinates of all points of inflection for the graph of f. Give a reason for your answer.

(d) Given that $f(0) = 9$, write an expression for $f(x)$ that involves an integral. Find $f(-2)$ and $f(3)$.

5. Consider the curve given by $x^2 + 3y^2 = 1 + 3xy$. It can be shown that $\dfrac{dy}{dx} = \dfrac{3y - 2x}{6y - 3x}$.

(a) Write an equation for the line tangent to the curve at the point $(1, 1)$.

(b) Find the coordinates of all points on the curve at which the line tangent to the curve at that point is vertical.

(c) Evaluate $\dfrac{d^2y}{dx^2}$ at the point on the curve where $x = 1$ and $y = 1$.

6. Consider the differential equation $\dfrac{dy}{dx} = x^2(2y + 1)$.

(a) On the axes provided, sketch a slope field for the given differential equation at the nine points indicated.

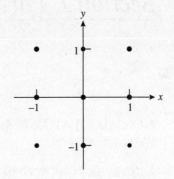

(b) While the slope field in part (a) is drawn at only nine points, it is defined at every point in the xy-plane. Describe all points in the xy-plane for which the slopes are positive.

(c) Find the particular solution $y = f(x)$ to the given differential equation with the initial condition $f(0) = 5$.

Calculus AB—Exam 2

Section I, Part A

Time: 60 minutes
Number of questions: 30

NO CALCULATOR MAY BE USED IN THIS PART OF THE EXAMINATION.

<u>Directions:</u> Solve each of the following problems. After examining the form of the choices, decide which is the best of the choices given.

<u>In this test:</u> Unless otherwise specified, the domain of a function f is assumed to be the set of all real numbers x for which $f(x)$ is a real number.

---

1. $\int_1^3 (3x^2 - 4x)\, dx =$

   (A) 4   (B) 8

   (C) 10   (D) 12

---

2. If $f(x) = x\sqrt{4x - 1}$, then $f'(x)$ is

   (A) $\dfrac{6x - 1}{\sqrt{4x - 1}}$ (B) $\dfrac{2x}{\sqrt{4x - 1}}$

   (C) $\dfrac{-6x + 2}{\sqrt{4x - 1}}$ (D) $\dfrac{9x - 2}{2\sqrt{4x - 1}}$

---

3. If $\int_a^b g(x)\, dx = 4a + b$, then $\int_a^b (g(x) + 7)\, dx =$

   (A) $8b + 11a$ (B) $8b - 3a$

   (C) $7b - 7a$ (D) $4a + b + 7$

4. If $f(x) = -x^5 + x + \dfrac{1}{x^2}$, then $f'(-1) =$

(A) 8   (B) -2

(C) -3 (D) -8

---

5. $y = 5x^4 - 24x^3 + 24x^2 + 17$ is concave down for

(A) $x < 0$ (B) $x < -2$ or $x > -\dfrac{2}{5}$

(C) $x < \dfrac{2}{5}$ or $x > 2$ (D) $\dfrac{2}{5} < x < 2$

---

6. $\dfrac{1}{3}\int e^{t/3}\, dt =$

(A) $3e^{t/3} + C$ (B) $e^{t/3} + C$

(C) $e^{-2t/3} + C$ (D) $e^{-t} + C$

---

7. $\dfrac{d}{dx}\cos^3(x^2) =$

(A) $\sin^3(x^2)$ (B) $6x\sin(x^2)\cos^2(x^2)$

(C) $-3\sin(x^2)\cos^2(x^2)$ (D) $-6x\sin(x^2)\cos^2(x^2)$

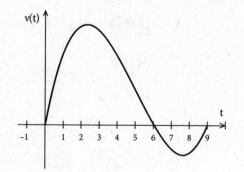

8. A spider begins to crawl up a vertical blade of grass at time $t = 0$. The velocity v of the spider at time t, $0 \le t \le 9$, is given by the function whose graph is shown above. Which of the following expressions measures the total distance the spider traveled from $t = 0$ to $t = 9$?

(A) $\int_0^9 v(t)dt$

(B) $\frac{1}{9}\int_0^9 v(t)dt$

(C) $\int_0^6 v(t)dt - \int_6^9 v(t)dt$

(D) $\left|\int_0^9 v(t)dt\right|$

9. The slope field above is for which of the following differential equations?

(A) $\dfrac{dy}{dx} = (x + 2)^2$

(B) $\dfrac{dy}{dx} = x^2 - 2x$

(C) $\dfrac{dy}{dx} = xy - 2y$

(D) $\dfrac{dy}{dx} = xy - 2x$

10. An equation of the line tangent to the graph of $y = \cos(3x)$ at $x = \dfrac{\pi}{6}$ is

(A) $y = 3\left(x - \dfrac{\pi}{6}\right)$

(B) $y = -\left(x - \dfrac{\pi}{6}\right)$

(C) $y = -3\left(x - \dfrac{\pi}{6}\right)$

(D) $y - 1 = -\left(x - \dfrac{\pi}{6}\right)$

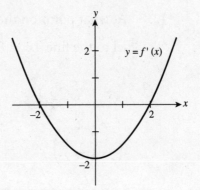

11. The graph of the derivative of *f* is shown in the figure above. Which of the following could be the graph of *f*?

(A)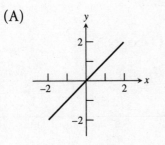

(B)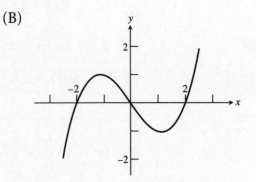

(C)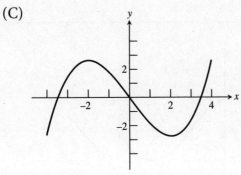

(D)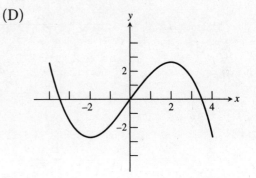

12. At what point on the graph of $y = \frac{1}{2}x^2 - \frac{3}{2}$ is the tangent line parallel to the line $4x - 8y = 5$?

(A) $\left(\frac{1}{2}, -\frac{3}{8}\right)$ (B) $\left(\frac{1}{2}, -\frac{11}{8}\right)$

(C) $\left(2, \frac{1}{2}\right)$ (D) $\left(-\frac{1}{2}, -\frac{11}{8}\right)$

---

13. Let f be a function defined for all real numbers x. If $f'(x) = \dfrac{\left|9 - x^2\right|}{x - 3}$, then f is decreasing on the interval

(A) $(-\infty, 3)$ (B) $(-\infty, \infty)$

(C) $(-3, \infty)$ (D) $(3, \infty)$

---

14. If $\dfrac{dy}{dx} = 4xy$ and $y(0) = 5$, find $y(1)$

(A) $\sqrt{29}$ (B) $20e$ (C) $5e$ (D) $5e^2$

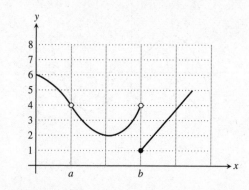

15. The graph of the function f is shown in the figure above. Which of the following statements about f is true?

(A) $\displaystyle\lim_{x \to a} f(x) = 4$ (B) $\displaystyle\lim_{x \to b} f(x) = 4$

(C) $\displaystyle\lim_{x \to b} f(x) = 1$ (D) $\displaystyle\lim_{x \to a} f(x)$ does not exist

16. The area of the region enclosed by the graph of $y = x^2 + 2$ and the line $y = 11$ is

(A) 18 (B) 30 (C) 36 (D) 72

17. If $x^2 = 25 - y^2$, what is the value of $\dfrac{d^2y}{dx^2}$ at the point $(3, 4)$?

(A) $\dfrac{-25}{64}$ (B) $\dfrac{-7}{64}$

(C) $\dfrac{25}{64}$ (D) $\dfrac{4}{3}$

18. $\displaystyle\int_{\pi/4}^{\pi/2} \dfrac{-e^{\cot x}}{\sin^2 x}\, dx$ is

(A) $-e$ (B) $1 - e$

(C) 0 (D) $1 + e$

19. If $f(x) = \ln|1 - x^2|$, then $f'(x) =$

(A) $\dfrac{-2|x|}{1 - x^2}$ (B) $\dfrac{-2x}{1 - x^2}$

(C) $\dfrac{1}{1 - x^2}$ (D) $\left|\dfrac{-2x}{1 - x^2}\right|$

20. The average value of $f(x) = -\sin x$ on the interval $[-2, 4]$ is

(A) $\dfrac{\cos 4 + \cos 2}{6}$ (B) $\dfrac{\cos 4 + \cos 2}{2}$

(C) $\dfrac{\cos 4 - \cos 2}{2}$ (D) $\dfrac{\cos 4 - \cos 2}{6}$

21. $\lim\limits_{x \to 1} \dfrac{\ln x}{3x}$

   (A) 0 (B) e

   (C) 3 (D) nonexistent

22. What are all values of x for which the function defined by $f(x) = (x^2 - 15)e^{-x}$ is increasing?

   (A) There are no such values of x.
   (B) $x < -3$ and $x > 5$
   (C) $-5 < x < 3$
   (D) $-3 < x < 5$

23. If the region enclosed by the y-axis, the line $y = 2$, and the curve $y = \sqrt[3]{x}$ is revolved about the y-axis, the volume of the solid generated is

   (A) 4π (B) 8π

   (C) $\dfrac{64\pi}{7}$ (D) $\dfrac{128\pi}{7}$

24. The expression
   $$\frac{1}{30}\left(\sin\left(\frac{1}{30}\right) + \sin\left(\frac{2}{30}\right) + \sin\left(\frac{3}{30}\right) + \cdots + \sin\left(\frac{30}{30}\right)\right)$$
   is a Riemann sum approximation for

   (A) $\int_0^1 \sin\left(\dfrac{x}{30}\right) dx$ (B) $\int_0^1 \sin x \, dx$

   (C) $\dfrac{1}{30}\int_0^1 \sin\left(\dfrac{x}{30}\right) dx$ (D) $\int_{1/30}^1 \sin x \, dx$

25. $\int x \sin(x^2)\, dx =$

   (A) $-\dfrac{1}{2}\cos(x^2) + C$ (B) $\dfrac{1}{2}\cos(x^2) + C$

   (C) $-x^2 \cos(x^2) + C$ (D) $x^2 \cos(x^2) + C$

26. Let $f(x) = \lim_{h \to 0} \dfrac{(x + h)^2 - x^2}{h}$. For what value of x does $f(x) = 4$?

   (A) -2 (B) -1

   (C) 2 (D) 4

27. Let $f(x) = \begin{cases} 3x^2 - 5 & \text{for } x \leq 1 \\ 6x + 2 & \text{for } x > 1 \end{cases}$

   Which of the following are true statements about this function?

   I. $\lim_{x \to 1} f(x)$ exists.

   II. $\lim_{x \to 1} f'(x)$ exists.

   III. $f'(1)$ exists.

   (A) II only   (B) III only

   (C) II and III   (D) I, II, and III

28. Let $g(x) = \dfrac{d}{dx}\displaystyle\int_0^x \sqrt{t^2 + 9}$. What is $g(-4)$?

   (A) -3 (B) 3

   (C) 4 (D) 5

29. Evaluate $\lim_{x \to \pi/2} \dfrac{1 - \sin x}{1 + \cos 2x}$

   (A) $-\dfrac{1}{4}$ (B) 0 (C) $\dfrac{1}{4}$ (D) 1

30. For what value of k, if any, is the function $f(x) = \begin{cases} 2x^2 + 7 & x < -1 \\ kx + 4 & x \geq -1 \end{cases}$ differentiable at $x = -1$?

   (A) -4 (B) -5 (C) 5 (D) There is no such value of k.

❖ **End of Part A of Section I** ❖

Calculus AB—Exam 2
Section I, Part B

Time: 45 minutes
Number of questions: 15

A GRAPHING CALCULATOR IS REQUIRED FOR SOME QUESTIONS IN THIS PART OF THE EXAMINATION.

<u>Directions:</u> Solve each of the following problems. After examining the form of the choices, decide which is the best of the choices given.

<u>In this test:</u>

1. The exact numerical value of the correct answer does not always appear among the choices given. When this happens, select from among the choices the number that best approximates the exact numerical value.
2. Unless otherwise specified, the domain of a function f is assumed to be the set of all real numbers x for which $f(x)$ is a real number.

---

31. If $f(x) = \dfrac{e^{3x}}{3x}$, then $f'(x) =$

(A) e^{3x}

(B) $\dfrac{e^{3x}(1 - 3x)}{3x^2}$

(C) $\dfrac{e^{3x}(3x + 1)}{3x^2}$

(D) $\dfrac{e^{3x}(3x - 1)}{3x^2}$

32. The graph of the function $y = \frac{1}{3}x^3 - x^2 - 5x + 3 \sin x$ changes concavity at $x =$

(A) 3.29   (B) 2.21   (C) 1.34   (D) -0.39

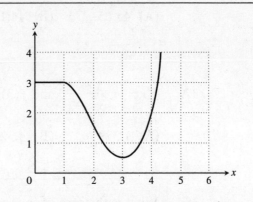

33. The graph of f is shown in the figure above. If $\int_1^4 f(x)\, dx = 3.8$ and $F'(x) = f(x)$, then $F(4) - F(0) =$

(A) 0.8   (B) 2.8

(C) 4.8   (D) 6.8

34. Let $f(x) = e^{\sin x}$ on the interval $1 \leq x \leq 3$. The Mean Value Theorem guarantees the existence of a value c, where $1 \leq c \leq 3$, such that $f'(c) =$

(A) -0.584 (B) -0.389

(C) 0   (D) 2.212

35. Let f be the function given by $f(x) = 5e^{3x^3}$. For what positive value of a is the slope of the line tangent to the graph of f at $(a, f(a))$ equal to 6?

(A) 0.142   (B) 0.344

(C) 0.393   (D) 0.714

36. Two roads cross at right angles, one running north/south and the other east/west. Eighty feet south of the intersection is an old radio tower. A car traveling at 50 feet per second passes through the intersection heading east. At how many feet per second is the car moving away from the radio tower 3 seconds after it passes through the intersection?

   (A) 43.65   (B) 44.12   (C) 44.59   (D) 56.67

37. $f'(x) = \dfrac{3 + 2x}{x^2 + 1}$ and $f(3) = 12$. Find $f(5)$.

   (A) 1.329   (B) 4.329   (C) 12.5   (D) 13.329

38. What is the area of the region in the first quadrant enclosed by the graphs of $y = \sin x$, $y = 2 - x$, and the y-axis?

   (A) 1.048   (B) 0.985   (C) 0.951   (D) 0.584

39. The base of a solid S is the region enclosed by the graph of $y = \sqrt{\ln(x - 1)}$, the line $x = 2e$, and the x-axis. If the cross sections of S perpendicular to the x-axis are squares, then the volume of S is

   (A) 1.587   (B) 3.173   (C) 3.185   (D) 3.501

40. If the derivative of f is given by $f'(x) = 2e^x - 5x^2$, at which of the following values of x does f have a relative maximum value?

   (A) −0.494   (B) 0.259   (C) 1.092   (D) 3.310

41. Let $f(x) = \sqrt{2x}$. If the rate of change of f at $x = c$ is four times its rate of change at $x = 1$, then $c =$

   (A) $\dfrac{1}{16}$ (B) $\dfrac{1}{2\sqrt{2}}$ (C) $\dfrac{1}{\sqrt{2}}$ (D) 1

42. At time $t \geq 0$, the acceleration of a particle that is moving along the x-axis is $a(t) = t + 2 \sin t$. At $t = 0$, the velocity of the particle is -4. For what value of t will the velocity of the particle be zero?

(A) 0   (B) 1.78   (C) 2.31   (D) 3.87

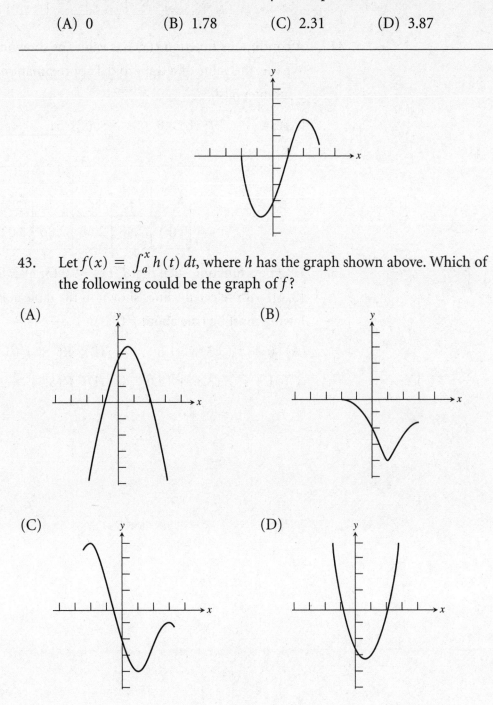

43. Let $f(x) = \int_a^x h(t)\, dt$, where h has the graph shown above. Which of the following could be the graph of f?

(A)

(B)

(C)

(D)

x	0	3	5	7
$f(x)$	8	4	5	8

44. A continuous function $f(x)$ has values as shown in the table above. What is the value of a trapezoidal approximation of $\int_0^3 f(x)\,dx$ using 3 subintervals?

(A) 34   (B) 40   (C) 51   (D) 80

x	3.2	3.3	3.4	3.5
$f(x)$	2.48	2.68	2.86	3.03

45. Let f be a function such that $f''(x) < 0$ for all x in the closed interval $[3, 4]$, with selected values shown in the table above. Which of the following must be true about $f'(3.3)$?

(A) $0 < f'(3.3) < 1.6$ (B) $1.6 < f'(3.3) < 1.8$

(C) $1.8 < f'(3.3) < 2.0$ (D) $f'(3.3) > 2.0$

Calculus AB—Exam 2
Section II, Part A

Time: 30 minutes
Number of problems: 2

A GRAPHING CALCULATOR IS REQUIRED FOR SOME PROBLEMS IN THIS PART OF THE EXAMINATION.

1. A security company shreds unwanted documents for other companies to protect their privacy. During a given day, the rate at which paper arrives at the shredder (in cubic feet per hour) is modeled by

    $G(t) = 110 - 90 \sin\left(\dfrac{t^2}{14}\right)$, where t is measured in hours and

    $0 \leq t \leq 8$. At the beginning of the day, the shredder already has 300 cubic feet of paper waiting to be shredded from the previous day. During the hours of operation, $0 \leq t \leq 8$, paper is shredded at a constant rate of 75 cubic feet per hour.

    (a) Find $G'(6)$. Using correct units, interpret your answer in the context of the problem.

    (b) Find the total amount of unshredded paper that arrives at the shredder during this day.

    (c) During what time interval(s) is the amount of unshredded paper at the shredder decreasing? Show the work that leads to your answer.

    (d) If the amount of unshredded paper exceeds 400 cubic feet at any time during the day, the shredders will have to be shut down. Will this happen on the day described? Justify your answer.

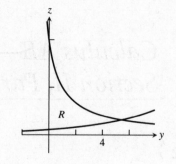

2. Let $f(x) = 2^{0.3x}$ and $g(x) = \dfrac{20}{x+1}$. Let R be the region in the first quadrant enclosed by the y-axis and the graphs of f and g, as shown in the figure above.

(a) Find the area of R.

(b) Find the volume of the solid generated when R is rotated about the horizontal line $y = -3$.

(c) The region R is the base of a solid. For this solid, each cross section perpendicular to the x-axis is a rectangle whose height is 3 times the length of its base in region R. Find the volume of this solid.

❖ **End of Part A of Section II** ❖

Calculus AB—Exam 2
Section II, Part B

Time: 60 minutes
Number of problems: 4

NO CALCULATOR MAY BE USED IN THIS PART OF THE EXAMINATION.

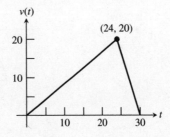

3. A speedboat travels in a straight line. For $0 \leq t \leq 30$ seconds, the boat's velocity $v(t)$, in meters per second, is modeled by the piecewise-linear function defined by the graph above.

    (a) Find $\int_0^{30} v(t)dt$. Using correct units, explain the meaning of this quantity.

    (b) Evaluate $v'(18)$ or explain why the value does not exist. Repeat this for $v'(24)$. Include units of measure with each value.

    (c) Let $a(t)$ be the boat's acceleration at time t, in meters per second. Write a piecewise-defined function for $a(t)$ over the interval $0 < t < 30$.

(d) Find the average rate of change of v over the interval $18 \le t \le 27$. Does the Mean Value Theorem guarantee a value of c such that $v'(c)$ is equal to this average rate of change? Why or why not?

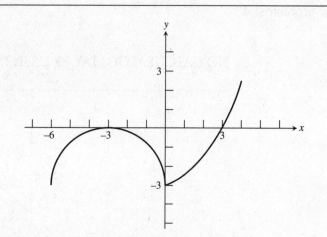

4. The derivative of a continuous function f is defined by

$$f'(x) = \begin{cases} g(x), & -6 \le x \le 0 \\ \dfrac{1}{3}x^2 - 3, & 0 \le x \le 4 \end{cases}$$

The graph of the continuous function f', shown in the figure above, has x-intercepts at $x = -3$ and $x = 3$. The graph of g on $-6 \le x \le 0$ is a semicircle, and $f(0) = 8$.

(a) For $-6 \le x \le 4$, find all values of x at which the graph of f has a point of inflection. Justify your answer.

(b) Find $f(-6)$ and $f(4)$.

(c) For $-6 \le x \le 4$, find the value(s) of x at which f has an absolute minimum. Justify your answer(s).

5. ACME Antenna Company builds cellphone antennas that sell for $200 per foot of height. Since taller antennas are more complicated to construct and support, the cost of constructing a portion of the antenna varies with its distance (height) from the base of the antenna. ACME has learned that their cost to produce a portion of the antenna that is x feet above the base is $3x$ dollars per foot.

(Note that profit is defined as the difference between the amount of money that ACME receives for selling the antenna and the company's cost to construct the antenna.)

(a) Find ACME's profit for selling a 50-foot antenna.

(b) Using correct units, explain the meaning of $\int_{50}^{55} 3x\,dx$ in the context of this problem.

(c) Write an expression, involving an integral, that represents ACME's profit on the sale of an antenna that is k feet high.

(d) What antenna height earns ACME the maximum amount of profit for the sale of a single antenna? Justify your answer.

t (days)	0	1	2	3	4	5
$A(t)$ (pounds)	0	3.1	6	9.7	14.3	19.9

6. A water holding tank has just been cleared of algae, but it tends to grow back quickly. The amount of algae in the tank at time t, $0 \le t \le 5$, is given by a differentiable function A, where t is measured in days. The amount of algae $A(t)$, measured in pounds, is recorded once a day and shown in the table above.

    (a) Use the data in the table to approximate $A'(3.5)$. Show the computations that lead to your answer, and include units of measure.

    (b) Is there a time t, $0 \le t \le 2$, at which $A'(t) = 3$? Justify your answer.

    (c) Use a right Riemann sum with 5 subintervals to approximate the value of $\frac{1}{5}\int_0^5 A(t)dt$. Using correct units, explain the meaning of $\frac{1}{5}\int_0^5 A(t)dt$ in the context of the problem.

    (d) The amount of algae in the tank, in pounds, can be modeled by $M(t) = \frac{1}{2}t^2 + \sqrt{t^2 + 6t}$. Using this model, find the rate at which the amount of algae in the tank is changing when $t = 2$.

Calculus BC—Exam 1

Section I, Part A

Time: 60 minutes
Number of questions: 30

NO CALCULATOR MAY BE USED IN THIS PART OF THE EXAMINATION.

<u>Directions:</u> Solve each of the following problems. After examining the form of the choices, decide which is the best of the choices given.

<u>In this test:</u> Unless otherwise specified, the domain of a function f is assumed to be the set of all real numbers x for which $f(x)$ is a real number.

---

1. $\int_1^2 x(3x + 2)\, dx =$

    (A) 10   (B) 11   (C) 14   (D) $\dfrac{71}{4}$

---

2. The graph of $g(x)$ is shown above. $\lim\limits_{x \to -1} g(x) =$

    (A) -1 (B) 1   (C) 3   (D) does not exist

3. If $x = e^{3t}$ and $y = \sin(5t)$, then $\dfrac{dy}{dx} =$

(A) $\dfrac{\cos(5t)}{e^{3t}}$

(B) $\dfrac{-3\cos(5t)}{5e^{3t}}$

(C) $\dfrac{5\cos(5t)}{3e^{3t}}$

(D) $15e^{3t}\cos(5t)$

---

4. Let P be the region between $y = e^{-3x}$ and the x-axis for $x \geq 2$. The area of region P is

(A) $-\dfrac{1}{3e^6}$

(B) $\dfrac{1}{3e^6}$

(C) $-\dfrac{3}{e^6}$

(D) $\dfrac{3}{e^6}$

---

5. Which of the following statements about the series $\displaystyle\sum_{n=1}^{\infty} \dfrac{(-1)^n}{2 + \sqrt[3]{n}}$ is true?

(A) The series is divergent.

(B) The series is conditionally convergent.

(C) The series is absolutely convergent.

(D) There is not enough information to determine convergence or divergence.

---

6. Given that y is a function of w, find $\dfrac{dy}{dw}$ in terms of y and w for the relation $w^2 + y^3 = wy + 4$.

(A) $\dfrac{y - 2w + 4}{3y^2 - w}$

(B) $\dfrac{y - 2w}{3y^2 - 1}$

(C) $\dfrac{-2w}{3y^2 - w}$

(D) $\dfrac{y - 2w}{3y^2 - w}$

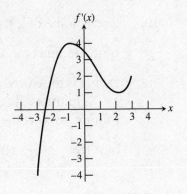

7. The graph of $f'(x)$, the derivative of f, is shown above. On the domain $[-3, 3]$, f has a local minimum value at $x =$

   (A) -3 (B) -2.5 (C) -1 (D) 2

---

8. Which of the following gives the area enclosed by one leaf of the polar curve $r = 2 \cos (2\theta)$?

   (A) $\int_0^{\frac{\pi}{4}} 4 \cos^2(2\theta)\, d\theta$ (B) $\frac{1}{2} \int_0^{\frac{\pi}{4}} [2 \cos(2\theta)]^2\, d\theta$

   (C) $\int_0^{\frac{\pi}{2}} [2 \cos(2\theta)]^2\, d\theta$ (D) $\int_0^{\frac{\pi}{2}} 2 \cos(2\theta)\, d\theta$

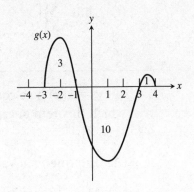

9. The graph of a continuous function $g(x)$, on the domain $[-3, 4]$, is shown above. The areas between $g(x)$ and the x-axis on the domains $[-3, -1]$, $[-1, 3]$ and $[3, 4]$ are 3, 10, and 1 respectively. If $f(x)$ is an antiderivative of $g(x)$, and $f(4) = 5$, then $f(-3) =$

   (A) -11 (B) -6 (C) 11   (D) 14

10. The volume of a sphere is $V = \frac{4}{3}\pi r^3$. For $t \geq 0$, the rate of increase of the radius of a certain sphere is given by $r'(t) = \frac{2}{t+1}$, where the radius is measured in inches and time is measured in minutes. At $t = 2$ minutes, the radius of the sphere is 6 inches. In cubic inches per minute, what is the rate of increase in the volume at $t = 2$ minutes?

(A) 16π (B) 24π (C) 96π (D) 144π

11. Let $y = h(x)$ be the solution to the differential equation $\frac{dy}{dx} = 2 + xy$ with the initial condition $h(0) = 3$. Use Euler's method to find the approximation of $h(1)$, starting at $x = 0$ with step size 0.5.

(A) 4   (B) 6   (C) 8   (D) 10

12. Which of the following limits is equal to $\int_1^5 x^2\, dx$?

(A) $\displaystyle\lim_{n \to \infty} \sum_{k=1}^{n} \left(1 + \frac{k}{n}\right)^2 \frac{1}{n}$ (B) $\displaystyle\lim_{n \to \infty} \sum_{k=1}^{n} \left(1 + \frac{4k}{n}\right)^2 \frac{1}{n}$

(C) $\displaystyle\lim_{n \to \infty} \sum_{k=1}^{n} \left(1 + \frac{k}{n}\right)^2 \frac{4}{n}$ (D) $\displaystyle\lim_{n \to \infty} \sum_{k=1}^{n} \left(1 + \frac{4k}{n}\right)^2 \frac{4}{n}$

13. Let $y = k(x)$ be a continuous function. If $k(-1) = 2$ and $k(5) = 9$, which theorem guarantees $k(x) = 7$ for at least one x in the domain $[-1, 5]$?

(A) Intermediate Value Theorem

(B) Mean Value Theorem

(C) Extreme Value Theorem

(D) Fundamental Theorem of Calculus

14. $\displaystyle \lim_{h \to 0} \frac{e^{(6+2h)} - e^6}{h} =$

   (A) 1　　　　(B) e^6　　　　(C) $2e^6$　　　　(D) $6e^6$

15. $\displaystyle \int \frac{2x - 9}{(x - 2)(x + 3)}\, dx =$

   (A) $3\ln|x + 3| - \ln|x - 2| + C$

   (B) $\ln|x + 3| - 3\ln|x - 2| + C$

   (C) $\ln|x + 3| - \ln|x - 2| + C$

   (D) $3\ln|x + 3| + \ln|x - 2| + C$

16. The first four terms of the infinite series $\displaystyle \sum_{n=1}^{\infty} \frac{(-1)^{n+1}}{n^2 + 1}$ are used to approximate the infinite sum. The least value below which bounds the absolute value of the error is

   (A) $\dfrac{1}{10}$　　　　(B) $\dfrac{1}{17}$　　　　(C) $\dfrac{1}{26}$　　　　(D) 0

17. A particle moves along the x-axis so that its acceleration at any time t is $a(t) = 2t - 3$. If the initial velocity of the particle is -4, at what time t in the interval $0 \le t \le 5$ is the particle farthest left?

   (A) 0　　　　(B) $\dfrac{3}{2}$　　　　(C) 4　　　　(D) 5

18. Identify all horizontal asymptotes of the graph of $y = \dfrac{4^x - 6}{2 + 4^x}$ in the xy-plane.

   (A) $y = 0$ only　　　　　　　(B) $y = 1$ only

   (C) $y = -3$ only　　　　　　(D) $y = -3$ and $y = 1$

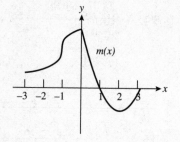

19. The graph of piecewise function $m(x)$ is shown. $m(x)$ is continuous on the domain $[-3, 3]$. There is a vertical tangent at $x = -1$ and a local minimum at $x = 2$. On $(-3, 3)$, $m'(x)$ fails to exist at $x =$

(A) $-1, 0$, and 2 only

(B) -1 and 0 only

(C) 2 only

(D) 0 only

x	1	2
$f(x)$	3	6
$f'(x)$	-5	1
$k(x)$	4	3
$k'(x)$	2	-1

20. The table above gives values of f, f', k, and k' for $x = 1$ and $x = 2$. If $\int_1^2 k'(x)f(x)dx = 8$, then $\int_1^2 k(x)f'(x)dx =$

(A) -2 (B) 0   (C) 2   (D) 4

21. At time $t \geq 0$, a particle moving in the xy-plane has position vector given by $s(t) = \langle -t^2 + 4t, e^{2t-2} \rangle$. What is the speed of the particle at time $t = 1$?

(A) $\frac{1}{3}$ (B) 1   (C) $\sqrt{5}$ (D) $\sqrt{8}$

22. If $g(x) = -x^2 e^x$, which of the following is the Maclaurin series for $g(x)$?

(A) $-x^2 - x^3 - \dfrac{x^4}{2!} - \dfrac{x^5}{3!} - \dfrac{x^6}{4!} - \cdots$

(B) $-x^2 - x^4 - \dfrac{x^6}{2!} - \dfrac{x^8}{3!} - \dfrac{x^{10}}{4!} - \cdots$

(C) $-x^3 - x^4 - \dfrac{x^5}{2!} - \dfrac{x^6}{3!} - \dfrac{x^7}{4!} - \cdots$

(D) $-x^2 + x^3 - \dfrac{x^4}{2!} + \dfrac{x^5}{3!} - \dfrac{x^6}{4!} + \cdots$

23. The average value of $f(x) = \dfrac{2}{\sqrt{x + 3}}$ on the interval $[1, 6]$ is

(A) $\dfrac{1}{5}$ (B) $\dfrac{4}{5}$ (C) $\dfrac{76}{15}$ (D) 4

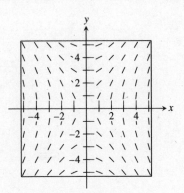

24. Which of the following could be the differential equation for the slope field given above?

(A) $\dfrac{dy}{dx} = x \cdot y$ (B) $\dfrac{dy}{dx} = \dfrac{y}{x}$

(C) $\dfrac{dy}{dx} = \dfrac{x}{y}$ (D) $\dfrac{dy}{dx} = 1 + x - y$

25. What are all the values of x for which the series $\sum_{n=1}^{\infty} \dfrac{(2x - 1)^n}{n \cdot 4^n}$ converges?

(A) $-\dfrac{3}{2} < x < \dfrac{5}{2}$

(B) $-\dfrac{3}{2} \le x \le \dfrac{5}{2}$

(C) $-\dfrac{3}{2} < x \le \dfrac{5}{2}$

(D) $-\dfrac{3}{2} \le x < \dfrac{5}{2}$

26. If $f'(x) = (x + 2)^2(x - 2)$, the graph of f is concave up on which interval(s)?

(A) $x > 2$

(B) $x < -2 \cup x > 2$

(C) $-2 < x < \dfrac{2}{3}$

(D) $x < -2 \cup x > \dfrac{2}{3}$

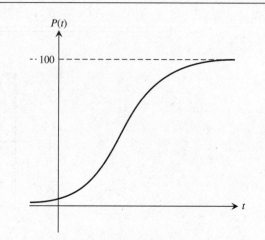

27. Which of the following differential equations for a population $P(t)$ could model the logistic graph shown above?

(A) $\dfrac{dP}{dt} = 0.3P^2 - 0.003P$

(B) $\dfrac{dP}{dt} = 0.3P - 0.003P^2$

(C) $\dfrac{dP}{dt} = 0.001P - 0.1P^2$

(D) $\dfrac{dP}{dt} = 0.2P - 0.001P^2$

28. Given $\displaystyle\sum_{n=1}^{\infty} a_n$ and $\displaystyle\sum_{n=1}^{\infty} b_n$ contain only positive terms. If $\displaystyle\lim_{n\to\infty} \frac{a_n}{b_n} = 7$,

and $\displaystyle\sum_{n=1}^{\infty} b_n$ converges, then $\displaystyle\sum_{n=1}^{\infty} a_n$

(A) must converge

(B) must diverge

(C) may converge or diverge

(D) has a sum exactly seven times as large as $\displaystyle\sum_{n=1}^{\infty} b_n$

---

29. $\displaystyle\lim_{x\to 1} \left[\frac{1}{x^3 - 1} \cdot \int_2^{2x} \tan(t)\,dt \right] =$

(A) $\dfrac{2\tan(2)}{3}$ (B) $\dfrac{\tan(2)}{3}$ (C) 1   (D) ∞

---

30. The sum of the infinite geometric series $\dfrac{7}{10} - \dfrac{21}{40} + \dfrac{63}{160} - \dfrac{189}{640} + \cdots$ is?

(A) $\dfrac{1}{5}$ (B) $\dfrac{2}{5}$

(C) $\dfrac{4}{7}$ (D) the series diverges

❖ **End of Part A of Section I** ❖

Calculus BC—Exam 1
Section I, Part B

Time: 45 minutes
Number of questions: 15

A GRAPHING CALCULATOR IS REQUIRED FOR SOME QUESTIONS IN THIS PART OF THE EXAMINATION.

<u>Directions:</u> Solve each of the following problems. After examining the form of the choices, decide which is the best of the choices given.

<u>In this test:</u>

1. The exact numerical value of the correct answer does not always appear among the choices given. When this happens, select from among the choices the number that best approximates the exact numerical value.
2. Unless otherwise specified, the domain of a function f is assumed to be the set of all real numbers x for which $f(x)$ is a real number.

---

31. Which of the following series converge?

    I. $\displaystyle\sum_{n=1}^{\infty} \frac{1}{n^2 + 1}$

    II. $\displaystyle\sum_{n=1}^{\infty} \frac{n}{n^2 - 1}$

    III. $\displaystyle\sum_{n=1}^{\infty} \frac{e^n}{n!}$

    (A) I and II only   (B) I and III only

    (C) II and III only   (D) I, II, and III

---

32. Find all values c that satisfy the Mean Value Theorem for the function $f(x) = \dfrac{2}{(1 + x^2)}$ on the interval $[-1, 2]$.

    (A) 0.050   (B) -0.050

    (C) 0.102 and 1.801   (D) 0.050 and 2.449

x	0	2	4	6	8
$g'(x)$	1	−1	3	6	−5

33. Function g is a twice differentiable function. The values of $g'(x)$ at selected integers are given in the table above. What is the fewest number of points of inflection g can have in the interval $[0, 8]$?

    (A) 0　　　　　(B) 1　　　　　(C) 2　　　　　(D) 3

34. If k is an antiderivative of $f(x) = \dfrac{x}{1 - x + x^4}$ and $k(0) = 4$, then $k(3) =$

    (A) 1.257　　　(B) 3.961　　　(C) 4.039　　　(D) 5.257

35. The position of an object oscillating along the x-axis is given by $x(t) = 2 \sin(2t) - 3 \cos(3t)$, where t is time in seconds. How many times is the velocity equal to 0 in the time interval $[0, 5]$?

    (A) 2　　　　　(B) 3　　　　　(C) 4　　　　　(D) 5

36. What is the area enclosed by the graphs of $y = 3x^2 - 8x + 1$ and $y = 2 \ln(x)$?

    (A) 8.132　　　(B) 12.578　　　(C) 25.547　　　(D) 52.902

37. Let h be a function of x. Using u-substitution, $\int_a^4 h(2x + 3)dx$ is equivalent to which of the following?

    (A) $\dfrac{1}{2} \int_{(2a+3)}^{11} h(u)du$ 　　　　　(B) $\int_{(2a+3)}^{11} h(u)du$

    (C) $2\int_{(2a+3)}^{11} h(u)du$ 　　　　　(D) $\int_a^4 h(u)du$

Derivative	$f'(x)$	$f''(x)$	$f'''(x)$	$f^{(4)}(x)$	$f^{(5)}(x)$
Maximum value	6	12	18	21	24

38. Let f be a function with only positive derivatives. The table above gives the maximum values of each of the five derivatives on the interval $[0, 2]$. If a third degree Taylor polynomial about $x = 0$ is used to approximate f, and $|P_3(2) - f(2)| < k$, the smallest possible value of k is

(A) 16   (B) 14   (C) 12   (D) 8

39. For $x > 0$, if $\dfrac{dy}{dx} = y(1 + \ln(x))$ and $y = 3$ when $x = 1$, then $y =$

(A) $3e^{x \ln(x)}$ (B) $1 + 2e^{x \ln(x)}$

(C) $3e^{-2+x+\frac{1}{x}}$ (D) $2 + e^{x \ln(x)}$

40. Let h be a function with $h(2) = 3$, $h'(2) = -1$, $h''(2) = 8$, and $h'''(2) = 18$. Which of the following is the third degree Taylor polynomial for h about $x = 2$?

(A) $3 - x + 8x^2 + 18x^3$

(B) $3 - x + 4x^2 + 3x^3$

(C) $3 - (x - 2) + 4(x - 2)^2 + 3(x - 2)^3$

(D) $3 - (x + 2) + 4(x + 2)^2 + 3(x + 2)^3$

41. Water drains from a tub at a rate of $D(t) = \dfrac{3}{\sqrt{1 + 2t^3}}$ gallons per minute where t is in minutes. How many gallons drain from the tub from time $t = 0$ to $t = 4$ minutes?

(A) 2.589   (B) 2.736   (C) 4.557   (D) 6.138

42. Let f be a twice-differential function such that $f(1) = 4$ and $f(3) = 10$. Which of the following must be true on the interval $1 \leq x \leq 3$?

(A) $f(2) = 7$

(B) $\int_1^3 f(x)dx < 20$

(C) $f''(x) < 0$ for some x in the interval

(D) The average value of f' is 3.

43. If $f(x) = \int_0^x \dfrac{2 - e^t + t}{e^t - t}\,dt$, find the first value of x greater than 0 for which f has a relative maximum.

(A) 0   (B) 1.146   (C) 1.623   (D) 1.848

44. The first quadrant region enclosed by the graphs of $y = e^x$, $y = 2 + \cos(x)$, and the y-axis is revolved around the x-axis. Find the volume of the solid generated.

(A) 1.658π (B) 4.922π (C) 5.387π (D) 10.592π

45. For $t \geq 0$, a particle moves through the xy-plane with a velocity vector function $v(t) = \langle t^2 - t + 1, \ln(t + 1) \rangle$. How far does the particle travel in the time interval $0 \leq t \leq 4$?

(A) 1.423   (B) 12.952   (C) 17.935   (D) 133.657

Calculus BC—Exam 1
Section II, Part A

Time: 30 minutes
Number of problems: 2

A GRAPHING CALCULATOR IS REQUIRED FOR SOME PROBLEMS IN THIS PART OF THE EXAMINATION.

1. A particle moving along a curve in the xy-plane has position $(x(t), y(t))$ at time t, with

$$\frac{dx}{dt} = \arctan(2 - t^2) \quad \text{and} \quad \frac{dy}{dt} = \frac{3t}{1 + e^t}$$

for $t \geq 0$. At time $t = 1$, the particle has position $(4, 2)$.

(a) Write the equation of the line normal to the curve at time $t = 1$.

(b) Find the speed of the particle and the acceleration vector at time $t = 1.5$.

(c) Is the particle moving right or left at $t = 2$? Explain your reasoning.

Is the speed of the particle increasing, decreasing, or doing neither <u>in the x-direction</u> at time $t = 2$? Justify your answer.

(d) Find the initial y-coordinate of the particle.

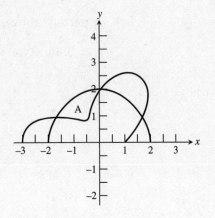

2. The graphs of the polar curves $r = 2$ and $r = 2 - \cos(3\theta)$ are shown in the figure above for $0 \le \theta \le \pi$.

(a) Find the area of region A, the second quadrant area outside $r = 2 - \cos(2\theta)$ and inside $r = 2$.

(b) For the curve $r = 2 - \cos(3\theta)$, find $\dfrac{dr}{d\theta}$ at $\theta = \dfrac{5\pi}{12}$ and explain its meaning.

(c) For the curve $r = 2 - \cos(3\theta)$, find the instantaneous rate of change of the y-coordinate with respect to θ when $\theta = \dfrac{\pi}{5}$.

Note: Problem 2, part (d) is on the next page.

(d) A particle moves along $r = 2 - \cos(3\theta)$ so that $\dfrac{dr}{dt} = 2$ for all $t \geq 0$. Find the value of $\dfrac{d\theta}{dt}$ when $\theta = \dfrac{\pi}{9}$.

✧ **End of Part A of Section II** ✧

Calculus BC—Exam 1
Section II, Part B

Time: 60 minutes
Number of problems: 4

NO CALCULATOR MAY BE USED IN THIS PART OF THE EXAMINATION.

3. Consider the differential equation $\frac{dy}{dx} = \frac{2x - 2}{y}$ for $y \neq 0$. Let $y = g(x)$ be the particular solution to this differential equation with the initial condition $g(1) = -3$.

    (a) Find the value of $\frac{d^2y}{dx^2}$ at $(1, -3)$.

    (b) Does the graph of $y = g(x)$ have a local maximum, local minimum, or neither at $(1, -3)$? Justify your answer.

    (c) Find the particular solution $y = g(x)$ to the differential equation $\frac{dy}{dx} = \frac{2x - 2}{y}$ with the initial condition $g(1) = -3$.

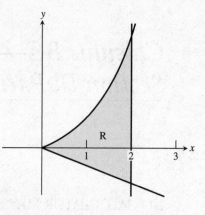

4. Let R be the shaded region bounded by the graphs of $y = e^x - 1$, the line $y = -x$, and the vertical line $x = 2$ as shown in the figure above.

(a) Find the area of region R.

(b) Write, but do not evaluate, an integral expression for the volume of the solid generated when R is rotated around the line $y = -3$.

(c) Region R is the base of a solid. The cross sections of the solid taken perpendicular to the y-axis are semicircles with diameters in the xy-plane. Write, but do not evaluate, an integral expression for the volume of the solid.

t (seconds)	0	5	12	16	21	23	27	30
v(t) (feet per second)	3	7	15	−5	−4	9	20	13

5. A remote control car moves along a straight track. Its velocity, measured in feet per second, is recorded for selected values of t over the interval $0 \leq t \leq 30$ seconds as shown in the table above. Velocity, $v(t)$, is a differentiable function over the given interval.

(a) Find the average acceleration of the car in the interval $21 \leq t \leq 27$. Indicate units of measurement. Justify that the car had that acceleration for at least one instant in the interval.

(b) Using correct units explain the meaning of $\int_0^{16} v(t)dt$. Use a trapezoidal sum with three subintervals to approximate $\int_0^{16} v(t)dt$.

(c) During what interval(s) must the car change directions? Justify your answer.

6. The Taylor series for a function f about $x = 2$ is given by
$$\sum_{n=1}^{\infty} (-1)^{n+1} \frac{(x - 2)^n}{n \cdot 3^n}.$$

(a) Find the open interval of convergence for the series.

(b) Determine if the series converges absolutely, converges conditionally, or diverges at the right endpoint of the interval found in part (a). Justify your choice.

(c) If the first three terms of the series are used to approximate $f(3)$, find a bound on the error using the alternating series error bound.

(d) Let g be defined by $g(x) = \int_2^x f(t)dt$. Write the sigma notation for $g(x)$.

Calculus BC—Exam 2

Section I, Part A

Time: 60 minutes
Number of questions: 30

NO CALCULATOR MAY BE USED IN THIS PART OF THE EXAMINATION.

<u>Directions:</u> Solve each of the following problems. After examining the form of the choices, decide which is the best of the choices given.

<u>In this test:</u> Unless otherwise specified, the domain of a function f is assumed to be the set of all real numbers x for which $f(x)$ is a real number.

1. What is the slope of the line tangent to the graph of $f(x) = \sin(2x)$ at the point where $x = \dfrac{\pi}{2}$?

   (A) -2 (B) -1 (C) 0 (D) 1

2. $\displaystyle\int \dfrac{4}{(x-1)(x+3)}\,dx =$

   (A) $\ln|x-1| + \ln|x+3| + C$

   (B) $\ln|x-1| - \ln|x+3| + C$

   (C) $2\ln\left(|x-1|\cdot|x+3|\right) + C$

   (D) $\ln(x^2 + 2x - 3) + C$

3. $\lim\limits_{x \to \frac{\pi}{2}} \dfrac{\left(x - \dfrac{\pi}{2}\right)^2}{1 - \sin x} =$

   (A) 0   (B) 1   (C) 2   (D) undefined

4. What is the value of $\sum\limits_{n=0}^{\infty} \dfrac{e^{n+1}}{(-3)^n}$?

   (A) $\dfrac{e}{-3}$ (B) $\dfrac{e}{1 + e}$ (C) $\dfrac{e}{3 + e}$ (D) $\dfrac{3e}{3 + e}$

5. Let f be the function defined by $f(x) = \begin{cases} 2x + 1, & x \le 1 \\ 5x - k, & x > 1 \end{cases}$.
   If f is continuous at $x = 1$, what is the value of k?

   (A) -1 (B) 1   (C) 2   (D) There is no such value of k.

6. $\displaystyle\int_0^1 \dfrac{x}{1 + x^2}\, dx =$

   (A) $\ln(2)$ (B) $\dfrac{\ln(2)}{2}$ (C) $\ln(4)$ (D) $\tan^{-1} x$

7. If y is the solution to the differential equation $\dfrac{dy}{dt} = .05y(250 - y)$, what are all values of y for which y is increasing at an increasing rate?

   (A) 125 only

   (B) $0 < y < 125$ only

   (C) $125 < y < 250$ only

   (D) $0 < y < 250$

8. The third-degree Taylor polynomial for a function f about $x = 0$ is $\dfrac{x^3}{24} - \dfrac{x^2}{8} + \dfrac{x}{2} + \ln(2)$. What is the value of $f'''(0)$?

(A) $\dfrac{1}{4}$ (B) $\dfrac{1}{6}$ (C) $\dfrac{1}{8}$ (D) $\dfrac{1}{24}$

9. Suppose $y^3 - xy = -1$, where y is a differentiable function of x, and $y = 1$ when $x = 2$. What is the value of $\dfrac{dy}{dx}$ when $y = 1$ when $x = 2$?

(A) 0   (B) $\dfrac{1}{4}$ (C) $\dfrac{1}{3}$ (D) 1

10. The function f has a first derivative given by $f' = (x - 3)(x - 1)^2(x + 2)$. At what values of x does f have a relative minimum?

(A) -2 only   (B) 3 only

(C) -2 and -3 only   (D) -2, 1, and 3 only

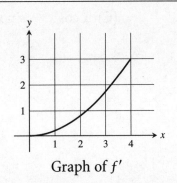

Graph of f'

11. The graph of f', the derivative of f, is shown in the figure above. If $f(0) = 15$, which of the following could be the value of $f(4)$?

(A) 12   (B) 16   (C) 20   (D) 24

12. If $\dfrac{dy}{dx} = \cos(x)\sin^2(x)$ and if $y = 1$ when $x = \dfrac{\pi}{2}$, what is the value of y when $x = 0$?

(A) $-\dfrac{2}{3}$ (B) $-\dfrac{1}{3}$ (C) $\dfrac{1}{3}$ (D) $\dfrac{2}{3}$

---

13. A particle moves on a plane curve so that at any time $t > 0$ its x-coordinate is $t^3 - 1$ and its y-coordinate is $(2t + 1)^3$. What is the acceleration vector of the particle when $t = 1$?

(A) $\langle 0, 27\rangle$ (B) $\langle 6, 18\rangle$ (C) $\langle 6, 72\rangle$ (D) $\langle 6, 36\rangle$

---

14. If $f(x) = \begin{cases} e^x, & x \le 2 \\ xe^2, & x > 2 \end{cases}$, then $\lim\limits_{x \to 2} f(x)$ is

(A) e (B) e^2 (C) $2e^2$ (D) nonexistent

---

15. $\int x \sin x \, dx =$

(A) $-x\cos x + \sin x + C$ (B) $-x\sin x + \sin x + C$

(C) $x\cos x + \sin x + C$ (D) $x\sin x + \sin x + C$

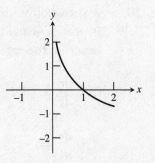

16. The graph of a twice differentiable function f is shown. Which of the following is true?

    (A) $f(1) < f'(1) < f''(1)$

    (B) $f'(1) < f(1) < f''(1)$

    (C) $f''(1) < f(1) < f'(1)$

    (D) $f''(1) < f'(1) < f(1)$

17. Which one of the following series converge?

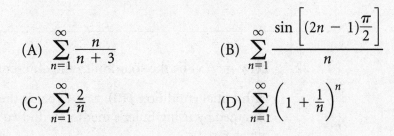

    (A) $\displaystyle\sum_{n=1}^{\infty} \frac{n}{n+3}$

    (B) $\displaystyle\sum_{n=1}^{\infty} \frac{\sin\left[(2n-1)\dfrac{\pi}{2}\right]}{n}$

    (C) $\displaystyle\sum_{n=1}^{\infty} \frac{2}{n}$

    (D) $\displaystyle\sum_{n=1}^{\infty} \left(1 + \frac{1}{n}\right)^n$

18. $\displaystyle\int_{0}^{\infty} \frac{3x^2}{(1+x^3)^2}\, dx =$

    (A) -1 (B) 0 (C) 1 (D) 3

19. What are all the values of x for which the series $\displaystyle\sum_{n=1}^{\infty} \frac{(-1)^n}{n}(x-1)^n$ converges?

    (A) $0 \le x < 2$

    (B) $0 < x < 2$

    (C) $0 < x \le 2$

    (D) $0 \le x \le 2$

20. A snowball with radius r melts so that the rate of change of its volume is proportional to its surface area. Which of the following could describe the rate at which the radius decreases?

(A) $\dfrac{dr}{dt} = -t$ (B) $\dfrac{dr}{dt} = -4\pi r^2$

(C) $\dfrac{dr}{dt} = -r$ (D) $\dfrac{dr}{dt} = -2$

21. Which of the following gives the length of the path described by the parametric equations $x = 1 + 2t$ and $y = t^3$ from $t = 0$ to $t = 1$?

(A) $\int_0^1 \sqrt{(1 + 2t)^2 + t^6}\, dt$ (B) $\int_0^1 \sqrt{2 + 3t^2}\, dt$

(C) $\int_0^1 \sqrt{4 + 9t^4}\, dt$ (D) $\int_0^1 \sqrt{1 + 9t^4}\, dt$

22. Let $y = f(x)$ be the solution to the differential equation $\dfrac{dy}{dx} = x + 2y$ with initial condition $f(0) = 1$. What is the approximation for $f(1)$ obtained by using Euler's method with two steps of equal length, starting at $x = 0$?

(A) 2   (B) 4   (C) 4.25   (D) 4.75

23. If $\displaystyle\lim_{h \to 0} \dfrac{\ln(a + h) - \ln(a)}{h} = 2$, which of the following could be the value of a?

(A) 0   (B) $\dfrac{1}{2}$ (C) 1   (D) 2

24. For $x > 1, \dfrac{d}{dx}\displaystyle\int_1^{x^2} \dfrac{\sin(t)}{t}\, dt =$

(A) $\cos(x^2)$ 　　　　　(B) $\sin(x^2)$

(C) $\dfrac{\sin(x^2)}{x^2}$ 　　　　(D) $\dfrac{2\sin(x^2)}{x}$

---

25. Which of the following is the Maclaurin series for $\cos(x^3)$?

(A) $1 - \dfrac{x^2}{2} + \dfrac{x^4}{4!} - \dfrac{x^6}{6!} + \cdots$ 　　(B) $1 - \dfrac{x^6}{2} + \dfrac{x^{12}}{4!} - \dfrac{x^{18}}{6!} + \cdots$

(C) $1 - \dfrac{x^5}{2} + \dfrac{x^7}{4!} - \dfrac{x^9}{6!} + \cdots$ 　　(D) $1 - \dfrac{x^3}{2} + \dfrac{x^6}{4!} - \dfrac{x^9}{6!} + \cdots$

---

26. If $f(x) = 3x^5 - 5x^4 + 2x - 1$, what are the x-coordinates of all points of inflection for the graph of f?

(A) 0 　　　(B) 1 　　　(C) 0 and 1 　　(D) $-1, 0,$ and 1

---

x	1	3	5	7	9
$f(x)$	8	10	14	16	24

27. The table above gives selected values for the continuous function f. Using a right Riemann sum with 4 subintervals of equal length, which of the following is an approximation of the average value of f on the interval $[1, 9]$?

(A) 16 　　(B) 32 　　　(C) 48 　　　(D) 64

---

28. A rectangle has its base on the x-axis and its upper two vertices on the parabola $y = 9 - x^2$. What is the largest area the rectangle can have?

(A) $\sqrt{3}$ 　　(B) $3\sqrt{3}$ 　　(C) $6\sqrt{3}$ 　　(D) $12\sqrt{3}$

29. What is the particular solution to the differential equation $\dfrac{dy}{dx} = 2xy$ with initial condition $y(0) = 3$?

(A) $y = 2e^{x^2}$

(B) $y = e^{x^2} + 3$

(C) $y = 3e^{x^2}$

(D) $y = e^{x^2+3}$

---

30. If $x = t^3$ and $y = \ln t$, what is $\dfrac{d^2y}{dx^2}$ in terms of t?

(A) $\dfrac{1}{6t}$

(B) $\dfrac{1}{3t^3}$

(C) $-\dfrac{1}{t^4}$

(D) $-\dfrac{1}{3t^6}$

❖ **End of Part A of Section I** ❖

Calculus BC—Exam 2
Section I, Part B

Time: 45 minutes
Number of questions: 15

A GRAPHING CALCULATOR IS REQUIRED FOR SOME QUESTIONS IN THIS PART OF THE EXAMINATION.

<u>Directions:</u> Solve each of the following problems. After examining the form of the choices, decide which is the best of the choices given.

<u>In this test:</u>

1. The exact numerical value of the correct answer does not always appear among the choices given. When this happens, select from among the choices the number that best approximates the exact numerical value.

2. Unless otherwise specified, the domain of a function f is assumed to be the set of all real numbers x for which $f(x)$ is a real number.

---

31. Let R be the region enclosed by the graph of $y = \sin e^{x^2}$ and the x-axis, between the lines $x = -1$ and $x = 1$. What is the closest integer approximation of the area of R?

    (A) 0   (B) 1   (C) 2   (D) 3

---

32. The Taylor series for e^x, centered at $x = 0$, is $\sum_{n=0}^{\infty} \frac{x^n}{n!}$. Let f be the function given by the sum of the first four nonzero terms of this series. The maximum value of $|e^x - f(x)|$ for $-0.6 \leq x \leq 0.6$ is

    (A) 0.0036   (B) 0.0048   (C) 0.0052   (D) 0.0061

33. The base of a solid is a region in the first quadrant bounded by the x-axis and the curve $y = \sin x$, where $0 \leq x \leq \pi$. If cross sections of the solid perpendicular to the x-axis are squares, what is the volume of the solid?

    (A) 0.785   (B) 1   (C) 1.571   (D) 2

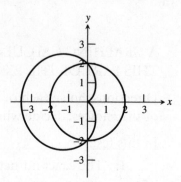

34. Let R be the region in the first quadrant that is inside the polar curve $r = 2$ and outside the curve $r = 2 - 2\cos\theta$, as shown in the figure above. What is the area of R?

    (A) 0.429   (B) 1.5708   (C) 2.429   (D) 4.858

35. A particle moves along the x-axis so that its velocity is given by $v(t) = -t^3 + 3t^2 - 2t + e^{-t}$ for $t \geq 0$. When is the particle furthest to the right?

    (A) $t = 0$ (B) $t = 0.61$ (C) $t = 1.51$ (D) $t = 2.059$

36. The population of fish in a lake grows at a rate given by $R(t) = 1500e^{0.14t}$ fish per year. If there are 1200 fish in the lake at time $t = 0$, what is the population at time $t = 4$?

    (A) 2626   (B) 3826   (C) 8043   (D) 9243

x	1	4	6	7
$f(x)$	20	40	50	30

37. The function f is continuous on the closed interval $[1, 7]$ and has values that are given in the table above. Using subintervals $[1, 4]$, $[4, 6]$, and $[6, 7]$, what is the trapezoidal approximation of $\int_1^7 f(x)dx$?

   (A) 130   (B) 180   (C) 210   (D) 220

38. The radius of a circle is increasing at a constant rate of 0.2 centimeters per second. In terms of the circumference C, what is the rate of change of the area of the circle, in square centimeters per second?

   (A) $2\pi(0.2)$ (B) $0.2C$ (C) $\pi(0.2)^2$ (D) $\pi(0.2)^2C$

39. For what values of k will $\sum_{n=1}^{\infty} \left(\frac{k}{3}\right)^n$ converge?

   (A) $-3 < k < 3$ (B) $-3 \leq k < 3$

   (C) $-3 < k \leq 3$ (D) $-3 \leq k \leq 3$

40. A function f is differentiable on the closed interval $[1, 7]$. If the value $c = 3$ satisfies the conclusion of the Mean Value Theorem applied to f on the open interval $(1, 7)$ and if $\int_1^7 f'(x)dx = 8$, what is the value of $f'(3)$?

   (A) $\frac{4}{3}$ (B) $\frac{7}{3}$ (C) 4   (D) 8

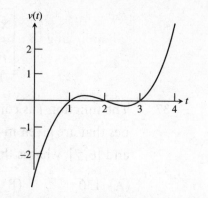

41. A particle moves along a line with velocity $v(t)$. The graph of the velocity is shown above. The velocity curve has roots at $t = 1$, $t = 2$, and $t = 3$, a maximum at $t = 1.423$, and a minimum at $t = 2.577$. On what intervals is the speed of the particle decreasing?

(A) $(1.423, 2.577)$

(B) $(0, 1) \cup (1.423, 2) \cup (2.577, 3)$

(C) $(1, 2) \cup (3, 4)$

(D) $(0, 1.423) \cup (2.577, 4)$

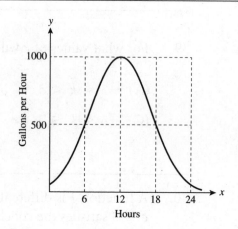

42. The rate of water pumped from a water storage tank is given by the graph shown. Of the following, which best approximates the total number of gallons pumped for the 24-hour period?

(A) 1000　　　(B) 6000　　　(C) 12,000　　　(D) 24,000

43. For $|x| < 1$ the series $1 - x^2 + x^4 - x^6 + \cdots$ converges to which of the following functions?

(A) $\dfrac{1}{1 + x^2}$ (B) $\dfrac{1}{1 - x^2}$ (C) $\cos x$ (D) $\ln x^2$

44. What is the volume of the solid generated when the region bounded by $y = 2 \sin x$ and the x-axis over the interval $[0, \pi]$ is rotated about the x-axis?

(A) 4.935   (B) 9.87   (C) 19.739   (D) 12.566

45. Which of the following limits is equal to $\int_1^4 x^2 dx$?

(A) $\displaystyle\lim_{n \to \infty} \sum_{k=1}^{n} \left(1 + \frac{3k}{n}\right)^2 \frac{3}{n}$

(B) $\displaystyle\lim_{n \to \infty} \sum_{k=1}^{n} \left(1 + \frac{k}{n}\right)^2 \frac{3}{n}$

(C) $\displaystyle\lim_{n \to \infty} \sum_{k=1}^{n} \left(1 + \frac{3k}{n}\right)^2 \frac{1}{n}$

(D) $\displaystyle\lim_{n \to \infty} \sum_{k=1}^{n} \left(1 + \frac{k}{n}\right)^2 \frac{1}{n}$

Calculus BC—Exam 2
Section II, Part A

Time: 30 minutes
Number of problems: 2

A GRAPHING CALCULATOR IS REQUIRED FOR SOME PROBLEMS IN THIS PART OF THE EXAMINATION.

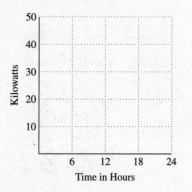

1. The power consumed in a house during a 24-hour period is described by

$$K(t) = 25 - 20 \cos \frac{\pi t}{12}$$

where $K(t)$ is measured in kilowatts and t is measured in hours.

(a) Sketch the graph of K on the grid provided.

(b) Find the average number of kilowatts between $t = 6$ and $t = 18$.

(c) Peak usage is considered to be 35 kilowatts or higher. For what values of t is the number of kilowatts above 35?

(d) There is a surcharge of $0.07 per kilowatt-hour for each kilowatt used beyond 35 kilowatts. What is the total cost, to the nearest cent, of the surcharge for this 24-hour period?

t (seconds)	0	5	10	18	30
$S(t)$ (degrees Celsius)	28	38	47	58	71

2. Water is heated on a camp stove. The temperature of the water in degrees Celsius is modeled by the differentiable function $S(t)$ for $0 \le t \le 30$. Selected temperatures are given in the table.

(a) Use the data in the table to estimate the rate at which the temperature is changing at $t = 14$. Show the calculations that lead to your answer.

(b) Using correct units, explain the meaning of $\frac{1}{30} \int_0^{30} S(t)dt$. Use a trapezoidal sum with four subintervals indicated by the table to estimate the value of $\frac{1}{30} \int_0^{30} S(t)dt$.

(c) Evaluate $\int_0^{30} S'(t)dt$. Explain the meaning of this expression.

(d) For $30 \leq t \leq 60$ the function S that models the temperature of the water has a first derivative given by $S'(t) = 2.16(0.970446)^t$. Based on this model, what is the temperature of the water at $t = 60$?

❖ **End of Part A of Section II** ❖

Calculus BC—Exam 2
Section II, Part B

Time: 60 minutes
Number of problems: 4

NO CALCULATOR MAY BE USED IN THIS PART OF THE
EXAMINATION.

---

3.   Let R be the region in the first quadrant bounded by the graph of
     $y = 4 - x^2$, the x-axis, and the y-axis.

     (a)   Find the area of the region R.

     (b)   Find the volume of the solid generated when R is revolved about
           the x-axis.

     (c)   Find the volume of the solid generated when R is revolved about
           the y-axis.

---

4.   Consider the differential equation given by $\dfrac{dy}{dx} = x^2 y$.

     (a)   On the axes provided, sketch a slope field for the given differential
           equation at the nine points indicated.

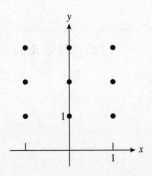

(b) Let $y = f(x)$ be the particular solution to the given differential equation with the initial condition $f(0) = 1$. Use Euler's method starting at $x = 0$, with a step size of 0.1, to approximate $f(0.2)$.

(c) Find the particular solution $y = f(x)$ to the given differential equation with the initial condition $f(0) = 1$.

5. A particle moves along the curve defined by the equation $y = x^2 - 2x$. The x-coordinate of the particle, $x(t)$, satisfies the equation $\dfrac{dx}{dt} = \dfrac{1}{\sqrt{t+1}}$, for $t \geq 3$ with the initial condition $x(3) = -1$.

(a) Find $x(t)$ in terms of t.

(b) Find $\dfrac{dy}{dt}$ in terms of t.

(c) Find the location of the particle at time $t = 8$.

(d) Find the speed of the particle at time $t = 8$.

6. Let f be a function that has derivatives of all orders for all real numbers. Assume $f(0) = 7$, $f'(0) = -4$, $f''(0) = 1$, and $f'''(0) = 6$.

(a) Write the third degree Taylor polynomial for f about $x = 0$ and use it to approximate $f(1)$.

(b) Write the fourth degree Taylor polynomial for g where $g(x) = f(x^2)$, about $x = 0$.

(c) Write the fourth degree Taylor polynomial for h, where $h(x) = \int_0^x f(t)dt$, about $x = 0$.

(d) Let h be defined as in part (c). Given that $f(1) = 5$, either find the exact value of $h(1)$ or explain why it cannot be determined.

Appendix

Precalculus Review of Calculus Prerequisites

If you are presently in a precalculus course, perhaps you have felt somewhat overwhelmed—so much to learn, so little time! All teachers know that many students struggle distinguishing important course content from the extremely important! *Preparing for the Calculus AP* Exam* will help you address the essential question:

What are the most important things to pay attention to in a precalculus course in order to be well prepared for an AP* Calculus course?

Precalculus—A Preparation for Calculus!

As the word implies, precalculus is a preparation for calculus. Whether your precalculus course uses *Precalculus: Graphical, Numerical, Algebraic* by Demana, Waits, Foley, Kennedy, and Bock (hereafter *Precalculus*) or some other textbook, the course should provide a good foundation for advanced mathematical study. If an AP* Calculus course is in your future, you should know the specific content, concepts, and skills taught in a precalculus course that will be encountered frequently throughout your calculus course.

The College Board's *AP Calculus AB and AP Calculus BC Course and Exam Description, Effective Fall 2016,* describes the following prerequisites needed for calculus:

> Before studying calculus, all students should complete the equivalent of four years of secondary mathematics designed for college-bound students: courses which should prepare them with a strong foundation in reasoning with algebraic symbols and working with algebraic structures. Prospective calculus students should take courses in which they study algebra, geometry, trigonometry, analytic geometry, and elementary functions. These functions include linear, polynomial, rational, exponential, logarithmic, trigonometric, inverse trigonometric, and piecewise-defined functions. In particular, before studying calculus, students must be familiar with the properties of functions, the composition of functions, the algebra of functions, and the graphs of functions. Students must also understand the language of functions (domain and range, odd and even, periodic, symmetry, zeros, intercepts, and descriptors such as increasing and decreasing). Students should also know how the sine and cosine functions are defined from the unit circle and know the values of the trigonometric functions at the numbers $0, \frac{\pi}{6}, \frac{\pi}{4}, \frac{\pi}{3}, \frac{\pi}{2}$, and their multiples. Students who take AP Calculus BC should have basic familiarity with sequences and series, as well as some exposure to polar equations.

AP Calculus AB and AP Calculus BC Course and Exam Description, Effective Fall 2016

This precalculus section is structured to identify the important precalculus Objectives, describe the importance of each in an Overview calculus context, provide succinct Content explanations, give Additional Practice problems, and point to resources if you Need More Help. Eleven topics—identified as Calculus Prerequisite Knowledge—are listed below and cross referenced to the *Precalculus* textbook.

299

AP* Preparation Topic	Calculus Prerequisite Knowledge	Precalculus Textbook
0	Basic functions	1.3
1	Functions	1.4
2	Transformations	1.6
3	Polynomial functions	2.3
4	Rational functions	2.6
5	Exponential functions	3.1, 3.2
6	Sinusoidal functions	4.4
7	Other trigonometric functions	4.5
8	Inverse trigonometric functions	4.7
9	Parametric relations	6.3
10	Numerical derivatives and integrals	11.4

For those using *Precalculus,* there are excellent features and calculus cues with the book. A few of them are noted below:

- Chapter P—Prerequisites. This wonderfully concise opening chapter identifies mathematical content, algebraic manipulation skills, and technology-related knowledge needed in both precalculus and calculus courses.

- Chapter 1, Section 1 provides a problem-solving process that incorporates the traditional algebraic methods as well as the graphical and numerical methods associated with graphing utilities.

- Chapter 1, Section 3 highlights the twelve basic functions that are used throughout calculus and captures their respective properties. This display is so useful that it is reprinted on the next pages of this book. Knowledge of these functions will be incredibly important because they are used constantly to illustrate calculus concepts and to model real-world phenomena (e.g., linearity, exponential growth, or periodicity).

- Throughout *Precalculus,* many examples and topics are marked with an icon, Σ, to point out concepts that foreshadow calculus concepts such as limits, extrema, asymptotes, and continuity. For your convenience, the table that follows shows each *Precalculus* icon location and references the AP* Calculus Concept Outline found in Part I.

Precalculus Icon Location	Precalculus Icon Reference Description	AP* Calculus Concept Outline Big Idea Number
1.2, p. 84	Continuity	1. Continuity as a property of functions.
1.2, p. 86	Increasing/Decreasing Functions	2. Relationship between the increasing and decreasing behavior of f and the sign of f'.
1.3, p. 99	What Graphs Can Tell Us	1. Analysis of graphs.
1.3, p. 103	Analyzing Functions Graphically	1. Analysis of graphs.
1.7, p. 142	Finding the Model and Solving	2. Modeling rates of change, including related rates problems.
2.1, p. 160	Average Rate of Change	2. Instantaneous rate of change as the limit of average rate of change.
2.1, p. 161	Rate of Change	2. Approximate rate of change from graphs and tables of values.
2.1, p. 166	Predicting Maximum Revenue	2. Optimization, both absolute (global) and relative (local) extrema.
2.1, p. 167	Vertical Velocity, Vertical Position	2. Interpretation of the derivative as a rate of change in varied applied contexts, including velocity, speed, and acceleration.
2.1, p. 167	Modeling Vertical Free-Fall Motion	2. Interpretation of the derivative as a rate of change in varied applied contexts, including velocity, speed, and acceleration.
2.3, p. 187	Local Extrema	2. Optimization, both absolute (global) and relative (local) extrema.
2.3, p. 190	Intermediate Value Theorem	1. Geometric understanding of graphs of continuous functions (Intermediate Value Theorem and Extreme Value Theorem).
2.7, p. 231	Finding a Minimum Perimeter	2. Optimization, both absolute (global) and relative (local) extrema.
2.7, p. 231	Designing a Juice Can	2. Optimization, both absolute (global) and relative (local) extrema.
3.1, p. 253	Computing Exponential Function Values for Rational Number Inputs	Relevant in Calculus but not listed specifically in the AP* Course Outline.
3.1, p. 253	Approximating Exponential Function Values for Irrational Number Inputs	Relevant in Calculus but not listed specifically in the AP* Course Outline.
3.1, p. 256	Natural Exponential Function	Relevant in Calculus but not listed specifically in the AP* Course Outline.
3.3, p. 277	Natural Logarithms	Relevant in Calculus but not listed specifically in the AP* Course Outline.
3.4, p. 285	Change of Base for Logarithms	Relevant in Calculus but not listed specifically in the AP* Course Outline.
3.4, p. 286	Graphs of Logarithmic Functions with Base b	Relevant in Calculus but not listed specifically in the AP* Course Outline.
3.5, p. 292	Solving an Exponential Equation	Relevant in Calculus but not listed specifically in the AP* Course Outline.
4.1, p. 323	Angular and Linear Motion	Relevant in Calculus but not listed specifically in the AP* Course Outline.
4.7, p. 383	Trigonometric Compositions	Relevant in Calculus but not listed specifically in the AP* Course Outline.
4.7, p. 383	Composing Trig Functions with Arcsine	Relevant in Calculus but not listed specifically in the AP* Course Outline.
5.1, p. 405	Pythagorean Identities	Relevant in Calculus but not listed specifically in the AP* Course Outline.
5.2, p. 417	Identities in Calculus	Relevant in Calculus but not listed specifically in the AP* Course Outline.
5.4, p. 428	Power-Reducing Identities	Relevant in Calculus but not listed specifically in the AP* Course Outline.
6.3, p. 480	Projectile Motion	Relevant in Calculus but not listed specifically in the AP* Course Outline.
8.6, p. 625	Quadratic Surfaces	3. Applications of integrals. Volumes of known cross sections.
9.4, p. 658	Summation Notation	4. Concepts of series.
9.5, p. 662	Infinite Series	4. Concepts of series.

Analysis of Graphs

Objectives:
- Predict and explain behavior of a function.
- Interplay between the geometric and analytic information.

Overview

Analyzing graphs is a critical tool in the study of calculus. With the use of graphs we can make conjectures, solve problems, and support our written work. The graphing calculator has enabled us to quickly and easily produce graphs of functions. It is very important, however, that we have an understanding of the graphs of basic functions and their behaviors in order to determine which function best models a given situation and to select an appropriate viewing window on our calculators or axis labels on our graphs. In precalculus, your studies included the following key function behaviors: domain and range, whether a function is odd or even, symmetry, whether a function is periodic or continuous, zeros, intercepts, asymptotes, extrema, translations, increasing, decreasing, boundedness, and end behavior.

Content and Practice

The AP Calculus Teacher's Guide states that as a prerequisite to calculus, students should be familiar with the properties of the graphs of linear, polynomial, rational, exponential, logarithmic, trigonometric, inverse trigonometric, and piecewise functions. In your precalculus class, you studied twelve basic functions. These twelve are very useful for understanding graphs and their transformations.

The Identity Function

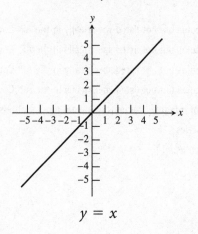

$y = x$

The Squaring Function

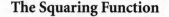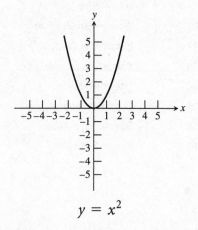

$y = x^2$

The Cubing Function

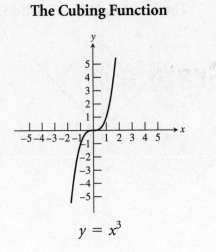

$$y = x^3$$

The Reciprocal Function

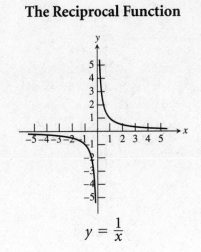

$$y = \frac{1}{x}$$

The Square Root Function

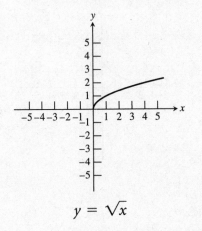

$$y = \sqrt{x}$$

The Exponential Function

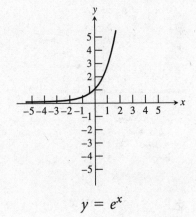

$$y = e^x$$

The Natural Logarithm Function

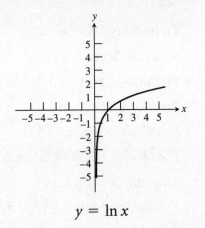

$$y = \ln x$$

The Sine Function

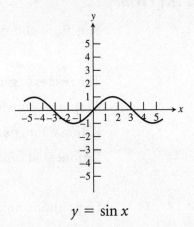

$$y = \sin x$$

The Cosine Function

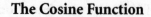
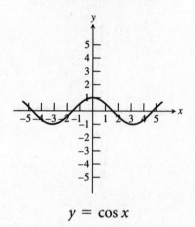

$$y = \cos x$$

The Absolute Value Function

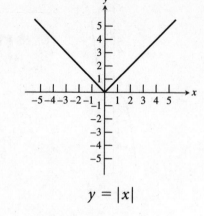

$$y = |x|$$

The Greatest Integer Function

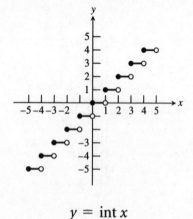

$$y = \operatorname{int} x$$

The Logistic Function

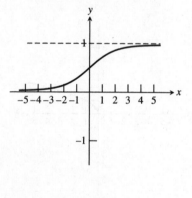

$$y = \frac{1}{1 + e^{-x}}$$

Need More Help With . . .

    Functions and their properties?

    The twelve basic functions?

    Graphical transformations?

    Rational functions?

    Exponential functions?

    Logarithmic functions?

    Sinusoids?

See . . .

Precalculus, Section 1.2

Calculus, Section 1.2

Precalculus, Section 1.3

Precalculus, Section 1.6

Precalculus, Section 2.6

Precalculus, Sections 3.1, 3.2, 3.5

Calculus, Section 1.3

Precalculus, Sections 3.3, 3.4, 3.5

Calculus, Section 1.5

Precalculus, Section 4.4

Calculus, Section 1.6

Functions

Objectives:

- Identify the domain and range for a given function.
- Compute the x- and y-intercepts for a given function.

Overview

Functions are the key mathematical concept in precalculus and calculus. You should understand the definition of a function and how functions are described by equations and tables. Every function has a corresponding graph. The ability to look at functions from an algebraic, numerical, and graphical perspective will be a great aid in understanding the concepts of precalculus and calculus.

Content and Practice

A *relation* is defined as a set of ordered pairs, usually of real numbers. A *function* is a relation for which each ordered pair (x, y) has a unique x-coordinate; that is, no two pairs may have the same x-coordinate. Some functions are not written as (x, y) pairs, but the definition still holds: the first coordinate, whatever the variable, must be unique.

The *domain* of a function is the set of all x-coordinates (first coordinates). It is understood that if a domain is not given for a function, we should select the largest domain possible—that is, all possible real values of x that can be used. Two very common reasons that restrict domains to only certain real numbers are zero denominators and square roots of negative numbers. The *range* of a function is the set of all y-coordinates (second coordinates). Sometimes the easiest way to confirm the range of a function is to inspect its graph.

The y-intercept of a function is the y-coordinate of the point whose x-coordinate is 0; the corresponding point of the graph intersects the y-axis. The x-intercepts of a function are the x-coordinates of the points that have a y-coordinate of 0. The corresponding points of the graph intersect the x-axis.

1. A function f is defined as $f(x) = \sqrt{x + 4}$.

    (a) Identify the domain of the function.

(b) Identify the range of the function.

(c) Compute the y-intercept.

(d) Compute the x-intercept(s).

(e) Sketch a graph of the function.

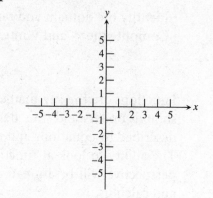

 2.   A function f is defined as $f(x) = x^2 - 2x - 3$.

(a) Identify the domain of the function.

(b) Identify the range of the function.

(c) Compute the y-intercept.

(d) Compute the x-intercept(s).

(e) Sketch a graph of the function.

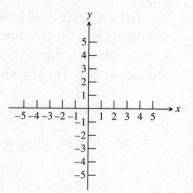

1.   The domain for the function $f(x) = \dfrac{1}{\sqrt{x-2}}$ is

(A) $x \geq 0$ (B) $x < 2$

(C) $x > 2$ (D) $x \geq 2$

2.   For each function below:

(i)   Sketch a graph. (Can you do it without the use of a calculator?)

(ii) Identify the domain.

(iii) Identify the range.

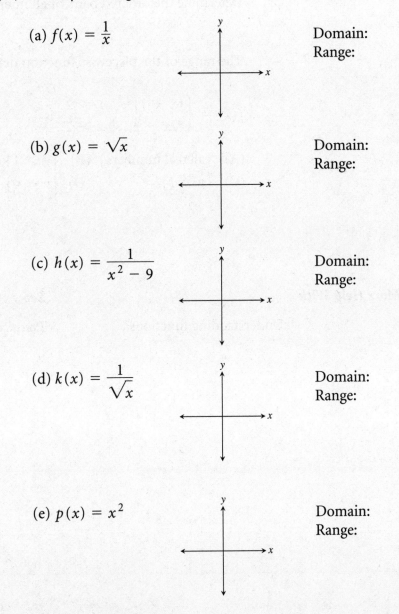

(a) $f(x) = \dfrac{1}{x}$ Domain:
Range:

(b) $g(x) = \sqrt{x}$ Domain:
Range:

(c) $h(x) = \dfrac{1}{x^2 - 9}$ Domain:
Range:

(d) $k(x) = \dfrac{1}{\sqrt{x}}$ Domain:
Range:

(e) $p(x) = x^2$ Domain:
Range:

(f) $q(x) = \sin x$

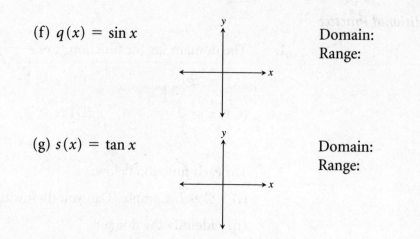

Domain:

Range:

(g) $s(x) = \tan x$

Domain:

Range:

3.   Determine the ordered pairs of all intercepts of $f(x) = x^3 - 9x$.

4.   The range of the piecewise function defined by

$$f(x) = \begin{cases} (x-1)^2, & x < 2 \\ 2x - 3, & x > 2 \end{cases} \text{ is}$$

(A) {all real numbers} (B) $\{y > 1\}$

(C) $\{y \neq 1\}$ (D) $\{y \geq 0\}$

Need More Help With . . .

Understanding functions?

See . . .

Precalculus, Section 1.2

Transformations

Objectives:

- Write the function rule, given a parent function and a set of transformations.
- Identify the transformations for a given function rule and parent function.

Overview

In addition to being familiar with a basic set of parent functions and their corresponding graphs, you should be able to describe important features of other functions in the family of functions associated with a particular parent function.

Content and Practice

We relate graphs using **transformations,** which are functions that map real numbers to real numbers. By acting on the *x*-coordinates and *y*-coordinates of points, transformations change graphs in predictable ways.

The key transformations are translations, reflections, stretches, and shrinks.

Translations

Let *c* be a positive real number. Then the following transformations result in translations (shifts) of the graph of $y = f(x)$:

Horizontal translations

$y = f(x - c)$ a translation to the right by *c* units

$y = f(x + c)$ a translation to the left by *c* units

Vertical translations

$y = f(x) + c$ a translation upward of *c* units

$y = f(x) - c$ a translation downward of *c* units

Reflections

The following transformations result in reflections of the graph of $y = f(x)$:

Across the x-axis
$$y = -f(x)$$

Across the y-axis
$$y = f(-x)$$

Stretches and Shrinks

Let c be a positive real number. Then the following transformations result in stretches or shrinks of the graph of $y = f(x)$:

Horizontal stretches or shrinks

$y = f\left(\frac{x}{c}\right)$ a stretch by a factor of c, if $c > 1$
a shrink by a factor of c, if $c < 1$

Vertical stretches or shrinks

$y = c \cdot f(x)$ a stretch by a factor of c, if $c > 1$
a shrink by a factor of c, if $c < 1$

When two vertical transformations are used, the order of operations prevails. For example, a vertical stretch would be done before a vertical shift. However, when two horizontal transformations are used, it is generally easier to describe the transformation in reverse—for example, a shift before a stretch.

1.   A function g is defined as $g(x) = 2\sqrt{x + 4} + 3$.

(a) Identify the domain of the function.

(b) Identify the range of the function.

(c) Describe the transformations that show how the graph of this function is obtained from the graph of the parent function $f(x) = \sqrt{x}$.

(d) Sketch a graph of the function.

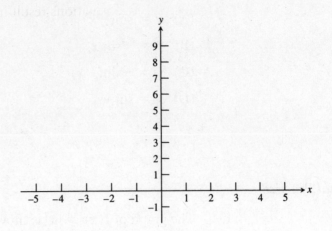

2.   The graph of a function $g(x)$ is obtained from the graph of the parent function $f(x) = x^2$ by an x-axis reflection, a vertical stretch by 3, a vertical shift down 4, and a horizontal shift right 1.

(a) Write the equation that describes the rule for the function.

(b) Sketch a graph of the function.

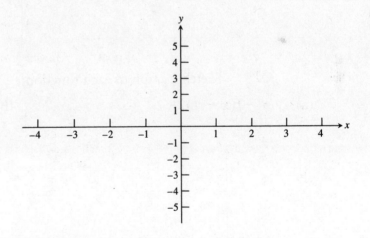

(c) Identify the range of the function.

3. The equation of the graph of $y = \sin x$ reflected across the x-axis is

(A) $y = \sin(-x)$

(B) $y = -\sin x$

(C) $y = -\sin(-x)$

(D) $x = \sin y$

Additional Practice

1. The graph of $f(x) = |x|$ is shown in the figure.

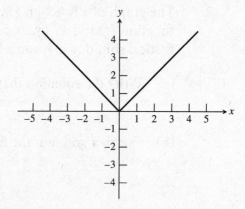

Sketch a graph of each function.

(a) $y = -f(x - 1) + 2$

(b) $y = 2f\left(\dfrac{x}{3} + 1\right)$

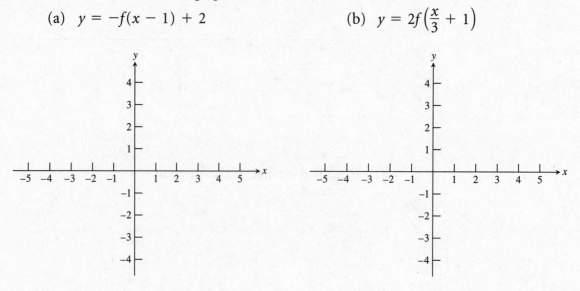

2. Which of the following represents a vertical shift up 3 and a horizontal shift left 4 of $f(x) = |x|$?

(A) $g(x) = |x + 4| - 3$ (B) $g(x) = |x - 4| + 3$

(C) $g(x) = |x + 4| + 3$ (D) $g(x) = |x + 3| - 4$

3. Which of the following represents the graph of $y = f(x)$ first shifted down 1 and then reflected in the x-axis?

(A) $y = f(-x) - 1$ (B) $y = -(f(x) - 1)$

(C) $y = -f(x) - 1$ (D) $y = f(-x) + 1$

Need More Help With . . .

Transformations?

See . . .

Precalculus, Section 1.6

Polynomial Functions

Objectives:

- Determine the possible number of real zeros for a polynomial function.
- Determine the possible number of extrema for a polynomial function.
- Determine the end behavior of a polynomial function.
- Determine the intervals where a polynomial function is increasing or decreasing.
- Compute zeros and extrema of a polynomial function.

Overview

You should be familiar with the family of functions known as *polynomial functions*. These functions are continuous. The degree and the leading coefficient describe specific patterns of increasing/decreasing and end behavior as well as the possible number of zeros and extreme points.

Content and Practice

For this section we are assuming polynomial functions with real coefficients and unrestricted domains.

A polynomial function of odd degree always has at least one real zero. (Since function "zeros" equate to graphical x-intercepts, that also guarantees that the graph of a polynomial of odd degree must intersect the x-axis at least once.) Because nonreal zeros occur in conjugate pairs, the possible number of real zeros increases by two, up to the degree of the function. Thus, a third-degree polynomial function has one or three real zeros, and a fifth-degree polynomial function has one, three, or five real zeros. Similarly, a fourth-degree polynomial function has zero, two, or four real zeros.

1. Use a graphing calculator to graph a variety of cubic equations: $y = x^3, y = x^3 - 3, y = x^3 - x^2, y = x^3 - x^2 - 2$, and others of your choice.

   (a) Note the number of distinct real zeros of each function.

   (b) Note the number of x-intercepts of the corresponding graph.

(c) Note the number of extrema of each function.

(d) Note the end behaviors of each function.

⊞ 2. Use a graphing calculator to graph a variety of fourth-degree equations: $y = x^4$, $y = x^4 - x$, $y = x^4 - x^2$, $y = x^4 - x^3 + 2x^2 - x - 1$, and others of your choice.

(a) Note the number of distinct real zeros of each function.

(b) Note the number of x-intercepts of the corresponding graph.

(c) Note the number of extrema of each function.

(d) Note the end behaviors of each function.

When a function such as $y = (x - 5)^3$ or $y = x^5$ has a single factor that is repeated, in general form $(x - c)^m$, we say that the respective zero has multiplicity m. So for $y = (x - 5)^3$ in which $(x - 5)$ is a repeated factor, 5 is a zero of multiplicity 3. For $y = x^5$, 0 is a zero of multiplicity 5.

The end behavior of a polynomial function of even degree is the same as x approaches both positive and negative infinity. When the leading coefficient is positive, the end behavior is: as $x \to \infty$, $y \to \infty$, and as $x \to -\infty$, $y \to \infty$. When the leading coefficient is negative, the end behavior is: as $x \to \infty$, $y \to -\infty$, and as $x \to -\infty$, $y \to -\infty$. Because of this behavior, a polynomial function of even degree has an odd number of extrema. For example, a fourth-degree function has three or one extrema.

The end behavior of a polynomial function of odd degree is different as x approaches both positive and negative infinity. When the leading coefficient is positive, the end behavior is: as $x \to \infty$, $y \to \infty$, and as $x \to -\infty$, $y \to -\infty$. When the leading coefficient is negative, the end behavior is: as $x \to \infty$, $y \to -\infty$, and as $x \to -\infty$, $y \to \infty$. Because of this behavior, a polynomial function of odd degree has an even number of extrema. For example, a fifth-degree function has four, two, or no extrema.

3. A function f is defined as $f(x) = 2x^3 - 9x^2 - 24x + 31$.

(a) Identify the *possible* number of real zeros.

(b) Identify the *possible* number of extreme points.

(c) Predict the end behavior of f.

(d) Compute all real zeros.

(e) Compute the coordinates of all extrema.

(f) Describe the rising/falling behavior of the graph.

(g) Sketch the graph of f. Confirm with a graphing calculator.

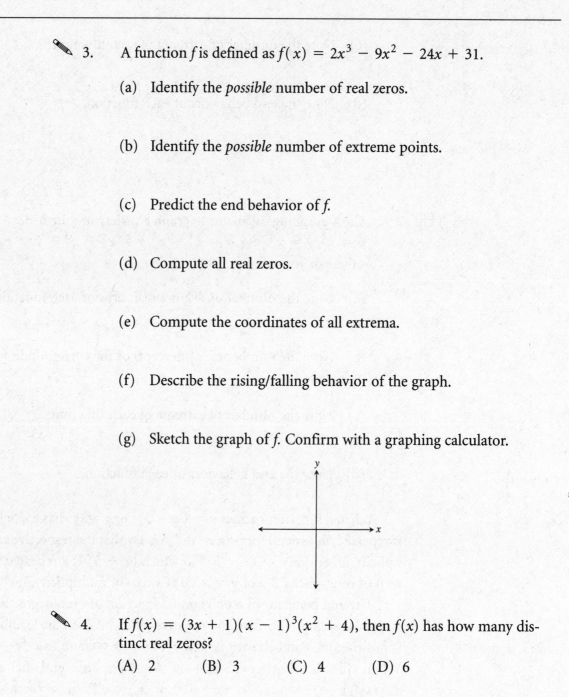

4. If $f(x) = (3x + 1)(x - 1)^3(x^2 + 4)$, then $f(x)$ has how many distinct real zeros?

(A) 2   (B) 3   (C) 4   (D) 6

1.   A function f is defined as $f(x) = x^4 - 8x^2 + 7$.

(a)   Identify the possible number of real zeros.

(b)   Identify the possible number of extreme points.

(c)   Predict the end behavior of f.

(d)   Compute all real zeros.

(e)   Compute the coordinates of all extrema.

(f)   Describe the rising/falling behavior of the graph.

(g)   Sketch the graph of f. Confirm with a graphing calculator.

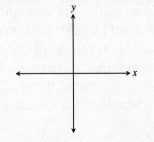

2.   Which of the following describes the possible number of real zeros and extrema for a fifth-degree polynomial function?

(A)   5 real zeros; 4 extrema

(B)   4, 2, or 0 real zeros; 3 or 1 extrema

(C)   5, 3, or 1 real zeros; 4 extrema

(D)   5, 3, or 1 real zeros; 4, 2, or 0 extrema

Need More Help With . . .

Polynomial functions?

See . . .

Precalculus, Section 2.3

Rational Functions

- Determine the domain for a rational function.
- Determine the vertical asymptotes and removable discontinuities.
- Determine the end behavior for a rational function, including horizontal asymptotes.

Overview

You should be familiar with the family of functions known as *rational functions*. These functions are usually continuous over their domain, but have values that are not in the domain. Thus, they are often not continuous everywhere. You should be able to determine the behavior of the function at these points. In addition, you should be able to describe the end behavior. All of this information should be used to sketch a graph. The ability to look at these functions from an algebraic, numerical, and graphical perspective will be a great aid in understanding the calculus concept of limits.

Content and Practice

A rational function is a ratio of two polynomial functions.

$$f(x) = \frac{5x}{x+3} \qquad g(x) = \frac{x^2-4}{x-2} \qquad h(x) = \frac{x^2-3x-18}{x^2-6x} \qquad k(x) = \frac{x+1}{(x+1)^3}$$

▪ *Domains:* If the function in the denominator has any real zeros, these values are not in the domain.

- The domain of $f(x)$ does not include -3.
- The domain of $g(x)$ does not include 2.
- The domain of $h(x)$ does not include 0 or 6.
- The domain of $k(x)$ does not include -1.

▪ *Removable discontinuities:* You should determine if the function has a removable discontinuity. You could factor the numerator and denominator separately. If a linear factor in the denominator appears at least as often in the numerator, then the function will have a removable discontinuity at the value that makes that factor zero.

- $g(x)$ has a removable discontinuity at 2 because it has a common factor of $(x - 2)$ in its numerator and denominator. Since $\lim\limits_{x \to 2} g(x) = 4$, $(2, 4)$ is identified as the ordered pair associated with the removable discontinuity.

- $h(x)$ has a removable discontinuity at 6 for a similar reason. Since $\lim\limits_{x \to 6} g(x) = \frac{3}{2}$, $\left(6, \frac{3}{2}\right)$ is identified as the ordered pair associated with the removable discontinuity.

▮ *Vertical asymptotes:* You should determine if the function has a vertical asymptote. Again, considering the linear factors in the numerator and denominator, if the factor is in the denominator only, or is a factor of the denominator more times than in the numerator, then the function has a vertical asymptote at the value that makes the factor zero.

  - $f(x)$ has a vertical asymptote at $x = -3$.
  - $h(x)$ has a vertical asymptote at $x = 0$.
  - $k(x)$ has a vertical asymptote at $x = -1$.

In the language of calculus, we wish to determine the values that are not in the domain. Then, we investigate the limit as x approaches that value. If the limit is finite, then we have a removable discontinuity; if it is infinite, then there is an asymptote.

▮ *End behavior:* You should also investigate the end behavior. If the degree of the numerator is less than the degree of the denominator, then the end behavior is zero and the function has a horizontal asymptote, $y = 0$.

  - $k(x)$ has a horizontal asymptote, $y = 0$.

▮ *Horizontal asymptotes:* If the degree of the numerator is the same as the degree of the denominator, the function has a horizontal asymptote but not at zero. The value is determined by the ratio of the leading coefficients.

  - $f(x)$ has a horizontal asymptote, $y = 5$.
  - $h(x)$ has a horizontal asymptote, $y = 1$.

▮ *Slant asymptotes:* If the degree of the numerator is one higher than the degree of the denominator, the function has a linear asymptote but it is not horizontal; rather, it is a slant (or oblique) asymptote.

- *Non-linear asymptotes:* If the degree of the numerator is more than one higher than the degree of the denominator, the function has an end behavior asymptote but it is not linear. For example, if the degree of the numerator is two higher, expect a parabolic asymptote.

In the case of either slant and parabolic asymptotes, the end behavior asymptote is determined by the quotient (without remainder) of the ratio of the two polynomials.

- $g(x)$ has a slant asymptote, $y = x + 2$.
- None of the functions f, g, h, or k has a non-linear asymptote.

1. A function f is defined as $f(x) = \dfrac{x^2 + 3x - 18}{x^2 - 9}$.

   (a) Write the domain.

   (b) Write the ordered pair for any removable discontinuities.

   (c) Write the equation for any vertical asymptotes.

   (d) Write the equation for any horizontal asymptotes.

   (e) Describe the end behavior of f.

   (f) Compute the y-intercept.

(g) Sketch the graph of f.

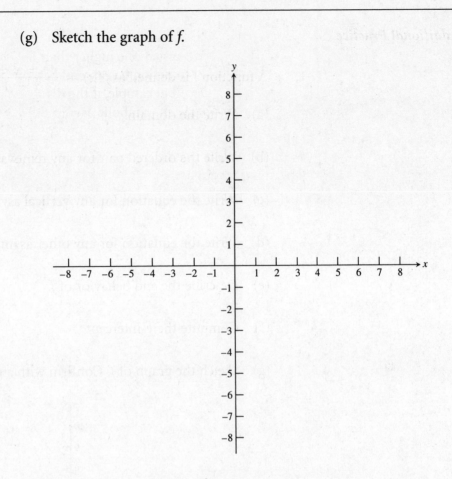

2. $f(x)$ is defined as $f(x) = \dfrac{x^2}{x-1}$.

(a) Complete the table of values for $f(x)$.

x	$f(x)$
0	
0.9	
0.99	
0.999	
1.001	
1.01	
1.1	
2	

(b) Referring to the table of values, describe the graph of f near $x = 1$.

1. A function f is defined as $f(x) = \dfrac{x^2 + x + 3}{x - 1}$.

    (a) Write the domain.

    (b) Write the ordered pair for any removable discontinuities.

    (c) Write the equation for any vertical asymptotes.

    (d) Write the equation for any other asymptotes.

    (e) Describe the end behavior of f.

    (f) Compute the y-intercept.

    (g) Sketch the graph of f. Confirm with a graphing calculator.

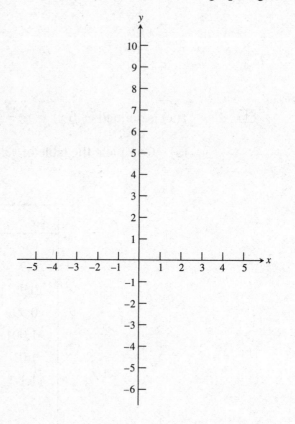

2. Which of the following best describes the behavior of the function $f(x) = \dfrac{x^2 - 2x}{x^2 - 4}$ at the values not in its domain?

(A) One vertical asymptote, no removable discontinuities

(B) Two vertical asymptotes

(C) One removable discontinuity, one vertical asymptote, $x = 2$

(D) One removable discontinuity, one vertical asymptote, $x = -2$

Need More Help With . . .	See . . .
Rational functions?	*Precalculus,* Section 2.6

Exponential Functions

Objectives:

- Determine the range for an exponential function.
- Determine the end behavior for an exponential function, including horizontal asymptotes.

Overview

You should be familiar with the family of functions known as *exponential functions*. These functions usually have a domain of all real numbers and are continuous over their domain. You should be able to describe the end behavior, which often includes a horizontal asymptote in one direction. All of this information should be used to sketch a graph.

Content and Practice

A basic exponential function has an equation of the form $f(x) = a \cdot b^x$. Transformed functions may have additional coefficients, such as $f(x) = a \cdot b^{x-h} + k$. For $a = \frac{1}{2}$, $b = 3$, $h = 0$, and $k = -4$, the function is $f(x) = \frac{1}{2} 3^x - 4$ and its graph is shown in the figure.

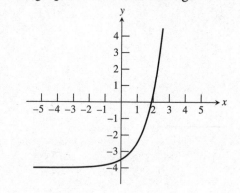

    The end behavior of such functions will always be infinite as $x \rightarrow \infty$ (if $b > 1$) or $x \rightarrow -\infty$ (if $0 < b < 1$) and have a horizontal asymptote for the other direction. Related behavior will mean that the function is either increasing or decreasing and that the graph of the function is rising or falling.

Exponential functions model many real phenomena, such as population growth, half-life decay, and Newton's law of cooling. For many of these models the y-intercept represents an initial value (at time 0) for the variable that y represents.

Example: A town's population is 3000 and projected to double every 10 years. An exponential model for the population, P, expected in d decades, would be $P = 3000 \cdot 2^d$.

1. A function f is defined as $f(x) = 24\left(\frac{1}{2}\right)^x + 4$.

   (a) Compute the y-intercept.

   (b) Compute $f(x)$ for $x \in \{-2, -1, 1, 2\}$.

   (c) Is f increasing or decreasing? Explain.

   (d) Write the equation for the horizontal asymptote.

   (e) Describe the end behavior of f.

   (f) Sketch the graph of f.

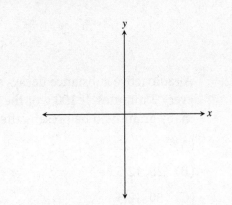

1. A function f is defined as $f(x) = 3 \cdot 2^x$.

    (a) Compute the y-intercept.

    (b) Compute $f(x)$ for $x \in \{-2, -1, 1, 2\}$.

    (c) Is f increasing or decreasing?

    (d) Write the equation for the horizontal asymptote.

    (e) Describe the end behavior of f.

    (f) Sketch the graph of f.

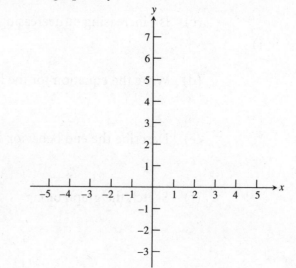

2. A radioactive substance decays so that half of the substance decays every 2 minutes. If 100 g of the substance are present initially, how many grams will be present after 4 minutes and 8 minutes, respectively?

    (A) 25, 6.25

    (B) 25, 12.5

    (C) 50, 12.5

    (D) 50, 25

Need More Help With . . .   *See . . .*

Exponential functions?   *Precalculus*, Sections 3.1–3.3

Sinusoidal Functions

- Determine the equations for a sinusoidal function for a particular graph.
- Determine the transformations for a sinusoidal function, given an equation.

Overview

Functions are the key mathematical concept in precalculus and calculus. You should be familiar with the family of functions known as *trigonometric functions*. The first type we investigate are *sinusoidal functions*, defined as a *sine* or *cosine function*. You should be able to sketch a graph for these types of functions, given the equation. You should also be able to describe the transformations that show how the graph compares to the basic sine or cosine graph. The ability to look at these functions from an algebraic, numerical, and graphical perspective will be a great aid in understanding the concepts of precalculus and calculus.

Content and Practice

The two basic sinusoidal functions are $y = \sin(x)$ and $y = \cos(x)$. Transformed functions will have additional coefficients, such as $y = a \cdot \sin[b(x - h)] + k$. The coefficient a determines the amplitude, the same transformation as a vertical stretch. The coefficient k determines the vertical shift. The coefficient h determines the horizontal shift, which in trigonometry is often referred to as a phase shift. The coefficient b determines the horizontal stretch or shrink. Because sinusoidal graphs are periodic, this coefficient also determines the period of the graph, found by computing $\frac{2\pi}{|b|}$.

1. A function f is defined as $f(x) = 3 \cos\left[\frac{1}{2}\left(x - \frac{\pi}{4}\right)\right] + 1$.

   (a) Determine the amplitude.

   (b) Determine the vertical shift.

   (c) Determine the range of the function.

(d) Determine the horizontal shift.

(e) Determine the period.

(f) Write the coordinates of two local maximum and two local minimum points.

(g) Sketch the graph.

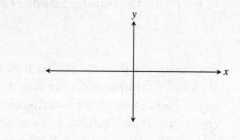

2. The graph of a sinusoidal function is shown.

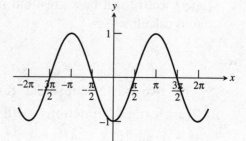

(a) Write the coordinates of two local maximum and two local minimum points.

(b) Determine the amplitude.

(c) Determine the vertical shift.

(d) Determine the period.

(e) Write the equation of a cosine function that has this graph. Identify the horizontal shift for this function.

(f) Write the equation of a sine function that has this graph. Identify the horizontal shift for this function.

Additional Practice

1. A sinusoidal function has a local maximum at $(2, 8)$ and the next local minimum at $(6, -2)$.

   (a) Determine the amplitude.

   (b) Determine the vertical shift.

   (c) Determine the range of the function.

   (d) Determine the period.

   (e) Write the equation of a cosine function that has this graph. Identify the horizontal shift for this function.

   (f) Write the equation of a sine function that has this graph. Identify the horizontal shift for this function.

   (g) Sketch the graph.

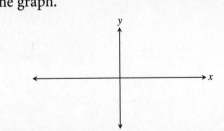

2. A sinusoidal function has a local maximum at $(0, 2)$ and the next minimum at $(\pi/4, -2)$. A correct equation for the function is

(A) $y = 2 \cos (4x)$

(B) $y = 2 \sin (4x)$

(C) $y = 4 \cos (x)$

(D) $y = 4 \cos (4x)$

3. The function $y = -3 \cos (x - \pi/4)$ has a local maximum at which point?

(A) $(\pi/4, 3)$

(B) $(3\pi/4, 3)$

(C) $(5\pi/4, 1)$

(D) $(5\pi/4, 3)$

Need More Help With . . .

Sinusoidal functions?

See . . .

Precalculus, Section 4.4

More Trigonometric Functions

Objectives:

- Sketch the graph of a trigonometric function.
- Determine the transformations for a trigonometric function, given an equation.

Overview

You should be familiar with the family of functions known as *trigonometric functions*. In the previous section, we explored sine and cosine functions. This section explores the other trigonometric functions, the *tangent, cotangent, secant,* and *cosecant functions*. You should be able to sketch a graph for these types of functions, given the equation. You should also be able to describe the transformations that show how the graph compares to the basic trigonometric graph. The ability to look at these functions from an algebraic, numerical, and graphical perspective will be a great aid in understanding the concepts of precalculus and calculus.

Content and Practice

The first new trigonometric function is $y = \tan(x)$. One definition states that $\tan(x) = \dfrac{\sin(x)}{\cos(x)}$. Therefore, the domain of this function does not include all real numbers; it excludes values where $\cos(x) = 0$, namely the odd multiples of $\pi/2$. The graph of $y = \tan(x)$ will have vertical asymptotes at these values. Transformed functions may have additional coefficients. However, the main transformations are those that transform these vertical asymptotes—the horizontal stretch, shrink, or shift. The basic function $y = \tan(x)$ has period π, and the function $y = \tan(bx)$ has period $\dfrac{\pi}{|b|}$.

Each of the sine, cosine, and tangent functions has a reciprocal function. They are the cosecant, secant, and cotangent functions, respectively. All of these reciprocal functions also have vertical asymptotes. The cotangent function has period $\frac{\pi}{|b|}$, but the secant and cosecant functions have period $\frac{2\pi}{|b|}$.

1.　A function f is defined as $f(x) = \tan\left(\frac{1}{2}x\right)$.

　(a)　Determine the period.

　(b)　Determine the domain.

　(c)　Determine the equations of the vertical asymptotes.

　(d)　Determine the x-intercepts.

　(e)　Sketch the graph, showing several periods.

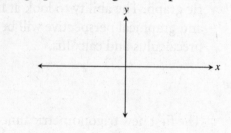

2.　Write the transformations that describe how the graph of $g(x) = 2\csc(3(x - \pi)) + 1$ compares to the graph of $f(x) = \csc(x)$.

3. Sketch each pair of functions on the same set of axes; show at least two periods and label the axes.

(a) $y = \cos x$ and $y = \sec x$

(b) $y = \sin x$ and $y = \sin\left(x - \dfrac{\pi}{2}\right) + 2$

(c) $y = \tan x$ and $y = \cot x$

Additional Practice

1. A function f is defined as $f(x) = 3 \sec(2x) + 1$.

(a) Determine the period.

(b) Determine the domain.

(c) Determine the equations of the vertical asymptotes.

(d) Determine the vertical shift.

(e) Write the coordinates of two local maximum and two local minimum points.

(f) Sketch the graph, showing several periods.

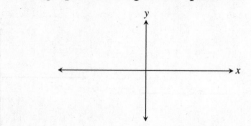

2. If the graph of $f(x) = \cot(x)$ is transformed by a horizontal shrink of $\frac{1}{4}$ and a horizontal shift left π, the result is the graph of

(A) $g(x) = \cot\left[\frac{1}{4}(x - \pi)\right]$

(B) $g(x) = \cot[4(x - \pi)]$

(C) $g(x) = \cot[4(x + \pi)]$

(D) $g(x) = \cot(4x + \pi)$

3. The function $y = \tan\left(\frac{x}{3}\right)$ has an x-intercept at

(A) $\frac{x}{3}$

(B) π

(C) 3π

(D) 6π

Need More Help With . . .   ***See . . .***

Trigonometric functions?   *Precalculus*, Sections 4.2–4.6

Inverse Trigonometric Relations and Functions

Objectives:

- Identify the domain and range of an inverse trigonometric function.
- Compute values for inverse trigonometric relations and functions.

Overview

Each of the trigonometric functions has an *inverse relation*. These relations are not functions because the original functions are not one-to-one. You should be familiar with the infinite set of values for an inverse relation. However, if the range of the inverse relation is properly restricted, then the inverse is a function with only one specific value. You should be familiar with the domain and range of each of these functions.

Content and Practice

The equation $\sin(x) = \frac{1}{2}$ has an infinite number of solutions. In the *Precalculus* textbook, the symbol $\sin^{-1}\left(\frac{1}{2}\right)$ denotes a single value, $\frac{\pi}{6}$. The function $f(x) = \sin^{-1}(x)$ is the inverse sine function and it has domain $[-1, 1]$ and range $[-\pi, \pi]$. The restricted range is selected so that the inverse will have the same domain, will actually be a function, and will pass the vertical line test. We wish to accomplish the same thing with the inverse cosine but cannot use the same range because it would not pass the vertical line test. Thus, each of the trigonometric functions has an inverse. The sine, cosine, and tangent are summarized in the table below. There are certain values, such as our $\sin^{-1}\left(\frac{1}{2}\right)$ example, that you should be able to compute without a calculator; others require the use of a calculator.

Function	Domain	Range
$\sin^{-1}(x)$	$[-1, 1]$	$\left[-\frac{\pi}{2}, \frac{\pi}{2}\right]$
$\cos^{-1}(x)$	$[-1, 1]$	$[0, \pi]$
$\tan^{-1}(x)$	$(-\infty, \infty)$	$\left(-\frac{\pi}{2}, \frac{\pi}{2}\right)$

Sometimes you are asked to solve an equation such as $\sin(x) = -\frac{\sqrt{3}}{2}$. You can use the inverse trig function to find a solution. However, the equation actually has an infinite number of solutions. For example, $\sin^{-1}\left(-\frac{\sqrt{3}}{2}\right) = -\frac{\pi}{3}$, but sine is also negative in Quadrant III so $\frac{4\pi}{3}$ is also a solution. The complete set of solutions could be written as $\left\{-\frac{\pi}{3} + 2n\pi, \frac{4\pi}{3} + 2n\pi\right\}$, where n is an integer.

1. Compute exact values.

   (a) $\cos^{-1}\left(-\frac{\sqrt{3}}{2}\right)$

   (b) $\tan^{-1}(-1)$

   (c) $\sin^{-1}\left(\frac{\sqrt{2}}{2}\right)$

2. Evaluate (3 decimal places).

   (a) $\cos^{-1}(0.873)$

   (b) $\tan^{-1}(2.4)$

   (c) $\sin^{-1}(-0.671)$

   (d) $\sec^{-1}(-0.511)$

3. Write all solutions.

   (a) $\cos(x) = \frac{1}{2}$

   (b) $\sin(x) = -1$

   (c) $\tan(x) = -\frac{\sqrt{3}}{3}$

1. Evaluate (3 decimal places).

   (a) $\cos^{-1}(-0.246)$

   (b) $\tan^{-1}(-1.5)$

   (c) $\sin^{-1}(0.379)$

2. Solve each equation.

   (a) $3 + \tan(x) = 2$

   (b) $4\cos^2(x) = 3$

   (c) $2\sin^2(x) = \sin(x)$

   (d) $\cos^2(x) = 4$

3. $\sin^{-1}\left(-\dfrac{1}{2}\right) =$

   (a) $-\dfrac{\pi}{6}$

   (b) $-\dfrac{\pi}{3}$

   (c) $\dfrac{5\pi}{6}$

   (d) $\dfrac{7\pi}{6}$

Need More Help With . . .

    Inverse trigonometric functions?

    Solving trigonometric equations?

See . . .

Precalculus, Section 4.7

Precalculus, Sections 5.1–5.4

Parametric Relations

Objectives:

- Given parametric equations, plot relations by hand or calculator.
- Control the speed and direction of the plot by varying t and its increments or by varying the equations.
- Produce parametric equations for Cartesian equations.
- Convert parametric equations to Cartesian equations (eliminate the parameter).
- Model motion problems.

Overview

Parametrics offer a powerful method to plot many relations whether or not they are functions. They also allow us to model motion, since we have more control over how points are plotted. Beyond this course, you will work with the calculus of parametrics, so gaining a high level of comfort with them now will ensure future success.

Content and Practice

When you first learned to plot lines, you probably used a chart where you chose x-values and plugged them into an equation to produce y-values. With parametrics, the x- and y-values are produced independently by substituting for a third variable, t, called the parameter. In modeling motion, t usually represents time.

1. Given the following parametric equations, produce a table of values and plot the relation. The table has been started for you.

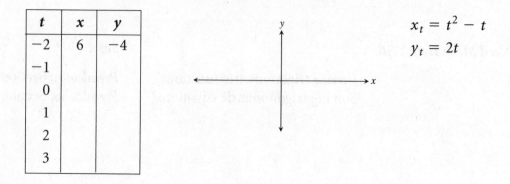

t	x	y
-2	6	-4
-1		
0		
1		
2		
3		

$$x_t = t^2 - t$$
$$y_t = 2t$$

2. Using substitution, convert the parametric equations in Problem 1 to Cartesian form. This is called eliminating the parameter. (*Hint:* Solve for x as a function of y.)

When parametric equations contain trigonometric functions, we often rely on a trigonometric identity rather than substitution to eliminate the parameter. Consider the parametric equations below.

$$x_t = \sec(t) \qquad y_t = \frac{1}{2}\tan^2(t)$$

If we use the trigonometric identity $1 + \tan^2\theta = \sec^2\theta$, the equation becomes $1 + 2y = x^2$.

3. Convert to Cartesian coordinates: $x = 3\sin(t)$, $y = 4\cos(t)$.
   (*Hint:* Divide each by the constant first.)

Any *function* can be converted to parametric form simply by letting the independent variable be t. So, for instance, $y = \sqrt{x^2 + 2x}$ can be converted to $x = t$ and $y = \sqrt{t^2 + 2t}$. We must realize, though, that due to limitations on the values of t we will not always produce a complete graph. For instance, $y = 2x - 1$ can be defined parametrically as $x = t$ and $y = 2t - 1$, but if t goes from -10 to 10, we would only see a plot of a segment from $(-10, -21)$ to $(10, 19)$.

4. Determine parametric equations to plot the right half of the parabola $y = (x - 2)^2$. Graph it on your calculator to see if you have achieved your goal.

$$x_t = \qquad\qquad t_{min} =$$
$$y_t = \qquad\qquad t_{max} =$$
$$\qquad\qquad\qquad t_{step} =$$

5. What is the effect of changing the increments of t, or t_{step} on the calculator? Find out by exploring. Try the following examples, comparing (a) to (b) and (a) to (c).

(a) $x_t = 2t - 1$ $t_{min} = 0$
     $y_t = \ t + 1$ $t_{max} = 3$
                      $t_{step} = 0.2$

(b) $x_t = 2t - 1$ $t_{min} = 0$
     $y_t = \ t + 1$ $t_{max} = 3$
                      $t_{step} = 0.02$

(c) $x_t = 2t - 1$ $t_{min} = \ \ 3$
     $y_t = \ t + 1$ $t_{max} = \ \ 0$
                      $t_{step} = -0.2$

i.   (a) compared to (b): What was the effect of making the t_{step} smaller? Explain why it caused that effect.

ii.   (a) compared to (c): What was the effect of a negative t_{step}? Explain why it caused that effect.

6. Compare the next two plots, where just the functions were changed slightly. (Make sure you plot in radians.) Explain the similarities and differences in the plots.

(a) $x_t = 3\cos(t)$ $t_{min} = 0$
     $y_t = 3\sin(t)$ $t_{max} = 6.3$
                      $t_{step} = 0.1$

(b) $x_t = \sin(t)$ $t_{min} = 0$
     $y_t = \cos(t)$ $t_{max} = 6.3$
                      $t_{step} = 0.1$

Parametric equations also allow us to model motion problems. We can model vertical motion, projectiles launched at an angle, circular motion, and many other kinds of motion.

To model vertical motion parametrically, let x equal any constant, e.g., $x = 1$. Let $y = -16t^2 + v_0 t + h_0$ where v_0 is the initial velocity in ft/sec and h_0 is the initial height in feet.

Projectile motion at an angle requires changing the equations slightly to $x = v_0 \cos(\theta) \cdot t$ and $y = -16t^2 + v_0 \sin(\theta) \cdot t + h_0$, where θ is the initial angle from the horizontal. These equations take into account the horizontal and vertical components of projectile motion as described in the *Precalculus* text. They ignore air resistance.

Circular motion is often modeled using $x = r \cdot \cos(b \cdot t) + c$ and $y = r \cdot \sin(b \cdot t) + d$, where r is the radius of motion, c is the horizontal shift, d is a vertical shift, and b is determined by the period.

7. A projectile is fired straight up from the ground with an initial velocity of 88 feet per second. Write parametric equations to model the motion.

8. A Ferris wheel has a diameter of 30 feet. Its lowest point is 8 feet off the ground. If it turns clockwise one full rotation each 20 seconds, write parametric equations to model a passenger's motion starting from the bottom and riding six full rotations.

Additional Practice

1. The parametric equations $x_t = 2t + 3$ and $y_t = \sqrt{t - 3}$ plot a portion of a/an
   (A) Line   (B) Parabola
   (C) Ellipse   (D) Hyperbola

2. A ball is thrown with an initial velocity of 48 feet per second at an angle of 35° with the ground. If the ball is released at an initial height of 5 feet off the ground, approximately how far will it travel horizontally before striking the ground?

(A) 45 feet

(B) 52 feet

(C) 68 feet

(D) 74 feet

Need More Help With . . .

Parametric equations?

See . . .

Precalculus, Section 6.3

Parametric, Polar, and Vector Functions

Objectives:

• Graph and evaluate functions defined in parametric, polar, and vector forms.

Overview

In function mode, y is a function of the independent variable x.

$$y = f(x)$$

In parametric mode, x and y are both functions of the independent parameter t.

$$x = f(t)$$
$$y = g(t)$$

In polar mode, r is a function of the independent variable θ.

$$r = f(\theta)$$

Vector-valued functions utilize parametric equations.

$$\mathbf{r}(t) = \langle f(t), g(t) \rangle \text{ with alternative notation}$$
$$\mathbf{r}(t) = f(t)\mathbf{i} + g(t)\mathbf{j}$$

Content and Practice

Parametric equations are often used to describe the motion of a particle in the plane. A graphing calculator can be used to see the path and direction of the particle.

1. During the time period from $t = 0$ to $t = 6$ seconds, a particle moves along the path given by

$$x(t) = 4 \cos \pi t$$
$$y(t) = 5 \sin \pi t$$

(a) Find the position of the particle when $t = 2.5$.

(b) Sketch the graph of the path of the particle from $t = 0$ to $t = 6$. Indicate the direction of the particle along its path.

(c) How many times does the particle pass through the point found in part (a)?

A calculator may be used on some problems to graph polar functions, but take care when using a graph to solve a system of polar equations.

⊞ 2.   Solve the following system.

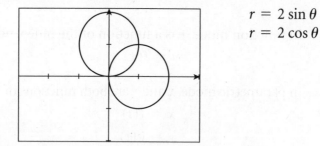

$$r = 2 \sin \theta$$
$$r = 2 \cos \theta$$

From the graph there appear to be two solutions: $(0, 0)$ and $\left(\dfrac{\pi}{4}, \sqrt{2} \right)$. However, substituting the ordered pairs in the system of equations shows only the second pair is a solution. This can be seen graphically if the calculator is placed in simultaneous mode before the graphs are drawn.

Vector-valued functions can be handled on the calculator using parametric mode.

⊞ 3.   The position of a moving particle is given by the vector function

$$\mathbf{r}(t) = \langle \cos(\pi t), t - 1 \rangle \text{ with alternate notation}$$
$$\mathbf{r}(t) = \cos(\pi t)\mathbf{i} + (t - 1)\mathbf{j}$$

(a) Find the position vector for the particle at $t = 1$.

(b) Graph the path of the particle for $0 \le t \le 2$.

Additional Practice

1. The position of a particle in a plane is described by the vector-valued function $r(t) = \langle e^{-t}, \cos t \rangle$. What is the position of the particle at $t = \frac{\pi}{2}$?

   (A) $\left(e^{-\frac{\pi}{2}}, 0 \right)$ (B) $\left(e^{-\frac{\pi}{2}}, 1 \right)$

   (C) $\left(-e^{-\frac{\pi}{2}}, 0 \right)$ (D) $\left(-e^{-\frac{\pi}{2}}, 1 \right)$

2. Consider the following polar functions.

$$r_1 = 4 \sin \theta$$
$$r_2 = 2$$

   (a) Graph the functions.

   (b) Find the points of intersection of the graphs of r_1 and r_2.

3. A particle moves along the path specified by the following parametric equations.

$$x(t) = \sin 2t$$
$$y(t) = \cos 2t$$

   Sketch the path of the particle.

Need More Help With . . .   **See . . .**

Need More Help With . . .	See . . .
Parametric equations?	*Precalculus,* Section 6.3
	Calculus, Section 11.1
Vector-valued functions?	*Calculus,* Section 11.2
Polar functions?	*Calculus,* Section 11.3

Numerical Derivatives and Integrals

Objectives:

- Estimate the slope of a curve at a particular point.
- Compute an average rate of change.
- Write an equation of the tangent line at a particular point on a particular curve.
- Estimate the area under a curve.

Overview

The two most fundamental concepts in all of calculus are those of a *derivative* and an *integral.* The derivative function tells us the slope of a curve at any point. A definite integral is used to compute the area under a curve.

Content and Practice

Your work with limits should have already developed the idea that places where a function looks "curved" may actually be locally linear (straight over infinitely small intervals). This allows us to talk about the slope of nonlinear functions. We define the slope of a secant on a function $f(x)$ to be

$$f(x) = \frac{f(x + h) - f(x)}{h}.$$

As the size of h gets smaller, the secant more and more accurately approximates the slope of the tangent line (if it exists) to the function at a given point $(x, f(x))$. The

$$\lim_{h \to 0} \frac{f(x + h) - f(x)}{h}$$

is the actual slope of the tangent to the function, when we can evaluate that limit.

When we cannot evaluate the limit, we can be satisfied with a fairly accurate numerical approximation we call the *numerical derivative.* Your calculator should have a built-in function to evaluate the numerical derivative. Most calculators use the symmetric difference quotient to estimate the derivative. The symmetric difference quotient uses points 0.001 units to the right and left of the place where we are trying to find the slope of the tangent. Calculating the

346

slope of the secant between those points usually provides a good approximation of the slope of the tangent:

$$m_{tan} \approx \frac{f(x + h) - f(x - h)}{2h}, \quad \text{with } h = 0.001.$$

The particular syntax for using a numerical derivative function on your calculator may be discussed in class or can be found in your calculator manual.

Be aware that built-in numerical derivatives work only on functions. A numerical derivative must be calculated manually when only discrete data are available. Under those circumstances, we find the slope on the smallest interval containing the point whose derivative we are seeking.

We also use the limit concept to compute the area under a curve. First we partition the domain of the function into small intervals. For each interval we draw a rectangle that estimates the area under the curve. The actual height used can be chosen from the left edge, the right edge, or the center of the interval. The sum of the area of the rectangles estimates the area under the curve. Your graphing calculator should also have a built-in function to estimate this area.

1. By using $f(0.999)$ and $f(1.001)$, find an approximation of the slope of the tangent to the function $f(x) = e^{2x}$ at $x = 1$. Use the built-in numerical derivative on your calculator to verify your answer.

2. Estimate the area under $f(x) = x^2 + 1$ over $[0, 3]$. Sketch a graph and shade the appropriate area.

Additional Practice

1. Which of the following is the equation of the line tangent to $y = \frac{1}{2}x^2 + 2x$ at the point where $x = 2$?
   (A) $y = 4x$ (B) $y = 4x + 6$
   (C) $y = 4x + 2$ (D) $y = 4x - 2$

2. The height of an object dropped from a 200-foot building is given by $h = 200 - 16t^2$, where t is measured in seconds and h is measured in feet. What is the velocity of the object 2 seconds after it is dropped?

(A) -64 ft/sec   (B) -32 ft/sec

(C) 32 ft/sec   (D) 64 ft/sec

3. The number of gallons of water in a tub t minutes after the plug is pulled is shown in the table.

Time (minutes)	0	0.5	1	1.5	2	2.5	3	3.5	4
Gallons	120	102	88	76	65	57	50	44	40

(a) Find the average rate of change in the volume in the first 4 minutes. (Include units.)

(b) Use the data to find an estimate of how fast the volume is changing at the 2.75-minute mark. Show your work.

Need More Help With . . .	*See . . .*
Numerical derivatives?	*Precalculus,* Section 11.4

Answers and Solutions

Part II: Review of AP* Calculus AB and BC Topics

Limits

Limits of Functions—Part II

Content and Practice, p. 25

1. $\lim\limits_{x \to 2} (x^3 - 5) = 3$

2. $\lim\limits_{x \to -4} \left(\dfrac{x^2}{x - 2} \right) = -\dfrac{8}{3}$

3. (a) $\lim\limits_{x \to 3} \left(\dfrac{x^2 - 9}{x^2 - 5x + 6} \right) = 6$

    (b) Substitution gives an answer of $\dfrac{0}{0}$.

    (c) $\lim\limits_{x \to 3} \dfrac{x^2 - 9}{x^2 - 5x + 6} = \lim\limits_{x \to 3} \dfrac{(x - 3)(x + 3)}{(x - 3)(x - 2)} = \lim\limits_{x \to 3} \dfrac{x + 3}{x - 2} = 6$

    (d)

x	$f(x)$
2.7	8.1429
2.8	7.25
2.9	6.5556
3	**6**
3.1	5.5455
3.2	5.1667

4. (a) $\lim\limits_{x \to -3^+} f(x) = -4$ (b) $\lim\limits_{x \to 8^-} f(x) = -3$

5. (a) $\lim\limits_{x \to -1^-} f(x) = -\infty$ (b) $\lim\limits_{x \to -1^+} f(x) = \infty$

    (c) $\lim\limits_{x \to 2^-} f(x) = \infty$ (d) $\lim\limits_{x \to 2^+} f(x) = -\infty$

    (e) $\lim\limits_{x \to -\infty} f(x) = 0$ (f) $\lim\limits_{x \to +\infty} f(x) = 0$

6. $\lim\limits_{x \to 0} \left(3 - x^4 \sin\left(\dfrac{1}{x}\right) \right)$

    $-1 \le \sin\left(\dfrac{1}{x}\right) \le 1$

    $-x^4 \le x^4 \sin\left(\dfrac{1}{x}\right) \le x^4$

    $x^4 \ge -x^4 \sin\left(\dfrac{1}{x}\right) \ge -x^4$

    $-x^4 \le -x^4 \sin\left(\dfrac{1}{x}\right) \le x^4$

    $3 - x^4 \le 3 - x^4 \sin\left(\dfrac{1}{x}\right) \le 3 + x^4$

    $\lim\limits_{x \to 0} (3 - x^4) \le \lim\limits_{x \to 0} \left(3 - x^4 \sin\left(\dfrac{1}{x}\right) \right) \le \lim\limits_{x \to 0} (3 + x^4)$

    $3 \le \lim\limits_{x \to 0} \left(3 - x^4 \sin\left(\dfrac{1}{x}\right) \right) \le 3$

    $\lim\limits_{x \to 0} \left(3 - x^4 \sin\left(\dfrac{1}{x}\right) \right) = 3$

Additional Practice, p. 30

1. (a) $\lim\limits_{x \to 2^-} f(x) = 1$

    (b) $\lim\limits_{x \to 2^+} f(x) = 3$

    (c) $\lim\limits_{x \to 2} f(x)$ does not exist since the left-hand limit and the right-hand limit are not equal.

2. $\lim\limits_{x \to 2^-} f(x) = 1$ and $\lim\limits_{x \to 2^+} f(x) = 4 + a$. Therefore, $a = -3$.

3. (a) $\lim_{x \to -\infty} f(x) = 0$ (b) $\lim_{x \to +\infty} f(x) = 0$

   (c) Conclusion: $y = 0$ is the horizontal asymptote.

4. (a) $\lim_{x \to -\infty} f(x) = 2$ (b) $\lim_{x \to +\infty} f(x) = 2$

   (c) $\lim_{x \to -2^-} f(x) = -\infty$ (d) $\lim_{x \to 2} f(x) = $ does not exist

   (e) Conclusions: $y = 2$ is the horizontal asymptote, and $x = -2$ and $x = 2$ are vertical asymptotes.

5. (a) $\lim_{x \to 0} f(x) = 2$ (b) $\lim_{x \to +\infty} f(x) = 0$

6. $\lim_{x \to -1.8} f(x) \approx -22.60$

7. (C)

8. (C)

9. (C)

10. (A)

11. (A)

12. $\dfrac{10}{3}$

Asymptotic and Unbounded Behavior—Part II

Content and Practice, p. 34

1. Vertical: $x = 4$; Horizontal: $y = 1$

2. Vertical: $x = 3$; Horizontal: none; Slant: $y = 2x + 9$

3. Vertical: none; Horizontal: $y = 0$

4. $h(x)$ in Problem 3

5. (B)

Additional Practice, p. 39

1. (D)

2. (B)

Function Magnitudes and Their Rates of Change—Part II

Additional Practice, p. 42

1. (B)

2. (C)

Continuity—Part II

Content and Practice, p. 43

1. Discontinuous at $x = \dfrac{\pi}{2} + k\pi$, where k is an integer.

2. Discontinuous at $x = -1$.

3. Discontinuous at $x = -1$.

4. f is undefined wherever $\cos x = 0$.

5. g is undefined when its denominator is zero.

6. h is discontinuous at $x = -1$ because $\displaystyle\lim_{x \to -1^-} h(x) = -5$ but $\displaystyle\lim_{x \to -1^+} h(x) = -4$.

7. For f, part I fails and part II fails.

8. For g, part I fails.

9. For h, part II fails.

Additional Practice, p. 44

1. Not continuous. $\displaystyle\lim_{x \to 3} f(x)$ does not exist.

2. Not continuous. $\displaystyle\lim_{x \to 0} g(x) = 5$, but $g(0) = 4$.

3. Continuous. $\displaystyle\lim_{x \to 2} h(x) = 4$, and $h(2) = 4$.

4. (a) No. $\displaystyle\lim_{x \to 3^-} f(x) = 1$, but $f(3) = 33$.

   (b) $b = \dfrac{1 - 9a}{3}$. $9a + 3b = 1 \Leftrightarrow b = \dfrac{1 - 9a}{3}$.

5. (D)

6. (A)

Intermediate and Extreme Value Theorems—Part II

Additional Practice, p. 49

1. We see that $f(x)$ is a continuous function on $[2, 3]$, so we can apply the IVT. Because $f(2)$ is positive and $f(3)$ is negative, the IVT tells us that between $x = 2$ and $x = 3$ the function has a value of zero.

2. Maximum 2.3, Minimum 0.5.

3. (A)

4. (B)

5. (B)

Derivatives

Concept of the Derivative—Part II

Content and Practice, p. 51

1. (a) Linear function $\Rightarrow m = \dfrac{f(0) - f(-3)}{0 - (-3)} = -1$

    (b) Linear function $\Rightarrow m = \dfrac{f(3) - f(0)}{3 - 0} = 1$

2. $f'(550) =$ the rate at which profit is changing (in dollars per basketball) when the number of basketballs being produced is 550.

Additional Practice, p. 53

1. (D) A derivative is an *instantaneous* rate of change.

2. (D) A derivative is an *instantaneous* rate of change.

Differentiability and Continuity—Part II

Content and Practice, p. 54

1. (a) Differentiable at all domain values *except* $\{-2, 0, 2\}$. Continuous functions will not be differentiable at corners or cusps (or places where the tangent line is vertical).

    (b) At $x = -2$ and $x = 0$. Continuous functions will not be differentiable at corners or cusps.

    (c) At $x = 2$. The function is not continuous at that point, so it also fails to be differentiable at that point.

Additional Practice, p. 55

1. (a) $\{-2, 2\}$. Jump discontinuity and removable discontinuity

    (b) $\{-3, -2, 2\}$. The function is discontinuous, and therefore not differentiable, at $x = -2$ and $x = 2$. The corner at $x = -3$ will cause the function to be not differentiable there either.

2. (A) Since $f'(x)$ has a derivative at $x = 5$, it must also be continuous there.

3. (C) A continuous function can still fail to be differentiable.

356

4. (C) A continuous function can still fail to be differentiable.

5. (D) Differentiability requires continuity, so a function that is not continuous will not be differentiable.

Slope of a Curve at a Point—Part II

Content and Practice, p. 57

1. (a) $m \approx 0$.   The tangent line at P is approximately horizontal.

    (b) $m \approx 2$.   If the origin and point P are both on the tangent then $m = \dfrac{2 - 0}{1 - 0} = 2$.

    (c) Undefined.   The tangent line at P is approximately vertical.

2. (a) 6.   Answers will vary. For example, $f(2.9) = 11.41$ and $f(3.1) = 12.61$

    $$f'(3) \approx \frac{12.61 - 11.41}{3.1 - 2.9} = \frac{1.2}{0.2} = 6$$

    (b) $m = \lim\limits_{h \to 0} \dfrac{f(3 + h) - f(3)}{h} = \lim\limits_{h \to 0} \dfrac{[(3 + h)^2 + 3] - (3^2 + 3)}{h} = \lim\limits_{h \to 0}(6 + h) = 6$

3. (D) No tangent line exists at a corner.

4. The left- and right-hand limits differ $\Rightarrow$ no two-sided limit $\Rightarrow$ no slope.

Additional Practice, p. 59

1. $m = \lim\limits_{h \to 0} \dfrac{f(x + h) - f(x)}{h} = \lim\limits_{h \to 0} \dfrac{\dfrac{1}{x + h} - \dfrac{1}{x}}{h} = \lim\limits_{h \to 0} \dfrac{\dfrac{x}{x(x + h)} - \dfrac{x + h}{x(x + h)}}{h}$

    $= \lim\limits_{h \to 0} \dfrac{\dfrac{-h}{x(x + h)}}{h} = \lim\limits_{h \to 0} \dfrac{-1}{x(x + h)} = -\dfrac{1}{x^2} \Rightarrow -\dfrac{1}{x^2} = -\dfrac{1}{4} \Leftrightarrow x = \pm 2$

2. (C) Because tangent lines at those points would be horizontal.

3. (D) Because the tangent line there is vertical.

Local Linearity—Part II

Content and Practice, p. 61

1. From the given information we know the slope is 0.5 and it passes through the point $(5, 3) \Rightarrow y - 3 = 0.5(x - 5) \Rightarrow y = 0.5x + 0.5$.

2. $f(5.023) \approx 0.5(5.023) + 0.5 = 3.0115$

Additional Practice, p. 62

1. From a calculator,
$f(2) = f'(2) \approx 7.389 \Rightarrow y - 7.389 = 7.389(x - 2) \Rightarrow y = 7.389x - 7.389.$

2. (a) (i) Yes (flattens out as you zoom in)
(ii) $f(1) = 2$ and $f'(1) = 2 \Rightarrow y - 2 = 2(x - 1) \Rightarrow y = 2x$

   (b) (i) Yes (slope $= 2$ everywhere, so differentiable)

   (ii) $y = 2x$. A linear function is its own tangent.

   (c) (i) Yes (flattens out as you zoom in)

   (ii) $f(1) = 2$ and $f'(1) = 2 \Rightarrow y - 2 = 2(x - 1) \Rightarrow y = 2x$

3. (D) $f(0) = 3$ and $f'(0) = k \Rightarrow y - 3 = k(x - 0) \Rightarrow y = kx + 3$. So,
$f(0.03) \approx k(0.03) + 3.$

4. (A) $f(1) = a \ln 3 \Rightarrow$ point: $(1, a \ln 3)$; $f'(1) = \dfrac{a}{3} =$ slope.

   Tangent line:

   $y - a \ln 3 = \dfrac{a}{3}(x - 1) \Rightarrow y = a \ln 3 + \dfrac{a}{3}(x - 1) \Rightarrow f(0.98) \approx a \ln 3 + \dfrac{a}{3}(-0.02)$

Instantaneous Rate of Change—Part II

Content and Practice, p. 64

1. (a) $\dfrac{f(1 + 5) - f(1)}{5} = \dfrac{108 - 3}{5} = 21$ units/sec

   (b) $\dfrac{f(1 + 3) - f(1)}{3} = \dfrac{48 - 3}{3} = 15$ units/sec

   (c) $\dfrac{f(1 + 1) - f(1)}{1} = \dfrac{12 - 3}{1} = 9$ units/sec

   Approximations of $f'(1)$ will vary, but should reflect the trend in the answers above, so should be ≤ 9. Students who explore using smaller intervals should see a limit of 6 units/sec (the actual rate).

2. $\lim\limits_{h \to 0} \dfrac{f(1 + h) - f(1)}{h} = \lim\limits_{h \to 0} \dfrac{3(1 + h)^2 - 3(1)^2}{h} = \lim\limits_{h \to 0}(6 + 3h) = 6.$ This is consistent
with our result in Problem 1.

3. (C) Slope at $x = 3$ is $\approx \dfrac{f(4) - f(2)}{4 - 2} = \dfrac{8.32 - 6.15}{4 - 2} = 1.085.$

Additional Practice, p. 65

1. $\displaystyle\lim_{h\to 0}\frac{f(-2+h)-f(-2)}{h}=\lim_{h\to 0}\frac{[6-(-2+h)^2]-[6-(-2)^2]}{h}=\lim_{h\to 0}(4-h)=4$

2. (a) $\dfrac{54.5-28.9}{2004-1994}=2.56$

   (b) $\dfrac{44.8-33.3}{2002-1996}=1.917$

   (c) $\dfrac{39-35.5}{2000-1998}=1.75$

   (d) 1.75.   The best approximation is an average slope over the smallest interval we can get that includes the target value; that is, the slope from part (C).

3. (D)   Sketch a tangent line at $x=2$. It appears to pass through the points $(1,-4)$ and $(3,4)\Rightarrow m=\dfrac{4-(-4)}{2}=4$.

Relationships between the Graphs of f and f'—Part II

Content and Practice, p. 67

1. (a) The values of f' are positive there.

   (b) The values of f' are negative there.

2. Positive slopes indicate an increasing function, whereas negative slopes indicate a decreasing function.

3. Whenever f' crosses the x-axis, f has an extreme point (maximum or minimum). f' represents the slope of f, so when it crosses the x-axis it means the slope of f is changing sign. Hence, f is changing from increasing to decreasing or vice versa, which creates an extreme value.

Additional Practice, p. 68

1. (C) f' has x-intercepts when the slope of f is zero (when f has a horizontal tangent line).

2. (C) f' will be negative over intervals when f is decreasing.

3. (D) A, B, and C can all be ruled out simply because the slope of those graphs at their x-intercepts is clearly not zero (so the values of $f(x)$ and $f'(x)$ can't be equal). $f(x)=e^{x-5}$, on the other hand, is always positive and always increasing; the values of the function appear to match up with the slope.

Basic Derivatives—Part II

Content and Practice, p. 70

1. See text.

2. The derivative of a constant is 0.

3. $\dfrac{dy}{dx} = \cos x$

4. $\dfrac{dy}{dx} = -\sin x$

5. $\dfrac{dy}{dx} = \sec^2 x$

6. $y = \cot x$

7. $\dfrac{dy}{dx} = \sec x \tan x$

8. $y = \csc x$

9. $\dfrac{dy}{dx} = \dfrac{1}{x}$

10. $y = e^x$

11. $\dfrac{dP}{dw} = \sec^2 w$

12. $\dfrac{dV}{dr} = \dfrac{2}{3}\pi rh$

13. $\dfrac{dE}{dm} = c^2$

14. $\dfrac{dS}{dt} = 12t$

Additional Practice, p. 71

1. (C) $\dfrac{dy}{dx} = \cos x$

    $\cos\dfrac{\pi}{3} = \dfrac{1}{2}$

2. (C) $\dfrac{dy}{dx} = e^x$

    At $x = a$, $\dfrac{dy}{dx} = e^a$.

3. (B) $\dfrac{dA}{dr} = 2\pi r$

    At $r = 2$, $\dfrac{dA}{dr} = 4\pi$ (Instantaneous)

    $\dfrac{A(3) - A(1)}{3 - 1} = \dfrac{9\pi - \pi}{2} = 4\pi$ (Average)

4. $\dfrac{1}{3}x = \sqrt{x}$

    $\dfrac{1}{9}x^2 = x$

    $x^2 - 9x = 0$

    $x = 9 \Rightarrow y = 3$

    Slope is $\dfrac{dy}{dx} = \dfrac{1}{2}x^{-1/2}$.

    At $x = 9$, slope is $\dfrac{1}{6}$.

    $y - 3 = \dfrac{1}{6}(x - 9)$

Derivative Rules—Part II

Content and Practice, p. 73

Formula Name	Derivative Formula	Word Description
Difference Formula	$y = f(x) - g(x)$ $\dfrac{dy}{dx} = f'(x) - g'(x)$	The derivative of a difference of functions is the difference of their individual derivatives.
Sum Formula	$y = f(x) + g(x)$ $\dfrac{dy}{dx} = f'(x) + g'(x)$	The derivative of a sum of functions is the sum of the derivative of each function.
Product Rule	$y = f(x) \cdot g(x)$ $\dfrac{dy}{dx} = f'(x) \cdot g(x) + f(x) \cdot g'(x)$	The derivative of a product of functions is the derivative of the first function times the second function, plus the derivative of the second function times the first function.
Quotient Rule	$y = \dfrac{f(x)}{g(x)}$ $\dfrac{dy}{dx} = \dfrac{g(x) \cdot f'(x) - f(x) \cdot g'(x)}{[g(x)]^2}$	The derivative of a quotient of functions is the denominator times the derivative of the numerator, minus the numerator times the derivative of the denominator, all over the square of the denominator.

1. $y = 5x^3 + \ln x$ $\qquad \dfrac{dy}{dx} = 15x^2 + \dfrac{1}{x}$

2. $y = x^3 \cdot \ln(x)$ $\qquad \dfrac{dy}{dx} = x^3 \cdot \dfrac{1}{x} + \ln x \cdot 3x^2 = x^2 + 3x^2 \ln x$

3. $s = \dfrac{5}{t^4}$ $\qquad \dfrac{ds}{dt} = -20t^{-5} = \dfrac{-20}{t^5}$ $\qquad$ Quotient rule is not required.

4. $k = \dfrac{\sin p}{\sqrt{p}}$ $\qquad \dfrac{dk}{dp} = \dfrac{\sqrt{p}\cos p - \dfrac{1}{2\sqrt{p}}\sin p}{(\sqrt{p})^2} = \dfrac{2p\cos p - \sin p}{2p^{3/2}}$

5. $w = z^4 - (z + 2)^7 \cos z$ $\quad \dfrac{dw}{dz} = 4z^3 - [(z + 2)^7 - \sin z + \cos z \, 7(z + 2)^6]$

$$= 4z^3 + \sin z (z + 2)^7 - 7 \cos z (z + 2)^6$$

6. $y = x^2(x^3 - 2)$ $\quad y = x^5 - 2x^2 \Rightarrow \dfrac{dy}{dx} = 5x^4 - 4x$

$$\dfrac{dy}{dx} = x^2 3x^2 + (x^3 - 2)2x$$

$$= 3x^4 + 2x^4 - 4x$$

$$= 5x^4 - 4x$$

Additional Practice, p. 74

1. (B) $f'(x) = e^x(-\sin x) + \cos x \, e^x = 0$

$e^x(-\sin x + \cos x) = 0$

$\sin x = \cos x$ and $e^x \neq 0$

$x = \dfrac{\pi}{4}$

2. (D) $y = \dfrac{x + 3}{x^2 + 1}\bigg|_{x=1} = 2$ $\qquad$ Ordered pair is $(1, 2)$.

$$\dfrac{dy}{dx} = \dfrac{(x^2 + 1)1 - (x + 3)2x}{(x^2 + 1)^2}$$

At $x = 1$, $\dfrac{dy}{dx} = \dfrac{2 - 8}{4} = -\dfrac{3}{2}$.

$$y - 2 = -\dfrac{3}{2}(x - 1)$$

$$y = -\dfrac{3}{2}x + \dfrac{7}{2}$$

3. (C) $\dfrac{d}{dx}(f \cdot g)\bigg|_{x=3} = f(3) \cdot g'(3) + g(3) \cdot f'(3)$

$$= 7 \cdot -1 + -4 \cdot \dfrac{3}{2}$$

$$= -13$$

4. (A) $\dfrac{d}{dx}\left(\dfrac{f}{g}\right)\bigg|_{x=1} = \dfrac{g(1) \cdot f'(1) - f(1) \cdot g'(1)}{[g(1)]^2}$

$$= \dfrac{2 \cdot 5 - 4 \cdot \dfrac{1}{2}}{2^2}$$

$$= 2$$

Chain Rule—Part II

Content and Practice, p. 76

1. $\dfrac{dy}{dx} = \dfrac{dy}{du} \cdot \dfrac{du}{dx} = (3u^2)(4) = 12u^2 = 12(4x + 2)^2$

2. Let $g(v) = 1 - \sin v$, $h(g) = g^{1/2}$.

$$\dfrac{dh}{dv} = \dfrac{dh}{dg} \cdot \dfrac{dg}{dv} = \left(\dfrac{1}{2} g^{-1/2}\right)\left(-\cos v\right) = -\dfrac{1}{2}\left(1 - \sin v\right)^{-1/2} \cos v$$

3. $y = [\sin(t^2 + 5)]^3$. Let $u = t^2 + 5$, $v = \sin u$, $y = v^3$.

$$\dfrac{dy}{dt} = \dfrac{dy}{dv} \cdot \dfrac{dv}{du} \cdot \dfrac{du}{dt} = (3v^2)(\cos u)(2t) = 6t \sin^2(t^2 + 5) \cos(t^2 + 5)$$

4. (D)

5. (a) $\dfrac{dy}{dx} = 0$

   (b) $\dfrac{dy}{dx} = -\sin u \cdot \dfrac{du}{dx}$

   (c) $\dfrac{dy}{dx} = \sec^2 u \cdot \dfrac{du}{dx}$

   (d) $y = \cot u$

   (e) $\dfrac{dy}{dx} = \sec u \cdot \tan u \cdot \dfrac{du}{dx}$

   (f) $y = \csc u$

   (g) $\dfrac{dy}{dx} = e^u \cdot \dfrac{du}{dx}$

   (h) $y = \ln u$

   (i) $\dfrac{dy}{dx} = a^u \ln(a) \cdot \dfrac{du}{dx}$

   (j) $\dfrac{dy}{dx} = \dfrac{1}{\sqrt{1 - u^2}} \cdot \dfrac{du}{dx}, |u| < 1$

   (k) $y = \cot^{-1} u$

   (l) $\dfrac{dy}{dx} = \dfrac{1}{|u|\sqrt{u^2 - 1}} \cdot \dfrac{du}{dx}, |u| > 1$

   (m) $y = \csc^{-1} u$

   (n) $\dfrac{dy}{dx} = \dfrac{1}{1 + u^2} \cdot \dfrac{du}{dx}$

   (o) $\dfrac{dy}{dx} = \dfrac{-1}{\sqrt{1 - u^2}} \cdot \dfrac{du}{dx}, |u| < 1$

   (p) $\dfrac{dy}{dx} = \dfrac{1}{u \cdot \ln a} \cdot \dfrac{du}{dx}$

1. (C) $y = \left[f(x) \right]^2 \Rightarrow y' = 2f(x)f'(x) \Rightarrow y'(2) = 2f(2)f'(2) = 2(7)\left(\frac{1}{3}\right) = \frac{14}{3}$

2. (C) $y' = f'(g(x))g'(x) \Rightarrow y'(1) = f'(g(1))g'(1) = f'(2)g'(1) = \frac{1}{4}$

Derivatives of Parametric, Polar, and Vector Functions—Part II

Content and Practice, p. 80

1. Solutions in text.

2. $\dfrac{dy}{dx} = -\dfrac{\cos 2t}{2 \sin t}, \dfrac{d^2y}{dx^2} = -\dfrac{2 \sin t \sin 2t + \cos 2t \cos t}{8 \sin^3 t}.$ At $t = \dfrac{\pi}{2}, \dfrac{d^2y}{dx^2} = 0.$

3. $f''(t) = (4e^{2t}, -\cos t)$

Additional Practice, p. 81

1. $y = -2.229x + 5.229.$ $\dfrac{dy/dt}{dx/dt} = \dfrac{-5}{3 + \sin 4} = -2.229.$

2. (C) $\dfrac{dy}{dx} = \dfrac{3}{2(2t - 1)\sqrt{3t + 1}}.$ At $t = 1, \dfrac{dy}{dx} = \dfrac{3}{4}.$

3. (A) $f''(1) = -i - \dfrac{1}{4}j.$ $f''(t) = -\dfrac{1}{t^2}i - \dfrac{1}{4}t^{-3/2}j.$

Equations Involving Derivatives—Part II

Content and Practice, p. 82

1. $W'(t) = -3$ inches/hour. $W'(t)$ measures how the water level changes with respect to time; it is negative because the water is falling.

2. (C) A 10% increase indicates that the *rate of change* at any moment in time is equal to 10% of the current population R.

3. The plane is descending at 200 feet per minute. The derivative measures the *rate of change* of the altitude, and a negative sign indicates the altitude is decreasing.

4. Since $\dfrac{\Delta S}{\Delta x} = 12x$, the sensitivity when $x = 3$ cm is 36. This means that when the side is 3 cm, a small additional change in the side, Δt cm, will result in an increase in the surface area of approximately $36\,\Delta x$ square centimeters.

Additional Practice, p. 84

1. $\Delta V = 8 \times \Delta r$ or $\dfrac{dV}{\Delta r} = 8$.

2. $C'(w) = 23$.   Here $C'(w)$ measures the *rate of change* of the cost, and the fact that it is positive shows the cost is increasing.

3.   (B)   The statement involves the rate of change of the populations, which is $A'(t)$. "Directly proportional" indicates that it is some constant multiple (k) of the expression.

Extreme Values of Functions—Part II

Content and Practice, p. 85

1.   A: local maximum; B: local and absolute minimum; C: local maximum; D: local minimum; E: local maximum and absolute maximum

2.   Yes. f could be increasing (or decreasing) on both sides, e.g., $f(x) = x^3$ at $x = 0$.

3.   Yes. f could be a function defined at $x = a$ with a corner or cusp, e.g., $f(x) = x^{2/3}$ at $x = 0$.

4. $5\frac{1}{3}$. Since $g'(x) = x^2 - 4$, the graph of g is decreasing on $[-1, 2]$ and increasing on $[2, 4]$. Therefore, either the left or right endpoint must be the absolute maximum. Evaluating $g(-1) = 3\,{}^2\!/_3$ and $g(4) = 5\,{}^1\!/_3$ shows that $x = 4$ generates the absolute maximum.

5.   (C)

Additional Practice, p. 87

1.   (A)

2.   (a) $f'\!\left(-\dfrac{1}{2}\right) = 0$ and f' changes from positive to negative at $x = -\frac{1}{2}$.

   (b)   Although $f'(-3) = 0$, f' does not change signs at $x = -3$.

   (c) f is increasing on the interval $[1, 5]$.

Concavity of Functions—Part II

Content and Practice, p. 88

1.   Concave down on the intervals (A, C) and (E, G)

2.   The x-coordinates of the points B, D, and F on the graph of $h'(x)$ would identify points of inflection on the graph of $h(x)$. Local extrema of $h'(x)$ on the interval (A, G) indicate points where $h''(x)$ changes signs, and are therefore points of inflection of $h(x)$.

3.   Yes. If f is any constant or linear function, $f''(x) = 0$ for all x yet there are no points of inflection.

4. Yes. The function $f(x) = x^{1/3}$ at $x = 0$ has a vertical tangent to the curve and $f''(0)$ is undefined.

5. Concave down on $(-\infty, -2) \cup (2, \infty)$

$$g(x) = \ln(4 + x^2) \Rightarrow g'(x) = \frac{2x}{4 + x^2} \Rightarrow g''(x) = \frac{2(4 - x^2)}{(4 + x^2)^2}. \quad g''(x) = 0 \Leftrightarrow x = \pm 2.$$

Analyzing the corresponding intervals leads to the answer.

6. (C)

7. $f'(x) = 3x^2 + 11x - 4$
$f'(x) = (3x - 1)(x + 4) = 0$

$f'(x) = 0$ when $x = \dfrac{1}{3}$ and $x = -4$.

$f''(x) = 6x + 11$

$f''\left(\dfrac{1}{3}\right) = 13 > 0$ so there is a local minimum at $x = \dfrac{1}{3}$.

$f''(-4) = -13 < 0$ so there is a local maximum at $x = -4$.

Additional Practice, p. 91

1. (D) Note that g is decreasing, so $g'(1) < 0$; $g(1) = 0$; and g is concave up, so $g''(1) > 0$.

2. $h(x) = x^2 \cdot e^x \Rightarrow h'(x) = xe^x(x + 2) \Rightarrow h''(x) = e^x(x^2 + 4x + 2)$. Since $h'(-2) = 0$ and $h''(-2) < 0$, there is a relative maximum at $x = -2$.

Points of Inflection—Part II

Content and Practice, p. 92

1. (a) $f'(x) = -4x^3 + 12x^2 + 3 \Rightarrow f''(x) = -12x^2 + 24x$

(b) $f''(x) = 0 \Rightarrow -12x^2 + 24x = 0 \Rightarrow -12x(x - 2) = 0 \Rightarrow x \in \{0, 2\}$. ($f''(x)$ is a polynomial function, so it is never undefined.)

(c) $f''(x) = -12x(x - 2)$

$$f'' \quad \overset{\text{- - - -}\;\;\text{+ +}\;\;\text{- -}}{\underset{0 \quad\;\; 2}{\longleftarrow\!\mid\!\!\mid\!\longrightarrow}}$$

$f''(x)$ is positive on $(0, 2)$ and negative on $(-\infty, 0) \cup (2, \infty)$.

(d) $(0, 5)$ and $(2, 27)$. f has points of inflection at $x = 0$ and $x = 2$. (f'' changes from negative to positive at $x = 0$, meaning that the graph changes from concave down to concave up; at $x = 2$, the concavity switches back again. We know f' exists at both of these points, so there is a tangent to the curve as well.)

Additional Practice, p. 93

1. (B)

$$f'' \xleftarrow[\substack{-1 \qquad 2}]{\overset{----\ \ +\ +\ +\ +}{\rule{4cm}{0.4pt}}}$$

There is a point of inflection at $x = -1$, where the concavity changes from concave down to concave up.

2. $\frac{1}{2}$. $f'(x) = 6x^2 - 6x + 6 \Rightarrow f''(x) = 12x - 6$. There is only one zero of $f''(x)$, at $x = \frac{1}{2}$.

   When $x < \frac{1}{2}, f''(x) < 0$ (making f concave down); when $x > \frac{1}{2}, f''(x) > 0$ (making f concave up). There is a point of inflection at $x = \frac{1}{2}$.

3. (a) (A)

   (b) The only point that could possibly be a point of inflection based on the information in the table is at $x = 5$, as it is the only place that $f''(x)$ changes signs (changing from negative to positive, thus making the graph change from concave down to concave up). Since $f'(5)$ has a value, there is a tangent line, and thus a point of inflection at that location.

Correspondences among the Graphs of *f*, *f'*, and *f"*—Part II

Content and Practice, p. 95

1. (a) Increasing.   (Slope is positive.)

   (b) Decreasing.   (Slope is negative.)

   (c) Local minimum.   (*f* is changing from decreasing to increasing.)

   (d) Local maximum.   (*f* is changing from increasing to decreasing.)

Additional Practice, p. 97

1. (a)

$$f' \xleftarrow[\substack{-2 \quad -1 \quad 0 \quad 1 \quad 2}]{\overset{++ \qquad -- \qquad\quad ++ \qquad --}{\rule{5cm}{0.4pt}}}$$

(b)

f''
$$--- \qquad +++ \qquad ---$$
$$\xleftarrow{\hspace{1cm} \underset{-2}{\;} \quad \underset{-1}{|} \quad \underset{0}{\;} \quad \underset{1}{|} \quad \underset{2}{\;} \hspace{1cm}}$$

(c) For the f' schematic, the sign is positive where the function is increasing and negative where it is decreasing. The zeros occur where the graph would have a horizontal tangent line. For the f'' schematic, the sign is positive where the graph is concave up, negative where it is concave down, and zero (or undefined) where there is a change of concavity (points of inflection).

2. (a) Approximately $[-3.1, 3.1]$. In general, a function is increasing when it has a positive derivative. (*Note*: Even though the derivative is zero at the endpoints and at a single point within this interval, the graph is said to be increasing on the entire closed interval.)

(b) Approximately $(-\infty, -3.1] \cup [3.1, \infty)$. In general, a function is decreasing when it has a negative derivative. (*Note*: For a continuous function, the points where a function switches between increasing and decreasing are included in both intervals.)

(c) At approximately $x = \pm 3.1$, where there is a change in sign in the derivative function. (There is a local *minimum* around $x = -3.1$ because the derivative (slope) is changing from negative to positive. There is a local *maximum* around $x = 3.1$ because the derivative (slope) is changing from positive to negative.)

3. (a) i. Definitely. Not only is there a change in sign in the second derivative, but since $f''(3)$ is defined, we know the first derivative exists and so there must be a tangent line at that point.

(b) ii. Possibly. There is a change in sign of the second derivative, but since $f''(5)$ is undefined, we can't be sure that a tangent line exists at that point.

(c) iii. Definitely not. There is no change in sign in the second derivative.

4. Shown in bold is one possible graph of f. Variations include any vertical translation of the graph. Based on the information from f', we know f will be increasing until about $x = -0.3$, where it has a maximum, then decreasing until about $x = 2.4$, where it has a minimum, and then increasing again. From f'' we know that the graph of f will be concave down until about $x = 1$, and then it will be concave up.

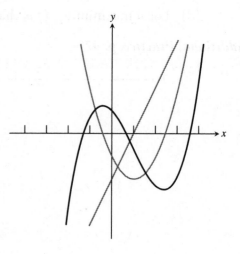

The Mean Value Theorem—Part II

Content and Practice, p. 99

1. (a) Yes; $f(x)$ is continuous on $[1, 5]$ and differentiable on $(1, 5)$.

    (b) $f'(x) = \lim\limits_{h \to 0} \dfrac{(x + h)^2 - x^2}{h} = \lim\limits_{h \to 0} \dfrac{2xh + h^2}{h} = \lim\limits_{h \to 0}(2x + h) = 2x$

    (c) $\dfrac{f(5) - f(1)}{5 - 1} = \dfrac{25 - 1}{4} = 6$

    (d) $2c = 6 \Rightarrow c = 3$

Additional Practice, p. 101

1. (C) $f(x)$ is continuous on $[2, 7]$ and differentiable on $(2, 7)$.

2. $f(x)$ is continuous on $[2, 11]$ and differentiable on $(2, 11)$, so the conditions of the MVT are met. Graph $y = f'(x)$ and $y = \dfrac{\sin 11 - \sin 2}{11 - 2} \approx -0.212$ on the same axes and find the points of intersection over the interval $[2, 11]$. $\{4.499, 8.068, 10.782\}$.

3. (D) The average rate of change over the interval $[-4, 4]$ is 0. For c to satisfy the MVT, $f'(c)$ must equal zero (that is, there must be a horizontal tangent at that point). This appears to happen around $x = 0$ and around $x = \pm 2$.

Optimization—Part II

Content and Practice, p. 102

1. Dimensions $2\sqrt[3]{3}$ by $2\sqrt[3]{3}$ by $\sqrt[3]{3}$ will minimize the surface area. Let the box dimensions be x by x by h. Volume $V = x^2 h$ and surface area $S = x^2 + 4xh$. Since $x^2 h = 12$, $h = \dfrac{12}{x^2}$, so $S = x^2 + \dfrac{48}{x}$. Finding S' and setting it equal to 0 yields $x = 2\sqrt[3]{3}$ as the only critical value. Since S' is negative to the left and positive to the right of $2\sqrt[3]{3}$, we have an absolute minimum.

Additional Practice, p. 104

1. $A(x) = \sin(x)(\pi - 2x)$
    $A'(x) = -2\sin(x) + \cos(x)(\pi - 2x)$
    $A'(x) = 0 \Rightarrow x = 0.710$
    Using the stored value from solving $A'(x) = 0$, $A(0.710) = 1.122$.

2. Maximum volume is approximately 52.5 in.^{3}. Let each square measure x by x (inches) with $x \in [0, 4]$.

$$V(x) = x(8 - 2x)(10 - 2x) \Rightarrow V'(x) = 4(3x^2 - 18x + 20). \ V'(x) = 0 \text{ for } x = \frac{9 \pm \sqrt{21}}{3}.$$

$$V(x) \text{ is maximized at } x = \frac{9 - \sqrt{21}}{3} \text{ with volume } V\left(\frac{9 - \sqrt{21}}{3}\right).$$

3. (A)

4. 7 Justify that your solution provides a maximum or minimum.

   5 Find the derivative of the varying quantities.

   4 If necessary, substitute from the fixed quantity into the varying quantity.

   8 Make sure you have answered the original question, with appropriate units of measure.

   2 Define variables to be used.

   1 Read and understand the problem, noting especially what is to be optimized.

   6 Find the zeros of the derivative equation.

   3 Write equations for all fixed and varying quantities.

Implicit Differentiation—Part II

Content and Practice, p. 106

1. $2x + 2y \dfrac{dy}{dx} = 6y^2 \dfrac{dy}{dx} \Rightarrow \dfrac{dy}{dx} = \dfrac{2x}{6y^2 - 2y}.$

2. (a) $(2)(1)^2 + 2(1)^4 = 4$ and $2^2 \cdot 1 = 4.$

    (b) $x2y \dfrac{dy}{dx} + y^2 + 8y^3 \dfrac{dy}{dx} = x^2 \dfrac{dy}{dx} + 2xy \Rightarrow \dfrac{dy}{dx} = \dfrac{2xy - y^2}{2xy + 8y^3 - x^2}.$ At $(2, 1)$, $\dfrac{dy}{dx} = \dfrac{3}{8}.$

Additional Practice, p. 108

1. (B) $\dfrac{dy}{dx} = \dfrac{2x - y}{x + 2y}.$ At $(2, 3)$, $\dfrac{dy}{dx} = \dfrac{1}{8}.$

2. (A) $\dfrac{dc}{da} = \dfrac{2a - c^2}{2ac - 3c^2}.$

3. (a) $2x - \left(x^2 \dfrac{dy}{dx} + 2xy\right) = 2y \dfrac{dy}{dx} \Rightarrow \dfrac{dy}{dx} = \dfrac{2x - 2xy}{x^2 + 2y}$.

   (b) Two points: $(2, -5)$ and $(2, 1)$. At $(2, 1)$, $\dfrac{dy}{dx} = 0 \Rightarrow$ a horizontal tangent.

4. $\dfrac{\frac{dy}{dx}}{1 + y} = x \Rightarrow \dfrac{dy}{dx} = x(1 + y) \Rightarrow \dfrac{d}{dx}\left(\dfrac{dy}{dx}\right) = x \dfrac{dy}{dx} + (1 + y) = x[x(1 + y)] + (1 + y)$

   $= x^2 + x^2 y + 1 + y$

Related Rates—Part II

Content and Practice, p. 109

1. Let $e = $ length of edge of cube and $V = $ volume of cube

   We know $\dfrac{de}{dt} = 2$ in/min and we are to find $\dfrac{dV}{dt}$ when $e = 3$ inches.

   $V = e^3 \Rightarrow \dfrac{dV}{dt} = 3e^2 \dfrac{de}{dt}$

   $\dfrac{dV}{dt} = 3(3 \text{ in.})^2 (2 \text{ in./min}) \Rightarrow \dfrac{dV}{dt} = 54 \text{ in.}^3/\text{min}$

2. (a) $y = (x - 3)^2, \dfrac{dx}{dt} = 4$ units/sec, find $\dfrac{dy}{dt}$ at $x = 1$.

   $\dfrac{dy}{dt} = 2(x - 3) \dfrac{dx}{dt} \Rightarrow$ at $x = 1$, $\dfrac{dy}{dt} = -16$ units/sec. This means that at the point $(1, 4)$

   the particle is moving downward along the parabolic path.

   (b) The particle's distance from any position (x, y) to the origin is determined by the distance

   formula $D = \sqrt{(x - 0)^2 + (y - 0)^2} = \sqrt{x^2 + y^2} = \sqrt{x^2 + (x - 3)^4}$. The rate of

   change of that distance will be $\dfrac{dD}{dt} = \dfrac{1}{2}\left(x^2 + y^2\right)^{-1/2}\left(2x \dfrac{dx}{dt} + 2y \dfrac{dy}{dt}\right)$. Evaluate at

   $x = 1$, replacing $\dfrac{dx}{dt}, \dfrac{dy}{dt}$ with the values from part (A). $\dfrac{dD}{dt} = \dfrac{-60}{\sqrt{17}}$ units/sec.

3. Ship W travels distance w and $dw/dt = 35$ mph

    Ship H travels distance h and $dh/dt = 28$ mph

    If the ships are distance a apart, find da/dt, when $t = 2$ hours.

    $$a^2 = w^2 + h^2 - 2wh\cos\theta \Rightarrow 2a\frac{da}{dt} = 2w\frac{dw}{dt} + 2h\frac{dh}{dt} - 2\cos\theta\left(w\frac{dh}{dt} + h\frac{dw}{dt}\right)$$

    Since $t = 2$ hours $\Rightarrow w = 70$ miles, $h = 56$ miles, $a = 54.74$ miles, $da/dt \approx 27.370$ mph.

4. $\frac{dr}{dt} = \frac{16}{25\pi}$ in./min. Given $\frac{dV}{dt} = 4$ in.^{3}/min. We know that $V = \frac{1}{3}\pi r^2 h$ and from the similar triangles (see diagram in text), $\frac{r}{h} = \frac{4}{16}$. Therefore, in terms of r, $V = \frac{4}{3}\pi r^3$. Find $\frac{dr}{dt}$ when $h = 5$ in. $\frac{dV}{dt} = 4\pi r^2\frac{dr}{dt}$, when $h = 5$ in., $r = 1.25$ in., $\frac{dr}{dt} = \frac{16}{25\pi}$ in./min.

Additional Practice, p. 113

1. (D) Let y = length of diagonal, $\frac{y}{\sqrt{2}}$ = length of sides of square. $\frac{dy}{dt} = 3$ in./min. Find $\frac{dp}{dt}$ when $A = 18$ in.^{2} (therefore, $y = 6$ in.)

    Perimeter:

    $$p = 2\sqrt{2}y \Rightarrow \frac{dp}{dt} = 2\sqrt{2}\frac{dy}{dt} \Rightarrow \frac{dp}{dt} = 6\sqrt{2} \text{ in./min.}$$

2. (D) $\frac{dV_{sphere}}{dt} = -2$ in.^{3}/min. If S is the surface area, find $\frac{dS}{dt}$ when $r = 1$ in. First, $\frac{dV}{dt} = 4\pi r^2\frac{dr}{dt}$. Substituting at $r = 1$ gives $\frac{dr}{dt} = \frac{-1}{2\pi}$ in./min. $S = 4\pi r^2 \Rightarrow \frac{dS}{dt} = 8\pi r\frac{dr}{dt}$. Substituting, $\frac{dS}{dt} = -4$ in.^{2}/min. $\Rightarrow$ decreases at 4 in.^{2}/min.

3. 2 Draw a diagram that illustrates the problem, identifying quantities that are variables and those that are constant.

    5 Substitute values for variables.

    6 Solve for the desired quantity, using appropriate units in your answer.

    4 Differentiate both sides of the equation implicitly with respect to time t.

    1 Read and understand the problem, identifying the variable(s) whose rate of change is known and the variable whose rate of change is to be found.

    3 Write an equation that relates the variables of the problem.

Derivative as a Rate of Change—Part II

Content and Practice, p. 115

1. (a) $v(t) = s'(t) = 2t - 3 \Rightarrow v(5) = 2(5) - 3 = 7$ in./sec.

    (b) $v_{\text{avg}} = \dfrac{s(4) - s(0)}{4 - 0} = \dfrac{4 - 0}{4} = 1$ in./sec.

    (c) Speed $= |v(1)| = |(2 \cdot 1)^2 - 3| = |-1| = 1$ in./sec.

2. (a) Approximately $(0, 2) \cup (4.7, 6)$. Acceleration is the slope of the velocity graph, so it is positive when the velocity graph is rising.

    (b) Speed is the absolute value of velocity (see the graph). This is decreasing on approximately $(2, 3) \cup (4.7, 6)$.

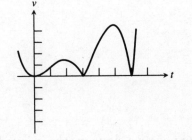

    (c) $a_{\text{avg}} = \dfrac{v(5) - v(1)}{5 - 1} \approx \dfrac{-4.2 - 1}{4} = \dfrac{-5.2}{4} = -1.3$ ft/sec^2.

Additional Practice, p. 117

1. (A) $v(t) = s'(t) = 1 + (-9)(t + 1)^{-2} = 1 - \dfrac{9}{(t + 1)^2} \Rightarrow v(1) = 1 - \dfrac{9}{2^2} = \dfrac{-5}{4}$.

2. (a) $v(13) \approx \dfrac{D(15) - D(10)}{15 - 10} = \dfrac{25 - 17}{15 - 10} = \dfrac{8}{5} = 1.6$ ft/sec.

    (b) $v_{\text{avg}} = \dfrac{D(20) - D(5)}{20 - 5} = \dfrac{30 - 7}{15} \approx 1.5$ ft/sec.

3. Acceleration is drawn in bold on the graph.

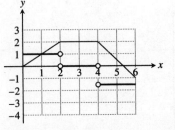

4. (C) Rate at which the volume of water in the tank is changing:
$R'(t) = 6t^2 - 40t - 72$. Minimize this.

$R''(t) = 12t - 40 = 0 \Rightarrow t = \dfrac{40}{12} = 3\dfrac{1}{3}$ min. R'' is changing from negative to positive at this value, so R' has a relative minimum there. Since $R'\left(3\dfrac{1}{3}\right) < 0$, the water is draining the fastest.

Slope Fields—Part II

Content and Practice, p. 119

1.
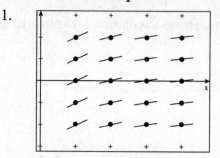

2. (C) Equations A and B both show negative slope marks in quadrants III and IV. Equation D would have slopes of zero along the *y*-axis. This rules out those three choices.

3. The slopes are zero whenever $x = 0$, positive in the first and third quadrants, and negative in the second and fourth quadrants.

4.
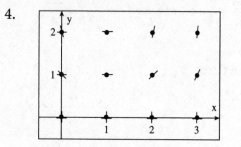

Additional Practice, p. 121

1. (a)
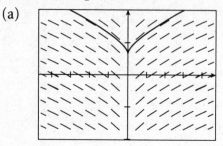

(b)

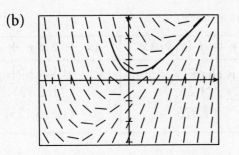

2. (A) The slope should be negative for $x < 0$, zero for $x = 0$, and positive for $x > 0$. The only graph with these properties is (A).

Euler's Method—Part II

Content and Practice, p. 123

1.

(x, y)	$f'(x, y)$	Δx or h	$\Delta y = f'(x, y)\Delta x$	$(x + \Delta x, y + \Delta y)$
$(1, 1)$	3	0.5	1.5	$(1.5, 2.5)$
$(1.5, 2.5)$	4	0.5	2	$(2, 4.5)$

$$f'(1, 1) = 2(1) + 1 = 3 \Rightarrow \Delta y = 3(0.5) = 1.5 \Rightarrow (x + \Delta x, y + \Delta y) = (1 + 0.5, 1 + 1.5)$$
$$f'(1.5, 2.5) = 2(1.5) + 1 = 4 \Rightarrow \Delta y = 4(0.5) = 2 \Rightarrow (x + \Delta x, y + \Delta y) = (1.5 + 0.5, 2.5 + 2)$$

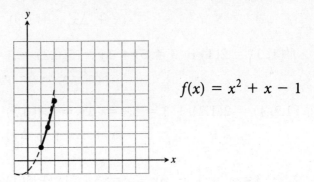

$$f(x) = x^2 + x - 1$$

2. Decreasing the value of Δx would provide a more accurate line.

3.

(x, y)	$f'(x, y)$	Δx or h	$\Delta y = f'(x, y)\Delta x$	$(x + \Delta x, y + \Delta y)$
$(0, 1)$	1	0.5	0.5	$(0.5, 1.5)$
$(0.5, 1.5)$	2.5	0.5	1.25	$(1, 2.75)$
$(1, 2.75)$	4.75	0.5	2.375	$(1.5, 5.125)$

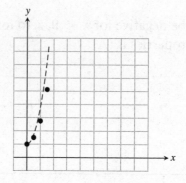

Additional Practice, p. 125

1. (C) $f'(2, 1) = \dfrac{2}{1} = 2 \Rightarrow \Delta y = 2(0.5) = 1 \Rightarrow$

$$(x + \Delta x, y + \Delta y) = (2 + 0.5, 1 + 1) = (2.5, 2).$$

$f'(2.5, 2) = \dfrac{2.5}{2} = 1.25 \Rightarrow \Delta y = 1.25(0.5) = 0.625 \Rightarrow$

$$(x + \Delta x, y + \Delta y) = (2.5 + 0.5, 2 + 0.625) = (3, 2.625).$$

2. (B) $f'(1, 3) = 2(1) + 3 = 5 \Rightarrow \Delta y = 5(0.2) = 1 \Rightarrow$

$$(x + \Delta x, y + \Delta y) = (1 + 0.2, 3 + 1) = (1.2, 4).$$

$f'(1.2, 4) = 2(1.2) + 3 = 5.4 \Rightarrow \Delta y = 5.4(0.2) = 1.08 \Rightarrow$

$$(x + \Delta x, y + \Delta y) = (1.2 + 0.2, 4 + 1.08) = (1.4, 5.08).$$

$\dfrac{dy}{dx} = 2x + 3 \Rightarrow y = x^2 + 3x + c \Rightarrow 3 = 1^2 + 3(1) + c \Rightarrow$

$$3 = 4 + c \Rightarrow c = -1 \Rightarrow y = x^2 + 3x - 1 \Rightarrow$$

$y(1.4) = (1.4)^2 + 3(1.4) - 1 = 5.16$

error $= |5.08 - 5.16| = 0.08.$

L'Hospital's Rule—Part II

Content and Practice, p. 127

1. $\lim\limits_{x\to\infty} \dfrac{\ln(x+1)}{\ln(3+x^2)} = \dfrac{1}{2}$ $\lim\limits_{x\to\infty} \dfrac{\ln(x+1)}{\ln(3+x^2)} = \lim\limits_{x\to\infty} \dfrac{\dfrac{1}{x+1}}{\dfrac{2x}{3+x^2}} = \lim\limits_{x\to\infty} \dfrac{3+x^2}{2x^2+2x} = \dfrac{1}{2}$

2. $\lim\limits_{x\to0} \dfrac{\sin x - 2x}{e^{3x}-1} = -\dfrac{1}{3}$ $\lim\limits_{x\to0} \dfrac{\sin x - 2x}{e^{3x}-1} = \lim\limits_{x\to0} \dfrac{\cos x - 2}{3e^{3x}} = -\dfrac{1}{3}$

3. $\lim\limits_{x\to0^+} (\csc x - \cot x) = 0$ $\lim\limits_{x\to0^+} (\csc x - \cot x) = \lim\limits_{x\to0^+} \left(\dfrac{1-\cos x}{\sin x} \right) = \lim\limits_{x\to0^+} \dfrac{\sin x}{\cos x} = 0$

4. $\lim\limits_{x\to\infty} \left(\dfrac{1}{x} \right)[\ln(x+1)+5x] = 5$ $\lim\limits_{x\to\infty} \left(\dfrac{1}{x} \right)[\ln(x+1)+5x] = \lim\limits_{x\to\infty} \left[\dfrac{\ln(x+1)}{x} + 5 \right]$

$$= \lim\limits_{x\to\infty} \left[\dfrac{\dfrac{1}{x+1}}{1} \right] + 5 = 5$$

Additional Practice, p. 128

1. (B) $\lim\limits_{x\to0} \dfrac{\sqrt[3]{1+x} - \frac{1}{3}x - 1}{x^2} = \cdots = \lim\limits_{x\to0} \left[-\dfrac{1}{9}(1+x)^{-5/3} \right] = -\dfrac{1}{9}.$

2. (C) $\lim\limits_{x\to\infty} \dfrac{\ln\sqrt{x}}{\ln(2+3x)} = \lim\limits_{x\to\infty} \dfrac{2+3x}{6x} = \dfrac{1}{2}.$

3. $\lim\limits_{x\to1} \dfrac{f(g(x))}{h(x)} = \dfrac{12}{7}$ $f(g(1)) = f(2) = 0$ and $h(1) = 0$ and so L'Hospital's Rule may be applied.

$$\lim\limits_{x\to1} \dfrac{f(g(x))}{h(x)} = \lim\limits_{x\to1} \dfrac{f'(g(x)) \cdot g'(x)}{h'(x)} = \dfrac{f'(g(1)) \cdot g'(1)}{h'(1)} = \dfrac{f'(2) \cdot 4}{7} = \dfrac{3 \cdot 4}{7} = \dfrac{12}{7}$$

Analysis of Parametric, Polar, and Vector Curves—Part II

Content and Practice, p. 130

1. (a) $\boldsymbol{v}(t) = \,<2t, 2\cos(2t)>$

   (b) $\boldsymbol{a}(t) = \,<2, -4\sin(2t)>$

   (c) $\dfrac{3}{\pi}$. $\dfrac{dy}{dx} = \dfrac{dy/dt}{dx/dt} = \dfrac{\cos 2t}{t}$. At $t = \dfrac{\pi}{6}, \dfrac{dy}{dx} = \dfrac{3}{\pi}.$

2. (a) $v(t) = \langle(3t^2 - 1), 6(2t - 1)^2\rangle$; $v(1) = \langle 2, 6\rangle$

   (b) $a(t) = \langle 6t, 24(2t - 1)\rangle$. When $(2t - 1)^3 = 0$, $t = \frac{1}{2}$. $a\left(\frac{1}{2}\right) = \langle 3, 0\rangle$.

3. $\dfrac{dy}{dx} = \dfrac{-\sin(\theta)\sin(\theta) + [1 + \cos(\theta)]\cos(\theta)}{-\sin(\theta)\cos(\theta) - \sin(\theta)[1 + \cos(\theta)]} = 0$

   $-\sin(\theta)\sin(\theta) + [1 + \cos(\theta)]\cos(\theta) = 0$

   $-\sin^2(\theta) + \cos(\theta) + \cos^2(\theta) = 0$

   $\cos^2(\theta) - 1 + \cos(\theta) + \cos^2(\theta) = 0$

   $2\cos^2(\theta) + \cos(\theta) - 1 = 0$

   $[2\cos(\theta) - 1][\cos(\theta) + 1] = 0$

   $\cos(\theta) = \dfrac{1}{2}$ or $\cos(\theta) = -1$

   $\theta = \left\{\dfrac{\pi}{3}, \pi, \dfrac{5\pi}{3}\right\}$.

   We reject $\theta = \pi$ since it produces a zero in the denominator of $\dfrac{dy}{dx}$, so the final answer is $\theta = \left\{\dfrac{\pi}{3}, \dfrac{5\pi}{3}\right\}$.

Additional Practice, p. 131

1. (a) $\left\langle 0, -\dfrac{1}{t^2}\right\rangle$

   (b) Speed is $2\sqrt{2}$. Speed is $|v(t)|$. Since $v(t) = \left\langle 2, \dfrac{1}{t}\right\rangle$, the speed at $t = \dfrac{1}{2}$ is $2\sqrt{2}$.

2. (B) $\dfrac{dy}{dx}$, a rational function, is infinite when $\dfrac{dx}{dt} = 0$ but $\dfrac{dy}{dt} \neq 0$. $\dfrac{dx}{dt} = 0$ for $t = -3$ and $t = 2$.

3. (C) Particle moves left when $\dfrac{dx}{dt} < 0$.

Integrals

Riemann Sums—Part II

Content and Practice, p. 133

1. (a) 10. Left-hand rectangles and four equal subdivisions: $[0 + 3 + 4 + 3] \cdot 1 = 10$

   (b) 10. Right-hand rectangles and four equal subdivisions: $[3 + 4 + 3 + 0] \cdot 1 = 10$

   (c) 11. Midpoint rectangles and four equal subdivisions:
   $[1.75 + 3.75 + 3.75 + 1.75] \cdot 1 = 11$

2. (a) Left-hand rectangles:
   $[0 + 6 + 10 + 16 + 14 + 12 + 18 + 22 + 12 + 4] \cdot 1 = 114$ inches

   (b) Right-hand rectangles:
   $[6 + 10 + 16 + 14 + 12 + 18 + 22 + 12 + 4 + 2] \cdot 1 = 116$ inches

Additional Practice, p. 134

1. (B) $[4.3 \cdot 1.2 + 3.1 \cdot 1.1 + 2.2 \cdot 1.5 + 1.5 \cdot 1.6] = 14.27$

2. 93°C   Left-hand Riemann sum, subintervals of length 5 minutes.

$$\frac{1}{25 - 0} [24 + 76 + 106 + 124 + 135]5 = 93°C$$

Definite Integral of a Rate of Change—Part II

Content and Practice, p. 136

1. (a) 4 cm.   The net change in position is 3 cm. The position after 3 seconds is
   $x = 1 + 3 = 4$.
   (b) $6\frac{1}{3}$ cm.   Net change in position $= \int_0^2 (4 - t^2) \, dt = 5\frac{1}{3}$. Given the $x = 1$ starting

   point, the particle position after 2 seconds is $6\frac{1}{3}$.

2. 34,925 bushels. $\int_0^{14} (1.3 + 1.025^t) \, dt = 34.925$ thousand bushels

Additional Practice, p. 137

1. (B) $\int_0^{24} 25e^{-0.05(t-15)^2} \, dt = 197.727$

2. (a) 1284 bison.   Herd growth from 2000 to 2015 is approximated by
$\int_0^{15} 26.7 \cdot 1.036^t \, dt = 528$. Therefore, the herd size at the beginning of 2015 will be approximately $756 + 528 = 1284$ bison.

   (b) 35 bison per year. $\dfrac{528}{15} \, dt = 35.220$ bison per year

Basic Properties of Definite Integrals—Part II

Content and Practice, p. 139

1. (a) 0. See Rule 2.
   (b) -8. $3 \int_1^2 f(x) \, dx + \int_1^2 1 \, dx = -9 + 1 = -8$. See Rule 4.
   (c) 8. $\int_1^5 f(x) \, dx - \int_1^2 f(x) \, dx = 5 - (-3) = 8$. See Rule 5.

2. 8. $4(3 - 1) = 8$. See Rule 6.

3. $-\pi$. $g(-2) = \int_0^{-2} f(t) \, dt = -\int_{-2}^0 f(t) \, dt = \dfrac{-\pi 2^2}{4} = -\pi$. $\int_{-2}^0 f(t) \, dt$ represents one-fourth of the circle's area; given radius 2 and the familiar area formula $\frac{1}{4} \pi r^2$, the value of the integral is $\dfrac{\pi 2^2}{4}$ in the calculation.

Additional Practice, p. 140

1. (D) $f(a)$ is a minimum and $f(b)$ is a maximum, so I and II are true.

2. (a) $\int_{-1}^3 h(r) \, dr - \int_{-1}^1 h(r) \, dr = 7 - (-2) = 9$. See Rule 5.
   (b) $\int_3^1 h(r) \, dr = -\int_1^3 h(r) \, dr = -9$. See Rule 1.

Fundamental Theorem of Calculus, Antiderivative Part—Part II

Content and Practice, p. 142

1. $\dfrac{dy}{dx} = x \cdot \ln(x - 1)$

2. $G'(x) = \sqrt{3 + \sin(x)}, G'(2) = \sqrt{3 + \sin(2)}$

3. $y = \int_x^5 t^2 \cdot e^t \, dt = -\int_5^x t^2 \cdot e^t \, dt, \quad \dfrac{dy}{dx} = -x^2 e^x$

4. (B) $f'(x) = \sqrt[3]{(\sin(x))^2 + 2} \cdot \dfrac{d}{dx}(\sin(x)) = \cos(x) \cdot \sqrt[3]{\sin^2(x) + 2}$

5. (a) $g(x)$ achieves its maximum value at $x = 1$.

   $g'(x) = f(x)$ is positive only on $[0, 1)$ and negative only on $(1, 3)$, so g increases before $x = 1$, then decreases after $x = 1$.

   (b) 6. $h(1) = 2 + g(1)$. Since $g(1) = A = 4$, $h(1) = 2 + 4 = 6$.

   (c) $g(x)$ achieves its minimum value at $x = 3$.

   $\int_0^1 f(t)dt = 4$ and $\int_1^3 f(t)dt = -5$, so g gains four units of area, then loses five units of area resulting in a minimum at $x = 3$.

   (d) g is concave down on $(0, 2)$.

   $g'(x) = f(x)$ so $g''(x) = f'(x)$. $g''(x) = f'(x)$ is less than zero and g is concave down where the graph of f is decreasing.

Additional Practice, p. 144

1. $y + 3 = 20(x - 2)$ $f'(x) = 2x \cdot g(x^2)$ so $f'(2) = 4 \cdot g(4) = 20$

2. (C) $h'(x) = \ln(x + 2) - x^2 + 4$ Solve $h'(x) = 0$ for critical points. The graph of $h'(x)$ changes from positive to negative at approximately 2.338.

3. $f(x) = \int_7^{2\sqrt{x}} g(t^2)dt$

   $f'(x) = \dfrac{d}{dx}\int_7^{2\sqrt{x}} g(t^2)dt = g(4x) \cdot x^{-1/2}$

   $f''(x) = g(4x)\left(\dfrac{-x^{-3/2}}{2}\right) + x^{-1/2} \cdot 4g'(4x) = \dfrac{-g(4x)}{2x\sqrt{x}} + \dfrac{4g'(4x)}{\sqrt{x}}$

4. (a) $H'(x) = p(x)$

   (b) $H(4) = \int_{-1}^4 p(t)dt = 1 - 2 + 3 = 2$

   (c) $H(-3) = \int_{-1}^{-3} p(t)dt = -\int_{-3}^{-1} p(t)dt = -2$

   (d) $H'(1) = p(1) = -2$

   (e) $H''(x) = p'(x)$ $H''(-2.3) = p'(-2.3) = 1$. (The slope of the segment at $x = -2.3$)

   (f) $[-3, 0]$ and $[2, 5]$ $H(x)$ is increasing where $H'(x) = p(x)$ is positive.
   (Note: Intervals may be open or closed as this convention is not universally agreed upon.)

   (g) $(-5, -1)$ and $(1, 3)$ $H(x)$ is concave up where $H''(x) = p'(x)$ is positive, where the graph of p is increasing.

Fundamental Theorem of Calculus, Evaluation Part—Part II

Content and Practice, p. 146

1. $\int_1^3 (2x + e^x)dx = x^2 + e^x \Big|_1^3 = (9 + e^3) - (1 + e) = 8 + e^3 - e$

2. (C) $\int_0^1 \dfrac{dx}{1 + x^2} = \tan^{-1}(x) \Big|_0^1 = \tan^{-1}(1) - \tan^{-1}(0) = \dfrac{\pi}{4}$

3. $\int_2^5 (2 + \cos^3(x))dx \approx 4.676$

4. $\int_{-4}^x t^3 e^{\sin(t)}dt = y(x) - y(-4)$ so $y = 2 + \int_{-4}^x t^3 e^{\sin(t)}dt$

   This says the new value of y will equal the initial value at $x = -4$, plus the accumulated change in y from -4 to x.

Additional Practice, p. 147

1. (a) $av(f') = \dfrac{1}{10 - 2} \int_2^{10} f'(x)dx = \dfrac{1}{8} f(x) \Big|_2^{10} = \dfrac{f(10) - f(2)}{8} = \dfrac{-22}{8} = \dfrac{-11}{4}$

   (b) The average rate of change of f on the interval $[2, 10]$ is $\dfrac{-11}{4}$.

2. $\int_0^3 x^2 \cdot \ln(x + 3)dx = 14.864$

3. (a) $x(5) = x(0) + \int_0^5 t \cdot \sin(t)dt \approx 6 + (-2.377) = 3.623$

   (b) $x(c) = x(0) + \int_0^c t \cdot \sin(t)dt$ or $x(c) = 6 + \int_0^c t \cdot \sin(t)dt$

4. $u = x, du = dx, dv = \sin(2x)dx, v = \dfrac{-1}{2}\cos(2x)$

$$\int_0^{\pi/2} x \sin(2x)dx = \dfrac{-x}{2}\cos(2x) \Big|_0^{\pi/2} + \int_0^{\pi/2} \dfrac{1}{2}\cos(2x)dx$$

$$= \dfrac{-x}{2}\cos(2x) \Big|_0^{\pi/2} + \dfrac{1}{4}\sin(2x) \Big|_0^{\pi/2}$$

$$= \left(\dfrac{-\pi}{4}\cos\pi - 0\right) + \left(\dfrac{1}{4}\sin(\pi) - \dfrac{1}{4}\sin 0\right)$$

$$= \dfrac{\pi}{4}$$

Alternative solution using the Tabular Method

$f(x)$ and its derivatives	$g(x)$ and its integrals
x	$\sin(2x)$
1	$-\frac{1}{2}\cos(2x)$
0	$-\frac{1}{4}\sin(2x)$

$$\int_0^{\pi/2} x\sin(2x)\,dx = -\frac{x}{2}\cos(2x) + \frac{1}{4}\sin(2x)\Big|_0^{\pi/2}$$

$$= \left(-\frac{\pi}{4}\cos\pi + \frac{1}{4}\sin\pi\right) - \left(0 + \frac{1}{4}\sin 0\right)$$

$$= \frac{\pi}{4}$$

5. Note: No absolute values are needed in the antiderivative because of the domain of the problem.

$$\int_1^3 \frac{12}{x^2 + 6x}\,dx = \int_1^3 \left(\frac{2}{x} - \frac{2}{x+6}\right)dx$$

$$= (2\ln(x) - 2\ln(x+6))\Big|_1^3$$

$$= 2\ln(3) - 2\ln(9) - (2\ln(1) - 2\ln(7))$$
$$= 2[\ln(7) + \ln(3) - \ln(9)]$$
$$= 2[\ln(7) - \ln(3)]$$
$$= 2\ln\left(\frac{7}{3}\right)$$

Antiderivative Basics—Part II

Content and Practice, p. 149

(a) $\cos x$

(b) $\sin x$

(c) $\sec^2 x$

(d) $\cot x + C$

(e) $\sec x \tan x$

(f) $\csc x + C$

(g) $\ln x + C, \quad (x > 0)$

(h) e^x

(i) $a^x + C, \quad (a > 0)$

1. Function: $\sin 2x$ Antiderivative: $-\frac{1}{2}\cos 2x + C$

2. Function: $8x^3 + \sqrt{x}$ Antiderivative: $2x^4 + \frac{2}{3}x^{3/2} + C$

3. Function: $3 + e^{5t}$ Antiderivative: $3t + \frac{1}{5}e^{5t} + C$

4. Function: $x\cos x^2$ Antiderivative: $\frac{1}{2}\sin x^2 + C$

5. Function: $8x - \csc x \cot x$ Antiderivative: $4x^2 + \csc x + C$

6. Function: $\sec^2 5x$ Antiderivative: $\frac{1}{5}\tan 5x + C$

7. Function: $6(2x + 7)^5$ Antiderivative: $\frac{1}{2}(2x + 7)^6 + C$

8. Function: $3^{4x}\ln(3)$ Antiderivative: $\frac{1}{4}3^{4x} + C$

9. A function $F(x)$ is an antiderivative of a function $f(x)$ if $F'(x) = f(x)$ for all x in the domain of f.

10. Functions differing by a constant have the same derivative.

Additional Practice, p. 150

1. (A) $x^2 + 7x + C$

2. (C) $\int_0^{\pi/6} \sin 2x\, dx = -\frac{1}{2}\cos 2x\Big]_0^{\pi/6} = -\frac{1}{2}\left(\cos\frac{\pi}{3} - \cos 0\right) = \frac{1}{4}.$

3. (A) $f(x) = 3 + \ln(x^2 + 1)$ is a possibility because the antiderivative of $f'(x)$ is $\ln(x^2 + 1) + C$.

Antidifferentiation by Substitution—Part II

Content and Practice, p. 152

1. $u = x^3$ and $du = 3x^2\, dx$, substitution transforms the original integral to $\int \sin(u)\, du$.

2. $u = 4x + 3$ and $du = 4\, dx$, substitution transforms the original integral to $\frac{5}{4}\int\frac{1}{u}\, du$.

3. $u = \tan x$ and $du = \sec^2 x\, dx$, substitution transforms the original integral to $\int 7u^5\, du$.

4. $u = x^2 - 4$ and $du = 2x\, dx$, substitution transforms the original integral to $2\int u^{-\frac{1}{2}}\, du$.

5. $u = x^2$ and $du = 2x\, dx$, substitution transforms the original integral to $4\int \csc u \cot u\, du$.

6. $u = \ln x$ and $du = \frac{1}{x}\, dx$, substitution transforms the original integral to $\int 3^u\, du$.

7. $u = x^3 + 5x$ and $du = (3x^2 + 5)\, dx$, substitution transforms the original integral to $2\int \frac{du}{u}$.

   From there, $2\int \frac{du}{u} = 2\ln|u| + C$. Substituting back gives

   $$\int \frac{6x^2 + 10}{x^3 + 5x}\, dx = 2\ln|x^3 + 5x| + C.$$

Additional Practice, p. 154

1. (C) $u = \cos x$ and $du = -\sin x\, dx$; the original integral becomes $-\int e^u\, du$, which integrates to (C).

2. (D) $u = \sin 2x$ and $du = 2\cos 2x\, dx$; the original integral becomes $\frac{1}{2}\int_0^{\frac{\sqrt{3}}{2}} u\, du$. Note the changes in the limits of integration.

3. (B) $u = x^4 + 2x$ and $du = (4x^3 + 2)\, dx$; the original integral becomes $\frac{1}{2}\int_3^{20} \frac{du}{u}$. Note the changes in the limits of integration. Integration yields

   $$\frac{1}{2}\left(\ln 20 - \ln 3\right) = \frac{1}{2}\ln\frac{20}{3} = \ln\left(\frac{20}{3}\right)^{1/2} \text{ or } \ln\sqrt{\frac{20}{3}}.$$

4. (C) Let $u = 2x$ and $du = 2\, dx$, then $\int_2^4 f(2x)\, dx$ becomes $\frac{1}{2}\int_4^8 f(u)\, du$. Note the changes in the limits of integration. So, $\int_2^4 f(2x)\, dx = \frac{1}{2}\int_4^8 f(u)\, du$. Therefore,

   $$\int_4^8 f(u)\, du = 2\int_2^4 f(2x)\, dx = 2(10) = 20.$$

Antidifferentiation by Parts—Part II

Content and Practice, p. 156

1. Let $u = \ln x$ and $dv = x^2\, dx$.

2. Let $u = \tan^{-1} x$ and $dv = x\, dx$.

3. Let $u = x$ and $dv = \cos x \, dx$.

4. Direct substitution; let $u = \sqrt{x} = x^{1/2}$ and $du = \frac{1}{2} x^{-1/2} \, dx$.

5. Let $u = x$ and $dv = 5^x \, dx$.

6. Let $u = \ln x^2$ and $dv = x \, dx$, so $du = \frac{2}{x} \, dx$ and $v = \frac{1}{2} x^2$.

$$\int x \ln x^2 \, dx = \frac{1}{2} x^2 \ln x^2 - \int \left(\frac{1}{2} x^2 \right) \frac{2}{x} \, dx = x^2 \ln x - \int x \, dx = x^2 \ln x - \frac{1}{2} x^2 + C$$

Additional Practice, p. 158

1. (B) Let $u = \ln x$ and $dv = x^{-2} \, dx$, so $du = \frac{1}{x} \, dx$ and $v = -x^{-1}$.

2. (C) Let $u = \sin^{-1} x$ and $dv = dx$, so $du = \dfrac{1}{\sqrt{1 - x^2}} \, dx$ and $v = x$.

$$\int \sin^{-1} x \, dx = x \sin^{-1} x - \int x \frac{1}{\sqrt{1 - x^2}} \, dx = x \sin^{-1} x + \sqrt{1 - x^2} + C$$

3. (A) Area $= \int_0^\pi [x \sin x - (x - \pi)] \, dx = \int_0^\pi x \sin x \, dx - \int_0^\pi (x - \pi) \, dx$. Integrate the first integral by parts, let $u = x$ and $dv = \sin x \, dx$.

Antidifferentiation by Simple Partial Fractions—Part II

Content and Practice, p. 160

1. $\dfrac{8}{2x^2 - 3x - 2} = \dfrac{8}{(2x + 1)(x - 2)} = \dfrac{A}{2x + 1} + \dfrac{B}{x - 2}$. Let $x = 2$ and the equation becomes $8 = 5B$. Let $x = -\frac{1}{2}$ and the equation becomes $8 = -\frac{5}{2} A$. Thus,

$$\frac{8}{2x^2 - 3x - 2} = \frac{-\dfrac{16}{5}}{2x + 1} + \frac{\dfrac{8}{5}}{x - 2}.$$

2. $\dfrac{7x - 1}{x^2 + 4x - 21} = \dfrac{7x - 1}{(x + 7)(x - 3)} = \dfrac{A}{x + 7} + \dfrac{B}{x - 3}$. Multiplying by the LCD we know that $7x - 1 = A(x - 3) + B(x + 7)$. Let $x = 3$ and the equation becomes $B = 2$. Let $x = -7$ and the equation becomes $A = 5$. Thus, $\dfrac{7x - 1}{x^2 + 4x - 21} = \dfrac{5}{x + 7} + \dfrac{2}{x - 3}$.

1. (B) First use simple partial fractions:

$$\frac{4}{x^2 + 8x + 15} = \frac{4}{(x+3)(x+5)} = \frac{2}{x+3} + \frac{-2}{x+5}.$$ Then integrate:

$$\int \frac{4}{x^2 + 8x + 15} = \int \frac{2}{x+3}\,dx - \int \frac{2}{x+5}\,dx = 2\ln|x+3| - 2\ln|x+5| + C.$$

2. (D) First use simple partial fractions: $\dfrac{3x+1}{x(x+1)} = \dfrac{1}{x} + \dfrac{2}{x+1}.$ Then integrate:

$$\int \frac{3x+1}{x(x+1)}\,dx = \int \frac{1}{x}\,dx + \int \frac{2}{x+1}\,dx = \ln|x| + 2\ln|x+1| + C = \ln\left|x(x+1)^2\right| + C.$$

Given that $y(1) = \ln 8$, $C = \ln 2$, $\ln\left|x \cdot (x+1)^2\right| + \ln 2 = \ln\left|2x(x+1)^2\right|.$

Applications of Integrals—Part II

Content and Practice, p. 163

1. $\displaystyle\int_0^{0.739} (\cos x - x)\,dx = 0.400$

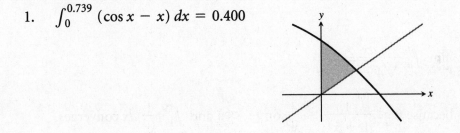

2. $\displaystyle\int_0^4 \left[\pi\left(\sqrt{x}\right)^2 - \pi\left(\frac{1}{2}x\right)^2\right] dx = \frac{8\pi}{3}$

3. $\displaystyle\int_0^1 \sqrt{(2t)^2 + (3t^2)^2}\,dt = \int_0^1 t\sqrt{4 + 9t^2}\,dt$

Additional Practice, p. 169

1. $\displaystyle\int_0^1 \frac{1}{2}\,\pi\left(\frac{1-x}{2}\right)^2 dx = \frac{\pi}{24}$

2. (A) $\displaystyle\frac{1}{2-0}\int_0^2 3x^2\sqrt{x^3+1}\,dx = \frac{26}{3}$

3. $\dfrac{4}{\pi}$ units. Since the function is negative on $[1, 2]$, the particle is reversing direction and the corresponding integral must be subtracted to find total distance: $2\displaystyle\int_0^1 \sin \pi t\,dt = \frac{4}{\pi}$.

387

4. $2\sqrt{3} + \dfrac{4}{3}\pi$.   Sketch the graph and identify the region.

$$\int_{-\pi/3}^{\pi/3}\left[\dfrac{1}{2}\,(4\cos\theta)^2 - \dfrac{1}{2}\,(2)^2\right]d\theta = 2\sqrt{3} + \dfrac{4}{3}\pi$$

5. (B)   Use the length of curve formula, $y'(x) = x^{1/2}$: $\int_0^3\sqrt{1 + (\sqrt{x})^2}\,dx = \dfrac{14}{3}$.

Improper Integrals—Part II

Content and Practice, p. 171

1. $\displaystyle\lim_{a\to\infty}\int_0^a\tan^{-1}x\,dx$

2. $\displaystyle\lim_{a\to 0^+}\int_a^5\dfrac{1}{e^x - 1}\,dx$

3. $\displaystyle\lim_{a\to 2^-}\int_0^a\dfrac{dx}{\sqrt[3]{4 - x^2}} + \lim_{a\to 2^+}\int_a^6\dfrac{dx}{\sqrt[3]{4 - x^2}}$

4. $\displaystyle\int_1^\infty\dfrac{dx}{1 + x^3}$ converges because $0 \le \dfrac{1}{1 + x^3} \le \dfrac{1}{x^3}$ on $[1, \infty)$ and $\displaystyle\int_1^\infty\dfrac{1}{x^3}\,dx$ converges.

5. $\displaystyle\int_0^1\dfrac{dx}{1 + \sqrt{x}}$ converges because $0 \le \dfrac{1}{1 + \sqrt{x}} \le \dfrac{1}{\sqrt{x}}$ on $[0, 1]$ and $\displaystyle\int_0^1\dfrac{1}{\sqrt{x}}\,dx$ converges.

6. $\displaystyle\int_2^\infty\dfrac{dx}{x}$ diverges because $0 \le \dfrac{1}{x} \le \dfrac{1}{\ln x}$ on $[2, \infty]$ and $\displaystyle\int_2^\infty\dfrac{dx}{\ln x}$ diverges.

Additional Practice, p. 173

1. (C) $\displaystyle\int_0^\infty\dfrac{3}{2}\,e^{-x/2}\,dx = \dfrac{3}{2}\lim_{a\to\infty}\int_0^a e^{-x/2}\,dx = \dfrac{3}{2}\lim_{a\to\infty}\left(-2e^{-x/2}\right)\Big]_0^a = 3$

2. (C) $\displaystyle\int_2^\infty\dfrac{dx}{x^2 + 5x + 6} = \int_2^\infty\dfrac{dx}{(x + 2)(x + 3)} =$

$\displaystyle\int_2^\infty\left(\dfrac{1}{x + 2} - \dfrac{1}{x + 3}\right)dx = \lim_{a\to\infty}\left(\ln\big|x + 2\big| - \ln\big|x + 3\big|\right)\Big]_2^a = \lim_{a\to\infty}\left(\ln\dfrac{a + 2}{a + 3} - \ln\dfrac{4}{5}\right) = \ln\dfrac{5}{4}$

3.   (C)   Applying integration by parts to the improper integral gives

$$\int_0^1 x \ln x \, dx = \lim_{a \to 0^+} \left(\frac{1}{2} x^2 \ln x - \frac{1}{4} x^2 \right)\Bigg|_a^1 = \lim_{a \to 0^+} \left[-\frac{1}{4} - \left(\frac{1}{2} a^2 \ln a - \frac{1}{4} a^2 \right) \right].$$

The trick here is to evaluate the expression $\lim_{a \to 0^+} a^2 \ln a = \lim_{a \to 0^+} \dfrac{\ln a}{a^{-2}} = 0$ using L'Hospital's Rule.

Initial Value Problems—Part II

Content and Practice, p. 174

1.   (a) $v(t) = -32t + 155$

     (b) $h(t) = -16t^2 + 155t + 5$

2.   The particular solution is $y = -\dfrac{1}{x} + \dfrac{1}{2}, x < 0$.

     $y = -\dfrac{1}{x} + C$

     Using initial conditions, $1 = \dfrac{1}{2} + C$, so $C = \dfrac{1}{2}$.

     The general solution is not continuous at $x = 0$, and the initial conditions pin down only the branch for $x < 0$ so we add this domain restriction.

3. $f(3) = \int_0^3 \sin(t^2)dt + 1 = 1.774$

     $f(x) = \int_0^x \sin(t^2)dt + C$

     Using initial conditions, $1 = \int_0^0 \sin(t^2)dt + C$ so $C = 1$.

Additional Practice, p. 176

1.   (A) $a(t) = t + \cos t, v(t) = \dfrac{1}{2}t^2 + \sin t + C$. $v(0) = -3 \Rightarrow C = -3$. Setting $v = 0$,

     $\dfrac{1}{2}t^2 + \sin t - 3 = 0$, and solving for t, $t = 2.057$.

2. $x(t) = -\cos t + 2$. $a = \cos t \Rightarrow v = \sin t + C_1$ and given $v(0) = 0, C_1 = 0$. Then
     $v = \sin t \Rightarrow x = -\cos t + C_2$ and since $x(0) = 1, C_2 = 2$.

3.   The particular solution is $y = x + \tan x + 1, -\dfrac{\pi}{2} < x < \dfrac{\pi}{2}$.
     $y = x + \tan x + C$
     $1 = 0 + \tan 0 + C$, so $C = 1$

     Since the general solution is discontinuous, the initial condition pins down only the branch on
     the interval $\left(-\dfrac{\pi}{2}, \dfrac{\pi}{2} \right)$ so we must add a domain restriction.

Separable Differential Equations—Part II

Content and Practice, p. 177

1. (a) $y = 2000e^{2.3t}$

   (b) $1.964 \cdot 10^{10}$

2. $y = (3x + 27)^{2/3}$ for $x > -9$

   $\int \sqrt{y}\, dy = \int 2\, dx \Rightarrow \frac{2}{3} y^{3/2} = 2x + C$

   $y^{3/2} = 3x + C \Rightarrow 9^{3/2} = C = 27$

   $y = (3x + 27)^{2/3}$

   This solution is not differentiable at $(-9, 0)$ and so has branches for $x < -9$ and $x > -9$. The initial condition only pins down the branch for $x > -9$; therefore the domain of the particular solution is $x > -9$.

3. (a) $\dfrac{dP}{dt} = \dfrac{1}{36} P(12 - P)$

   (b) $\lim\limits_{t \to \infty} P(t) = 12$

Additional Practice, p. 179

1. $y(t) = 2e^{\left(\frac{t}{3} - \frac{t^2}{24}\right)}$. $\int \dfrac{dy}{y} = \int \left(\dfrac{1}{3} - \dfrac{t}{12}\right) dt \Rightarrow y = C \cdot e^{\left(\frac{t}{3} - \frac{t^2}{24}\right)}$. Since $y(0) = 2$, $C = 2$.

2. (A) Solving $y = y_0 e^{kt}$ using the given information gives

   $2y_0 = y_0 e^{8k} \Rightarrow k = \dfrac{\ln 2}{8} \approx .0866434.$

3. $y = 4e^{1-x^2}$. $\int \dfrac{dy}{y} = \int -2x\, dx$. Integrating both sides and solving for y gives $y = Ce^{-x^2}$. Since $y(1) = 4$, $C = 4e$ and $4e \cdot e^{-x^2} = 4e^{1-x^2}$.

4. (A) $\dfrac{dP}{dt} = 0.012P(500 - P)$ so by comparison to $\dfrac{dP}{dt} = kP(M - P)$, carrying capacity is $M = 500$.

Numerical Approximations to Definite Integrals—Part II

Content and Practice, p. 181

1. (a) 10. $\int_{-2}^{2} f(x)\,dx \approx \frac{1}{2}\,[f(-2) + 2f(-1) + 2f(0) + 2f(1) + f(2)] = 10$

    (b) Left Riemann sum = 10; right = 10, average = 10

2. 115 in. From the data: $\frac{1}{2}\,[v(0) + 2v(1) + 2v(2) + \cdots + 2v(8) + 2v(9) + v(10)] = 115$

Additional Practice, p. 182

1. 6. From the graph: $\frac{1}{2}\left[f(-2) + 2f(-1) + 2f(0) + 2f(1) + f(2)\right] = 6$

2. (C) $\int_{1}^{7} f(x)\,dx \approx \left[\frac{1}{2} \cdot 3 \cdot (10 + 20) + \frac{1}{2} \cdot 2 \cdot (20 + 40) + \frac{1}{2} \cdot 1 \cdot (40 + 30)\right] = 140$

Series

Concept of Series—Part II

Content and Practice, p. 184

1. Converges to just over 1.6

k	$\sum_{k=1}^{\infty}\frac{1}{k^2}$
1	1
2	1.25
3	1.3611
4	1.4236
5	1.4636
6	1.4914
7	1.5118

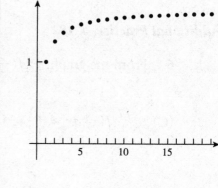

2. Diverges

k	$\sum_{k=1}^{\infty}\frac{k}{k+2}$
1	.33333
2	.83333
3	1.4333
4	2.1
5	2.8143
6	3.5643
7	4.3421

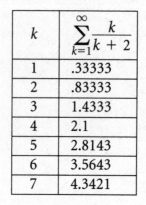

Additional Practice, p. 186

1. Converges

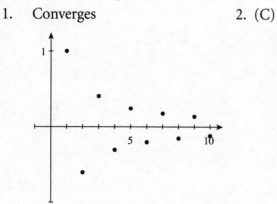

2. (C)

k	$\sum_{k=0}^{\infty}\left(\frac{-1}{3}\right)^k$
0	1
1	.66667
2	.77778
3	.74074
4	.75309
5	.74897
6	.75034
7	.74989

392

3. The series diverges by the nth-Term Test since $\displaystyle\lim_{k\to\infty}\left(1 + \frac{1}{k}\right)^k = e$.

Geometric, Harmonic, and Alternating Series—Part II

Content and Practice, p. 187

1. (B) I is a geometric series with $r > 1$, so it diverges.
         II converges by the Alternating Series Test.
         III is harmonic, so it diverges.

2. 15. $\dfrac{5}{1 - \dfrac{2}{3}} = 15$

Additional Practice, p. 188

1. (B) $S_\infty = \dfrac{\dfrac{3}{2}}{1 - \dfrac{3}{8}} = \dfrac{12}{5}$

2. 3. $S_\infty = \dfrac{4}{1 + \dfrac{1}{3}} = 3$

Power Series—Part II

Content and Practice, p. 195

1. $a = x; r = -3x; f(x) = \dfrac{x}{1 + 3x}$

2. (a) $f(x) = \dfrac{2}{1 - \dfrac{3}{2}x} = 2 + 3x + \dfrac{9}{2}x^2 + \dfrac{27}{4}x^3 + \cdots$

   (b) $f(x) = \dfrac{4}{1 - (3x - 1)} = 4 + 4(3x - 1) + 4(3x - 1)^2 + 4(3x - 1)^3 + \cdots$

Additional Practice, p. 197

1. (C) Note that $f(x) = \dfrac{x}{\sqrt{1 - x^2}}$, the product of x and $g'(x)$. Therefore, a seventh-order

   power series of $f(x)$ can be found by $x\left(1 + \dfrac{x^2}{2} + \dfrac{3x^4}{8} + \dfrac{5x^6}{16}\right)$.

2. (C)

3. (A) The power series is geometric with $r = \dfrac{x-3}{2}$.

$$\left| \frac{x-3}{2} \right| < 1 \Rightarrow -2 < x - 3 < 2 \Rightarrow 1 < x < 5$$

Taylor Polynomials—Part II

Content and Practice, p. 192

1. (a) At $x = 2$

    (b) Yes

    (c) Domain: $(1, 3]$

2. (a) (v) on domain all Real numbers

    (b) (iv) on domain $[-1, 1]$

    (c) (ii) on domain all Real numbers

    (d) (i) on domain $(-2, 2)$

    (e) (iii) on domain $(-\pi/2, \pi/2)$

Additional Practice, p. 194

1. (C) The error for the nth partial sum is $\left| \dfrac{0.4}{3 - 0.4} - \left(\dfrac{0.4}{3} + \dfrac{0.4^2}{9} + \cdots + \dfrac{0.4^n}{3^n} \right) \right|$. By trial and error, this quantity is less than $\dfrac{1}{1000}$ when $n = 3$.

2. (A) $\cos x = 1 - \dfrac{x^2}{2!} + \dfrac{x^4}{4!} - \dfrac{x^6}{6!} + \cdots$. Therefore,

$$\cos 2x = 1 - \frac{(2x)^2}{2!} + \frac{(2x)^4}{4!} - \frac{(2x)^6}{6!} + \cdots = P(x)$$

Maclaurin and Taylor Series—Part II

Additional Practice, p. 198

1. $4 + 7x - x^2 + \dfrac{5x^3}{3!} - \dfrac{8x^4}{4!}$

2. $\sum_{k=0}^{\infty}(-1)^k(x-1)^k = 1 - (x-1) + (x-1)^2 - (x-1)^3 + \cdots + (-1)^k(x-1)^k + \cdots$

3. (B) Set $\dfrac{h^{12}(0)}{12!} = \dfrac{1}{3960}$ and solve for $h^{12}(0)$.

Manipulating Taylor Series—Part II

Content and Practice, p. 199

1. $\tan^{-1} x = x - \dfrac{x^3}{3} + \dfrac{x^5}{5} - \dfrac{x^7}{7} + \cdots = \sum_{n=1}^{\infty} \dfrac{x^{2n-1}}{2n-1}(-1)^{n+1}$; center at 0.

2. No. Substitution would produce a series that is centered at $\dfrac{1}{2}$, not 0.

Additional Practice, p. 202

1. $xe^{x^2} = x\left(1 + x^2 + \dfrac{x^4}{2!} + \cdots + \dfrac{x^{2n}}{n!} + \cdots\right) = x + x^3 + \dfrac{x^5}{2!} + \cdots + \dfrac{x^{2n+1}}{n!} + \cdots$

2. (C)

3. (B) Antidifferentiation yields $g(x) = \left[7t - \dfrac{3}{2}(t-4)^2 + \dfrac{5}{3}(t-4)^3\right)\Big]_4^x$. Substituting x and 4 and taking the difference produces answer (B).

Integral Test, Ratio Test, and Comparison Test—Part II

Content and Practice, p. 203

1. Ratio test: $\displaystyle\lim_{n\to\infty} \dfrac{3^{n+1}}{(n+1)!} \cdot \dfrac{n!}{3^n} = \lim_{n\to\infty} \dfrac{3}{n+1} = 0$. Since this limit is less than 1, the series converges.

2. This series is less than $\displaystyle\sum_{n=1}^{\infty} \dfrac{1}{n^2}$, which is a convergent p-series. Therefore the original series converges by comparison.

Additional Practice, p. 205

1. (C) I is a p-series with $p = \dfrac{1}{2}$, so it diverges.

   II Ratio test: $\displaystyle\lim_{n\to\infty} \dfrac{(n+1)!}{(n+1)^{n+1}} \cdot \dfrac{n^n}{n!} = \lim_{n\to\infty} \left(\dfrac{n}{n+1}\right)^n = \dfrac{1}{e} < 1$, so the series converges.

   III This series is less than $\displaystyle\sum_{n=1}^{\infty} \dfrac{1}{n^3}$, which is a convergent p-series, so the series converges.

Limit Comparison Test—Part II

Content and Practice, p. 206

1. (a) The $\lim\limits_{n\to\infty} \dfrac{a_{n+1}}{a_n} = 1$ for this series. The Ratio Test is inconclusive.

   (b) The terms of the given series are smaller than $\dfrac{n}{n^2}$ for each n, but $\sum\limits_{n=1}^{\infty} \dfrac{n}{n^2}$ diverges.

   (c) The $\sin^2(n)$ in the denominator makes antidifferentiation difficult, if not impossible.

2. For very large n, $\dfrac{n}{\sin^2(n) + n^2} \approx \dfrac{n}{n^2}$.

$$\lim_{n\to\infty} \frac{\dfrac{n}{\sin^2(n) + n^2}}{\dfrac{n}{n^2}} = \lim_{n\to\infty} \frac{n}{\sin^2(n) + n^2} \cdot \frac{n^2}{n}$$

$$= \lim_{n\to\infty} \frac{n^3}{n \cdot \sin^2(n) + n^3}$$

$$= 1$$

The resulting limit is positive and finite, and $\sum\limits_{n=1}^{\infty} \dfrac{n}{n^2} = \sum\limits_{n=1}^{\infty} \dfrac{1}{n}$ diverges (harmonic series),

therefore $\sum\limits_{n=1}^{\infty} \dfrac{n}{\sin^2(n) + n^2}$ also diverges by the Limit Comparison Test.

Additional Practice, p. 208

1. Ratio Test (often good with factorials and exponentials)

2. nth-Term Test for divergence

3. Ratio Test, Limit Comparison Test with $\sum\limits_{n=1}^{\infty} \left(\dfrac{3}{5}\right)^n$

4. Ratio Test, Limit Comparison Test with $\sum\limits_{n=1}^{\infty} \dfrac{1}{e^{2n}}$

5. Direct Comparison Test with $\sum\limits_{n=2}^{\infty} \dfrac{1}{n}$, Integral Test, Limit Comparison Test with $\sum\limits_{n=2}^{\infty} \dfrac{1}{n}$

6. Use the end behavior model $\dfrac{1}{\sqrt{n^3}} = \dfrac{1}{n^{(3/2)}}$ for $n \geq 2$.

$$\lim_{n\to\infty} \frac{\dfrac{1}{\sqrt{n^3 - n}}}{\dfrac{1}{\sqrt{n^3}}} = \lim_{n\to\infty} \frac{\sqrt{n^3}}{\sqrt{n^3 - n}} = 1$$

The limit is finite and positive and $\displaystyle\sum_{n=1}^{\infty} \frac{1}{\sqrt{n^3}} = \sum_{n=1}^{\infty} \frac{1}{n^{(3/2)}}$ converges by the p-Series Test, so

$\displaystyle\sum_{n=2}^{\infty} \frac{1}{\sqrt{n^3 - n}}$ also converges by the Limit Comparison Test.

7. Use $\dfrac{1}{\sqrt{n}}$.

$$\lim_{n \to \infty} \frac{\dfrac{1}{\sqrt{n} + \sqrt{n+1}}}{\dfrac{1}{\sqrt{n}}} = \lim_{n \to \infty} \frac{\sqrt{n}}{\sqrt{n} + \sqrt{n+1}}$$

$$\lim_{n \to \infty} \frac{\sqrt{n}}{\sqrt{n} + \sqrt{n+1}} \cdot \frac{\dfrac{1}{\sqrt{n}}}{\dfrac{1}{\sqrt{n}}} = \lim_{n \to \infty} \frac{1}{1 + \sqrt{1 + \dfrac{1}{n}}} = \frac{1}{2}$$

The limit is positive and finite, and $\displaystyle\sum_{n=1}^{\infty} \frac{1}{\sqrt{n}} = \sum_{n=1}^{\infty} \frac{1}{n^{(1/2)}}$ diverges by the p-Series Test, so

$\displaystyle\sum_{n=1}^{\infty} \frac{1}{\sqrt{n} + \sqrt{n+1}}$ also diverges by the Limit Comparison Test.

Absolute and Conditional Convergence—Part II

Content and Practice, p. 209

1. The given series converges conditionally.

$\displaystyle\sum_{n=1}^{\infty} \left| \frac{(-1)^{n+1}}{\sqrt{n}} \right| = \sum_{n=1}^{\infty} \frac{1}{\sqrt{n}}$ Diverges by the p-Series Test.

Alternating series test: $u_n = \dfrac{1}{\sqrt{n}} > 0$ for $n \geq 1$

$\dfrac{1}{\sqrt{n+1}} \leq \dfrac{1}{\sqrt{n}}$ for $n \geq 1$

$\displaystyle\lim_{n \to \infty} \frac{1}{\sqrt{n}} = 0$ Converges as an alternating series.

2. The absolute series diverges by the nth-Term Test for divergence. Since $\displaystyle\lim_{n \to \infty} \frac{2^n}{n^2} \neq 0$ the series cannot converge as an alternating series.

$\displaystyle\lim_{n \to \infty} \frac{2^n}{n^2} = \infty$ by L'Hospital's Rule.

3. If $x = 4$, $\displaystyle\sum_{n=1}^{\infty} \frac{(x - 3)^n}{n + 1} = \sum_{n=1}^{\infty} \frac{1}{n + 1}$. The series diverges. (Harmonic series)

If $x = 2$, $\displaystyle\sum_{n=1}^{\infty} \frac{(x - 3)^n}{n + 1} = \sum_{n=1}^{\infty} \frac{(-1)^n}{n + 1}$. The series converges. (Alternating harmonic series)

The series is conditionally convergent at $x = 2$.

Additional Practice, p. 210

1. $\displaystyle\sum_{n=1}^{\infty} \frac{\cos(n\pi)}{\sqrt{n^2 + 1}}$ converges conditionally.

$\displaystyle\sum_{n=1}^{\infty} \frac{1}{\sqrt{n^2 + 1}}$ diverges by the Limit Comparison Test with $\displaystyle\sum_{n=1}^{\infty} \frac{1}{n}$.

$$\lim_{n \to \infty} \frac{\dfrac{1}{\sqrt{n^2 + 1}}}{\dfrac{1}{n}} = \lim_{n \to \infty} \frac{n}{\sqrt{n^2 + 1}} = 1$$

Alternating Series Test: $\qquad u_n = \dfrac{1}{\sqrt{n^2 + 1}} > 0$ for $n \geq 1$

$$\frac{1}{\sqrt{(n + 1)^2 + 1}} < \frac{1}{\sqrt{n^2 + 1}} \text{ for } n \geq 1$$

$$\lim_{n \to \infty} \frac{1}{\sqrt{n^2 + 1}} = 0$$

2. (D) II and III only

I. $\displaystyle\sum_{n=1}^{\infty} \frac{(-1)^{n+1}}{n^2}$ converges absolutely by p-Series Test.

II. $\displaystyle\sum_{n=1}^{\infty} \frac{(-1)^{n+1}}{n}$ is the alternating harmonic series, which converges conditionally.

III. $\displaystyle\sum_{n=2}^{\infty} \frac{(-1)^{n+1}}{\ln(n)}$ converges conditionally since it diverges absolutely and converges as an alternating series.

$\dfrac{1}{\ln(n)} > \dfrac{1}{n}$ for $n \geq 2$, so $\displaystyle\sum_{n=2}^{\infty} \frac{1}{\ln(n)}$ diverges by the Direct Comparison Test with $\displaystyle\sum_{n=2}^{\infty} \frac{1}{n}$.

$u_n = \dfrac{1}{\ln(n)}$ for $n \geq 2$ meets all three conditions of the Alternating Series Test.

3. (B) $-\dfrac{7}{2} \le x < \dfrac{9}{2}$

$$\sum_{n=1}^{\infty} \frac{(2x-1)^n}{n \cdot 2^{3n}} = \sum_{n=1}^{\infty} \frac{(2x-1)^n}{n \cdot 8^n}$$

At $x = \dfrac{9}{2}$, $\displaystyle\sum_{n=1}^{\infty} \frac{(2x-1)^n}{n \cdot 8^n} = \sum_{n=1}^{\infty} \frac{1}{n}$. Diverges (harmonic series)

At $x = -\dfrac{7}{2}$, $\displaystyle\sum_{n=1}^{\infty} \frac{(2x-1)^n}{n \cdot 8^n} = \sum_{n=1}^{\infty} \frac{(-8)^n}{n \cdot 8^n} = \sum_{n=1}^{\infty} \frac{(-1)^n}{n}$. Converges (alternating harmonic series)

Radius and Interval of Convergence—Part II

Content and Practice, p. 212

1. (a) $f(x) = \dfrac{1}{4-x}$

   (b) $2 < x < 4$

   (c) $a = 3$

   (d) Radius is 1.

2. (B)

3. $\dfrac{3}{2} < x < \dfrac{11}{2}$

4. $-4 < x < 6$. The Ratio Test: $\displaystyle\lim_{n \to \infty} \left| \frac{\dfrac{(n+1)(x-1)^{n+1}}{5}}{\dfrac{n(x-1)^n}{5^n}} \right| < 1 \Rightarrow -1 < \frac{1}{5}(x-1) < 1$

Additional Practice, p. 214

1. (A)

2. (C)

3. (D) $\displaystyle\lim_{n\to\infty}\left|\frac{(x+2)^{n+1}}{n+2}\cdot\frac{n+1}{(x+2)^n}\right| = |x+2| < 1$, so $-3 < x < -1$

Endpoints:

At $x = -3$ the series becomes $\displaystyle\sum_{n=0}^{\infty}\frac{(-1)^n}{n+1}$, which converges by the Alternating Series Test.

At $x = -1$ the series becomes $\displaystyle\sum_{n=0}^{\infty}\frac{(1)^n}{n+1}$, which is harmonic and diverges.

Error Bounds—Part II

Content and Practice, p. 216

1. The error is less than the first unused term $\frac{1}{5!}$, which is less than $\frac{1}{100}$. Since the first unused term is positive, the error is positive and the approximation is an underestimate.

2. Error is less than or equal to $e^{0.5}\dfrac{(0.5)^3}{3!} \approx 0.0344$.

3. The Lagrange Error formula is $\dfrac{f^{(4)}(c)}{4!}(x-2)^4$. The maximum value of $(x-2)^4$ on the interval $[1, 3]$ occurs at $x = 3$ and the maximum value of $f^{(4)}(c)$ on the interval is 1.65. The error is less than or equal to $\dfrac{1.65}{4!}(3-2)^4 = 0.06875 < 0.07$.

Additional Practice, p. 217

1. 8 terms.   We need $4\left(\dfrac{-1}{3}\right)^n < 0.001$. By trial and error we find $n = 8$.

2. (D) The fourth derivative is $\dfrac{e^x - e^{-x}}{2}$ so the Lagrange Error is $\dfrac{e^c - e^{-c}}{2}\cdot\dfrac{x^4}{4!}$. This error takes on its maximum value on the interval $|x| < 2$ when $c = 2$ and $x = 2$, giving an error bound of 2.418.

3. (B) The Lagrange Error is $\dfrac{e^{c-1}(x-1)^{n+1}}{(n+1)!}$. This takes on its maximum value on $-1 \le x \le 3$ when $c = 3$ and $x = 3$, giving an error bound of $\dfrac{e^2 \cdot 2^{n+1}}{(n+1)!}$. By trial and error, this error bound is less than 1 when $n = 5$.

Practice Examinations
Calculus AB—Exam 1

Section I

Part A—No Calculator

Problem	Answer	Key Concept
1.	(A)	Differentiability
2.	(B)	Graph analysis for extrema
3.	(D)	Definite integral
4.	(C)	Continuity/Differentiability
5.	(C)	Definite integral
6.	(B)	Implicit differentiation
7.	(A)	Definite integral
8.	(B)	Slope field
9.	(D)	L'Hospital's Rule
10.	(D)	Instantaneous rate of change
11.	(A)	Relationships of derivatives
12.	(D)	Limit
13.	(B)	Graph analysis for differentiability
14.	(B)	Velocity/Position
15.	(D)	Fundamental Theorem of Calculus
16.	(B)	Derivative with Chain Rule
17.	(C)	Area approximations
18.	(D)	Tangent line
19.	(C)	Points of inflection
20.	(B)	Integration rules
21.	(B)	Exponential growth derivative
22.	(D)	Graph analysis for points of inflection
23.	(C)	Velocity/Acceleration optimization
24.	(A)	Derivative graph
25.	(D)	Area between curves
26.	(A)	Analysis of derivative data
27.	(D)	Average value
28.	(C)	Numerical derivative
29.	(A)	Rate of change
30.	(A)	Graph analysis for Positon/Velocity

Part B—Calculator Allowed

Problem	Answer	Key Concept
31.	(D)	Graph analysis
32.	(A)	Numerical derivative with calculator
33.	(C)	Derivative graph analysis for extrema
34.	(A)	Critical values
35.	(D)	Continuity/Differentiability
36.	(D)	Fundamental Theorem of Calculus
37.	(B)	Limit
38.	(A)	Exponential growth derivative
39.	(C)	Trapezoidal Rule
40.	(C)	Volume by cross section
41.	(A)	Tangent line
42.	(D)	Fundamental Theorem of Calculus
43.	(A)	Velocity/Acceleration
44.	(C)	Mean Value Theorem/Intermediate Value Theorem
45.	(B)	Area under curve

Calculus AB—Exam 1: Section II, Part A

1. $f(x) = g(x)$ at $x = 0$, $x = 1.8109294$, and $x = 3.7724666$. Let $A = 1.8109294$ and $B = 3.7724666$

    (a) Area $= \int_0^A [f(x) - g(x)]dx + \int_A^B [g(x) - f(x)]dx = 9.931$

    (b) Volume $= \pi \int_0^A [(f(x))^2 - (g(x))^2]dx = 64.325$

    (c) Volume $= \int_A^B (g(x) - f(x))^2 dx = 31.790$

2. (a) $v(2.4) \approx -1.452 < 0$ and $a(2.4) \approx 0.884 > 0$. Since the velocity and acceleration have opposite signs, the speed is decreasing at $t = 2.4$.

    (b) Average velocity $= \frac{1}{4} \int_0^4 v(t)dt = 1.158$

    (c) Total Distance $= \int_0^4 |v(t)| \, dt = 7.309$

    (d) The particle changes from moving left to moving right when the velocity changes from negative to positive.

    $x(2.865) = 2.7 + \int_0^{2.865} v(t)dt = 3.967$

3. (a) $h'(3.5) \approx \dfrac{h(4) - h(3)}{4 - 3} = \dfrac{13.5 - 11}{1} = 2.5$ cm/day

    (b) $\frac{1}{6} \int_0^6 h(t)dt$ is the average length of a leaf in centimeters during the first six days of the data collection.

    $\frac{1}{6} \int_0^6 h(t)dt \approx \frac{1}{6}[1(6.8) + 2(11) + 1(13.5) + 2(20.1)] = \frac{82.5}{6} = 13.75$ cm

    (c) Since the graph of $h(t)$ is strictly increasing on $[0, 6]$, the right Riemann sum is an overestimate, and therefore greater than the true area.

    (d) $\int_0^6 h'(t)dt = h(6) - h(0) = 20.1 - 5.1 = 15$. The leaf grew a total of 15 cm in the first six days.

Calculus AB—Exam 1: Section II, Part B

4. (a) $f'(x) = 0$ at $x = -2$, $x = 0$, and $x = 3$. $x = 0$ is the only critical point where f' changes from negative to positive. Therefore, f has a relative minimum at $x = 0$.

   (b) f is concave up when f'' is positive, which is where f' is increasing. f is increasing where f' is positive. Therefore, f is both concave up and increasing on $0 < x < 1.4$ because f' is both increasing and positive on this interval.

   (c) The graph of f has inflection points at $x = -0.8$, where f' changes from decreasing to increasing and at $x = 1.4$, where f' changes from increasing to decreasing.

   (d) $f(x) = 9 + \int_0^x f'(t)dt$

   $f(-2) = 9 + \int_0^{-2} f'(t)dt = 9 + 2 = 11$

   $f(3) = 9 + \int_0^3 f'(t)dt = 9 + 7 = 16$

5. (a) $\left.\dfrac{dy}{dx}\right|_{(1,\,1)} = \dfrac{3-2}{6-3} = \dfrac{1}{3} \Rightarrow y - 1 = \dfrac{1}{3}(x-1)$

   (b) $6y - 3x = 0 \Rightarrow 2y = x$

   $(2y)^2 + 3y^2 = 1 + 3(2y)y$

   $4y^2 + 3y^2 = 1 + 6y^2$

   $y^2 = 1$

   $y = \pm 1 \Rightarrow x = \pm 2$

   $(-2, -1)$ and $(2, 1)$

   (c) $\dfrac{d^2y}{dx^2} = \dfrac{dy}{dx}\left(\dfrac{3y-2x}{6y-3x}\right) = \dfrac{(6y-3x)\left(3\dfrac{dy}{dx}-2\right) - (3y-2x)\left(6\dfrac{dy}{dx}-3\right)}{(6y-3x)^2}$

   $\left.\dfrac{d^2y}{dx^2}\right|_{(1,\,1)} = \dfrac{(6-3)\left(3\cdot\dfrac{1}{3}-2\right) - (3-2)\left(6\cdot\dfrac{1}{3}-3\right)}{(6-3)^2} = \dfrac{3(-1)-1(-1)}{9} = -\dfrac{2}{9}$

6. (a)

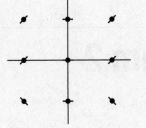

(b) Slopes are positive for points where $x \neq 0$ and $y > -\frac{1}{2}$.

(c) $\displaystyle\int \frac{dy}{2y+1} = \int x^2 dx$

$\displaystyle\frac{1}{2}\int \frac{2dy}{2y+1} = \int x^2 dx$

$\displaystyle\frac{1}{2}\ln|2y+1| = \frac{1}{3}x^3 + C$

$\displaystyle\ln|2y+1| = \frac{2}{3}x^3 + C$

$\displaystyle|2y+1| = e^{\frac{2}{3}x^3+C}$

$\displaystyle|2y+1| = Ce^{\frac{2}{3}x^3}$

$\displaystyle|2(5)+1| = Ce^0$

$11 = C$

$\displaystyle 2y+1 = 11e^{\frac{2}{3}x^3}$

$\displaystyle 2y = 11e^{\frac{2}{3}x^3} - 1$

$\displaystyle y = \frac{1}{2}\left(11e^{\frac{2}{3}x^3} - 1\right)$

Calculus AB—Exam 2

Section I

Part A—No Calculator

Problem	Answer	Key Concept
1.	(C)	Antiderivative of a polynomial
2.	(A)	Derivative—product rule
3.	(B)	Properties of definite integrals
4.	(B)	Derivative—polynomial
5.	(D)	Use derivatives to analyze graph properties
6.	(B)	Antiderivative—substitution
7.	(D)	Derivative—chain rule
8.	(C)	Definite integrals—motion problems from graph
9.	(C)	Slope Fields
10.	(C)	Tangent line to function
11.	(C)	Relating graphs of f and f'
12.	(B)	Tangent line to function
13.	(A)	Use derivatives to analyze graph properties
14.	(D)	Separable differential equations
15.	(A)	Limit from a graph
16.	(C)	Area using definite integrals
17.	(A)	Higher-order derivatives, implicit differentiation
18.	(B)	Antiderivative—substitution
19.	(B)	Derivative—chain rule
20.	(D)	Average value of a function
21.	(A)	Evaluate limit using limit properties
22.	(D)	Use derivatives to analyze graph properties
23.	(D)	Volume of revolution
24.	(B)	Riemann sum approximation for definite integral
25.	(A)	Antiderivatives—substitution
26.	(C)	Identify limit of difference quotient as derivative
27.	(A)	Differentiability and continuity—piecewise function
28.	(D)	Fundamental Theorem of Calculus
29.	(C)	L'Hospital's Rule
30.	(D)	Continuity and Differentiability

Part B—Calculator Allowed

Problem	Answer	Key Concept
31.	(D)	Derivative—quotient rule
32.	(B)	Use derivatives to analyze graph properties
33.	(D)	Fundamental Theorem of Calculus, integral as area
34.	(A)	Mean Value Theorem
35.	(B)	Slope of tangent line
36.	(B)	Related rates
37.	(D)	Definite integral as net change
38.	(A)	Area using definite integrals
39.	(B)	Volume using known cross sections
40.	(C)	Use derivatives to analyze graph properties
41.	(A)	Derivative as rate of change
42.	(B)	Integral as net change—motion problem
43.	(C)	Fundamental Theorem of Calculus, relating graphs of f and f'
44.	(B)	Riemann sum approximation from a table, trapezoidal rule
45.	(C)	Estimating $f'(x)$ from a table, connecting $f'(x)$ and $f''(x)$

Calculus AB—Exam 2: Section II, Part A

1. (a) $G'(t) = -90 \cos\left(\frac{t^2}{14}\right)\left(\frac{t}{7}\right) \Rightarrow G'(6) = -90 \cos\left(\frac{36}{14}\right)\left(\frac{6}{7}\right) \approx 69.940$

   The rate at which paper arrives at the shredder is increasing by 64.940 cubic feet per hour at time $t = 6$ hours.

   (b) $\int_0^8 G(t)dt \approx 650.690$ cubic feet

   (c) Amount of unshredded paper at time t: $A(t) = 300 + \int_0^t (G(x) - 75)dx$. Using FTC, $A'(t) = G(t) - 75$. $A(t)$ is decreasing on the interval $[2.365, 6.196]$ because $A'(t)$ is negative on the interval $(2.365, 6.196)$.

   (d) The amount of unshredded paper has a relative maximum value at time $t = 2.365$ because $A'(t)$ changes from positive to negative there, and also at $t = 8$ because it is a right endpoint and $A'(t)$ is positive to the left.

   $$A(2.365) = 354.751$$
   $$A(8) = 350.690$$

   This is a continuous function on a closed interval, so the Extreme Value Theorem tells us that 354.751 is the absolute maximum, and this is less than 400, so the shredders will not have to be shut down.

2. (a) f and g intersect when $x \approx 5.445$. Area $= \int_0^{5.445}(g(x) - f(x))dx \approx 27.154$

   (b) Volume $= \pi \int_0^{5.445}\left((g(x) + 3)^2 - (f(x) + 3)^2\right)dx \approx 1{,}508.345$

   (c) Volume $= \int_0^{5.445} 3(g(x) - f(x))^2 dx \approx 724.226$

Calculus AB—Exam 2: Section II, Part B

3. (a) $\int_0^{30} v(t)dt = \frac{1}{2}(30)(20) = 300$. The boat travels 300 meters in those 30 seconds.

    (b) $v'(18) = \dfrac{20 - 0}{24 - 0} = \dfrac{5}{6}$ meters/sec

    $v'(24)$ does not exist. The velocity graph has a corner at that location, causing it to be non-differentiable. (Since $\displaystyle\lim_{t \to 24^-} \dfrac{v(t) - v(24)}{t - 24} = \dfrac{5}{6} \neq \dfrac{-10}{3} = \lim_{t \to 24^+} \dfrac{v(t) - v(24)}{t - 24}$ no two-sided limit, nor derivative, exists at $t = 24$.)

    (c) $a(t) = \begin{cases} \dfrac{5}{6} & 0 < t < 24 \\[2mm] \dfrac{-10}{3} & 24 < t < 30 \end{cases}$

    $a(t)$ does not exist at $t = 24$.

    (d) $\dfrac{v(27) - v(18)}{27 - 18} = -\dfrac{5}{9}$ meters/sec. No, the MVT does not apply to the interval $[18, 27]$ because v is not differentiable at $t = 24$.

4. (a) f' changes from increasing to decreasing at $x = -3$ and from decreasing to increasing at $x = 0$. Therefore, the graph of f has points of inflection at $x = -3$ and $x = 0$.

    (b) $f(-6) = f(0) + \int_0^{-6} g(x)$
    $$= 8 + \left[18 - \tfrac{1}{2}\pi(3)^2\right] = 26 - \tfrac{9\pi}{2}$$
    $$f(4) = f(0) + \int_0^4 \left(\tfrac{1}{3}x^2 - 3\right)dx$$
    $$= 8 + \left(\tfrac{1}{9}x^3 - 3x\right)\Big|_0^4 = \tfrac{28}{9} \quad \text{or} \quad 3\tfrac{1}{9}$$

    (c) Since $f'(x) < 0$ on the intervals $-6 < x < -3$ and $-3 < x < 3$, f is decreasing on the interval $-6 \leq x \leq 3$. Since $f'(x) > 0$ on the interval $3 < x < 4$, f is increasing on the interval $3 \leq x \leq 4$. Therefore f has an absolute minimum at $x = 3$.

5. (a) Profit $= 200 \cdot 50 - \int_0^{50} 3x\,dx = \$6{,}250$

    (b) $\int_{50}^{55} 3x\,dx$ is the difference in cost, in dollars, between building an antenna that is 55 feet high and building an antenna that is 50 feet high.

    (c) Profit $= 200k - \int_0^k 3x\,dx$ dollars

(d) $P(k) = 200k - \int_0^k 3x \, dx$

$P'(k) = 200 - 3k = 0$ when $k = \frac{200}{3}$ or $66\frac{2}{3}$ feet high.

This is the only critical point for P, and P' changes from positive to negative at $k = 66\frac{2}{3}$, therefore this height will yield the maximum profit for selling a single antenna.

6. (a) $A'(3.5) \approx \dfrac{A(4) - A(3)}{4 - 3} = \dfrac{14.3 - 9.7}{1} = 4.6$ lbs/day

(b) Yes. A is differentiable and therefore continuous on the closed interval $0 \leq t \leq 2$, and the average rate of change on that interval is $\dfrac{A(2) - A(0)}{2 - 0} = \dfrac{6 - 0}{2 - 0} = 3$ lbs/day.

Therefore, by the Mean Value Theorem, there is at least one time t, $0 < t < 2$, for which $A'(t) = 3$.

(c) $\dfrac{1}{5}\int_0^5 A(t)\,dt \approx \dfrac{1}{5}[1 \cdot A(1) + 1 \cdot A(2) + 1 \cdot A(3) + 1 \cdot A(4) + 1 \cdot A(5)]$

$= \dfrac{1}{5}[3.1 + 6 + 9.7 + 14.3 + 19.9] = \dfrac{1}{5}(53) = \dfrac{53}{5}$ or $10\frac{3}{5}$

$\dfrac{1}{5}\int_0^5 A(t)\,dt$ is the average amount of algae in the tank, in pounds, over the 5-day period from $t = 0$ to $t = 5$.

(d) $M'(t) = t + \dfrac{1}{2}(t^2 + 6t)^{-\frac{1}{2}}(2t + 6)$

$M'(2) = 2 + \dfrac{1}{2}((2)^2 + 6(2))^{-\frac{1}{2}}(2(2) + 6) = 2 + \dfrac{1}{2\sqrt{16}}(10)$

$= 2 + \dfrac{5}{4} = \dfrac{13}{4}$ or $3\frac{1}{4}$

Calculus BC—Exam 1

Section I

Part A—No Calculator

Problem	Answer	Key Concept
1.	(A)	Antiderivative of a polynomial
2.	(D)	Limit from a graph
3.	(C)	Derivative of a parametric function
4.	(B)	Integral as area and improper integral
5.	(B)	Conditional vs. absolute convergence and limit comparison test
6.	(D)	Implicit differentiation
7.	(B)	Behavior of a graph determined from the graph of its derivative
8.	(A)	Area inside a polar curve
9.	(C)	Fundamental Theorem of Calculus
10.	(C)	Related rates
11.	(B)	Euler's method
12.	(D)	Definition of an integral as the limit of a Riemann sum
13.	(A)	Intermediate Value Theorem
14.	(C)	Limit definition of a derivative or L'Hospital's Rule
15.	(A)	Antidifferentiation by partial fractions
16.	(C)	Alternating series error bound
17.	(C)	Position, velocity, acceleration relationships (integration)
18.	(D)	Asymptote as a limit as x goes to infinity and negative infinity
19.	(B)	Ways a derivative can fail to exist
20.	(A)	Integration by parts (conceptual)
21.	(D)	Speed as the magnitude of the velocity vector
22.	(A)	Creating a new series from a familiar series
23.	(B)	Average value
24.	(C)	Slope field represented by differential equation
25.	(D)	Convergence using ratio test and testing endpoints
26.	(D)	Intervals of concavity
27.	(B)	Logistic differential equations
28.	(A)	Limit comparison test
29.	(A)	L'Hospital's Rule and Fundamental Theorem of Calculus
30.	(B)	Sum of an infinite geometric series

Part B—Calculator Allowed

Problem	Answer	Key Concept
31.	(B)	Series convergence tests
32.	(A)	Mean Value Theorem
33.	(C)	Points of inflection
34.	(D)	Accumulation of function value by integrating its derivative
35.	(C)	Particle velocity from position
36.	(A)	Area between graphs
37.	(A)	U-substitution forms
38.	(B)	LaGrange error bound
39.	(A)	Separable differential equation with initial condition
40.	(C)	Generation of Taylor polynomials
41.	(C)	Accumulation of a rate of change
42.	(D)	Analysis of functions and average value
43.	(B)	Local max/min with Fundamental Theorem of Calculus
44.	(B)	Volume by washers
45.	(C)	Length of a path of a vector function

Calculus BC—Exam 1: Section II, Part A

1. (a) The slope of the tangent is

$$\left.\frac{dy}{dx}\right|_{t=1} = \frac{\left.\dfrac{dy}{dt}\right|_{t=1}}{\left.\dfrac{dx}{dt}\right|_{t=1}}$$

$$= \frac{\dfrac{3}{1+e}}{\arctan(1)}$$

$$\approx 1.027$$

The slope of the normal is the opposite reciprocal, or approximately -0.973.

The equation of the normal line is $y - 2 = -0.973(x - 4)$.

(b) Speed is $\left|\left\langle \dfrac{dx}{dt}, \dfrac{dy}{dt} \right\rangle\right|_{t=1.5} = \sqrt{[x'(1.5)]^2 + [y'(1.5)]^2}$

$$\approx 0.856 \text{ or } 0.857$$

Acceleration vector is $\langle x''(t), y''(t)\rangle|_{t=1.5} \approx \langle -2.823, -0.123\rangle$

(c) $\left.\dfrac{dx}{dt}\right|_{t=2} \approx -1.107$

The particle is moving left at $t = 2$, since $x'(2)$ is less than zero.

$x''(2) \approx -0.800$

Since $x'(2)$ and $x''(2)$ have the same sign (both negative), the speed of the particle in the x-direction is increasing at $t = 2$.

(d) $y(0) + \displaystyle\int_0^1 \frac{dy}{dt}\, dt = y(1)$

$$y(0) = 2 - \int_0^1 \frac{3t}{1 + e^t}\, dt$$

$$\approx 1.488$$

2. (a) Area $= \dfrac{1}{2}\displaystyle\int_{\frac{\pi}{2}}^{\frac{5\pi}{6}} (2^2 - [2 - \cos(3\theta)]^2)\,d\theta \approx 1.071$ or 1.072

(b) Note: The symbolic derivative is not required. The answer may be found by taking the derivative on your calculator.

$$\dfrac{dr}{d\theta}\bigg|_{\theta=\frac{5\pi}{12}} = 3\sin(3\theta)\bigg|_{\theta=\frac{5\pi}{12}}$$

$$= 3\sin\left(\dfrac{5\pi}{4}\right)$$

$$\approx -2.121$$

As θ increases, at the instant $\theta = \dfrac{5\pi}{12}$, the distance from the curve to the pole is decreasing at 2.121 units per radian.

(c) $y = r \cdot \sin(\theta) = [2 - \cos(3\theta)]\sin(\theta)$

$$\dfrac{dy}{d\theta}\bigg|_{\theta=\frac{\pi}{5}} \approx 3.545$$

(d) $\dfrac{d\theta}{dt} = \dfrac{dr}{dt} \div \dfrac{dr}{d\theta}$

$$\dfrac{dr}{d\theta}\bigg|_{\theta=\frac{\pi}{9}} \approx 2.598$$

$$\dfrac{d\theta}{dt} = 2 \div 2.598$$

$$\approx 0.769 \text{ or } 0.770$$

Calculus BC—Exam 1: Section II, Part B

3. (a) $\dfrac{d^2y}{dx^2} = \dfrac{d}{dx}\left(\dfrac{2x-2}{y}\right)$

$$= \dfrac{y \cdot 2 - (2x-2)\dfrac{dy}{dx}}{y^2}$$

At $(1, -3), \dfrac{dy}{dx} = 0$ so $\dfrac{d^2y}{dx^2} = \dfrac{2y}{y^2} = -\dfrac{2}{3}.$

(b) The graph of $y = g(x)$ has a local maximum. At $(1, -3), \dfrac{dy}{dx} = 0$ and $\dfrac{d^2y}{dx^2} < 0.$ By the second derivative test, $y = g(x)$ has a local maximum.

(c) $\int y\, dy = \int (2x-2)dx$

$\dfrac{y^2}{2} = x^2 - 2x + C$

Using $g(1) = -3, \dfrac{9}{2} = 1 - 2 + C \Rightarrow C = \dfrac{11}{2}.$

$\dfrac{y^2}{2} = x^2 - 2x + \dfrac{11}{2}$

$y^2 = 2x^2 - 4x + 11$

$y = -\sqrt{2x^2 - 4x + 11}$ since $g(1) = -3.$

4. (a) Area $= \displaystyle\int_0^2 [(e^x - 1) - (-x)]dx$

$e^x - x + \dfrac{1}{2}x^2 \Big|_0^2 = (e^2 - 2 + 2) - (e^0 - 0 + 0)$

Area $= e^2 - 1$

(b) $V = \pi \displaystyle\int_0^2 [(e^x - 1 + 3)^2 - (-x + 3)^2]\, dx$

(c) Perpendicular to y-axis requires dy.

$y = e^x - 1 \Rightarrow x = \ln(y + 1)$ for $0 \le y \le e^2 - 1$.

$y = -x \Rightarrow x = -y$ for $-2 \le y \le 0$.

This requires integrals for the region above the x-axis and below.

Diameter above $= 2 - \ln(y + 1)$, so upper radius is $1 - \frac{1}{2}\ln(y + 1)$.

Diameter below $= 2 - (-y)$, so lower radius is $1 + \frac{1}{2}y$.

Since they are semicircles, integrate $\frac{1}{2}\pi r^2$ for each region.

$$V = \frac{1}{2}\pi \int_0^{e^2-1} \left(1 - \frac{1}{2}\ln(y + 1)\right)^2 dy + \frac{1}{2}\pi \int_{-2}^{0} \left(1 + \frac{1}{2}y\right)^2 dy$$

5. (a) $\dfrac{20 - (-4) \text{ ft./sec.}}{27 - 21 \text{ sec.}} = \dfrac{24}{6} = 4 \dfrac{\text{ft.}}{\text{sec}^2}$

(b) $\int_0^{16} v(t)dt$ is the displacement of the car in feet over the time interval $[0, 16]$ seconds.

$\dfrac{5}{2}(3 + 7) + \dfrac{7}{2}(7 + 15) + \dfrac{4}{2}(15 + (-5)) = 122$ feet

(c) The car must change directions in the intervals $12 < t < 16$ and $21 < t < 23$. The velocity is a differentiable function, so it is continuous over the given domain. By the Intermediate Value Theorem, as velocity changes from positive to negative in $12 < t < 16$ and negative to positive in $21 < t < 23$, the velocity must change signs in the interval, causing the car to change direction.

6. (a) Apply the ratio test.

$$\lim_{n \to \infty} \left| \frac{(x - 2)^{n+1}}{(n + 1) \cdot 3^{n+1}} \cdot \frac{n \cdot 3^n}{(x - 2)^n} \right| < 1 \Rightarrow \lim_{n \to \infty} \left| \frac{n}{n + 1} \cdot \frac{(x - 2)}{3} \right| < 1$$

$$-1 < \frac{x - 2}{3} < 1 \Rightarrow -1 < x < 5$$

(b) At $x = 5$, $\displaystyle\sum_{n=1}^{\infty}(-1)^{n+1}\frac{(x-2)^n}{n\cdot 3^n} = \sum_{n=1}^{\infty}(-1)^{n+1}\frac{3^n}{n\cdot 3^n}$

Test $\displaystyle\sum_{n=1}^{\infty}(-1)^{n+1}\frac{1}{n}$ for convergence.

$\dfrac{1}{n} > 0$ for all n in the summation.

$\dfrac{1}{n+1} < \dfrac{1}{n}$ for all n in the summation.

$\displaystyle\lim_{n\to\infty}\frac{1}{n} = 0$ so the series converges as an alternating series.

As an absolute series, $\displaystyle\sum_{n=1}^{\infty}\frac{1}{n}$ is the harmonic series which diverges.

The given series converges conditionally at the right endpoint, $x = 5$.

(c) The series is alternating, so the bound is the absolute value of the first unused term, in this case the fourth term. The error is less than $|a_4| = \dfrac{(3-2)^4}{4\cdot 3^4} = \dfrac{1}{324}$.

(d) $\displaystyle\int_2^x (-1)^{n+1}\frac{(t-2)^n}{n\cdot 3^n}\,dt = (-1)^{n+1}\frac{(t-2)^{n+1}}{n(n+1)\cdot 3^n}\bigg|_2^x$

$g(x) = \displaystyle\sum_{n=1}^{\infty}(-1)^{n+1}\frac{(x-2)^{n+1}}{n(n+1)\cdot 3^n}$

Calculus BC—Exam 2

Section I

Part A—No Calculator

Problem	Answer	Key Concept
1.	(A)	Solve problems involving the slope of a tangent line
2.	(B)	Calculate antiderivatives using partial fractions
3.	(C)	L'Hospital's Rule
4.	(D)	Geometric Series
5.	(C)	Continuity
6.	(B)	Evaluate definite integrals
7.	(B)	Logistic differential equations
8.	(A)	Taylor Series
9.	(D)	Implicit differentiation
10.	(B)	Use derivatives to analyze properties of a function
11.	(C)	Fundamental Theorem of Calculus
12.	(D)	Specific solution to a differential equation
13.	(C)	Vectors, parametric equations
14.	(D)	Determine limits of functions
15.	(A)	Integration by parts
16.	(B)	Derivatives to analyze properties of a function
17.	(B)	Determine whether a series converges or diverges
18.	(C)	Improper integrals
19.	(C)	Interval of convergence
20.	(D)	Related rates
21.	(C)	Length of a parametric curve
22.	(C)	Euler's method
23.	(B)	Definition of the derivative
24.	(D)	Fundamental Theorem of Calculus
25.	(B)	Maclaurin series
26.	(B)	Points of inflection
27.	(A)	Numerical approximations of definite integrals
28.	(D)	Optimization problems
29.	(C)	Differential equations, separation of variables
30.	(D)	Chain rule for parametric equations

Part B—Calculator Allowed

Problem	Answer	Key Concept
31.	(C)	Area between two curves
32.	(D)	Error analysis of Taylor series
33.	(C)	Volumes of known cross section
34.	(C)	Area bounded by polar curves
35.	(D)	Rectilinear motion
36.	(D)	Analyze differential equations to obtain specific solutions
37.	(D)	Trapezoidal Rule
38.	(B)	Related rates
39.	(A)	Convergence of geometric series
40.	(A)	Mean Value Theorem
41.	(B)	Rectilinear motion
42.	(C)	Definite integral of a rate of change
43.	(A)	Geometric series
44.	(C)	Volumes of revolution
45.	(A)	Definite integral defined as the limit of a Riemann sum

Calculus BC—Exam 2: Section II, Part A

1. (a)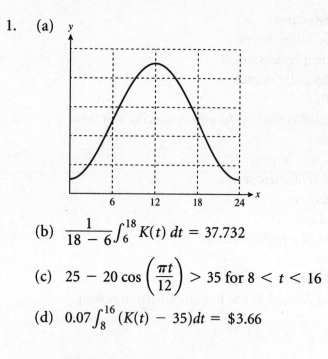

    (b) $\dfrac{1}{18 - 6}\displaystyle\int_6^{18} K(t)\, dt = 37.732$

    (c) $25 - 20 \cos\left(\dfrac{\pi t}{12}\right) > 35$ for $8 < t < 16$

    (d) $0.07\displaystyle\int_8^{16} (K(t) - 35)dt = \$3.66$

2. (a) $\dfrac{58 - 47}{18 - 10} = \dfrac{11}{8} = 1.375$°C per sec

    (b) $\dfrac{1}{30}\displaystyle\int_0^{30} S(t)dt$ is the average temperature of the water in degrees Celsius per second for the first 30 seconds.

    $$T = \frac{5}{2}(28 + 38) + \frac{5}{2}(38 + 47) + \frac{8}{2}(47 + 58) + \frac{12}{2}(58 + 71) = 1571.5$$

    $$\frac{1}{30}\int_0^{30} S(t)dt \approx \frac{1}{30} T = 52.383\text{°C}$$

    (c) $\displaystyle\int_0^{30} S'(t)dt = S(30) - S(0) = 71 - 28 = 43$°C

    This is the change in temperature from $t = 0$ to $t = 30$.

    (d) $71 + \displaystyle\int_{30}^{60} 2.16(0.970446)^t\, dt = 88.372$°C

Calculus BC—Exam 2: Section II, Part B

3. (a) $\int_0^2 (4 - x^2)dx = \frac{16}{3}$

    (b) Use the method of disks about the x-axis: $\pi \int_0^2 (4 - x^2)^2 dx = \frac{256}{15}\pi$

    (c) Use the method of disks about the y-axis: $\pi \int_0^4 (4 - y)dy = 8\pi$

4. (a)

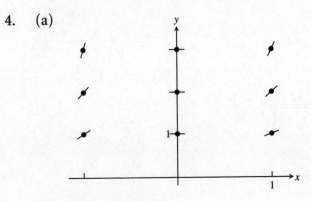

    (b) $f(0.2) \approx 1.001$

x	y	$f'(x)$
0	1	0
0.1	1	0.01
0.2	1.001	

    (c) $\dfrac{dy}{dx} = x^2 y$

    $\dfrac{dy}{y} = x^2 dx$

    $\ln|y| = \dfrac{x^3}{3} + C$

    $|y| = Ce^{x^3/3}$

    $1 = Ce^0$

    $1 = C$

    $y = e^{x^3/3}$

5. (a) $\dfrac{dx}{dt} = (t + 1)^{-1/2}$

    $x = 2\sqrt{t + 1} + C$

    Initial conditions:

    $-1 = 2\sqrt{4} + C$

    $-5 = C$

    $x = 2\sqrt{t + 1} - 5$

    (b) $\dfrac{dy}{dt} = 2x\dfrac{dx}{dt} - 2\dfrac{dx}{dt} = 4 - \dfrac{12}{\sqrt{t + 1}}$

    (c) From (a), $x(8) = 1$. $y(1) = 1^2 - 2 = -1$
    Location $(1, -1)$

    (d) $\text{Speed} = \sqrt{\left(\dfrac{1}{\sqrt{t + 1}}\right)^2 + \left(4 - \dfrac{12}{\sqrt{t + 1}}\right)^2}$

    At $t = 8$, speed $= \dfrac{1}{3}$

6. (a) $7 - 4x + \dfrac{1}{2}x^2 + x^3$; $f(1) \approx 4\dfrac{1}{2}$

    (b) $7 - 4x^2 + \dfrac{1}{2}x^4$

    (c) $7x - 2x^2 + \dfrac{x^3}{6} + \dfrac{x^4}{4}$

    (d) $h(1)$ cannot be determined because $f(t)$ is known only for $t = 0$ and $t = 1$.

Appendix: Precalculus Review of Calculus Prerequisites

Functions—Appendix

Content and Practice, p. 305

1. (a) $[-4, \infty)$

    (b) $[0, \infty)$. Since $x + 4 \geq 0$, $\sqrt{x + 4} \geq 0$, therefore $f(x) \geq 0$.

    (c) 2. To find a y-intercept, let $x = 0$. $f(0) = 2$.

    (d) -4. To find x-intercepts, let $f(x) = 0$. $\sqrt{x + 4} = 0 \Rightarrow (x + 4) = 0 \Rightarrow x = -4$.

    (e)
    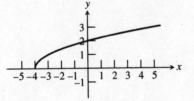

2. (a) $(-\infty, \infty)$

    (b) $[-4, \infty)$. The graph of $f(x)$ is a parabola with vertex $(1, -4)$. Since the parabola opens upward, the ordinate of the vertex is the least value of the function, -4.

    (c) -3. y-intercept: let $x = 0, f(0) = -3$

    (d) x-intercepts: 3 and -1. Set $f(x) = 0$.

    $$x^2 - 2x - 3 = (x - 3)(x + 1) = 0 \Rightarrow x - 3 = 0, x + 1 = 0 \Rightarrow x = 3, x = -1$$

    (e)
    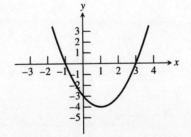

Additional Practice, p. 307

1. (C) $\dfrac{1}{\sqrt{x-2}} \geq 0 \Rightarrow (x-2) > 0 \Rightarrow x > 2$

2. (a) $f(x) = \dfrac{1}{x}$; Domain: $x \neq 0$. Range: $y \neq 0$.

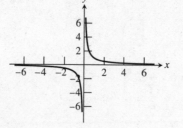

(b) $g(x) = \sqrt{x}$; Domain: $[0, \infty)$. Range: $[0, \infty)$.

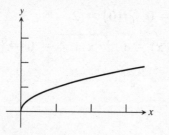

(c) $h(x) = \dfrac{1}{x^2 - 9}$; Domain: $x \neq \pm 3$. Range: $\left(-\infty, -\dfrac{1}{9}\right] \cap (0, \infty)$

(d) $k(x) = \dfrac{1}{\sqrt{x}}$; Domain: $(0, \infty)$. Range: $(0, \infty)$.

(e) $p(x) = x^2$; Domain: $(-\infty, \infty)$. Range: $[0, \infty)$.

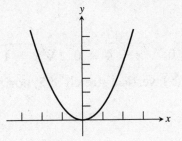

(f) $q(x) = \sin x$; Domain: $(-\infty, \infty)$. Range: $[-1, 1]$.

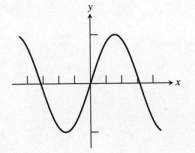

(g) $s(x) = \tan x$; Domain: all $x \neq \dfrac{\pi}{2} + k\pi$, where k is an integer. Range: $(-\infty, \infty)$.

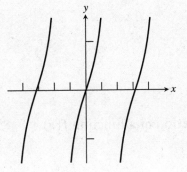

3. $(0, 0)$ is both an x-intercept and a y-intercept, $(3, 0)$ and $(-3, 0)$ are additional x-intercepts.

$$f(x) = x^3 - 9x = x(x - 3)(x + 3) = 0 \Rightarrow x = 0, x = \pm 3$$

4. (D). The range of a piecewise function is the union of the ranges of its separate parts. Since the range of $(x - 1)^2$, on its defined domain $x < 2$, is the set of nonnegative real numbers and the range of $2x - 3$ on $x > 2$, is $(1, \infty)$, then the range of f must be $[0, \infty)$. Confirm with a graph.

Transformations—Appendix

Content and Practice, p. 309

1. (a) $[-4, \infty)$

 (b) Range: $[3, \infty)$. Since $x + 4 \geq 0$, $\sqrt{x + 4} \geq 0, 2\sqrt{x + 4} + 3 \geq 3$.

 (c) $g(x)$ is a transformation from $f(x)$: vertical stretch of 2, horizontal shift of -4, and vertical shift of 3.

 (d)

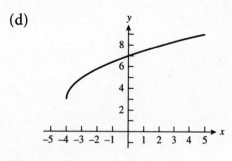

2. (a) $g(x) = -3(x - 1)^2 - 4$

 (b)

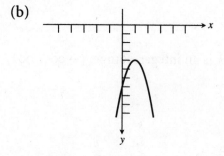

 (c) Range of function $g(x)$: $(-\infty, -4]$.

3. (B) $-f(x)$ produces an x-axis reflection of a function $f(x)$.

Additional Practice, p. 312

1. (a) $y = -f(x - 1) - 2$, where $f(x) = |x|$

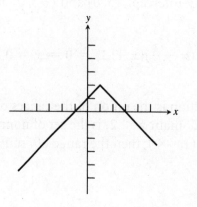

(b) $y = 2f\left(\dfrac{x}{3} + 1\right)$, where $f(x) = |x|$

2. (C)

3. (B)

Polynomial Functions—Appendix

Content and Practice, p. 314

1. (a) 1, 1, 2, 1

   (b) 1, 1, 2, 1

   (c) 0, 0, 2, 2

   (d) For each function, as $x \to -\infty$, $y \to -\infty$ and as $x \to \infty$, $y \to \infty$

2. (a) 1, 2, 3, 2

   (b) 1, 2, 3, 2

   (c) 1, 1, 3, 1

   (d) as $x \to -\infty$, $y \to \infty$ and as $x \to \infty$, $y \to \infty$

3. (a) 1 or 3 real zeros

   (b) 0 or 2 extrema

   (c) as $x \to \infty$, $y \to \infty$ and as $x \to -\infty$, $y \to -\infty$

   (d) $\left\{1, \dfrac{7 \pm 3\sqrt{33}}{4}\right\}$. The Rational Root Theorem helps us identify that 1 is a root. Dividing the given cubic by $(x - 1)$ produces the quadratic factor $(2x^2 - 7x - 31)$, which yields the two additional roots.

   (e) $(-1, 44)$ and $(4, -81)$

   (f) Function $f(x)$ is rising on both $(-\infty, -1]$ and $[4, \infty)$, and falling on $[-1, 4]$.

(g)

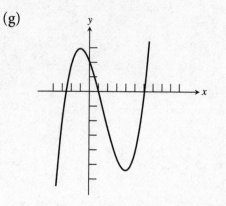

4. **(A)** $f(x)$ was expressed as the product of three distinct factors. Consider the zeros of each factor: $(3x + 1)$ has a single zero, $(x - 1)$ has a single zero (of multiplicity 3), and $x^2 + 4$ has no real zeros. Therefore, there are two distinct real zeros of $f(x)$.

Additional Practice, p. 317

1. (a) 0, 2, or 4 real zeros

   (b) 1 or 3 extrema

   (c) as $x \to \pm\infty, f(x) \to \infty$

   (d) $\left\{ \pm 1, \pm \sqrt{7} \right\}$. $f(x)$ easily factors into $(x - 1)(x + 1)(x^2 - 7)$.

   (e) $(0, 7), (2, -9), (-2, -9)$

   (f) Function $f(x)$ rising on both $[-2, 0]$ and $[2, \infty)$, and falling on $(-\infty, -2]$ and $[0, 2]$.

   (g)

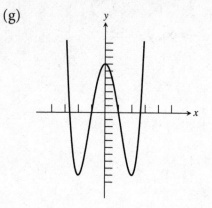

2. **(D)**

Rational Functions—Appendix

Content and Practice, p. 318

1. (a) $x \neq \pm 3$

   (b) $\left(3, \dfrac{3}{2} \right)$. $f(x) = \dfrac{x^2 + 3x - 18}{x^2 - 9} = \dfrac{(x + 6)(x - 3)}{(x + 3)(x - 3)}$. The factor $(x - 3)$ appears in both the numerator and denominator exactly once.

(c) $x = -3$. The factor $(x + 3)$ appears only in the denominator.

(d) $y = 1$. The degree of the numerator equals the degree of the denominator, and the ratio of the two leading coefficients is 1. Therefore $y = 1$ will be a horizontal asymptote.

(e) As $x \rightarrow \pm\infty, f(x) \rightarrow 1$.

(f) 2

(g)

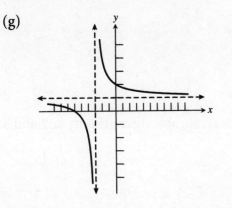

2. (a)

x	$f(x)$
0	0
0.9	-8.1
0.99	-98.01
0.999	-998.001
1.001	1002.001
1.01	102.01
1.1	12.1
2	4

(b) As $x \rightarrow 1^-$, the graph of f falls toward $-\infty$. As $x \rightarrow 1^+$, the graph of f rises toward $+\infty$.

Additional Practice, p. 322

1. (a) $x \neq 1$

(b) No removable discontinuities. There are no common factors in the numerator and denominator to consider.

(c) $x = 1$

(d) $y = x + 2$ is a slant asymptote. The degree of the numerator is 1 greater than the degree of the denominator. The linear asymptote can be confirmed by graphing.

(e) $x \rightarrow \infty, y \rightarrow \infty$, and $x \rightarrow -\infty, y \rightarrow -\infty$

(f) -3

(g)

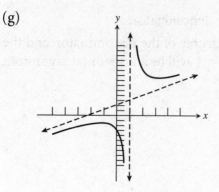

2. (D) $f(x) = \dfrac{x^2 - 2x}{x^2 - 4} = \dfrac{x(x - 2)}{(x + 2)(x - 2)}$ implies a removable discontinuity at 2 and a vertical asymptote at $x = -2$.

Exponential Functions—Appendix

Content and Practice, p. 324

1. (a) 28

    (b)

x	$f(x)$
-2	100
-1	52
1	16
2	10

    (c) f is decreasing. As x increases, the function value decreases because $0 < b < 1$ and $a > 0$.

    (d) $y = 4$

    (e) As $x \to +\infty, f(x) \to 4$. As $x \to -\infty, f(x) \to \infty$.

    (f)

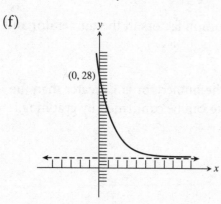

(0, 28)

Additional Practice, p. 326

1. (a) 3. Let $x = 0, f(0) = 3$.

    (b)

x	$f(x)$
-2	0.75
-1	1.5
1	6
2	12

    (c) Increasing. As x increases, the values of $f(x)$ increases, because $b > 1$ and $a > 0$.

    (d) $y = 0$

    (e) As $x \to -\infty, f(x) \to 0$.

    As $x \to +\infty, f(x) \to \infty$.

    (f)

2. (A) $A(t) = 100\left(\dfrac{1}{2}\right)^{\frac{t}{2}}$. $A(4) = 25$ and $A(8) = 6.25$.

Sinusoidal Functions—Appendix

Content and Practice, p. 327

1. (a) Amplitude is 3.

    (b) Vertical shift of $+1$.

    (c) Range: $[-2, 4]$

    (d) Horizontal shift of $\dfrac{\pi}{4}$ to the right.

    (e) Period is 4π since $\dfrac{2\pi}{\frac{1}{2}} = 4\pi$.

    (f) Local maxima determined by $\left(\dfrac{\pi}{4} + 4k\pi, 4\right)$, where k is an integer.

    Local minima determined by $\left(\dfrac{9\pi}{4} + 4k\pi, -2\right)$, where k is an integer.

(g)

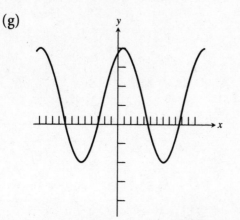

2. (a) Local maxima determined by $(\pi + 2k\pi, 1)$, where k is an integer. Local minima determined by $(2k\pi, -1)$, where k is an integer.

(b) Amplitude is 1

(c) Vertical shift: none

(d) Period is 2π.

(e) Example: $f(x) = -\cos x$. No horizontal shift.

(f) Example: $f(x) = \sin\left(x - \left(\frac{\pi}{2}\right)\right)$. Horizontal shift: right $\frac{\pi}{2}$

Additional Practice, p. 329

1. (a) Amplitude is $\dfrac{(8 - {}^{-}2)}{2} = 5$.

(b) Vertical shift: $+3$

(c) Range: $[-2, 8]$

(d) Period $= (6 - 2) \cdot 2 = 8$.

(e) Example: $y = 5 \cos\left[\dfrac{\pi}{4}(x - 2)\right] + 3$. Horizontal shift: right 2.

(f) Example: $y = 5 \sin \dfrac{\pi}{4} x + 3$.   No horizontal shift.

(g)

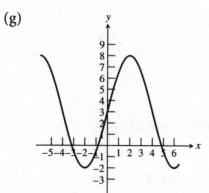

2. (A)

3. (D)

More Trigonometric Functions—Appendix

Content and Practice, p. 331

1. (a) Period: 2π

   (b) Domain: $x \neq \pi + 2k\pi$, where k is an integer.

   (c) Equations of vertical asymptotes: $x = (2k + 1)\pi$, where k is an integer.

   (d) $2k\pi$, where k is an integer.

   (e)
   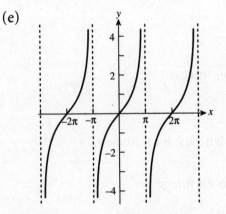

2. Vertical stretch by a factor of 2, vertical shift up 1; horizontal shift right π, horizontal shrink by $\frac{1}{3}$

3. (a)
   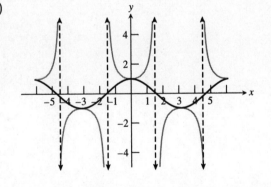

   (b)
   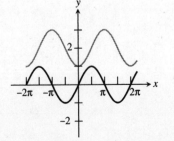

(c)

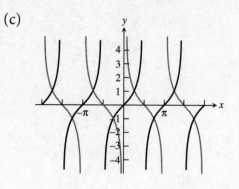

Additional Practice, p. 333

1. (a) Period: π

    (b) Domain: $x \neq \dfrac{\pi}{4} + k \cdot \dfrac{\pi}{2}$, where k is an integer.

    (c) Vertical asymptotes: $x = \dfrac{\pi}{4} + \dfrac{k\pi}{2}$, where k is an integer.

    (d) Vertical shift: $+1$.

    (e) Local minima determined by $\left(\dfrac{\pi}{2} + k\pi, -2 \right)$, where k is an integer.

    Local maxima determined by $(k\pi, 4)$, where k is an integer.

    (f)

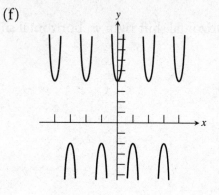

2. (C)

3. (C)

Inverse Trigonometric Relations and Functions—Appendix

Content and Practice, p. 335

1. (a) $\dfrac{5\pi}{6}$

    (b) $-\dfrac{\pi}{4}$

    (c) $\dfrac{\pi}{4}$

2. (a) 0.509

    (b) 1.176

    (c) -0.736

    (d) No solution

3. (a) $x = \pm\dfrac{\pi}{3} + 2k\pi$, where k is an integer.

    (b) $x = -\dfrac{\pi}{2} + 2k\pi$, where k is an integer.

    (c) $x = -\dfrac{\pi}{6} + k\pi$, where k is an integer.

Additional Practice, p. 337

1. (a) 1.819
    (b) -0.983
    (c) 0.389

2. (a) $x = -\dfrac{\pi}{4} + k\pi$, where k is an integer. $3 + \tan x = 2 \Rightarrow \tan x = -1$.

    (b) $x = \pm\dfrac{\pi}{6} + k\pi$, where k is an integer. $4\cos^2 x = 3 \Rightarrow \cos x = \pm\dfrac{\sqrt{3}}{2}$.

    (c) $x = k\pi$ or $x = \dfrac{\pi}{6} + 2k\pi$ or $\dfrac{5\pi}{6} + 2k\pi$, where k is an integer.

      $2\sin^2 x = \sin x \Rightarrow \sin x(2\sin x - 1) = 0$.

    (d) No solutions. $\cos^2 x = 4 \Rightarrow \cos x = \pm 2$ but $-1 \le \cos x \le 1$!

3. (a) $\sin^{-1} x$ is defined only on $\left[-\dfrac{\pi}{2}, \dfrac{\pi}{2}\right]$, where it has the single solution, $-\dfrac{\pi}{6}$.

Parametric Relations—Appendix

Content and Practice, p. 338

1.

t	x	y
-2	6	-4
-1	2	-2
0	0	0
1	0	2
2	2	4
3	6	6

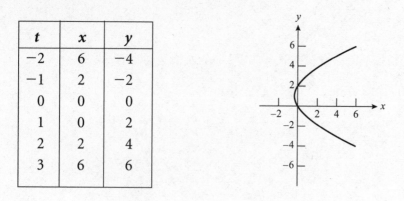

2. $x = t^2 - t, y = 2t; y = 2t \Rightarrow t = \dfrac{1}{2}\,y$. Therefore,

$$x = \left(\frac{1}{2}\,y\right)^2 - \left(\frac{1}{2}\,y\right)$$

$$x = \frac{1}{4}\,y^2 - \frac{1}{2}\,y$$

3. Utilizing the identity assuring that $\sin^2 t + \cos^2 t = 1$,

$$x = 3\sin t \Rightarrow \sin t = \frac{x}{3} \quad \text{and} \quad y = 4\cos t \Rightarrow \cos t = \frac{y}{4}.$$

$$\sin^2 t + \cos^2 t = \left(\frac{x}{3}\right)^2 + \left(\frac{y}{4}\right)^2 = 1 \quad \text{or} \quad \frac{x^2}{9} + \frac{y^2}{16} = 1, \text{ an ellipse.}$$

4. $x_t = t \qquad\qquad t_{\min} = 2$
   $y_t = (t - 2)^2 \quad\; t_{\max} = \infty$
   $\qquad\qquad\qquad\; t_{\text{step}} = 0.1$

5. (i) (a) compared to (b): The smaller parametric t_{step} in (b) caused the graph to be generated more slowly. This was because the calculator was generating about ten times as many points in graphing (b).

   (ii) (a) compared to (c): The negative t_{step} in (c) and the reversal of values in $t_{\min}$ and $t_{\max}$ caused the graph to be generated right to left, rather than left to right as it was in (a). This was because the calculator begins generating points by using the $t_{\min}$ and incrementing that value by t_{step}.

6. Similarities: Plots (a) and (b) generate circles with centers (0, 0). Differences: The plot (a) has radius 3 and is generated in a counterclockwise fashion beginning with the point (3, 0), while plot (b) has radius 1 and is generated clockwise from (0, 1). The radius differences were caused by the constant factor of 3 in (a). The point generation differences were caused by the reversal of trig functions within x_t, y_t.

7. $x_t = 88 \cos \dfrac{\pi}{2}, \quad y_t = -16t^2 + 88t + 0$

  $x_t = 0, \qquad\quad y_t = -16t^2 + 88t$

8. $x_t = 15 \cos\left(-\dfrac{\pi}{10}\left(t + 5\right)\right), y_t = 15 \sin\left(-\dfrac{\pi}{10}\left(t + 5\right)\right) + 23$, with $t_{\min} = 0$ and $t_{\max} = 120$.

  Radius is 15 feet, height off the ground is 8 feet, and the period is given as 20, so

  $20 = \dfrac{2\pi}{|B|}, |B| = \dfrac{\pi}{10}$. For clockwise motion, $B < 0$, so $B = -\dfrac{\pi}{10}$.

Additional Practice, p. 341

1. (B) Eliminate the parameter: $x = 2t + 3 \Rightarrow t = \dfrac{x - 3}{2} \Rightarrow y = \sqrt{\left(\dfrac{x - 3}{2}\right) - 3}$, which is a

  portion (half) of the parabola $y^2 = \dfrac{1}{2}x - \dfrac{9}{2}$.

2. (D) The parametric equations are $x = 48 \cos(35°) t$ and $y = -16t^2 + 48 \sin(35°)t + 5$.
  When the ball hits the ground, $y = 0$. Solving the second equation for t, setting $y = 0$, tells us
  that $t = 1.886$ seconds. Evaluating the first equation for x at 1.886 seconds indicates a distance
  of about 74 feet.

Parametric, Polar, and Vector Functions—Appendix

Content and Practice, p. 343

1. (a) $(0, 5)$

  (b) The particle moves counterclockwise from initial point $(4, 0)$.

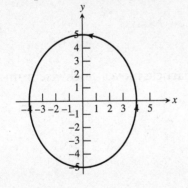

  (c) 3 times

2. $\theta = \dfrac{\pi}{4} + k\pi$. $r = 2\sin\theta$, $r = 2\cos\theta \Rightarrow \sin\theta = \cos\theta = \pm\dfrac{\sqrt{2}}{2}$, so $r = \pm\sqrt{2}$.

   Thus $\left\{(\theta, r): \theta = \dfrac{\pi}{4} + 2k\pi \text{ and } r = \sqrt{2}, \text{ or } \theta = \dfrac{5\pi}{4} + 2k\pi \text{ and } \right.$

   $r = -\sqrt{2} \left.\text{ where } k \text{ is an integer.}\right\}$

3. (a) $\mathbf{r}(1) = \langle -1, 0 \rangle$ or $\mathbf{r}(1) = -\mathbf{i} + 0\mathbf{j}$

   (b)

   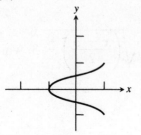

Additional Practice, p. 345

1. (A)

2. (a)

   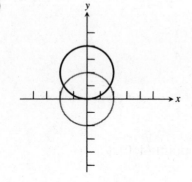

   (b) $(2, \pi/6), (2, 5\pi/6)$

3. The path of the particle is a circle with radius 1. The particle moves clockwise from initial point $(0, 1)$. $x^2 + y^2 = \sin^2 2t + \cos^2 2t = 1$.

   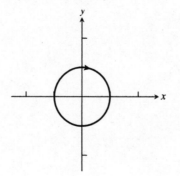

Numerical Derivatives and Integrals—Appendix

Content and Practice, p. 346

1. 14.778. $m_{\tan} = \dfrac{f(1.001) - f(0.999)}{1.001 - 0.999} = 14.778$

2. Exact area = 12. Built-in graphing calculator functions give many approximate answers. The exact area is 12.

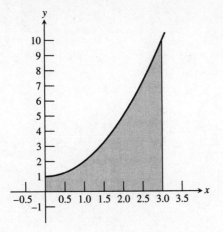

Additional Practice, p. 347

1. (D) Numerical derivative gives a slope value of 4 and the point (2, 6).
   $y - 6 = 4(x - 2) \Rightarrow y = 4x - 2$.

2. (A) Evaluating the numerical derivative of $h = 200 - 16t^2$ at $t = 2$ yields -64 feet/second.

3. (a) -20 gal/min.   Avg. $= \dfrac{G_4 - G_0}{t_4 - t_0} = \dfrac{40 - 120}{4 - 0} = -20$ gal/min.

   (b) -14 gal/min.   Avg. $= \dfrac{G_3 - G_{2.5}}{t_3 - t_{2.5}} = \dfrac{50 - 57}{3 - 2.5} = \dfrac{-7}{0.5} = -14$ gal/min.